Food and Culture in America

Food and Culture
in America

A Nutrition Handbook

Pamela Goyan Kittler, M.S.
Food and Nutrition Education Consultant

Kathryn Sucher, Sc.D., R.D.
Associate Professor, San Jose State University

VNR | VAN NOSTRAND REINHOLD
_____ New York

Library of Congress Catalog Card Number 88-20460
ISBN 0-442-28322-9

Printed in the United States of America

Designed by Nan K. Smith

Van Nostrand Reinhold
115 Fifth Avenue
New York, New York 10003

Van Nostrand Reinhold International Company Limited
11 New Fetter Lane
London EC4P 4EE, England

Van Nostrand Reinhold
480 La Trobe Street
Melbourne, Victoria 3000, Australia

Macmillan of Canada
Division of Canada Publishing Corporation
164 Commander Boulevard
Agincourt, Ontario M1S 3C7, Canada

16 15 14 13 12 11 10 9 8 7 6 5 4 3 2 1

Library of Congress Cataloging in Publication Data

Kittler, Pamela Goyan, 1953—
  Food and culture in America.

  Bibliography: p.
  Includes index.
  1. Nutrition—United States—Cross-cultural stud-
ies. 2. Food habits—United States. I. Sucher, Kathryn
P. II. Title.
TX357.K58 1989   641′.0973   88-20460
ISBN 0-442-28322-9

*This book is dedicated to
Peter, Richard, Erika, Adrienne, and Alexander,
with affection.*

CONTENTS

PREFACE   ix
ACKNOWLEDGMENTS   xiii

1. FOOD AND CULTURE IN AMERICA   1
Food and Culture   3
Factors that Influence Food Habits   5
The Study of Foods and Food Habits   9
Nutrition and Food Habits   15
The American Melting Pot   17

2. FOOD AND RELIGION   19
Western Religions   20
Eastern Religions   41

3. NATIVE AMERICANS   51
Cultural Perspective   52
Traditional Food Habits   57
Contemporary Food Habits   74

4. EUROPEANS   81
Early European History   81
Northern Europeans   85

Southern Europeans   112
Central Europeans and the People of the Soviet Union   131
Scandinavians   156

5. BLACK AMERICANS   171
Cultural Perspective   172
Traditional Food Habits   179
Contemporary Food Habits   193

6. LATINOS   200
Mexicans   201
Caribbean Islanders   226

7. ASIANS   248
Chinese   248
Japanese   269
Southeast Asians   285

8. PEOPLE OF GREECE AND THE MIDDLE EAST   312
Cultural Perspective   312
Traditional Food Habits   318
Contemporary Food Habits   330

9. ASIAN INDIANS   333
Cultural Perspective   334
Traditional Food Habits   342
Contemporary Food Habits   357

ADDITIONAL REFERENCES ON FOOD AND CULTURE   363

INDEX   371

PREFACE

The topic of food and culture is inherently complex. It has been approached nutritionally, anthropologically, psychologically, historically, sociologically, ecologically, and even geographically. Research in the field has ranged from anecdotal to academic. Yet despite these efforts, information that can be used by practicing health professionals has been lacking.

The need for culturally sensitive information that health professionals can use when providing nutrition education is undisputed. The United States population is heterogeneous, including uncounted numbers of racial, ethnic, and religious minority groups. And each of these groups has traditional foods and food habits that may vary significantly from the so-called typical American diet. Effective education requires that these variations be acknowledged.

Foods and food habits must be understood within the context of culture. It is our goal to provide nutritionists and dietitians with both the cultural overview necessary to avoid ethnocentric assumptions and the reported nutritional data concerning the foods and food habits of each minority group discussed. Thus we attempt to combine the conceptual with the technical in a way that will prove useful to other health professionals as well.

The first chapter details the methods and approaches that can be used to study culturally based foods and food habits. Chapter 2 describes the major Western and Eastern religions, discussing their dietary practices in depth. Each subsequent chapter concerns a minority group. We have chosen to cover the major cultural populations in America in depth, rather than to include a little information on all ethnic and racial groups. The order of presentation is historical, determined by the approximate arrival sequence of the various groups in the United States.

The first section in each of these chapters outlines the history of the country of origin, the history of immigration to the United States, current demographics and socioeconomic status, and the prevailing worldview (outlook on life) expressed by members of the minority group. This background information is essential to understanding food habits within the cultural context. The second section of each chapter describes traditional food habits, including ingredients and common foods, meal patterns, special-occasion foods, the role of food in the society, and therapeutic uses of food. The third section explains contemporary food habits, such as adaptations made in the United States and the impact the group has had on the American diet, and reported nutritional status. Information about counseling members of the minority population concludes each chapter (although it is beyond the scope of this book to report comprehensively on cross-cultural communication techniques, which is a specialty in itself).

Each of these chapters also includes one or more cultural food groups tables. The focus is on ingredients common to the populations of each region. For example, although the cuisines of Great Britain and France differ greatly, the foods that go into their dishes are similar. Each emphasizes protein foods and feature milk and milk products; each uses many of the same temperate-zone fruits and vegetables. Thus they are listed together as northern European. Important differences within each region, as well as unique food habits, are noted in the "Comments" section of each table. Foods are divided into protein (including milk and milk products, meats, poultry, fish, eggs, and legumes), cereals and grains, fruits and vegetables, and additional foods, including seasonings, nuts and seeds, beverages, fats and oils, and sweeteners. Known adaptations common in the United States are noted. The tables are intended as a starting point for the reader; they do not replace either chapter content nor an in-depth interview with a patient or client.

There are many difficulties in attempting to provide dietary data within the context of culture. First, food is integral to ethnic and religious identity. Descriptions of food habits must be as objective as possible to avoid inadvertent criticisms of the underlying culture. Any instances of cultural bias on our part are unintentional. Second, any definition of ethnic or religious foods and food habits implies cultural homogeneity. In reality, however, each member of a minority group has an individually distinctive diet. The food habits of minority groups influence the majority American diet, and vice versa. Each person practices traditional culturally based food habits to a different degree. Thus we do not intend to stereotype the foods and food habits of minority groups. Rather, we hope to provide a basis for understanding specific dietary practices compared to general trends.

Further, research on food and culture is multidisciplinary. We have tried to go beyond our backgrounds in nutritional science to explore the wealth of information found in other fields. Even so, the data on foods and food habits of minority groups in the United States are scanty and sporadic. It is not unusual to find only one or two current studies on the diet or nutritional status of a given ethnic or religious group. Our references, by necessity, include numerous citations of research conducted 10, 20, and even 30 years ago. And, as is usually the case with studies on nutrition, the cautions necessary when extrapolating data from small samples to large populations apply to research in culturally based food habits. In our continuing effort to obtain additional dietary information on the minority groups discussed, we invite the readers to forward any personal observations or data, so that we may share it in future editions.

We believe that this book will do more than introduce the concepts of food and culture in America. It should also encourage self-examination and individual cultural identification. We hope that it will help dietitians and nutritionists work effectively with members of different ethnic and religious groups in a culturally sensitive manner. If it sparks a gustatory interest in the foods of other cultures too, we will personally be pleased.

ACKNOWLEDGMENTS

The authors wish to thank the many colleagues who have graciously given support and advice in the development of this book: Dileep Bal, M.D.; Lillian Estrada-Castillo, R.D.; Chuck Darrah, M.P.H.; Pat Goyan; K. C. Kraven, Ph.D.; Norma Jeanne Downes, M.S.; James Freeman, Ph.D.; Shiriki Kumanyiki, Ph.D.; Melinda Poliarco, R.D.; Naswa Saah, M.S.; Tar Toyafuka; Rose Y. Tseng, Ph.D., R.D.; Irene Tupper; and Virginia Ziegler, M.S.

De Gustibus Non Est Disputandum

1

FOOD AND CULTURE IN AMERICA

W hat do Americans eat? Meat and potatoes, according to popular myth. There's no denying that more beef is consumed than any other protein food in the United States and that franchise restaurants sell over $3 billion worth of hamburgers and french fries each year. Yet the American diet cannot be so simply described.

Just as the population of the United States contains many different ethnic and cultural groups, so are the foods and food habits of Americans diverse. It can no more be said that the typical U.S. citizen is white, Anglo-Saxon, and Protestant than it can be stated that meat and potatoes are what this typical citizen eats.

Data from the 1980 U.S. census show that one in every five Americans is either black, of "Spanish descent," or belongs to some other non-white category. These figures greatly underestimate the number and diversity of American minority groups, however. For instance, they do not list members of white ethnic or religious groups, nor do they count the many U.S. residents who are not citizens. Additionally, the census category "Spanish descent" is vague. It is thought that many Latinos, who do not consider themselves as Spanish, are categorized as "white" instead. Thus the proportion of American minority group members is larger than statistics indicate, and, more important, it is rapidly increasing.

Asian Indians are one of the fastest growing immigrant group in America. Their population more than doubled between 1980 and 1984, from 200,000 to 500,000. Blacks are

As suggested by their names, not even hamburgers and french fries are American in origin. Chopped beef steaks were introduced to the United States from the German city of Hamburg in the late nineteenth century. They became popularized as a sandwich at the St. Louis World's Fair. Although the potato is a New World vegetable, it was brought to America by the Irish in 1719. The term *French fried potatoes*, first appeared in the United States in the 1860s and may have come from the way in which the potatoes are cut or the method in which they are cooked. In France, fries are known as *pomme frites*. Other foods considered typically American also have foreign origins, such as hot dogs (*frankfurters*), apple pie, and ice cream.

1

An American restaurant: The eclectic specialties of this restaurant demonstrate the diversity of American cuisine: seafood from the coast, Cajun cooking from Louisiana, Italian pasta, mesquite-grill meats from the southwest, and all-American beef. (Courtesy California Cafe Bar & Grill.)

numerically the largest minority group (approximately ten percent of the total U.S. population) although Latinos, with a growth rate close to 30 percent between 1982 and 1986, are expected to surpass blacks by the middle of the next century.

Each American minority group has its own culturally based

foods and food habits. Many of these traditions have been influenced and modified through contact with the majority culture. The foods and food habits of the majority culture have, in turn, been affected by those of the minority groups. Today, a fast food restaurant or street stand is as likely to offer pizza, tacos, egg rolls, croissants, or falafels as hamburgers.

The American diet encompasses the numerous varied cuisines of the U.S. population. To understand it fully, one must study not only the traditional foods and food habits of the many minority groups but also the interactions between these traditions and those of the majority culture.

*The term *majority* describes the culture shared by the dominant white, Anglo-Saxon, Protestant population in the U.S. *Minority* refers to any ethnic or religious group in America that culturally differs from the majority.*

FOOD AND CULTURE

Food, as defined in the dictionary, is any substance that provides the nutrients necessary to maintain life and growth when ingested. When animals feed, they repeatedly consume those foods necessary for their well-being, and they do so in a similar manner at each feeding. Humans, however, do not feed. They eat. Eating is distinguished from feeding by the ways in which humans use food.

To begin with, humans not only gather or hunt food, they also cultivate plants and raise livestock. Food is thus regularly available to most humans, permitting the development of food habits, such as the setting of mealtimes. In addition, humans cook food, which greatly expands the number and variety of edible substances available. Choice of what to eat follows. Humans use utensils to eat food and create complex rules, commonly called manners, about how food is actually ingested. Humans share food. Standards for who may dine with whom in each eating situation are well-defined. The term *food habits* refers to the ways in which humans use food, including how food is obtained and stored, how it is prepared, how it is served and to whom, and how it is consumed.

A. H. Maslow's theory of human maturation as applied to food habits (Lowenberg 1970) explains how food use progresses from eating for existence to eating for self-actualization:

1. *Physical needs for survival:* this is the most basic use of food, nearly equivalent to feeding. Daily needs for nutrients must be met before more complex food use can occur.
2. *Social needs for security:* once the immediate need for

food is satisfied, future needs can be considered. The storage of food represents security.

3. *Belongingness:* this use of food shows that an individual belongs to a group. The need to belong is satisfied by consuming the foods that are eaten by the social group as a whole. These foods represent comfort and happiness for many people; for example, during periods of stress or illness, people often want the foods they ate during childhood.

Sometimes people adopt a special diet to demonstrate belongingness. For example, black Americans, who live outside the South may choose to eat what is called *soul food* (typically Southern black cuisine, such as pork ribs and greens) as an expression of ethnic identity. Etiquette, the appropriate use of food, is also a way of demonstrating belongingness. Lunching with business associates at an expensive restaurant requires entirely different manners from those eating with a lover at a picnic.

4. *Status:* in general, eating with someone connotes social equality with that person. Many societies regulate who can dine together as a means of establishing class relationships. Women and children may eat separately from men, or servants may eat in the kitchen, away from their employers. This attempted separation by class was also seen in some U.S. restaurants that excluded blacks before the civil rights legislation of the 1960s.

What foods are eaten can be used to define social position as well. Caviar implies wealth; mesquite-grilled foods and goat cheese suggest upward mobility.

5. *Self-realization:* this stage of food use occurs when all previous stages have been achieved to the individual's satisfaction. Personal preference takes precedence, and the individual may experiment with the foods of different economic or ethnic groups.

The correlation between what people eat, how others perceive them, and how they characterize themselves is striking. In one study, researchers listed foods typical of five diets: vegetarian (broccoli quiche, brown rice, avocado and bean sprout sandwich); gourmet (oysters, caviar, French-roast coffee); health food (protein shake, wheat germ, yogurt); fast food (Kentucky fried chicken, Big Mac, pizza); and synthetic food (Carnation Instant Breakfast, Cheez Whiz), it was found that each category was associated with a certain personality type. Vegetarians were considered to be pacifists, drug users, and likely to drive foreign cars. Gourmets were also thought to be drug users, liberal, and sophisticated. Health-food fans were described as drug users, anti-nuclear activists, and Democrats. Fast-food and synthetic-food eaters were believed to be religious, conservative, and wearers of polyester clothing. These stereotypes were confirmed by self-description and personality tests completed by persons whose diet fell within each of the five categories (Sadalla & Burroughs, 1981).

It is clear from these uses of food that for humans, food is more than simply nutrients. Humans use foods symbolically, and it is this symbolic use of food that is important to each cultural group. The foods and food habits of each group are often associated with religious beliefs or ethnic behaviors. Eating, like dressing in traditional clothing or speaking in a native language, is a daily reaffirmation of cultural identity. Culturally based food habits are often one of the last traditions people change when they move to a new country. This process of change, called *acculturation*, takes place when an individual is repeatedly exposed to the influences of another culture. The lack of available native ingredients may force immediate acculturation, or convenience or cost factors may speed change. Asian Indians readily replace traditional home-made flatbreads with store bought loaves when living in the United States, for example. Foods that are tasty are easily accepted, such as pastries, candies, and soft drinks; conversely, unpopular traditional foods may be the first to go. Mexican children living in America quickly reject the variety cuts of meat, such as tripe, that their parents still enjoy. It is the foods that are most associated with cultural identity that are most resistant to acculturation. Muslims will probably never eat pork, regardless of where they live. People from China may insist on eating rice with every meal, even if it is the only Asian food on the table.

A *symbol* is something that suggests something else due to relationship, association, or convention. Bread is an excellent example of symbolic use of food. Bread is the "staff" of life; one "breaks bread" with friends; bread represents the body of Christ in the Catholic sacrament of communion; white bread was traditionally eaten by the upper classes, dark bread by the poor; a person of wealth has a lot of "bread"; and whole-wheat bread is eaten by people in the United States who are concerned more with health than with status.

Culture is defined as the knowledge, beliefs, customs, and habits a group of people share. These patterned behaviors are learned, not inherited. Culture is passed on from generation to generation through the process known as *enculturation*.

FACTORS THAT INFLUENCE FOOD HABITS

There are numerous factors that affect the food habits of each person within culture. Many operational models have been developed to describe these influences, including the lifestyle model of dietary habits (Pelto, 1981), which attempts to explain how these factors interact to result in specific food behaviors.

Societal Factors

The food production and distribution system is responsible for the availability of foods, which differs from region to re-

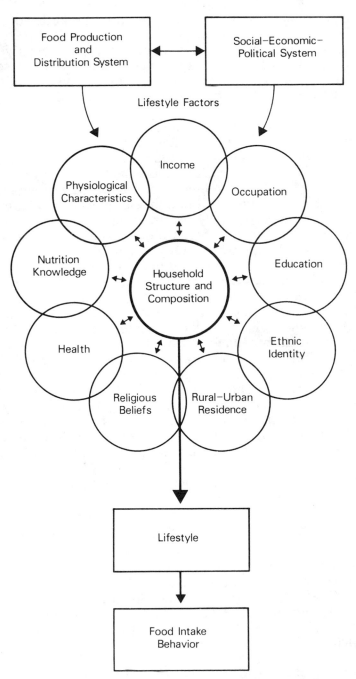

Factors that influence food habits. (From Pelto 1981 with permission from the Society for Nutrition Education.)

gion and country to country. Individuals may have access only to home-grown food, or they may be able to purchase exotic products from around the world.

Food availability influences, and in turn is influenced by, the socioeconomic and political systems. These serve to control the production and distribution of food in the culture. For example, farm subsidies in both the United States and in Europe promote the production of dairy and grain foods far in excess of what can be used by these societies. Advertising is another form of control, greatly affecting some food habits, such as the cereal preferences of children.

Lifestyle Factors

Both availability and control of food at the societal level affect the lifestyle factors of individuals. These factors include income, which limits what foods can be purchased. Even when abundant nutritious food can be bought, the prestige of certain food items is often linked to affordability, such as champagne and lobster. Occupation influences food habits in several ways. The amount of activity involved in a job affects the actual number of calories a person requires each day, for example. The location of the job also influences meal patterns. In some cultures, where everyone's job is near home, the whole family joins in a leisurely lunch at midday. In urbanized societies, people often work far from home; therefore, lunch is eaten with fellow employees. Instead of a large, home-cooked meal, employees may eat a quick, light, fast-food meal. Further, who is employed is also important. In the United States, the greater the number of hours a wife spends on a job outside the home each day, the fewer the hours she spends in meal preparation.

Income is directly affected by occupation, and occupation is in turn affected by education. The status and self-realization phases of food use are usually, though not always, dependent on higher levels of education. Educational attainment may also influence other lifestyle factors that affect food habits, such as nutrition knowledge. Nutrition knowledge, however, may or may not translate into knowledgeable behavior. Other lifestyle factors often exert greater influence over what someone eats than what he or she knows about nutrition.

Ethnic identity can be overt, as in those who have recently arrived in the United States, or it can be subtle, a distant heritage that has been modified or lost over the generations.

The degree of ethnic identity directly influences food habits. An individual who has just immigrated from China, for example, is more likely to prefer traditional Chinese cuisine than is a third-or fourth-generation Chinese American. Place of residence (rural versus urban) may also affect which foods people eat. A poor farmer, for example, may have access to more fresh ingredients than a person with the same income who lives in a ghetto apartment.

Religious beliefs are similar to ethnic identity in that they may greatly affect food habits or they may have no influence at all. It depends on both what religion is followed and the degree of adherence. Many Christian religions have no food restrictions, but some, such as the Seventh-Day Adventists, have strict guidelines about what church members can eat. Judaism requires that only certain foods be consumed in certain combinations, yet most Jews do not follow these rules strictly. Health beliefs also influence food habits in varying ways. For instance, some women avoid specific foods during pregnancy and lactation: some people believe that eating strawberries causes birthmarks. Vegetarianism is another way in which health beliefs can affect food habits.

One of the lifestyle factors most influential on how food is used is a person's physiological characteristics. This term includes each person's age, sex, and state of health. Food preferences and the ability to eat and digest foods vary with age. Where a person is in the life cycle affects food habits. Most cultures have rules regarding what foods are appropriate for infants; milk is generally considered wholesome, and frequently any liquid resembling milk, such as nut "milks," is also thought to be nourishing. Pregnant and lactating women commonly have different food habits from other adults. In the United States, women are urged to consume more food when they are pregnant, especially dairy products. They are also believed to crave unusual food combinations, such as pickles and ice cream. In some societies with subsistence economies, pregnant women may be allowed to eat more meat than other people, whereas in others, pregnant women avoid beef, because it is feared that the cow's cloven hoof may cause a cleft palate in the child.

Puberty is a time for special food rites in some cultures. In America, adolescents are especially susceptible to advertising and peer pressure at this time in their lives. They tend to eat quite differently from both children and adults, consuming more fast foods and soft drinks. A fast rate of growth at this time also affects the amount of food that teenagers consume. The opposite is true of older adults. As their metabolism slows, their caloric needs decrease. In addition, they may find that their tolerance for fatty foods or highly spiced foods decreases. The elderly often face other eating problems related to age, such as inability to chew certain foods or a disinterest in cooking and dining alone.

Sex has also been found to influence what a person eats. In some cultures women are prohibited from eating specific foods or are expected to serve the best pieces of food to the men. In other societies, food preference is related to sex. Some people in the United States consider steak to be a masculine food, and salad to be a feminine one.

A person's state of health affects what he or she eats. Chronic diseases, such as diabetes, require people to restrict or omit certain foods. An individual who is sick may not be hungry or may find it difficult to eat. Even minor illnesses may result in dietary changes, such as chicken soup or hot tea for a cold.

Finally, at the center of all the lifestyle factors is household structure and composition. Lifestyle is defined by and organized around the family unit, which may be an extended family, a nuclear family, a single-parent family, a couple with no children, a group of unrelated adults, or an adult living alone. In each household, food behavior develops from the complex interaction of lifestyle factors. Although the lifestyle of each family is unique, similar household composition, influenced by similar societal and lifestyle factors, results in similar food habits.

In many homes, few meals are eaten together as a family. The term grazing *refers to individuals who eat small amounts throughout the day, consuming a doughnut here and a hot dog there, usually on the go.*

THE STUDY OF FOODS AND FOOD HABITS

As may be seen from the numerous factors that influence food habits, the study of any one person's diet is more complicated than simply recording what that person eats for 24 hours or 3 days. Food habits must be examined within a cultural context. Researchers from the fields of anthropology, nutrition, and psychology have all contributed methods and approaches to the study of food habits.

Cultural Perspective

Everyone is intimately involved with his or her own culture; therefore, it is difficult for anyone to study another culture objectively. There are two different theoretical ways in which

Grazing Americans: Many Americans no longer sit down for three full meals. Instead, they eat a little here and a little bit there, snacking throughout the day. (Photo by Pat Goyan.)

a culture may be viewed. The first and most common method is the *etic* approach, which is the viewpoint of an outsider to the culture. The other method is the *emic* approach, which is the viewpoint of an insider to the culture. Some anthropologists live in a cultural group for months or years in order to gain an insider's perspective.

Food habits that appear illogical to an outsider usually make sense to insiders. Complex symbolic, economic, sociologic, ecologic, or even physiologic reasons for how a culture uses food often escape an outsider's recognition. A frequently cited example of well-meaning but misguided outsider viewpoint was the U.S. Agency for International Development's provision of powdered milk to undernourished peoples in developing nations after World War II. Complaints by recipients that drinking the milk caused stomach aches, bloating, gas, and diarhhea were attributed to eating the powder without mixing it with water, improper dilution, or impure water sources. It was assumed that if milk was nutritious food for most Americans, it was nutritious food for hungry people elsewhere in the world. Not until 1965 was it discovered that most adults in the world cannot digest milk.

The assumption that powdered milk was an excellent food for malnourished populations also illustrates another aspect of cultural perspective, the concept of *cultural relativity*. This refers to understanding a culture within the context of that culture, avoiding the biases of the one's own culture. The bias in favor of milk was so strong that it prevented the donors from recognizing that the milk was causing illness, not alleviating hunger, even after the clinical discovery of lactose intolerance (inability to digest milk sugar) was made.

The study of culturally based food habits is not an exact science; further, there are no absolute right or wrong ways to use food. It is sometimes difficult not to apply value judgments to other peoples' food habits, especially those that are repugnant within the context of one's own culture. The use of dog meat in some Asian cultures is an example. It is tempting to label such food habits as immoral or disgusting, yet this is cultural bias. Most Asians do not share Americans' adoration of dogs as pets. Instead, within the context of their cultures, dogs are considered an acceptable food source. *Ethnocentric* is the term applied to a person who does not practice cultural relativity and who feels that his or her own habits or beliefs are superior in some way to those of another culture.

Methodology

Given the appropriately sensitive cultural perspective, the next step in studying culturally based food habits is to describe what one observes systematically so as to allow for further analysis. In the United States, food has typically been classified by food group (as in the Basic Four Food Groups: protein, dairy, cereal and grain, fruit and vegetables) or by important nutrients (such as exchange systems that rank foods according to protein, carbohydrate, and fat content). The way in which food is classified is also a matter of culture. For instance, the Four Food Groups, which includes a category for dairy foods is useful only with those groups who consume significant amounts of milk and milk products. In addition, these categories are limited when applied to food use in different cultures. Although they list what foods people eat, they tell us nothing about how, when, or why.

Researchers have suggested many other ways of categorizing foods and food habits. Some models have been developed based on cross-cultural uses of food, such as the culinary triangle (Levi-Strauss, 1969) of raw, cooked, and rotten food. Raw food is transformed culturally by cooking, or naturally by decomposition. Other categories, found in both developing and industrialized societies, include cultural superfoods, usually staples that have a dominant role in the diet; prestige foods, often protein foods, usually expensive or rare; body-image foods, those thought to influence health and well-being; sympathetic magic foods, which by their form or color are associated with specific effects on the body; and physiologic group foods (those that are reserved for, or forbidden to, groups with certain physiologic status, such as sex, age, or health condition (Jelliffe, 1967)). Foods and food habits can also be classified according to their content or their context (Hertzler, Wenkam, & Standal, 1982). Content includes the observable expressions of food use, such as ingredients, preparation methods, equipment, and food-handling roles. All content has meaning within context. Context can be connotative (physical and economic properties of food, such as appearance, aroma, flavor, convenience, and availability) and image-based (communicating cultural or social identity). The complexity of food habits can be ranked in both content and context categories.

Some classification approaches that help us understand the food habits of a culture include (1) which foods are considered edible, and (2) how often those foods are consumed.

Further, the daily, weekly, and yearly use of food in a culture can be characterized through meal patterns and meal cycles.

EDIBLE OR INEDIBLE?

One approach (National Research Council, 1945) describes the classification process each person uses to determine what is considered to be food.

1. *Inedible foods:* those foods that are poisonous or are not eaten because of strong beliefs or taboos. Which foods are defined as inedible varies from culture to culture. Examples of foods that are frequently taboo ("taboo" is Polynesian, from the Tongan term "tabu," meaning "marked as Holy") include: animals that are useful to the cultural group, such as cattle in India; animals that are dangerous to catch; animals that have died of unknown reasons or of disease; animals that consume garbage or excrement; and plants or animals that resemble a human ailment (such as strawberries or beef during pregnancy, as described above). The reasons behind food taboos are often unknown.

2. *Edible by animals, but not by me:* for example, foods such as insects in the United States or corn in France (where it is used only as a feed grain). Again, the foods in this category vary widely by culture.

3. *Edible by humans, but not by my kind:* these are foods that are recognized as acceptable in some societies, but not in one's own culture. Examples of unacceptable foods in the United States which are acceptable elsewhere are dog meat in Asia (as discussed above), and horse meat in Europe.

4. *Edible by humans, but not by me:* these foods include all those that are acceptable by a person's cultural group but not by the individual, due to such factors as preference (e.g., brussels sprouts, raw oysters), expense or health reasons (a low-sodium or low-cholesterol diet may eliminate many traditional American foods). Other factors, such as religious restrictions, may also influence food choices.

5. *Edible by me:* Finally, all of those foodstuffs accepted as a part of an individual's diet.

CORE FOODS

Those foods that are defined as edible within a culture can be grouped according to their frequency of consumption by an individual (Passim & Bennett, 1943). These writers' ex-

Children under the age of two will try to eat anything and everything. Children between three and six years of age begin to reject culturally unacceptable food items, such as insects in the U.S. By age seven, children are completely repulsed by foods that their culture catagorizes as repugnant (Rozin et al. 1985).

There are always exceptions to the ways we categorize food habits. It is assumed, for instance, that poisonous plants and animals are not eaten. But in Japan, fugu (blowfish or globefish) is considered a delicacy, despite the fact that there is a deadly toxin in the liver and ovaries. These organs must be deftly removed by a certified chef as the last step of cleaning (if they are accidently damaged, the poison spreads rapidly throughout the flesh). The fugu's testes are tidbits prized by Japanese men. Several people die each year after eating fugu.

According to a 1987 Roper poll, the foods Americans like least are tofu, liver and yogurt. Brussels sprouts, lamb, and prunes were also frequently mentioned.

panded concept of *core foods* states that the staples regularly included in the diet, in unmodified form, are at the core of food habits. Foods that are widely but less frequently eaten are termed *secondary core foods*. Foods that are eaten only sporadically are called *peripheral foods*. These foods are characteristic of individual food preference, not cultural or group habit. It is hypothesized that changes in food behaviors happen most often with peripheral foods and least often with core foods. A Mexican American who is adapting to life in the United States, for example, is much more likely to give up some peripheral food item such as *nopalitos* (cactus) than to eliminate core foods, such as *tortillas* or beans.

MEALS AND MEAL CYCLES

A more comprehensive method of categorizing food habits has been developed through analysis of eating patterns (Douglas, 1974). Food can be considered a code that transmits messages about social relations and events in a culture by means of meals and meal cycles.

The first step in decoding eating patterns is to determine what constitutes a meal. In each culture, a meal is made up of certain elements. In the United States, for instance, cocktails and appetizers, or coffee and dessert, are not considered meals. A meal contains a main course and side dishes. In many Asian cultures, a meal is not considered a meal unless rice is included, no matter how much other food is served.

The elements that define a meal must also be served in their proper order. In the United States, appetizers come before soup or salad, followed by the entree and then by dessert. In addition, the foods served should be appropriate for the meal or situation. Although some cultures do not differentiate among foods that can be served at different meals, eggs and bacon are considered breakfast foods in the United States, not lunch or dinner foods. Soup is commonly served at breakfast in Southeast Asia; in the United States, it is a lunch or dinner food.

Other aspects of the meal message include who prepares the meal and what culturally specific preparation rules are used. In the United States, catsup goes with french fries; in Great Britain, vinegar is sprinkled on chips (fried potatoes). Orthodox Jews consume meat only if it has been slaughtered by an approved butcher in an approved manner and has been prepared in a particular way (see Chapter 2 for more information on Judaism).

Who eats the meal is also important. A meal is frequently used to define the boundaries of interpersonal relationships. Americans feel comfortable inviting friends for dinner, but they usually invite acquaintances only for drinks and hors d'oeuvres. For a family dinner, people may include only some of the elements that constitute a meal, but serving a meal to guests requires that all elements be included in their proper order.

Beyond the individual meal is the cycle in which meals occur. These include the everyday routine, such as how many meals are usually eaten and when. In Europe, a large main meal is traditionally consumed at noontime, for example, while in the United States, the main meal is eaten in the evening. In poor societies only one meal a day may be eaten, whereas in wealthy cultures three or four meals are standard.

In most cultures, the meal cycle also includes either fasting or feasting, and often both. Fasting my be partial, the elimination of just some items from the diet, such as the traditional Catholic omission of meat on Fridays or a Hindu personal fast day, when only foods cooked in milk are eaten. Complete fasts are less common. During the holy month of *Ramadan*, Muslims are prohibited from taking food or drink from sunrise to sunset, but they may eat in the evening. *Yom Kippur*, the day of atonement observed by Jews, is a total fast from sunset to sunset.

Feasting celebrates special events. Religious holidays such as Christmas and Passover, secular holidays such as Thanksgiving and the Vietnamese New Year's day, known as Tet, and even personal events such as birth, marriage, and death, are observed with appropriate foods. In many cultures, feasting means simply more of the foods consumed daily and is considered a time of plenty when even the poor have enough to eat. Special dishes that include costly ingredients or are time-consuming to prepare are characteristic of feasting in other cultures. The elements of a feast rarely differ from those of an everyday meal. There may be more of an everyday food or several main courses with additional side dishes and a selection of desserts, but the meal structure does not change.

NUTRITION AND FOOD HABITS

The study of culturally based foods and food habits has specific applications to determining nutritional status and imple-

Sometimes culturally based food combinations have important nutritional benefits. One example is the use of corn tortillas with beans in Mexico. Either corn or beans eaten alone supplies insufficient essential amino acids (the chemical building blocks of protein) to maintain optimum health. Combined, however, they supply complete protein.

menting dietary change. Even the act of obtaining a diet record has cultural implications. Questions such as what was eaten at breakfast, lunch, and dinner not only ignore other daily meal patterns but also make assumptions about what constitutes a meal. Snacks and consumption of food not considered a meal may be overlooked. Cultural perspective is particularly important when evaluating the nutritional impact of a person's food habits.

Ethnocentric assumptions about dietary practices should be avoided. A food behavior that on first observation is judged detrimental may actually have limited impact on a person's physical health. Sometimes other moderating food habits are overlooked. For example, a dietitian may be concerned that an Asian patient is getting insufficient calcium because she eats few dairy products. Undetected sources of calcium in this case might be the daily use of fermented fish sauces or broth rich in minerals made from vinegar-soaked bones.

Likewise, a food habit that the investigator finds repugnant may have some redeeming nutritional benefits. Examples include the consumption of raw meat and organs by the Eskimos, which provide a source of vitamin C that would have been lost during cooking, and the use of mineral-rich ashes or clay in certain breads and stews in Africa and Latin America (Wilson, 1985).

In addition, physiologic differences among populations can affect nutritional needs. The majority of the research on dietary requirements has been conducted on young, white, middle-class American males. Extrapolation of findings to other populations should be done with caution.

Finally, immigrant groups that have changed their traditional food habits to those of the majority American diet have not always improved their health. The classic epidemiologic study of Japanese immigrants to Hawaii demonstrated that the change from a diet high in vegetables and low in meats to one high in meats and lower in vegetables resulted in increased incidence of coronary disease. Native Americans, who are believed to be genetically adapted to a feast-and-famine lifestyle, suffer high rates of obesity when they regularly consume a high-calorie, high-fat diet.

Thus, diet should be carefully evaluated within the context of culture and food habits classified according to nutritional impact (Jelliffe & Bennett, 1961): (1) food use that has positive health consequences and that should be encouraged; (2) neutral food behaviors that have neither adverse nor benefi-

Tofu lasagne: Japanese tofu *is the main ingredient in this new American adaptation of Italian lasagne.* (Courtesy Potter and Mack, Inc.)

cial effects on nutritional status; (3) food habits that are unclassified due to insufficient culturally specific information; and (4) food behaviors that have demonstrable harmful effects on health and that should be discouraged. When modification of diet is found to be necessary, it should be attempted with culturally based foods and food habits in mind.

THE AMERICAN MELTING POT

The term *melting pot* has been used to describe the wonderful mix of population groups living in the United States. It suggests not just separate ethnic and religious minority groups residing in the same country, but a physical and spiritual blending of cultures.

Foods and food habits are a part of this mix. Although Americans of every cultural background enjoy hamburgers and fries, American cuisine goes far beyond meat and potatoes. Just as it is impossible to describe "the American diet," it cannot be said that members of American minority groups eat only their traditional foods. Exotic combinations of ingredients and preparation techniques result in new American dishes, such as tofu lasagna and croissant tuna sandwiches. It is this unique blending of the traditional and the new that makes American foods and food habits so exciting and challenging to study.

REFERENCES

Axelson, M. L. 1986. The impact of culture on food-related behavior. *Annual Review of Nutrition, 6,* 345–363.

Douglas, M. 1972. Deciphering a meal. *Daedalus, 101,* 61–81.

Hertzler, A. A., Wenkam, N., & Standal, B. 1982. Classifying cultural food habits and meanings. *Journal of the American Dietetic Association, 80,* 421–425.

Jelliffe, D. B. 1967. Parallel food classifications in developing and industrialized countries. *American Journal of Clinical Nutrition, 20,* 279–281.

Jelliffe, D. B., & Bennett, F. J. 1961. Cultural and anthropological factors in infant and maternal nutrition. Proceedings of the Fifth International Congress of Nutrition. *Federation Proceedings, 20* (3) 185–188.

Levi-Strauss, C. 1969. *The Raw and the Cooked.* New York: Harper & Row.

Lowenberg, M. E. 1970. Socio-cultural basis of food habits. *Food Technology, 24,* 27–32.

National Research Council. 1945. Cited by M. E. Lowenberg. Socio-cultural basis of food habits. *Food Technology, 24,* 27–32

Passim, H., & Bennett, J. W. 1943. Social process and dietary change. In *The Problem of Changing Food Habits.* National Research Council Bulletin, *108.*

Pelto, G. H. 1981. Anthropological contributions to nutrition education research. *Journal of Nutrition Education, 13* (supplement), S2–S8.

Rozin, P., Fallon, A., & Augustoni-Ziskind, M. 1985. The child's conception of food: the development of contamination sensitivity to "disgusting" substances. *Developmental Psychology, 21,* 1,075–1,079.

Sadella, E., & Burroughs, J. 1981. Profiles in eating: Sexy vegetarians and other diet-based social stereotypes. *Psychology Today,* Oct., 51–57.

Wilson, C. S. 1985. Nutritionally beneficial cultural practices. *World Review of Nutrition and Diet, 45,* 68–96.

2

FOOD AND RELIGION

The function of religion is to explain the inexplicable and thus to give humans a sense of control over a chaotic world. Food, because it sustains life, is an important part of religious rituals, symbols, and customs, those acts of daily life that are intended to bring about an orderly relationship with the supernatural. This chapter discusses the beliefs, and food practices of the world's major religions.

In the West, Judaism, Christianity, and Islam are the most prevalent religions, whereas Hinduism and Buddhism are most prevalent in the East. The western religions, originating in the Middle East, are equated with the worship of a single God and the belief that that God is omnipotent and omniscient. It is for God to command and for humankind to obey. This life is a time of testing, and a preparation for life everlasting, when humans will be held accountable to God for their actions on earth.

The eastern religions, Hinduism and Buddhism, developed in India. Unlike the western religions, they do not teach that God is the lord and maker of the universe who demands that humankind be righteous. Rather, the principal goal of the Indian religions is deliverance or liberation of the human soul, which is immortal, from the bondage of the body. Moreover, nearly all Indian religions teach that liberation, given the right disposition and training, can be experienced in the present life.

19

WESTERN RELIGIONS

Judaism

The Jewish religion, estimated to be four thousand years old, started when Abraham received God's earliest covenant with the Jews. Judaism was originally a nation as well as a religion. However, after the destuction of its capital, Jerusalem, and its principle sanctuary, the Temple of Solomon, in A.D. 70 by the Romans, it had no homeland until the birth of Israel in 1948.

During the Diaspora (the dispersion of Jews outside the state of Israel), Jews scattered and settled all over the ancient world. Two sects of Judaism eventually developed: the Ashkenazi, who prospered in Germany, Northern France, and the Slavic countries, and the Sephardim, originally from Spain, who now inhabit most Mediterranean and Middle Eastern countries. Hasidic Jews are very religous Ashkenazic Jews who believe salvation is to be found in joyous communion with God as well as in the Bible. Hasidic men are evident in larger U.S. cities by their dress, which includes long black coats and black or fur-trimmed hats (worn on Saturdays and holidays only), and by their long beards with side curls.

The cornerstone of the Jewish religion is the Hebrew Bible, particularly the first five books of the Bible, the Pentateuch, also known as the books of Moses, or the *Torah*. It consists of Genesis, Exodus, Leviticus, Numbers, and Deuteronomy. The Torah chronicles the beginnings of Judaism and contains the basic laws that express the will of God to the Jews. The Torah not only sets down the Ten Commandments but also describes the right way to prepare food, give to charity, and conduct one's life in all ways. The interpretation of the Torah and commentary on it is found in the *Talmud*.

The basic tenet of Judaism is that there is only one God, and His will must be obeyed. Jews do not believe in original sin (that humans are born sinful), but rather that all people can choose to act in a right or wrong way. Sin is attributed to human weakness. Humans can achieve, unaided, their own redemption by asking for God's forgiveness (if the have sinned against God), or asking forgiveness of the person they sinned against. The existence of the hereafter is recognized, but the main concern in Judaism is with this life and adherence to the laws of the Torah.

Many Jews belong to or attend a *synagogue* (temple), which is lead by a *rabbi*, who is a scholar, teacher, and spiritual leader. In the United States, congregations are usually classified as Orthodox, Conservative, or Reform, although American Jews represent a spectrum of beliefs and practices. The main division between the three groups is their position on the Jewish laws. Orthodox Jews believe that all Jewish laws, as the direct commandments of God, must be observed in all details. Reform Jews do not believe that the laws are permanently binding, but that the moral law is valid. They believe that the laws are still being interpreted and that some laws may be irrelevant or out of date, and they observe only certain religious practices. Conservative Judaism holds a middle ground between Orthodox and Reform beliefs.

IMMIGRATION TO THE UNITED STATES

In the early nineteenth century, Jews, primarily from Germany, sought economic opportunities in the New World. By 1860, there were approximately 280,000 Jews living in the United States. Peak Jewish immigration occurred around the turn of the century (1880–1920); vast numbers of Jews moved from Eastern Europe because of poverty and pogroms (organized massacres practiced by the Russians against the Jews before World War II).

During the Depression, Jews continued to immigrate into the United States, primarily to escape from Nazi Germany. Their numbers were few, however, because of restrictions in the immigration quota system. Today, Jews continue to come to the United States, especially from the Soviet Union and other Soviet block countries. Some come from Israel as well.

The Jewish population in the United States is approximately six million; most live in major cities. Large populations are found in New York, Chicago, and Los Angeles. Most Jews in the United States are Ashkenazi and are either Reform or Conservative, but may not belong to a congregation.

KASHRUT, THE JEWISH DIETARY LAWS

Some people in the United States believe that Jewish food consists of dill pickles, lox and bagels, chicken soup, and matzo balls. In actuality, the foods Jews eat reflect where their families originally came from. Because most Jews in the United States are Ashkenazi, their diet reflects the foods of Germany and Eastern Europe. Sephardic Jews tend to eat foods similar to those of Mediterranean and Middle Eastern countries, while Jews from India prefer curries and other Asian foods.

All Orthodox and some Conservative Jews follow the dietary laws, *kashrut*, that were set down in the Torah and explained in the Talmud. *Kosher* or *kasher* means "fit" and is a popular term for Jewish dietary laws and permitted food. *Glatt kosher* means that the strictest kosher standards are used in obtaining and preparing the food.

Kashrut is one of the pillars of Jewish religious life and is concerned with the fitness of food. Many health-related explanations have been postulated about the origins of the Jewish dietary laws; however, it is spiritual health, not physical health or any other factor, that is the sole reason for their observance. Jews who "keep kosher" are expressing their sense of obligation to God, to their fellow Jews, and to themselves.

The dietary laws governing the use of animal foods may be classified into the following categories:

Most gelatin is obtained from processed pig tissues. Kosher gelatin-like products are available.

1. *Which animals are permitted for food and which are not*: Any mammal that has a completely cloven foot and also chews the cud may be eaten, and its milk may be drunk. Examples of permitted, or clean, animals are all cattle, deer, goats, oxen, and sheep. Unclean animals include swine, carnivorous animals, and rabbits. Clean birds must have a crop, gizzard, and an extra talon, such as chickens, ducks, geese, and turkeys. Their eggs are also considered clean. All birds of prey, and their eggs, are unclean and cannot be eaten. Among fish, everything that has fins and scales is permitted, everything else is unclean. Examples of unclean fish are catfish, eels, rays, sharks, and all shellfish. All reptiles, amphibians, and invertebrates are also unclean.

Kosher cheese must be made with rennin obtained from a calf which was killed according to the Jewish laws of slaughtering.

2. *Method of slaughtering animals:* the meat of permitted animals can be eaten only if the life of the animal is taken by a special process known as *shehitah*. If an animal dies a natural death or is killed by any other method, it may not be eaten. The *shohet* (person who kills the animal) must be trained and licensed to perform the killing, which is done by slitting the neck with a sharp knife, cutting the jugular vein and trachea at the same time. This method, which is quick and painless, also causes most of the blood to be drained from the carcass.

3. *Examination of the slaughtered animal:* after the animal is slaughtered, it is examined by the shohet for any blemishes in the meat or the organs that would render the animal *trefah*,

or unfit for consumption. Disease in any part of the animal makes the whole animal unfit to eat.

4. *The parts of a permitted animal that are forbidden:* two parts of the animal body that are prohibited as food are blood and a certain kind of fat, called *heleb*. This is fat that is not intermingled with the flesh and forms a separate solid layer that may be encrusted with skin or membrane and can easily be peeled off. This prohibition of heleb applies only to four-footed animals. Blood from any animal is strictly forbidden; even an egg with a small bloodspot in the yolk must be discarded.

5. *The preparation of the meat:* for meat to be kosher, the *heleb*, blood, blood vessels, and sciatic nerve must be removed. Much of this work is now done by the Jewish butcher, although some Jewish housewives still choose to remove the blood. This is known as koshering, or kashering, the meat. It is accomplished by soaking the meat (within 72 hours after killing) in water and then covering it with kosher salt. After the blood has been drawn out, the meat is rinsed several times with water. Because it is not known how much salt remains on the meat after rinsing, Orthodox Jews with hypertension may have to restrict their meat consumption.

The liver cannot be made kosher in the ordinary way because it contains too much blood. Instead, its surface must be cut across or pierced several times, then it must be rinsed in water, and finally, it must be grilled on an open flame until it turns a greyish white color.

6. *The law of meat and milk:* meat (*fleischig*) and dairy (*milchig*) products may not be eaten together. It is generally accepted that after eating meat a person must wait six hours before eating any dairy products. Only one hour is necessary if dairy products are consumed first. Many Jews are lactose intolerant and do not drink milk. However other dairy items such as cheese, sour cream, and yogurt are often included in the diet. Separate sets of dishes, pots, and utensils for preparing and eating meat and dairy products are usually maintained. Often there are separate linens and washing implements. Eggs, fruits, vegetables, and grains are *pareve*, neither meat nor dairy, and can be eaten with both.

7. *Products of forbidden animals:* the only exception to the rule that products of unclean animals are also unclean is honey. Although bees are not fit for consumption, honey is kosher because it is believed that it does not contain any parts from the insect.

8. *Examination of fruit and vegetables for insects and worms:*

"Whoever it be that eateth any blood, that soul shall be cut off from his people"— Lev. 7, 27.

The prohibition of the sciatic nerve is based on the biblical passage that tells the story of Jacob's nighttime fight with a mysterious being who touched him on the thigh and made him limp. This story is thought to be symbolic of the moral law represented by Jacob versus brutal force as practiced by the mysterious being. Because the nerve is hard to remove, the entire animal's hindquarter is usually not eaten.

"Thou shalt not seethe a kid in its mother's milk." Exod. 23, 19; Exod. 34, 26; and Deut. 14, 21.

because small insects and worms can hide on fruits, vegetables, and grains, they must be carefully examined before being eaten.

A processed food product (including therapeutic dietary formulas) is considered kosher only if a reliable rabbinical authority's name or insignia appears on the package. The three most common insignias are the Ⓤ (Union of Orthodox Jewish Congregations of America), Ⓚ (Organized Kasrus Laboratories) and just "K" indicating rabbinical supervision by the company.

JEWISH RELIGIOUS HOLIDAYS

The Sabbath

Two breads, or one bread with a smaller one braided on top, are usually served on the Sabbath, symbolic of the double portion of manna (a nourishing food), provided by God to help sustain the Israelites when they wandered in the desert for 40 years after their exodus from Egypt. A double portion was collected by the Israelites on Friday.

The Jewish Sabbath, the day of rest, is observed from shortly before sundown on Friday until after nightfall on Saturday. Traditionally, the Sabbath is a day devoted to prayer and rest, and no work is allowed. All cooked meals must be prepared before sundown on Friday, since no fires can be kindled on the Sabbath. *Challah,* a braided bread, is commonly served with the Friday night meal. In most Ashkenazi homes, the meal would also contain chicken.

Rosh Hashanah

The Jewish religious year begins with the New Year, or *Rosh Hashanah*, which means "head of the year." Rosh Hashanah is also the beginning of the ten days of penitence, which ends with the Day of Atonement, *Yom Kippur*. Rosh Hashanah occurs in September or October; as with all Jewish holidays, the actual date varies from year to year because the Jewish calender is based on lunar months counted according to Biblical custom and does not coincide with the secular calendar.

For this holiday, the challah is baked in a round shape that symbolizes life without end and a year of uninterrupted health and happiness. Apples are dipped in honey, and a special prayer is said for a sweet and pleasant year. No sour or bitter foods are served on this holiday and special sweets and delicacies, such as honey cakes, are usually prepared.

Yom Kippur, The Day of Atonement

Yom Kippur falls ten days after Rosh Hashanah and is the holiest day of the year. On this day, every Jew atones for the sins committed against God and resolves to improve and once again follow all the Jewish laws.

Yom Kippur is a complete fast day (no food or water; medications are allowed) from sunset to sunset. Everyone fasts, except boys under 13 years old, girls under 12 years old, persons who are very ill, and women in childbirth. The meal before Yom Kipppur is usually not highly seasoned in order to avoid thirst. The meal that breaks the fast is usually light and is composed of dairy foods or fish, fruit, and vegetables.

Sukkot, Feast of Tabernacles

Sukkot is a festival of thanksgiving. It occurs in September or October and lasts one week. On the last day, *Simchat Torah*, the reading of the Torah (a portion is read every day of the year) is completed for the year and started again. Both these festivals are very joyous, and there is much singing and dancing. Orthodox families build a *sukkah* (hut) in their yards, and hang fruit and flowers from the narrow rafters, which are built far enough apart so that the sky and stars are visible. Meals are eaten in the sukkah during Sukkot.

Hanukkah, the Festival of Lights

Hanukkah is celebrated for eight days, usually during the month of December, to commemorate the recapture of the Temple in Jerusalem in 169 B.C. Families celebrate Hanukkah by lighting one extra candle on the *menorah* (candelabra) each night, so that on the last night all eight candles are lit. Traditionally, potato pancakes, called *latkes*, are eaten during Hanukkah.

Purim

Purim, a joyous celebration that takes place in February or March, commemorates the rescue of the Persian Jews from the wicked Haman by Queen Esther. One traditional Purim recipe is for cookies filled with fruit preserves or poppy seeds called *hamantashen* (named after Haman's — the villain — pocket, but made in the triangular shape of his hat).

Passover

Passover, *Pesach* in Hebrew, is the Festival of spring and of freedom. It occurs in March or April and celebrates the anniversary of the Jewish exodus from Egypt. The Passover, *seder*,

The **seder** plate: All symbolic elements of the traditional seder plate used at the Jewish Passover are shown in this advertisement. Matzah is in the center. Note the insignia designating the coffee as Kosher. (Courtesy General Foods Corporation. SANKA is a registered trademark of the General Foods Corporation.)

a ceremony carried out at home, includes the recounting of the exodus and a festive meal. The seder book, the *Haggaddah*, is read aloud. It tells the story of the exodus, of the Jews' redemption from slavery, and of the God-given right of all humankind to life and liberty. A festive meal is a part of the seder; the menu usually includes chicken soup, matzo balls, and meat or chicken.

When Moses led the Jews out of Egypt, they left in such haste that there was no time for their bread to rise. Today, *matzah*, a white flour cracker, is the descendant of the unleavened bread or "bread of affliction." During the eight days of Passover, no food that can become subject to a leavening process, *hametz,* or that has come in contact with leavened foods can be eaten. The foods that are forbidden are wheat, barley, rye, and oats. Wheat flour can be eaten only in the form of matzah or matzah meal. In addition, beans, peas, lentils, maize, millet, and mustard are also avoided. No leavening agents or malt liquors and beers can be used.

Observant Jewish families have special dishes, silver, and pots and pans that are used only for Passover. Since milk and meat cannot be mixed at any time, there are two sets of Passover utensils and dishes. The entire house, especially the kitchen, must be cleaned and any hametz removed before Passover. It is customary for Orthodox Jews to sell their leavened products and flours to a non-Jew before Passover. It is very important that all processed foods, including wine, be prepared for Passover use and be marked "Kosher for Passover."

The seder table is set with the best silverware and china and must include candles, kosher wine, Haggadah, three pieces of matzot (the plural of matzah) covered separately in the folds of a napkin or special Passover cover, and a seder plate. The following items go on the seder plate:

1. *Z'roah.* A roasted shank bone, symbolic of the ancient paschal lamb in Egypt which was eaten roasted.
2. *Beitzah.* A roasted egg, symbolic of the required offering brought to the Temple at Festivals. Although the egg itself was not sacrificed, it is used in the seder as a symbol of mourning. In this case, it is for loss of the Temple in Jerusalem.
3. *Marror.* Bitter herbs, usually horseradish (although not an herb), symbolic of the Jews bitter suffering under slavery. The marror is usually eaten between two small pieces of matzot.

"When a stranger resides with you in your land, you shall not wrong him. . . . You shall love him as yourself, for you were strangers in the land of Egypt." Lev. 19:33–34. It is customary to invite strangers or single people to Passover.

4. *Haroset.* A mixture of chopped apple, nuts, cinnamon, and wine. Its appearance is a reminder of the mortar used by the Jews to build the palaces and pyramids of Egypt during centuries of slavery. The haroset is also eaten on a small piece of matzo.

5. *Karpas.* A green vegetable, such as lettuce or parsley, is placed to the left of the haroset, symbolic of the meager diet of the Jews in bondage. It is dipped into salt water in remembrance of the tears shed during this time. It also symbolizes springtime, the season of Passover.

6. A special cup, usually beautifully decorated, is set out on the seder table for Elijah, the prophet who strove to restore purity of Divine worship and labored for social justice. (Elijah is also believed to be a messenger of the Almighty, whose task it will be to announce the coming of the Messiah, and consequent peace and divine kingdom of righteousness on Earth).

Fast Days

There are several Jewish fast days in addition to Yom Kippur (see Table 2.1). On Yom Kippur and on Tisha b'Av, the fast lasts from sunset to sunset and no food or water can be consumed. All other fast days are observed from sunrise to sunset. Most Jews usually fast on Yom Kippur, but other fast days are observed only by Orthodox Jews. All fasts can be broken

TABLE 2.1. Jewish Fast Days.

Fast Day	Time of Year	Purpose
Ninth of Ave	August	Commemorates the destruction of the Temple in Jerusalem.
Tzom Gedaliah	Day after Rosh Hashanah	In memory of Gedaliah, who ruled after the First Temple was destroyed.
Tenth of Tevet Seventeenth of Tamuz	December July	Commemorates an assortment of national calamities listed in the Talmud.
Ta'anit Ester	Eve of Purim	In grateful memory of Queen Esther, who fasted when seeking divine guidance.
Ta'anit Bechorim	Eve of Passover	Gratitude to God for having spared the first born of Israel. Usually only the first-born son fasts.

if it is dangerous to one's health; those who are pregnant and nursing are exempt from fasting.

Additional information about Jewish dietary laws and customs associated with Jewish holidays can usually be obtained from the rabbi at a local synagogue. The Union of Orthodox Jewish Congregations of America also publishes a directory of kosher products.

Christianity

Throughout the world, more people follow Christianity than any other single religion. The three dominant Christian religions are Roman Catholicism, Eastern Orthodoxy, and Protestantism. Christianity is founded on actual events surrounding the life of Christ, believed to be the Son of God and the Messiah, that are chronicled in the New Testament. The central convictions of the Christian faith are found in the Apostles' and the Nicene Creed. The creed expresses the belief of the faith that people are saved through God's grace and Christ's life and death.

For most Christians, the sacraments mark the key stages of worship and sustain the individual worshiper. A *sacrament* is an outward act derived from something Christ did or said, by whose performance and observation the individual receives God's grace. The seven sacraments are baptism (entering Christ's church), confirmation (the soul receiving the Holy Ghost), communion (partaking of the sacred presence by sharing bread and wine), marriage, unction (sick and dying are reassured of salvation), penance (confession), and ordination of the clergy. Which sacraments are observed and in what manner varies among Christian groups.

ROMAN CATHOLIC

The largest number of persons adhering to one Christian faith in the United States are Roman Catholics (approximately 53 million people in 1983). The head of the worldwide church is the Pope, and he is considered to be infallible when defining faith and morals. The seven sacraments are conferred on the faithful.

Immigration to the United States

Although some Roman Catholics immigrated to the United States during the colonial period, substantial numbers came from Germany, Poland, Italy, and Ireland in the 1800s and from Mexico and the Caribbean in the twentieth century. There are small groups of French Catholics in New England (primarily in Maine) and in Louisiana. In addition, most Filipinos and some Vietnamese people living in the United States are Catholics.

Dietary Practices

Before 1966, abstinence was observed on every Friday that did not fall on a holy day of obligation. In the U.S. the six days of obligation are: New Year's Day (January 1), Ascension Thursday (40 days after Easter), Assumption (August 15), All Saints' Day (November 1), Immaculate Conception (December 8), and Christmas (December 25). In addition, fasting and abstinence were observed on Ash Wedneday (the first day of Lent) and Good Friday (the Friday before Easter). Abstinence forbids the use of meat but not of eggs, milk products, or condiments made of animal fat; fasting permits only one full meal a day. Fasting does not prohibit the taking of some food in the morning and evening; however, local custom as to the quantity and quality of this supplementary nourishment varies. Only Catholics over the age of 14 and under the age of 60 are required to observe the dietary laws. In 1966, the U.S. Catholic Conference abolished most dietary restrictions, although Catholics are still required to abstain from eating meat on the Fridays of Lent in remembrance of the sacrificial death of Christ, and to fast and abstain on Ash Wednesday and Good Friday. Some older or more devout Catholics still observe the previous rules of fasting and abstinence. Catholics are also required to avoid liquids (except water) and food one hour before receiving communion.

Lent is the 40 days before Easter and the word originally meant spring.

Roman Catholic Holidays and Feasts

Most Americans are familiar with Christmas (the birth of Christ) and Easter (the day Christ rose after the crucifixion). Other holidays that are observed by more devout Catholics are the Annunciation (March 25), Palm Sunday (the Sunday before Easter), Ascension (40 days after Easter), and Pentecost (Trinity) Sunday (50 days after Easter). Holiday fare depends on the family's country of origin. For example, the French traditionally serve *bûche de Noël* (a rich cake in the shape of a Yule log) on Christmas for dessert, while the Italians may serve *panettone,* a fruited sweet bread (refer to the chapter on each country for specific foods associated with holidays).

Eastern Orthodox

The Eastern Orthodox Church is not familiar to most Americans, but it is as old as the Roman Catholic branch of Christianity. In the year A.D. 300 there were two centers of Christianity, one in Rome and the other in Constantinople (now Istanbul, Turkey). Differences arose over theological interpretations of the Bible and the governing of the church, and in A.D. 1054 the fellowship between the Latin and Byzantine churches was finally broken. Some of the differences between the two churches concern the interpetation of the Trinity (the Father, the Son, and the Holy Ghost), the use of unleavened bread for the communion, the celibacy of the clergy, and the authority of the Pope. In the Eastern Orthodox Church leavened bread is used for communion, the clergy are allowed to marry before entering the priesthood, and the authority of the Pope is not recognized.

In the Eastern Orthodox religion the leavened communion bread, called *Phosphoron*, is prepared by the women of the Church.

Today the Orthodox Church consists of 14 self-governing churches, five of which, Constantinople, Alexandria (the Egyptian Coptic Church), Antioch, Jerusalem, and Cyprus, date back to the time of the Byzantine Empire. Six other churches represent the nations where the majority of people are Orthodox (Russia, Rumania, Yugoslavia, Bulgaria, Greece, and Soviet Georgia). Three other churches exist independently in countries where only a minority profess the religion. The beliefs of the churches are similar; only the language of the service differs.

The first Eastern Orthodox church in America was started by Russians on the West Coast in the late 1700s. In 1977 it was estimated that 3 million persons in the United States adhered to the Eastern Orthodox religion, with the largest following (2 million persons) being Greek. Most Eastern Orthodox churches in the United States recognize the patriarch of Constantinople as their spiritual leader.

Eastern Orthodox Dietary Practices

In the Eastern Orthodox religion there are numerous fast days (see Table 2.2). Further, those receiving Holy communion on Sunday abstain from food and drink before the service. Fasting is considered an opportunity to prove that the body can rule the soul. On fast days, no meat or animal prod-

Koliva, boiled whole grain wheat mixed with nuts, dried fruit and sugar, must be offered before the Church altar 3, 9, and 40 days after the death of a family member and then whenever desired. After the Koliva is blessed by the Priest it is distributed to the friends of the deceased. The boiled wheat symbolizes everlasting life and the fruit sweetness and plenty.

TABLE 2.2. Eastern Orthodox Fast Days and Periods.

Fast Day

Every Wednesday and Friday except during fast-free weeks:
  Week following Christmas till Eve of Theophany (12 days after Christmas)
  Bright Week, week following Easter
  Trinity Week, week following Trinity Sunday
Eve of Theophany (Jan. 6 or 18*)
Beheading of John the Baptist (Aug. 29 or Sept. 27)
The Elevation of the Holy Cross (Sept. 14 or 27)

Fast Periods

Nativity Fast (Advent): Nov. 15 or 28 to Dec. 24 or Jan. 6
Great Lent and Holy Week: 7 weeks before Easter
Fast of the Apostles: May 23 or June 5 to June 16 or 29
Fast of the Dormition of the Holy Theotokos (Aug. 1 or 14 to Aug. 15 or 28)

* Date depends on whether the Julian or Gregorian calendar is followed.

ucts (milk, eggs, butter, and cheese) are consumed. Fish is also avoided, but shellfish is allowed. Older or more devout Greek Orthodox followers do not use olive oil on fast days but will eat olives.

Feasts

All the feast days are listed in Table 2.3. Easter is the most important holiday in the Eastern Orthodox religion and is celebrated on the first Sunday after the full moon after March 21, but not before the Jewish Passover. Lent is preceded by a pre-Lenten period lasting 10 weeks before Easter or 3 weeks before Lent. On the third Sunday before Lent (Meat Fare Sun-

TABLE 2.3. Eastern Orthodox Feast Days.

Feast Day	Date*
Christmas	Dec. 25, Jan. 7
Theophany	Jan. 6, Jan. 19
Presentation of Our Lord into the Temple	Feb. 2, Feb. 15
Annunciation	Mar. 25, Apr. 7
Easter	See text for date
Ascension	40 days after Easter
Pentecost (Trinity) Sunday	50 days after Easter
Transfiguration	Aug. 6, Aug. 19
Dormition of the Holy Theotokos	Aug. 15, Aug. 28
Nativity of the Holy Theotokos	Sept. 8, Sept. 21
Presentation of the Holy Theotokos	Nov. 21, Dec. 4

* Exact date depends on whether the Julian or Gregorian calendar is followed.

day) all the meat in the house is eaten. On the Sunday before Lent (Cheese Fare Sunday) all the cheese, eggs, and butter in the house are eaten. On the next day, Clean Monday, the Lenten fast begins. Fish is allowed on Palm Sunday and on the Annunciation Day of the Virgin Mary. The Lenten fast is traditionally broken after the midnight services on Easter Sunday. Easter eggs in the Eastern Orthodox religion range from the highly ornate (Eastern Europe and Russia) to the solid red ones used by the Greeks.

The red Easter egg symbolizes the tomb of Christ (the egg) and is a sign of mourning (red). The breaking of the eggs on Easter morning represents the opening of the tomb and the belief in the resurrection.

PROTESTANTS

The sixteenth-century religious movement known as the Reformation established the Protestant churches by questioning the practices of the Catholic Church and eventually breaking away from its teachings. The two men most responsible for the Reformation were Martin Luther and John Calvin.

Martin Luther, a German Augustinian monk who taught theology, started the movement when, in 1517, he nailed a document containing 95 protests against certain Catholic practices on the door of the Castle Church in Wittenberg. He later broadened his position, and a decade later several countries and German principalities organized the Protestant Lutheran church based on his teachings.

Luther placed great emphasis on the individual's direct responsibility to God. He believed that every person can reach God through direct prayer without the intercession of a priest or saint; thus every believer is in effect a minister. Although everyone is prone to sin and is inherently wicked, a person can be saved by faith in Christ, who by His death on the Cross had atoned for the sins of all people. Consequently, to Luther, faith was all-important and good works alone could not negate evil deeds. Luther's theology took away the priest's mystic function and encouraged everyone to read the Bible and interpret the Scriptures.

John Calvin, a French theologian who fled France to settle in Geneva, gave theological coherence to Protestant revolt in his book *Institutes of Christian Religion*. It includes the doctrine of *predestination:* those who have been chosen for salvation cannot resist or fall from that fate, but those who have been chosen for damnation are doomed to everlasting hell (including infants who die before they have committed any conscious acts). The Presbyterian and Reformed churches regard themselves as the spiritual heirs of Calvinism but do not strictly adhere to the doctrine of predestination.

In addition to the Protestant churches already mentioned, other denominations in the United States include Congregationalists (started by the Puritans); Methodists; Baptists; Episcopalians (related to the English Anglican Church started under King Henry VIII); Seventh-Day Adventists; Jehovah's Witnesses; Disciples of Christ; Church of Jesus Christ of Latter Day Saints (Mormons); Church of Christ, Scientist (Christian Scientists); and Friends (Quakers). Only a few of the Protestant denominations, such as the Seventh-Day Adventists and the Mormons, have dietary practices integral to the religion.

Mormons

The Church of Jesus Christ of Latter Day Saints is a purely American institution that emerged in the early 1800s. Its founder, Joseph Smith, Jr., had a vision of the Angel Moroni, who told him of golden plates hidden in a hill and the means by which to decipher them. The resulting *Book of Mormon* was published in 1829, and in 1830 a new religious faith was born.

The *Book of Mormon* details the story of two bands of Israelites who settled in America and from whom certain Native Americans are descended. Christ visited them after His resurrection, and thus they preserved Christianity in its pure form. The tribes did not survive, but the last member, Moroni, hid the nation's sacred writings, compiled by his father, Mormon.

The Mormons believe that God reveals Himself and His will through His apostles and prophets. The Mormon Church is organized along biblical lines. Members of the priesthood are graded upward in six degrees (deacons, teachers, priests, elders, seventies, and high priests). From the priesthood are chosen, by the church at large, a council of twelve apostles, which constitutes a group of ruling elders; from these, by seniority, a church president rules with life tenure. There is no paid clergy. Sunday services are held by groups of Mormons, and selected church members give the sermon.

Because of persecution, Brigham Young led the people of the Mormon Church to Utah in 1847. Today, Utah is over 80 percent Mormon and many western states have significant numbers of church members. The main branch of the church is headquartered in Salt Lake City, but a smaller branch, the Reorganized Church of Jesus Christ of Latter Day Saints, is centered in Independence, Missouri. All Mormons believe that Independence will be the capital of the world when Christ returns.

Joseph Smith, through a revelation, prescribed the Mormon laws of health, dealing particularly with dietary matters. They prohibit the use of tobacco, strong drink, and hot drinks. Strong drink is defined as alcoholic beverages; hot drinks mean tea and coffee. Many Mormons do not use any product that contains caffeine. In addition, all Mormons are required to store a year's supply of food and clothing for each person in the family. Many also fast one day per month.

Seventh-Day Adventists

In the early 1800s, many people believed that the Second Coming of Christ was imminent. In the United States, William Miller predicted that Christ would return in 1843 or 1844. When both years passed and the prediction did not materialize, many of his followers became disillusioned. However, one group continued to believe that the prediction was not wrong but that the date was actually the beginning of the world's end preceding the coming of Christ. They became known as the Seventh-Day Adventists and were officially organized in 1863.

The spiritual guide for the new church was Ellen G. Harmon, who later became Mrs. James White. Her inspirations were the result of over 2,000 prophetic visions and dreams she reportly had during her life. Mrs. White claimed to be not a prophet but a conduit that relayed God's desires and admonitions to humankind.

Today there are over one-half million Seventh-Day Adventists in the United States and over one million worldwide. Besides the main belief in Christ's advent, or second coming, the Seventh-Day Adventists practice the principles of Protestantism. They believe that the advent will be preceded by a monstrous war, pestilence, and plague, resulting in the destruction of wicked people and Satan and the purification of the earth by holocaust. Although the hour of Christ's return is not known, they believe that dedication to His work will hasten it.

The church adheres strictly to the teachings of the Bible. The Sabbath is observed from sundown on Friday to sundown on Saturday and is wholly dedicated to the Lord. Food must be prepared on Friday and dishes washed on Sunday. Church members dress simply, avoid ostentation, and wear only functional jewelry.

The church's headquarters are in Takoma Park, Maryland, near Washington, D.C., where they were moved after a series

The American breakfast cereal industry is the result of the dietary and health practices of the Seventh-Day Adventists. Dr. Kellogg studied medicine at Johns Hopkins University and became director of the Adventists' sanitarium in Battle Creek, Michigan. In his efforts to find a tasty meat substitute, he invented corn flakes.

of fires ravaged the previous center in Battle Creek, Michigan. Each congregation is led by a pastor (a teacher more than a minister), and all the churches are under the leadership of the president of the general conference of Seventh-Day Adventists.

Adventists follow Apostle Paul's teaching that the human body is the temple of the Holy Spirit. Many of Mrs. White's writings are concerned with health and diet and have been compiled into such books as *The Ministry of Healing, Counsels on Diet and Foods,* and *Counsels on Health.*

Adventists believe that sickness is a result of the violation of the laws of health. One can preserve health by eating the right kinds of foods in moderation and by getting enough rest and exercise. Overeating is discouraged. Vegetarianism is widely practiced, because the Bible states that the diet in Eden did not include flesh foods. Most Adventists are lacto-ovo-vegetarians (eating milk products and eggs but not meat), but some do consume meat, although they avoid pork and shellfish. Mrs. White advocated the use of nuts and beans instead of meat, substituting vegetable oil for animal fat, and using whole grains in breads. Like the Mormons, the Adventists do not consume tea, coffee, or alcohol and do not use tobacco products. Water is considered the best liquid and should be consumed only before and after the meal, not during the meal. Meals are not highly seasoned, and condiments such as mustard and pepper are avoided. Eating between meals is discouraged so that food can be properly digested. Mrs. White recommended that 5 or 6 hours should elapse between meals.

Islam

Islam is the second largest religious group in the world. Although not widely practiced in the United States, Islam is the dominant religion in the Middle East, North Africa, Pakistan, Indonesia, and Malaysia. Large numbers of people also practice the religion in parts of Africa, India, the Soviet Union, and Southeast Asia. Islam, which means "submission" (to the will of God) is not only a religion but also a way of life. One who adheres to Islam is called a Muslim, "he who submits."

Islam's founder, Mohammed, was neither a savior nor a messiah but rather a prophet through whom God delivered His messages. He was born in A.D. 570 in Mecca, Saudi Arabia, a city located along the spice trade route. Early in Mohammed's life he acquired a respect for Jewish and Christian monotheism. Later, the archangel Gabriel appeared to him in many visions. These revelations continued for a decade or more, and the archangel told Mohammed that he was a prophet of Allah, the one true God.

Mohammed's teachings met with hostility in Mecca, and in A.D. 622 he fled to Yathrib. The year of the flight (*hegira*) is the first year in the Muslim calendar. At Yathrib, later named Medina, Mohammed became a religious and political leader. Eight years after fleeing Mecca, he returned a triumphant warrior and declared Mecca a holy place to Allah. The most sacred writings of Islam are found in the *Koran*, believed to contain the words spoken by Allah through Mohammed. It includes many legends and traditions that parallel those of the Old and New Testaments, as well as Arabian folktales. The Koran also contains the basic laws of Islam, and its analysis and interpretation by religious scholars has provided the guidelines by which Muslims lead their day-to-day lives.

The Muslims believe that the one true God, Allah, is basically the God of Judaism and Christianity, but that His word was incompletely expressed in the Old and New Testaments and was only fulfilled in the Koran. Similarly, they believe that Mohammed was the last prophet, superseding Christ, who is considered a prophet and not the Son of God. The primary doctrines of Islam are monotheism and the concept of the last judgment, the day of final resurrection when all will be judged worthy of either the delights of heaven or the terrors of hell.

Mohammed did not institute an organized priesthood or sacraments but instead advocated the following ritualistic observances, known as the Five Pillars of Islam:

1. *Faith,* shown by the proclamation of the unity of God, and belief in that unity, as expressed in the creed "There is no God but Allah; Mohammed is the Messenger of Allah."

2. *Prayer,* performed five times daily (at dawn, noon, mid-afternoon, sunset, and nightfall), facing Mecca, wherever one may be; and on Fridays, the day of public prayer, in the mosque (a building used for public worship). On Fridays sermons are delivered in the mosque after the noon prayer.

3. *Almsgiving, zakat,* as an offering to the poor and an act of piety. In some Islamic countries Muslims are expected to give 2.5 percent of their net savings or assets in money or goods. The money is used to help the poor or to support the religious organization in countries were Islam is not the dom-

If one is unable to attend a mosque, the prayers are said on a prayer rug facing Mecca.

The *Kaaba* is the holiest shrine of Islam and contains the Black Stone. The Muslims believe that the stone was given to Abraham and Ishmael by the Archangel Gabriel.

inant religion. In addition, *zakat* is given to the needy on certain feast and fast days (see the section on dietary practices for more details).

4. *Fasting,* to fulfill a religious obligation, to earn the pleasure of Allah, to wipe out previous sins, and to appreciate the hunger of the poor and the needy.

5. *Pilgrimage to Mecca, hadj,* once in a lifetime if means are available. No non-Muslim can enter Mecca. Pilgrims must wear seamless white garments, go without head covering or shoes, practice sexual continence, abstain from shaving or having their hair cut, and avoid harming any living thing, animal or vegetable.

There are no priests in Islam; since every Muslim can communicate directly with God, a mediator is not needed. The successors of the prophet Mohammed and the leaders of the Islamic community were the *caliphes* (kalifah). No caliphes exist today. A *mufti*, like a lawyer, gives legal advice based on the sacred laws of the Koran. An *imam* is the person appointed to lead prayer in the mosque and deliver the Friday sermon.

The following prominent sects in Islam have their origin in conflicting theories on the office of caliph:

1. The *Sunni,* who form the largest number of Muslims and hold that the caliphate is an elected office that must be occupied by a member of the tribe of Koreish, the tribe of Mohammed.

2. The *Shi'ites,* the second largest group, who believe that the caliphate was a God-given office held rightfully by Ali, Mohammed's son-in-law, and his descendants. The Shi'ites are found primarily in Iran, Iraq, Yemen, and India.

3. The *Khawarij,* who believe that the office of caliph is open to any believer whom the faithful consider fit for it. Followers of this sect are found primarily in eastern Arabia and North Africa.

4. The *Sufis,* are ascetic mystics who seek a close union with God now, rather than in the hereafter. Only 3 percent of present-day Muslims are Sufis.

It is estimated that 3 million Muslims live in the United States; the majority came from the Middle East. In addition, there is a group of American blacks that believes Allah is the one true God and that uses the Koran and traditional Muslim rituals in their temple services. The movement was originally known as the Nation of Islam and its followers identified as Black Muslims. Under the leadership of Wallace D. Muhammad, this formerly black nationalist group became an orthodox Islamic religion and is now called the World Community of Al-Islam in the West. It is accepted as a branch of the Islamic world community. Membership claims vary from 100,000 to 750,000, consisting primarily of young blacks living in urban ghettos.

MUSLIM DIETARY PRACTICES

In the Islamic religion, eating is considered to be a matter of worship. Muslims are expected to eat for survival and good health; self-indulgence is not permitted. Muslims are advised not to eat more than two-thirds of their capacity, and sharing food is recommended. Food is never to be thrown away, wasted, or treated with contempt. The hands and mouth are washed before and after meals. If eating utensils are not used, only the right hand is used for eating, since the left hand is considered unclean.

Unlawful foods

Unless specifically prohibited, all food is edible. The Koran prohibits the following foods:

1. All swine, four-footed animals that catch their prey with their mouths, and birds of prey that seize their prey with their talons.

2. Improperly slaughtered animals: an animal must be killed in a manner similar to that described in the Jewish laws, by slitting the front of the throat, cutting the jugular vein, carotid artery, and windpipe, and allowing the blood to drain completely. Additionally, the person who kills the animal must repeat at the instant of slaughter, "In the name of God, God is great." Fish and seafood are exempt from this requirement.

Some Muslims believe that a Jew or a Christian can slaughter an animal to be consumed by Muslims as long as it is done properly. Others will eat only kosher meat, while some abstain from meat unless they know it is properly slaughtered by a Muslim or can arrange to kill the animal themselves. Meat of animals slaughtered by people other than Muslims, Jews, or Christians is prohibited. Meat is also prohibited if it came from an animal that was slaughtered when any name besides God's was mentioned.

3. Alcoholic beverages and intoxicating drugs; unless medically necessary. The drinking of stimulants, such as coffee and tea, is discouraged, as is smoking; however, these prohibitions are practiced only by the most devout Muslims.

A Muslim can eat or drink prohibited food under certain conditions, such as when the food is taken by mistake, is forced by others, or there is fear of dying by hunger or disease.

Fast Days

On fast days Muslims abstain from food, drink, smoking, and coitus from dawn to sunset. Food can be eaten before the sun comes up and again after it sets. Muslims are required to fast during Ramadan, the ninth month of the Islamic calendar. During Ramadan, it is believed that "the gates of Heaven are open, the gates of Hell closed, and the devil put in chains." At sunset the fast is usually broken by taking a liquid, along with an odd number of dates.

All Muslims past the age of puberty (15 years old) are required to fast during Ramadan. A number of groups are exempt from fasting, but most must make up the days before the next Ramadan. They include sick individuals with a recoverable illness; people who are traveling; women during pregnancy, lactation, or menstruation; elderly people who are physically unable to fast; insane people; and those engaged in hard labor.

During Ramadan it is customary to invite guests to break the fast and dine in the evening; special foods are eaten, especially sweets. Food is often given to neighbors, relatives, and needy individuals or families.

Muslims are also encouraged to fast six days during Shawwal, the month following Ramadan; the tenth day of the month of Muhurram; and the ninth day of Zul Hijjah, but not during the pilgrimage to Mecca. A Muslim may fast voluntarily, preferably on Mondays and Thursdays. Muslims are not allowed to fast on two festival days, *Eid al-Fitr* (Feast of Fast Breaking) and *Eid al-Azhă (Festival of Sacrifice)* (see the next section for more information). It is also undesirable for Muslims to fast excessively or to fast on Fridays.

The month of Ramadan can fall during any part of the year. The Muslim calendar is lunar, but does not have a leap month, thus the months fall at different times each year.

Feast days

The following are the feast days in the Islamic religion:

1. *Eid al-Fitr, the Feast of Fast Breaking:* the end of Ramadan is celebrated by a feast and the giving of alms.
2. *Eid al-Azhă, the Festival of Sacrifice:* the commemoration of Abraham's willingness to sacrifice his son, Ishmael, for God. It is customary to sacrifice a sheep and distribute its meat to friends, relatives; and the needy.
3. *Shab-i-Barăt, the night in the middle of Shaban:* originally a fast day, this is now a feast day, often marked with fireworks. It is believed that God determines the actions of every person for the next year on this night.
4. *Nau-Roz, New Year's Day:* primarily celebrated by the Iranians, it is the first day after the sun crosses the vernal equinox.
5. *Maulud n'Nabĭ:* the birthday of Mohammed.

EASTERN RELIGIONS

Hinduism

Hinduism is considered to be the world's oldest religion and like Judaism it is the basis of other religions, such as Buddhism. Although Hinduism was once popular throughout much of Asia, most Hindus now live in India, its birthplace.

The common Hindu scriptures are the *Vedas*, the *Epics* and the *Bhagavata Purana.* The Vedas form the supreme authority for Hinduism. There are four Vedas: the *Rigveda*, the *Samaveda*, the *Yajurveda* and the *Aatharvaveda.* Each consists of four parts.

The goal of Hinduism is not to make humans perfect beings or life a heaven on earth but to make humans one with the universal spirit or supreme being. When this state is achieved, there is no cause and effect, no time and space, no good and evil: all dualities are merged into oneness. This goal cannot be reached by being a good person, but it can be obtained by transforming human consciousness or liberation, *moksha*, into a new realm of divine consciousness that sees individual parts of the universe as deriving their true significance from the central unity of spirit. The transformation of human consciousness into divine consciousness is not achieved in one lifetime, and Hindus believe that the present life is only one in a series of lives, or reincarnations. Hindus believe in the law of rebirth, which postulates that every person passes through a series of lives before he obtains liberation, the law of *karma,* and that one's present life is the result of what one thought or did in one's past life. In each new incarnation, an individual's soul moves up or down the spiritual scale; the goal for all souls is liberation.

There is one supreme being, Brahmin, and all the various gods worshiped by men are partial manifestations of him. The worshiper chooses the form of the supreme being that satisfies the spirit and makes it an object of love and adoration. This aspect of worship makes Hinduism very tolerant of other gods and their followers; many different religions have been absorbed into Hinduism.

The three most important functions of the supreme being are the creation, protection, and destruction of the world, and these functions have become personified as three great gods: Brahma, Vishnu, and Siva (the Hindu triad or trinity). The supreme being as Vishnu is the protector of the world. Vishnu is also an avatara, meaning he can take on human forms whenever the world is threatened by evil. Rama and Krishna are regarded as two such incarnations and are also objects of worship.

The Hindus believe that the world passes through repeating cycles; the most common version of the creation is connected to the life of Vishnu. From Vishnu's navel grows a lotus, and from its unfolding petals is born the god Brahma who creates the world. Vishnu governs the world until he sleeps, then Siva destroys it and the world is absorbed into Vishnu's body to be created once again.

The moral ideals of Hinduism are purity, self-control, detachment, truth, and nonviolence. Purity is both a ceremonial goal and a moral ideal. All rituals for purification and the elaborate rules regarding food and drink are meant to lead to purity of mind and spirit. Self-control is both the flesh and the mind. Hinduism does not teach its followers to suppress the flesh completely, but to regulate its appetites and cravings. The highest aspect of self-control is detachment. Complete liberation from this world and union with the divine is not possible if one clings to the good or evil of this existence.

Pursuit of truth is indispensable to the progress of man, and truth is always associated with nonviolence, *ahimsa.* These are considered to be the highest virtues. India's greatest exponent of this ideal was Mahatma Gandhi, who taught that nonviolence must be practiced not only by individuals but also by communities and nations.

One common belief of Hinduism is that the world evolved in successive stages, beginning with matter and going on through life, consciousness, and intelligence, to spiritual bliss or perfection. Spirit first appears as life in plants, then as consciousness in animals, intelligence in humans, and finally bliss in the supreme spirit. A good person is closer to the supreme spirit than a bad person, and a person is closer than an animal. Truth, beauty, love, and righteousness are of higher importance than intellectual values (such as clarity, cogency, subtlety, and skill) or biological values (such as health, strength, and vitality). Material values (riches, possessions, and pleasure) are valued least.

Depending on a person's level of consciousness, Hinduism prescribes the kind of discipline that will enable one to pass to the the next stage. If the metaphysical ideal (transformation of human consciousness into divine consciousness) is too advanced and abstract for a particular person, then the theological ideal is used. In this stage, the impersonal God becomes personal, the perfect becomes good, liberation becomes life in heaven, and love takes the place of knowledge. If one is not fit for this stage either, a course of ritualistic and moral action is prescribed. At this level the personal God is represented by an image in a temple, ritual and prayer take the place of meditation, and righteous conduct takes the place of love.

The organization of society grows from the principle of spiritual progression. The Hindu lawgivers tried to construct an ideal society in which people are ranked not according to wealth or power but by their spiritual progress and culture. The social system reflects this ideal, which is represented by castes. The four castes are the *Brahmans* (teachers and priests), the *Kshatriyas* (soldiers), the *Vaisyas* (merchants and farmers), and the *Sundras* (laborers). Untouchables (such as butchers and leather workers) are a group of persons who do not fall into the above four categories; this class was outlawed by the Indian government in 1950.

The four classes are represented as forming parts of the Creator's body, respectively his mouth, arms, thighs, and feet. The untouchables were created from darkness that Brahma discarded in the process of creation. The castes also conform to the law of spiritual progression, in that the most spiritual caste occupies the top and the least spiritual the bottom. The Hindus believe that nature has three fundamental qualities: purity, energy, and inertia. Those in whom purity predominates form the first caste, energy the second caste, inertia the third and fourth caste. Each caste should perform its own duties, follow its hereditary occupation, and cooperate with the others for the common welfare. A person's good actions in this life earns him promotion to a higher caste in the next life.

There are thousands of subdivisions of the four main castes. The subcastes often reflect a trade or profession, but some scholars contend that the latter was imposed on the former. In reality, the subcaste is very important to daily life, while what major caste one belongs to makes little difference to non-Brahmans. (See the chapter on India for more information on castes.)

The ideal life of a Hindu is divided into four successive stages, called *asramas*. The first stage is the student and is devoted entirely to study and discipline. The *guru* becomes one's spiritual parent. After this period of preparation, the student should marry, settle down, and serve his marriage, community, and country. When this period of active life and citizenship is over, he should retire to a quiet place in the country and meditate on the higher aspects of the spirit (a recluse). The recluse then becomes a *sannyasin*, one who has renounced all earthly possessions and ties. This stage is the crown of human life. The goals of life are *dharma* (righteousness), *artha* (worldly prosperity), *kama* (enjoyment), and *moksha* (liberation). The ultimate aim of life is liberation, but on their way to this final goal people must satisfy the animal wants of the bodies, as well as the economic and other demands of their families and communities. However, all should be done within the moral law of dharma.

Common practices in Hinduism include rituals and forms of mental discipline. Every Hindu is advised to choose a deity on whose form, features, and qualities he can concentrate his mind and whose image he can worship every day with flowers and incense. The deity is only a means of realizing the supreme being by means of ritualistic worship. Externally, the deity is worshipped as a king or honored guest. Internal worship consists of prayer and meditation. Mental discipline is indicated by the word *yoga*. Along with mental discipline, *yoga* has come to mean a method of restraining the functions of the mind and their physiologic consequences.

Hindus can be divided into three broad sects according to their view of the supreme being. They are the *Vaishnava*, the *Saiva*, and the *Sakta*, who maintain the supremacy of Vishnu, Siva, and the Sakti (the female and active aspects of Siva),

Yoga means yoke, as in yoking together or union.

respectively. Different sects are popular in different regions of India. Many Hindus do not worship one God exclusively. Vishnu may be worshiped in one of his full (Krishna or Rama) or partial incarnations. In addition there are hundreds of lesser deities, much like saints. One is Siva's son, the elephant-headed Ganash, who is thought to be a bringer of good luck and a remover of obstacles.

It is not known how many Hindus live in the United States, since the religion is not centered around a temple nor are its affairs conducted by priests. It is assumed that a significant percentage of the Indian population of the United States is Hindu. A small percentage of non-Indian Americans have become followers of the Hindu religion. The International Society for Krishna Consciousness (ISKON), founded in 1966 by devotees of a sixteenth-century Bengali ascetic, has the largest number of converts.

HINDU DIETARY PRACTICES

In general, Hindus avoid foods that are thought to hamper the development of the body or mental abilities. Bad food habits will prevent one from reaching mental purity and communion with God. Dietary restrictions and attitudes vary among the castes.

The Laws of Manu state that "no sin is attached to eating flesh or drinking wine, or gratifying the sexual urge, for these are the natural propensities of men; but abstinence from these bears greater fruits." Inherent in the Hindu's vegetarian diet is the concept of *ahimsa*. By not eating meat, a Hindu avoids inflicting pain on an animal. Although eating meat is allowed, the cow is considered sacred and is not to be killed or eaten. Fish that have ugly forms, and the heads of snakes, are forbidden. Snails, crabs, fowl, cranes, ducks, camels, and boars are also forbidden. No fish or meat should be eaten until it has been sanctified by the repetition of mantras offering it to the gods.

Pious Hindus may also abstain from drinking alcohol. Garlic, turnips, onions, mushrooms, and red-colored foods such as tomatoes, red lentils, and red-colored juices may be avoided. If meat is eaten, pork as well as beef is usually avoided. Students who are studying the Vedas and other celibates are vegetarians and may restrict irritating or exciting foods, such as honey.

Intertwined in Hindu food customs is the concept of purity and pollution. All elaborate rules regarding food and drink are meant to lead to purity of mind and spirit. Pollution is the opposite of purity and should be avoided or ameliorated. To remain pure is to remain free from pollution; to become pure is to remove pollution.

Certain substances are considered both pure in themselves and purifying in their application. These include the products of the living cow, such as milk products, dung, and urine, and water from sources of special sanctity, such as the Ganges River. They also include materials commonly employed in rituals, such as tumeric and sandalwood paste. All body products (feces, urine, saliva, menstrual flow, and afterbirth) are polluting. Use of water is the most common method of purification, because water easily absorbs pollution and carries it away.

Fasting

The Indian calendar is lunar, thus its religious days do not always fall on the same day in the Western calendar. Every five years the Hindu calender adds a 13th leap month (a very auspicious month) in order to reconcile the months with the seasons.

In India, fasting practices vary according to one's caste, family, age, sex, and degree of orthodoxy. A devoutly religious person may fast more often and more strictly than one who is less religious. Fasting may mean eating no food at all or abstaining from only specific foods or meals. It is rare for an individual to go without any food at all, because there are numerous fast days in Hinduism.

The fast days in the Hindu calendar include the first day of the new and full moon of each lunar month; the tenth and eleventh day of each month; the feast of *Sivaratri*; the ninth day of the lunar month *Cheitra*; the eighth day of *Sravana*; days of eclipses, equinoxes, solstices, and conjunction of planets; the anniversary of the death of one's father or mother, and Sundays.

Feasts

The Hindu calendar has 18 major festivals every year. Additional important feast days are those of marriages, births, and deaths. Each region of India has its own special festivals; it has been said that there is a festival going on somewhere in India every day of the year. All members of the community eat generously on festive occasions, and these may be the only days that very poor people eat adequately. Feasting is a way of sharing food among the population, because the wealthy are responsible for helping the poor celebrate the festivals.

One of the gaiest and most colorful of the Hindu festivals is *Holi*, the spring equinox and the celebration of one of Krishna's triumphs. According to legend, Krishna had an evil uncle who sent an ogress named Holika to burn down Krishna's house. Instead, Krishna escaped and Holika burned in the blaze. It is traditional for Indians to throw colored water or powder at passersby during this holiday.

Divali, celebrated throughout India in November, marks the darkest night of the year, when souls return to earth and must be shown the way by the lights in the houses. For many, Divali is also the beginning of the new year, when everyone should buy new clothes, settle old debts and quarrels, and wish everyone else good fortune.

The ten-day celebration of *Dasehra* in late September or early October commemorates the victory of Prince Rama (one of Vishnu's incarnations) over the army of the demon Ravana and is a grateful tribute to the goddess Durga, who aided Rama. The first nine days of Dasehra are spent in worshiping the deity, and the tenth day is spent celebrating Rama's victory.

Prince Rama was aided by Hanuman, a monkey hero, thus monkeys are revered all over India and are not killed even though they cause serious crop damage.

Buddhism

Siddhartha Gautama, who later became known as Buddha (the Enlightened One), founded this Eastern religion in India

Buddhist church Betsuin of San Jose, California.

in the sixth century B.C. Buddhism flourished in India until A.D. 500, when it declined and gradually became absorbed into Hinduism. Meanwhile, it had spread throughout Southeast and central Asia. Buddhism remains a vital religion in many Asian countries, where it has been adapted to local needs and traditions.

Buddhism was a protestant revolt against orthodox Hinduism, but it accepted certain Hindu concepts, such as the idea that all living beings go through countless cycles of death and rebirth; the doctrine of karma; spiritual liberation from the flesh; and that the path to wisdom includes taming the appetites and passions of the body. Buddha disagreed with the Hindus about the methods by which these objectives were to be achieved. He advocated the "Middle Way" between asceticism and self-indulgence, stating that both extremes in life should be avoided. He also disagreed with the Hindus on caste distinctions, believing that all persons were equal in spiritual potential.

The basic teachings of Buddha are found in the Four Noble Truths and the Noble Eightfold Path. The Four Noble Truths are:

The spokes of the Wheel of the Law, a symbol of Buddhism, represent the Eightfold Path.

1. *The Noble Truth of Suffering:* suffering is part of living. Persons suffer when they experience birth, old age, sickness, and death. They also suffer when they fail to obtain what they want.
2. *The Noble Truth of the Cause of Suffering:* suffering is caused by a person's craving for life, which causes rebirth.
3. *The Noble Truth of the Cessation of Suffering:* a person no longer suffers if all cravings are relinquished.
4. *The Noble Truth to the Path that Leads to the Cessation of Suffering:* this is the Eightfold Path. By following this path (right view, right thought, right speech, right action, right livelihood, right effort, right mindfulness, and right concentration), craving is extinguished and deliverance from suffering ensues.

The third and fourth phrases of the Eightfold Path, right speech and right action, have been extended into a practical code of conduct which is known as the Five Precepts. These are: (1) to abstain from the taking of life; (2) to abstain from the taking of what is not given; (3) to abstain from all illegal sexual pleasures; (4) to abstain from lying; and (5) to abstain from consumption of intoxicants, because they tend to cloud the mind.

For the person who perfects Buddha's teachings, the outcome is *nirvana*, a state of calm insight, passionlessness, and wisdom. In addition, the person is no longer subject to rebirth into the sorrows of existence.

Because the ideal practice of Buddhism is impractical in the turmoil of daily life, Buddhism has encouraged a monastic lifestyle. The ideal Buddhists are monks, following a life of simplicity and spending considerable time in meditation. They own no personal property and obtain food by begging. They are usually vegetarians and are permitted to eat only before noon. The monk confers a favor or merit (good karma) on those who give him food.

There are numerous sects in Buddhism and two great schools of doctrine: *Hinayana* (or *Theravada*) Buddhism, which is followed in India and Southeast Asia, and *Mahayana* Buddhism, which is followed in China, Japan, Korea, Tibet, and Mongolia.

Hinayana Buddhism is primarily a spiritual philosophy and system of ethics. It places little or no emphasis on deities, teaching that the goal of the faithful is to achieve nirvana. In Mahayana, a later form of Buddhism, Buddha is eternal and cosmic, appearing variously in many worlds in order to make known his truth, called dharma. This has resulted in a pantheon of Buddhas who are sometimes deified, and, for some sects, a hierarchy of demons. Some sects promise the worshiper a real paradise, rather than the perfected spiritual state of nirvana.

The number of Buddhists in the United States is probably fewer than 200,000; the majority are immigrants from Japan, China, and Southeast Asia and their descendants. There is also a small number of non-Asians who have more recently converted to Buddhism. Zen Buddhism, a Chinese sect that spread to Japan around the year 1200, has gained followers in the West.

BUDDHIST DIETARY PRACTICES

Buddhist dietary restrictions vary considerably depending on the sect and country. Buddhist doctrine forbids the taking of life; therefore many followers are lacto-ovo-vegetarians, but some eat fish and others abstain only from beef. Others believe that if they were not personally responsible for killing the animal, it is permissible to eat its flesh.

Fasting and Feasting

Buddhist monks may fast twice a month, on the days of the new and full moon. They also do not eat any solid food after

A Zen Buddhist monastery, Tassajara, located in Carmel Valley, California, runs a vegetarian restaurant in San Francisco called Greens and has also published a popular cookbook. Zen macrobiotics has nothing to do with Zen Buddhism. It was created in this century by George Oshawa, who advocated a diet (mainly brown rice and miso soup) that he said would produce spiritual enlightenment.

noon. Buddhist festivals vary according to region. Most Buddhists celebrate *pravarana*, the end of the rainy season; this is an occasion for offering gifts to the monks, inviting them to a meal, and organizing processions.

REFERENCES

Anon. 1957. *The World's Great Religions.* New York: Time, Inc.

Cole, W. O., & Singh Sambhi, P. 1978. *The Sikhs.* Boston, MA: Routledge & Kegan Paul.

Lowenberg, M. E., Todhunter, E. N., Wilson, E. D., Savage, J. R., & Lubawski, J. L. 1979. *Food and People* (3rd ed.). New York: John Wiley & Sons.

Marsh, C. E. 1984. *From Black Muslims to Muslims: The Transition from Separatism to Islam, 1930–1980.* Metuchen, NY: Scarecrow Press.

Natow, A. B., Heslin, J. & Raven, B. C. 1975. Integrating the Jewish dietary laws into a dietetic program. *Journal of American Dietetic Association 67,* 13–16.

Nelson, M. S., & Javanovic, L. 1987. Pregnancy, diabetes, and Jewish dietary law: The challenge for the pregnant diabetic women who keep Kosher. *Journal of American Dietetic Association 87,* 1,054–1,058.

Robinson, R. H., & Johnson, W. L. 1982. *The Buddhist Religion.* Belmont, CA: Wadworth.

Roth, C. 1972. Dietary habits. In *Encyclopedia Judaica.* Jerusalem: Keter Publishing.

Rau, S. R. 1969. *Cooking of India.* New York: Time-Life Books.

Sakr, A. H. 1971. Dietary regulations and food habits of Muslims. *Journal of American Dietetic Association 58,* 123–126.

Sakr, A. H. 1975. Fasting in Islam. *Journal of American Dietetic Association 67,* 17–21.

Sarma, D. S. 1953. The nature and history of Hinduism. In *The Religion of the Hindus,* K. W. Morgon (Ed.). New York: Ronald Press.

Spence, H. 1960. *The Story of America's Religions.* New York: Holt, Rinehart & Winston.

3

NATIVE AMERICANS

Included in the designation "Native American" is the greatest number of ethnic groups of any minority population in the United States. Each of the approximately 400 Indian and Alaskan Native nations has its own distinct cultural heritage. There are nearly 1.5 million self-declared Native Americans in the United States, approximately 0.6 percent of the total population.

Traditional Native American foods have made significant contributions to today's American diet. Corn, squash, beans, cranberries, and maple syrup are just a few of the items Indians introduced to European settlers. Historians question whether the original British colonists would have survived their first years in America without the supplies they obtained and cooking methods they learned from the Indians.

The vast majority of Native Americans today live west of the Mississippi River. Roughly half live in rural areas, either on government reservations or on nearby farms. Native American ethnic identity varies tremendously, from tenacious maintainence of heritage to total adoption of the majority culture. The diet of the Native American has changed dramatically from its origins, yet recent renewed interest in Native American culture has prevented the complete disappearance of many traditional foods and food habits. This chapter will review both the past and present diet of Native American ethnic groups.

Traditional Native American foods: Some typical foods in traditional Native American regional diets include beans, berries, corn, fish, jerky, *maple syrup, squash, and tomatoes.* (Photo by Laurie Macfee.)

CULTURAL PERSPECTIVE

History of Native Americans

It is hypothesized that the Indians came to North America approximately 20,000 to 50,000 years ago across the Bering Strait, which links Asia to Alaska, although some evidence suggests earlier migrations may have occurred. Archaeological research provides little insight into the settlement patterns and diversification of Indian culture in the years before European contact in the 1600s. In addition, the Indian languages are entirely verbal, so written historical records are nonexistent. There are, consequently, enormous gaps in knowledge of early Native American society.

In contrast, the observations of the Indians by white settlers have been well documented. They identified three centers of Indian culture during the seventeenth century. In the southeast, the sophisticated social organization of the Cherokees, Chickasaws, Choctaws, Creeks, and Seminoles led the Europeans to call them the "Five Civilized Tribes." The Iro-

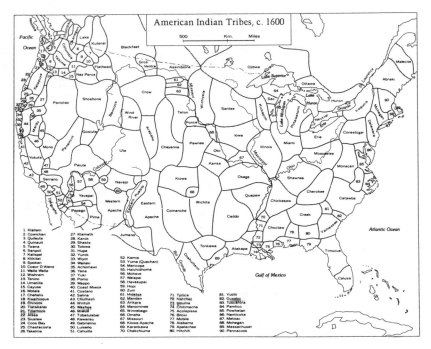

Native American nations in the seventeenth century. (From Thernstrom et al. 1980 with permission from Harvard University Press ©1980 by The President and Fellows of Harvard College.)

quois, in what is now New York State, ruled a democratic confederacy of five nations. Religion and the arts flourished in Pueblo Indian communities adjacent to the Rio Grande and Little Colorado Rivers in the Southwest.

The introduction of horses, firearms, and metal knives changed the lifestyles of many nations, especially those that used the new tools to exploit the resources of the Great Plains. This initial interaction between white settlers and Native Americans resulted in the development of the stereotype of the buffalo-hunting horseman with feathered headdress who came to represent all Indian ethnic groups in the white imagination.

European diseases and the massacre of whole nations reduced the number of both Native American individuals and ethnic groups. Additionally, many Indians were forced to migrate west to accommodate white expansion. It is estimated that the hardships of involuntary relocation and the deaths caused by illness and assault caused the extinction of nearly one-quarter of all Indian ethnic groups.

The Navajo are the largest surviving Indian nation. The total Native American population doubled between the 1950s and 1970s, and there are now more people of Indian heritage in the U.S. than there were when the Europeans arrived.

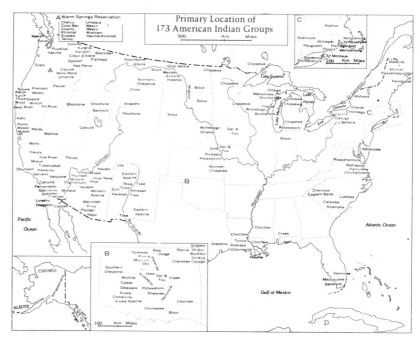

Native American nations in the twentieth century. (From Thernstrom et al. 1980 with permission from Harvard University Press ©1980 by The President and Fellows of Harvard College.)

Indian lands dwindled as white settlers moved westward. By the late nineteenth century, the majority of Native Americans lived on lands held in trust for them by the U.S. government called federal reservations. Still others resided in state reservation communities. Although they were not required by law to live on reservations, there were few other viable Indian communities.

The Bureau of Indian Affairs (BIA) took over the administration of the reservations near the turn of the century. They established a program of cultural assimilation designed to bring the Indian residents into mainstream American society. Before the 1930s, Indian children were sent to off-reservation boarding schools where white values were encouraged. Later, public reservation schools attempted similar indoctrination. The BIA program usually failed to force Native Americans to accept white values, however. The Indians changed their dress, occupation, and social structure, but they did not fully assimilate. In many cases, their religious beliefs, crafts, music, and dance were strengthened to support their ethnic identity.

CURRENT DEMOGRAPHICS

Many Indians left the reservations for the employment opportunities available during World War II. Some joined the armed services, where they became fluent in English and the ways of the majority society. Others took war-related industry jobs. In the 1950s and 1960s, the BIA Employment Assistance Program was a major factor in the continuing outmigration of Indians from the reservations to the cities. By 1980, just over half of all Native Americans resided in urban areas and towns outside of reservations. The cities with the largest Indian populations are (in descending order): Los Angeles, the San Francisco Bay Area, Tulsa, Minneapolis-St. Paul, Oklahoma City, Chicago, and Phoenix. The remainder of the Indian population resides in rural areas, including reservations. Many first-generation urban Indians maintain close ties with the reservation of their ethnic group and travel often between the cities and the reservation. Members of the second generation living in urban regions are more likely to think of the city as their permanent home.

SOCIOECONOMIC STATUS

The socioeconomic status of Native Americans declined drastically with the forced migrations of the nineteenth century. Even those Indian nations that were agriculturally self-sufficient suffered when relocated to regions with poor growing conditions. Further, there were few native occupations that were valued in the job market outside the reservations. BIA education efforts were generally unsuccessful, and most Native Americans did not begin to find employment until World War II and the development of the BIA Employment Assistance Program. More recently, the Indian Self-Determination and Education Act of 1975 was enacted to promote Native American participation in government and education.

Economic improvement has been slow. Nearly one-fourth (24%) of Native American families fell below the poverty level in the 1980 Census. Unemployment at that time among Indians was nearly ten times that of the national average. Although rates of formal education have been improving, over one-half of all adult Indians have not attended high school.

NATIVE AMERICAN ORGANIZATIONS

Few Native American neighborhoods develop in urban areas. Indians who settle in the cities usually arrive as individuals or small family groups and rarely live near others of their nation. Sometimes long-time city residents exhibit a sense of superiority over recent arrivals from the reservations. In general, the difficulties of adjusting to urban white society stimulate many young Indians to identify not only with Indians of other nations but also with people from other minority groups. Activists for Native American rights often come from the cities and are not always supported by Indians who live on reservations.

Indian organizations have done much to maintain Native American identity. Most areas with large Indian populations have Indian clubs and service associations. Organizations to promote ethnic identity have been founded by the Navajo, Pueblos, Tlingit, Haida, and Pomo. Other groups serve the social needs of the pan-Indian community, such as athletic clubs and dance groups. The National American Indian Council was founded in 1982 to represent the needs of urban Indians.

Worldview

Harmony best describes the Native American approach to life. Each individual strives to maintain a balance between spiritual, social, and physical needs. Only what is necessary for life is taken from the natural environment; it is believed that the earth should be cared for and treated with respect. Generosity is esteemed and competitiveness is discouraged, yet individual rights are also highly regarded; personal autonomy is protected by means of the principal of noninterference. Among the Navajo, for example, an individual would never presume to speak for another, even a close family member. For most Indians, time is conceptualized as being without beginning or end, and the culture is present-oriented, meaning that the needs of the moment are emphasized over the possible rewards of the future.

RELIGION

Traditional Native American religions vary from simple belief in the magic of a self-declared practitioner to elaborate theological systems with organized hierarchies of priests. Yet they all share one characteristic: the religion permeates all aspects of life. Rather than a separate set of beliefs practiced at certain times in specific settings, religion is an integral part of the Native American holistic worldview. Religious concepts influence both the physical and emotional well-being of the individual.

Many Indian nations have rejected all attempts at Christian conversion, especially in the Southwest. The Navajo, Arizona Hopi, Rio Grande Pueblos, Potawatomi and the Sioux have retained most of their native religious values and rituals. Other religions unique to Native Americans emerged after European contact, such as the Drum Dance cult and the Medicine Bundle religions, which combine spiritual elements from several different ethnic groups. In addition, religions that mix Christianity with traditional beliefs have been popular since the late nineteenth century; the Native American Church has been especially successful. Other groups claim Christian fellowship but continue to practice native religions as well. Finally, many Native Americans now adhere to Roman Catholicism or some form of Protestantism, especially in urban areas, where churches have been established to serve all-Native American congregations.

FAMILY

The primary social unit of Native Americans is the extended family; most show great respect for age and value children highly. All blood kin of all generations are considered equal; there is no differentiation between close and distant relatives. Aunts and uncles are often considered like grandparents and cousins are viewed as brothers or sisters. Even other tribal members are sometimes accepted as close kin. In many Native American societies, an individual without relatives is considered poor.

TRADITIONAL FOOD HABITS

The traditional food habits of Native Americans were influenced primarily by geography and climate. Each Indian nation adopted a way of life that allowed it to maximize indigenous resources. Many were agriculturally based societies, others were predominantly hunters and gatherers, and some survived mainly on fish. Most of each day was spent procuring food.

Ingredients and Common Foods

NATIVE AMERICAN FOODS

The tradition of the Pacific Northwest Indian *potlatch* reflects the abundance of the region. Commonly held for important events such as marriage or birth of a son, these ostentatious feasts with excessive amounts of foods were followed by gift-giving of items such as blankets, canoes, edible oils, furs, jewelry, and wood carvings. The *potlatch* served to demonstrate the wealth and socioeconomic status of the host. These nations were the only native American groups to develop a class system based on possession of material goods. Anthropologists suggest that the *potlatch* was also a method of food distribution among nations from different areas.

Archaeological records and early descriptions of America by the European settlers indicate that Native Americans on the East Coast enjoyed an abundance of food. Fruits, including blueberries, cranberries, currants, grapes, persimmons, plums, and strawberries, as well as vegetables, such as beans, corn, and pumpkins, were mentioned by the New England colonists. They also describe rivers so full of fish that they could be caught with frying pans, sturgeon so large they were called "Albany beef," and lobster so plentiful that they were considered the food of the poor. Game included deer, moose, partridge, pigeon, rabbit, raccoon, squirrel, and turkey. Maple syrup was used to sweeten foods.

Farther south Native Americans cultivated peanuts, potatoes, sweet potatoes, and tomatoes and collected wild Jerusalem artichokes (a starchy tuber related to the sunflower). Indians of the Pacific Northwest coast collected enough food, such as salmon and fruit, during the summer to support them for the remainder of the year. Peoples of the plains hunted buffalo and those of the northwest woodlands gathered wild rice; nations of the Southwest cultivated chilis, melons, and squash amidst their corn.

Native Americans not only introduced whites to indigenous foods; they shared their methods of agriculture and food preparation as well. Legend has it that the Pilgrims nearly starved despite the plentiful food supply because they were unfamiliar with the local foods. One version of the tale is that Squanto, the sole surviving member of the Pautuxet Indians (the other members had succumbed to smallpox following contact with earlier European explorers), saved the Pilgrims, who were mostly merchants, by teaching them to grow corn. He showed them the Indian method of planting corn kernels in mounds with a fish head for fertilizer and using the cornstalks as supports for beans. In Virginia, Indians are attributed with providing the Cavaliers, also from England, with enough food to ensure their survival.

Although the wild turkey was found in the Plymouth area, it may not have been eaten at the first Thanksgiving. Goose was the preferred holiday bird during colonial times.

FOODS INTRODUCED FROM EUROPE

Foods introduced by the Europeans, especially the French Jesuits in the North and the Spanish in the South, were well-accepted by Native Americans. Apples, apricots, carrots, lentils, peaches, purslane, and turnips were some of the more successful new foods. Settler William Penn noted that he found peaches in every large Indian farm he encountered, barely 100 years after they were introduced to the Iroquois. The Europeans also brought rye and wheat. However, few Indian nations replaced corn with these new grains.

Livestock made a much greater impact on Native American life than did the new fruits and vegetables. Cattle, hogs, and sheep reduced the Indians' dependence on game meats. The Creeks and Cherokees of the Southeast fed their cattle on corn and fattened their suckling pigs and young lambs on apples and nuts. The Powhatans of Virginia fed their hogs peanuts, then cured the meat over hickory smoke. Lamb and mutton became a staple in the Navajo diet after the introduction of sheep by the Spanish.

In addition, the Europeans brought horses and firearms, which made hunting easier, and metal knives and iron pots, which simplified food preparation. They also introduced the Native Americans to distilled spirits.

Carrots escaped vegetable gardens in many areas, reverting to the uncultivated flowering form, known as Queen Anne's lace.

STAPLES

The great diversity of Native American cultures has resulted in a great variety of cuisines. The cooking of one region was as different from that of another as French food is from German food today. Indian cooking featured local ingredients and often reflected the need to preserve foods for future shortages. The only staple foods common to many, though not all, Native American nations were beans, corn, and squash. The Cultural Food Groups list is found in Table 3.1.

REGIONAL VARIATIONS

Native American cuisine has been divided by region into five major types: northeastern, southern, plains, southwestern; and Pacific Northwest/Alaskan Native. Although each area encompasses many different Indian nations, they share many similarities in foods and food habits.

Corn is the largest crop grown in the U.S. today. It is the American staple grain, although most is used for animal feed and is ultimately consumed in the form of meat and poultry.

Northeastern

The northeastern region of the United States was heavily wooded, with numerous freshwater lakes and a long Atlantic coastline. It provided the local Indians, including the Iroquois and Powhatan, with abundant indigenous fruits, vegetables,

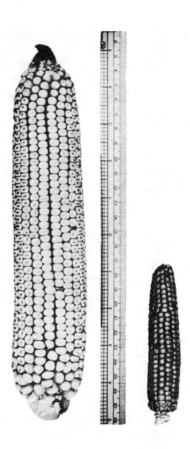

Modern Indian corn compared to Indian corn circa A.D. 500. (From La Farge 1956 with permission from Crown Publishers, Inc.)

One Indian tale about the discovery of maple syrup is that a woman who was cooking a pot of moose stew was too busy to go to the creek for water, so she filled the pot with "water" dripping from a nearby tree. As it cooked she found that the meat was in a delicious, thick, sweet syrup instead of gravy.

fish, and game. Most nations also cultivated crops, such as beans, corn, and squash.

Many of the foods that are associated with the cooking of New England have their origins in northeastern Indian recipes. The clambake was created when the Narragansett and the Penobscot steamed their clams in beach pits lined with hot rocks and seaweed. Dried beans were simmered for days with maple syrup (considered the precursor of Boston baked beans). The dish that today is called *succotash* comes from a stew common in the diet of most Native Americans; it combined corn, beans, and fish or game. In the Northeast, it was usually flavored with maple syrup. Clam chowder, codfish balls, brown bread, corn pudding, pumpkin pie, and the des-

Cooking succotash: This early engraving shows Indians of the Northeast boiling corn, beans, and fish together in the dish now known as succotash. (From La Farge with permission from Crown Publishers, Inc.)

sert known as Indian pudding are all variations of northeastern Indian recipes.

In addition to clams, the Indians of the region ate lobster, oysters, mussels, eels, and many kinds of fish. Game, such as deer and rabbit, was eaten when available. Wild ducks, geese, and turkeys were roasted with stuffings featuring crabapples, grapes, cranberries, or local mushrooms. Corn was the staple food. It was prepared in many ways, such as roasting the young ears, cooking the kernels or meal in soups, gruels, and breads, or steaming it in puddings. Pumpkins and squash were baked almost daily, and beans were added to soups and stews. Local green leafy vegetables were served fresh. Sweets included cherries stewed with maple syrup, cranberry pudding, crab applesauce, and hazelnut cakes.

Southern

The great variety of foods found in the northeastern region of the United States is matched in the plentiful fauna and lush flora of the South. Oysters, shrimp, and blue crabs washed up on the warm Atlantic beaches during tropical storms. The woodlands and swamplands teemed with fish, fowl, and game, including bear, deer, raccoon, and turtle, as well as ample fresh fruit, vegetables, and nuts. The Indians of this

TABLE 3.1. Cultural Food Groups: Native American

Group	Comments
PROTEIN FOODS	
Milk/milk products	High incidence of lactose intolerance among Native Americans with a high pecentage of Indian heritage.
Meats/poultry/fish/eggs/ legumes	Meat highly valued, considered healthful.
	Meats mostly grilled or stewed, preserved through drying and smoking.
	Beans an important protein source.
CEREALS/GRAINS	Corn primary grain; wild rice available in some areas.
FRUITS/VEGETABLES	Indigenous plants major source of calories in diet of some Indian nations.
	Fruits and vegetables either gathered or cultivated.

Common Foods	Post-Contact Adaptations
No common milk products in traditional diets.	Powdered milk and evaporated milk are typical commodity products; usually added to coffee, cereal, and traditional baked goods. Some reports of frequent milk consumption.
Meat: bear, buffalo (including jerky, pemmican) deer, elk, moose, oppossum, otter, porcupine, rabbit, raccoon, squirrel. *Poultry and Small Birds:* duck, goose, grouse, lark, pheasant, quail, seagull, wild turkey. *Fish, Seafood, and Marine Mammals:* bass, catfish, clams, cod, crab, eel, flounder, frogs, halibut, herring, lobster, mussels, olechan, oysters, perch, red snapper, salmon, seal, shrimp, smelts, sole, sturgeon, trout, turtle, walrus, whale. *Eggs:* bird, fish. *Legumes:* many varieties of the common bean (kidney, navy, pinto, etc.), *tepary* beans.	Beef well-accepted, lamb and pork also popular. Canned and cured meats (bacon, luncheon meat) may be common if income is limited. Game rarely eaten. Meats remain a favorite food. Chicken eggs commonly eaten.
Cornmeal breads (fry bread, *piki,* bean bread), gruels, corn tortillas, toasted corn; wild rice.	Wheat has widely replaced corn; store-bought or commodity breads and sugared cereals common. Cakes, cookies, pastries popular.
Fruits: blackberries, blueberries, buffalo berries, cactus fruit *(tuna),* chokeberries, cherries, crab apples, cranberries, currants, elderberries, grapes, ground cherries, huckleberries, muskmelons, persimmons, plums, raspberries, salal, salmonberries, strawberries (beach and wild), thimbleberries, watermelon, wild rhubarb.	Apples common after European introduction. Apples, bananas, oranges, peaches, pineapple well-accepted; canned fruits popular. Wild berries still gathered in rural areas.

TABLE 3.1.   Cultural Food Groups: Native American (*continued*)

Group	Comments
ADDITIONAL FOODS	
Seasonings	
Nuts/seeds	Nuts often an important food source, acorns sometimes a staple.
Beverages	
Fats/oils	
Sweeteners	

Common Foods	Post-Contact Adaptations
Vegetables: camass root, cacti *(nopales),* chilis, fiddleheads, Jerusalem artichokes, lichen, moss, mushrooms, nettles, onions, potatoes, pumpkin, squash, squash blossoms, sweet potatoes, tomatoes, wild greens (cattail, clover, cow parsnip, creases, dandelion, ferns, milkweed, pigweed, pokeweed, purslane, saxifrage, sunflower leaves, watercress, winter cress), wild potatoes, wild turnips, *yuca* (cassava).	Some traditional vegetables eaten when available. Green peas, string beans, instant potatoes common commodity items. Intake of vegetables low; variety limited.
Chilis, garlic, hickory nut cream, onions, peppermint, sage, salt, sassafras, seaweed, spearmint, and other indigenous herbs and spices.	
Acorn meal, black walnuts, buckeyes, chestnuts, hazelnuts, hickory nuts, mesquite tree beans, pecans, peanuts, *piñon* nuts (pine nuts), pumpkin seeds, squash seeds, sunflower seeds, seeds of wild grasses.	
Teas of buffalo berries, mint, peyote, rose hip, sassafras, spicebush, sumac berries, *yerba buena;* honey and water.	Coffee, tea, soft drinks common beverages. Alcoholism prevalent.
Fats rendered from buffalo, caribou, moose, and other land mammals; seal and whale fat.	Butter, lard, margarine, vegetable oils have replaced rendered fats in most regions; seal and whale fat still consumed by Inuits and Aleuts.
Maple syrup, other tree saps, honey.	Sugar primary sweetener; candy, jams, and jellies popular.

When blacks were first brought to America from Africa, they were often housed at the periphery of farms. There was initially a great deal of interaction between blacks and local Indians, who taught them how to hunt the local game without guns and to use the native plants. Some of the Indian cooking techniques were later introduced into white southern cuisine by black cooks.

Dried, ground sassafras was called *filé* (meaning "thread") powder by the French settlers of the South due to the stringly consistency it gave to soups and stews when boiled. Filé powder, which often includes ground thyme in addition to sassafras, is still used in southern cooking today.

region, such as the Cherokee, Creek, and Seminole, were accomplished farmers, growing crops of beans, corn, and squash.

Many of the flavors typical of modern southern cooking come from traditional Indian foods. *Hominy* (dried corn kernels with the hulls removed) and *grits* (made of coarsely ground hominy) were introduced to the settlers by the Indians. The chicken dish known as Brunswick stew is an adaptation of a southern Indian recipe for squirrel. The Indians also made sophisticated use of native plants for seasoning, and they thickened their soups and stews with sassafras.

The staple foods of corn, beans, and squash were supplemented with the indigenous woodland fruits and vegetables. Blackberries, elderberries, gooseberries, huckleberries, raspberries, strawberries, crab apples, grapes, ground cherries, Jerusalem artichokes, green leafy vegetables, persimmons (pounded into a paste for puddings and cakes), and plums were some of the numerous edible native plants. The Indians of the South also used beechnuts, hazelnuts, hickory nuts, pecans, and walnuts in their cooking. The thick, creamlike oil extracted from hickory nuts was used to flavor corn puddings and gruels. Honey was the sweetener used most frequently, and it was mixed with water for a cooling drink. Teas were made from mint, sassafras, and spicebush *(Lindera benzoin)*, and during the summer Indian "lemonade" was made from citrus-flavored sumac berries.

Plains

The Indians who lived in the area that is now the American Midwest were mostly nomadic hunters, following the great herds of bison across the flat plains for sustenance. The land was rugged and generally unsuitable for agriculture. Those nations that settled along the fertile Mississippi and Missouri river valleys, however, developed farm-based societies supported by crops of beans, corn, melons, squash, and tomatoes.

Bison meat was the staple food for most plains nations, such as the Arapaho, Cheyenne, Crow, Dakota, and Pawnee. The more tender cuts were roasted or broiled, while the tougher ribs, joints, and other bones with marrow were prepared in stews and soups. Pieces of meat, water, and sometimes vegetables would be placed in a hole in the ground lined with cleaned buffalo skin. The stew would then be

Early European rendition of a bison, Rome, 1651. (Courtesy Rare Books and Manuscripts Division, The New York Public Library, Astor, Lenox and Tilden Foundations.)

"stone-boiled:" rocks that had been heated in the fire would be added to the broth until the mixture was thoroughly cooked. All parts of the bison were eaten, including the liver and kidneys (which were consumed raw immediately after the animal was slaughtered), udder, tongue, and hump. Extra meat was preserved by cutting it into very thin strips and then dehydrating it in the sun or over the fire. This tough, dried meat would keep for several years and was known as *jerked* buffalo or *jerky.* The jerky would be pulverized and mixed with water or corn gruel, or, in emergencies, eaten dry. Most often it was shredded and mixed with buffalo fat and berries, then formed into cakes called *pemmican.*

When bison were unavailable, the plains Indians would hunt deer, rabbit, and game birds. Fresh green leafy vegetables were consumed in season and root vegetables, such as wild onions, throughout the year. Wild rice was collected in the northern parts of the Midwest, where it was served with bison or venison and used as a stuffing for grouse, partridge, and duck. Blackberries, cherries, crab apples, grapes, persimmons, and plums were available in some areas, but the most popular fruit was the scarlet buffalo berry *(Shepherdia canadensis),* so called because it was so often served in sauces for bison meat or dried for pemmican.

The term "jerked" or "jerky" is believed to have come from the Spanish word for meat dried in the sun, *charqui.*

Southwestern

Some of the oldest Indian settlements in North America were located along the river valleys of the arid Southwest. Despite the semidesert conditions, many Indians, such as the Hopi, Pima, Pueblo, and Zuni, lived in *pueblo* (Spanish for "town" or "village") communities and were predominantly farmers, cultivating beans, chilis, corn, melons, and squash. Others, including the Apache and Navajo, were originally roving hunters and gatherers. After the Spanish introduced livestock, some of these nomadic groups began to raise sheep.

Until the arrival of livestock, the diet of the region was predominantly vegetarian. Agriculture provided a nourishing diet when supplemented with small game, such as rabbit and turkey. Corn was the primary food and at least five different colors of corn were cultivated. Each symbolized one of the cardinal points for the Zuni, and each had its own use in cooking. White corn (East) was ground into a fine meal and was used in gruels and breads. Yellow corn (North) was roasted and eaten in kernel form or off the ear. The rarer red (South), blue (West) and black (the nadir) corn was used more for special foods, such as the lacy, flat Hopi bread made from blue cornmeal known as *piki*. Multicolored corn represented the zenith. The Hopi also attached importance to the color of corn and cultivated 20 different varieties. In many areas, corn was prepared in ways similar to those of the northern Mexican Indians: *tortillas* (flat, griddle-fried cornmeal bread), *pozole* (hominy), and the *tamale*like *chukuviki* (stuffed cornmeal dough packets).

Beans were the second most important crop of the southwestern region. Many varieties were grown, including the domesticated indigeneous *tepary* beans and pinto beans from Mexico. Both squash and pumpkins were commonly consumed, and squash blossoms were fried or added to soups and salads. Squash and pumpkin seeds were also used to flavor foods. Green and red chilis were used as vegetables and to season stews. Yellow-fleshed watermelons were prized; muskmelons (what are now called cantaloupe) were also grown after they were introduced by the Spanish.

When the crops failed or were insufficient, the southwestern Indians relied on wild plants. *Piñon* seeds (also called pine nuts) flavored stews and soups. Both the fruit *(tunas)* and the pads *(nopales)* of the prickly pear cactus were eaten, as were the pulp and fruit of other cacti. The beans of the mesquite tree saved many Indians from starvation during times of hun-

It was up to the Hopi woman to propose marriage to a man. She did this by preparing a blue cornmeal cake called a piki and placing it on her intended's doorstep. If the piki was taken into his house, her proposal was accepted.

ger; they were ground into a flour and used in gruels, breads, and sun-baked cakes.

Northwest Coast/Alaskan Natives

This culinary region incorporates a diverse geographical area. The climate of the Pacific Northwest coast is temperate. The luxuriantly forested hills and mountain slopes abound with edible plants and game, and the sea supplies fish, shellfish, and marine mammals. Farther north, in Alaska and Canada, the growing season shortens to only a few summer months and temperatures in the winter regularly plunge to −50°F. Two-thirds of Alaska is affected by permafrost and the vast stretches of tundra are inhospitable to humans.

The Native American ethnic groups that inhabit this region include Indians as well as Inuits (Eskimos) and Aleuts, known as Alaskan Natives. Indian nations such as the Tlingit and Kwakiutl inhabit the northwest coastal area and some interior Alaskan regions. The Aleuts live on the 1,000-mile-long chain of volcanic islands that arch into the Pacific from Alaska called the Aleutians. The Inuits live in the northern

The word Eskimo comes from the Algonquin Indian word *eskimantik,* meaning "eater of raw flesh." Inuit, meaning "the people," is the preferred name.

Traditional Alaskan Native seal-hunting method.

Adult salmon, which are normally ocean-dwelling fish, swim up rivers to spawn and then die. The Indians of the Pacific Northwest believed that salmon were immortal. It was thought that the salmon came yearly to the rivers to feed the people, then returned to the oceans, where they were reborn. The Indians would ceremoniously return the fishes' skeletons to the river so that this rebirth could take place.

Recent research suggests that a diet high in fish oils that contain large amounts of omega-3-fatty acids may lower serum cholesterol and triglyceride levels, thus reducing the risk of heart disease. The low rate of cardiovascular illness among Inuits is attributed to the large amount of these fatty acids in their traditional diet.

and western areas of Alaska, as well as in Canada, Greenland, and Siberia.

The Indians of the Northwest Coast had no need for agriculture. Food was plentiful, and salmon was their primary food. The fish were caught annually in the summer as they swam upstream to spawn. They were roasted over the fire when fresh, and the eggs, known today as red caviar, were a favorite treat when dried in the sun into chewy strips. Extra fish were smoked to preserve them for the winter. In addition, cod, clams, crabs, halibut, herring, shrimp, sole, smelt, sturgeon, and trout were consumed. Ocean mammals such as otter, seal, and whale were also hunted. Bear, deer, elk, and mountain goats were eaten, as were numerous wild fowl and game birds.

Despite the abundant fish and game, wild plants comprised over half the diet of the Northwest Coast Indians. Over 100 varieties of indigenous fruits, vegetables, and even lichen were consumed, including acorns, blackberries, blueberries, camass roots (*Camassia quamash*), chokecherries (*Prunus virginiana*), desert parsley, leafy green vegetables, hazelnuts, huckleberries, mint, raspberries, salal (*Gaultheria shallon*), and strawberries. Roots were roasted or baked and fresh greens were popular.

In contrast to the plenty of the Northwest Coast, the diet of many Alaskan Natives was often marginal. The Inuits and Aleuts were usually seminomadic, traveling as necessary to fish and hunt. Fish and sea mammals such as seal, walrus, and whale were the staple foods. Arctic hare, caribou, ducks, geese, mountain goats, moose, musk oxen (hunted to extinction in Alaska by the 1870s), polar bear, and mountain sheep were consumed when available. Most of these foods were eaten raw due to the lack of wood or other fuel. The fat of animals was especially valued as food. *Akutok*, a favored dish, was a mixture of seal oil, berries, and caribou fat. Even the stomachs of certain game were examined for edible undigested foods, such as lichen in elk and clams in walruses. Wild plants were limited to mosses, lichen, and a few blueberries and cranberries.

Other Native American Cuisines

Many traditional Indian diets do not fit conveniently within the five major regional cuisines. Among them were the food habits of the population found in what is now Nevada and parts of California, called Digger Indians by the first whites to encounter them because they subsisted mostly on dug-up roots, supplemented by small game and insects. In central California, numerous nations, such as the Miwok and Pomo, had an acorn-based diet. In the rugged northern mountains and plains lived Indian nations such as the Blackfeet, Crow, Shoshone, and Sioux who were nomadic hunters of large and small game. Although many may have hunted bison at one time, they were limited to the local bear, deer, moose, rabbits, wildfowl, and freshwater fish when the expansion of other Indians and whites into the Midwest pushed them northward and westward. Wild plants added variety to their diet.

Acorns contain tannic acid, a bitter-tasting substance that is toxic in large quantities. To make the acorns edible, the Indian woman would first crack and remove the hard hull, then grind the meat into a meal, add water to make a dough, then leach the tannic acid from the dough by repeatedly pouring hot water through it.

Meal Composition and Cycle

DAILY PATTERNS

Traditional meal patterns varied according to ethnic group and locality. In the northeast, one large, hearty meal was consumed before noon, and snacks were available throughout the day. Two meals a day were more common in the southwest. The women would rise before dawn to prepare breakfast, eaten at sunrise. The afternoon was spent cooking the evening meal, which was eaten before sunset. Two meals a day were also the pattern among the Indians of the Pacific northwest.

In regions with limited resources, meals were often monotonous. The two daily meals of the southwestern Indians, for example, regularly consisted of cornmeal gruel or bread and boiled dehydrated vegetables. No distinction was made between morning or evening menus. Other dishes, such as game, fresh vegetables, or fruit, were included when seasonally available. The single meal of the northeastern Indians often included roasted game; the Northwest Coast Indians frequently included some form of salmon twice a day in addition to the many local edible greens and roots.

Food was simply prepared. It was roasted over the fire or in the ashes or cooked in soups or stews. The northeastern and Northwest Coast Indians steamed seafood; southwestern Indians baked cornmeal bread in adobe ovens called *hornos* (after the introduction of hogs, flat breads were commonly fried in lard). All nations liked sweets, but they were limited to fruits and dishes flavored with maple syrup, honey, or other indigenous sweeteners.

Baking bread in a southwestern outdoor oven. (Courtesy Calleros Estate, El Paso, TX copy from Institute of Texan Cultures.)

SPECIAL OCCASIONS

Many Indian religious ceremonies were accompanied by feasts. Among the northeastern Iroquois Indians, seasonal celebrations were held for the maple, planting, strawberry, green corn, harvest and new year's festivals. The southern Indians held an elaborate green corn festival in thanks for a plentiful autumn harvest. No one was allowed to eat any of the new corn until the ceremony was complete. Each home was thoroughly cleaned, the fires were extinguished, and all old pieces of pottery and clothing were replaced with newly made items. The adult men bathed and purged with an emetic. When everything and everyone was thoroughly clean in body and thought, the central fire was lit and each hearth fire was relit with its flames. The feasting on new corn then began.

Role of Food in Native American Societies

Native American nations, especially in the inland regions, experienced frequent food shortages. Food is valued as sacred and in the holistic worldview shared by most Indian ethnic groups, food is also considered a gift of the natural realm. In some nations, elaborate ceremonies accompanied cultivation of crops, and prayers were offered for a successful hunt.

Traditionally in many nations, the men were responsible for hunting or the care of livestock. The job of food gathering, preparation, and storage usually belonged to the women; they also made the cooking utensils, such as watertight baskets or clay pots. In predominantly agricultural societies, both men and women were frequently involved in cultivation of the crops. Among the nations of the Northeast, the men ate first, followed by women and children. In the Southwest, men prepared the game they caught and served it to the women.

Sharing food is an important aspect of most Native American societies. Food is usually offered to guests, and extra food is often given to members of the extended family. In some nations of the Southwest, meals are prepared and eaten communally. Each woman makes a large amount of one dish and shares it with the other families, who in turn share what they have prepared.

Among the nations of the Southwest, food is considered a valuable gift from a woman to a man or from a woman to another woman. A present of firewood, clothing, or game is considered more appropriate from a man to a woman.

Therapeutic Uses of Food

The role of food in spiritual and physical health is still important for many Indians. They commonly believe that an individual who is ill is out of balance with nature. Most native Indian health practitioners attempt to restore harmony to the body so that healing may begin. Religion, medicine, and well-being are not separate concepts in many Native American cultures but instead are deeply interrelated.

Corn holds special significance in some healing ceremonies. Cornmeal may be sprinkled around the bed of a patient to protect against further illness. Corn pollen may be used to ease heart palpitations and fine cornmeal rubbed on children's rashes. Navajo women drink blue cornmeal gruel to promote the production of milk after childbirth, and Pueblo women use a mixture of water and corn ear smut (a corn fungus) to relieve diarrhea and to cure irregular menstruation. A similar drink was given to Zuni women to speed childbirth and to prevent postpartum hemorrhaging.

Numerous other indigenous plants are used by Native Americans for medicinal purposes. For example, *agave* leaves (from a succulent common in the Southwest) are chewed as a general tonic, and the juice is applied to fresh wounds. Chilis are used in compresses for arthritis and applied directly to warts. Mint tea is thought to ease colic, indigestion, and nausea. Often the concept of "like cures like" is used in se-

Some Indians steeped willow bark as a tea for use as a pain killer. It is high in salicylic acid, the active ingredient in aspirin.

lecting medicinal plants: bloodroot is used to stop bleeding because its juice is red, and wormroot is given for intestinal parasites (worms). Bitter purges and emetics are also sometimes administered.

Food restrictions are still common during illness. Depending on the nation, many Indians believe that cabbage, eggs, fish, meat, milk, onions, or organ meats should be eliminated from a patient's diet. Some foods are prohibited after childbirth, such as cod, halibut, huckleberries, and spring salmon for Nootka women of the northwest coast.

CONTEMPORARY FOOD HABITS

Native American food is becoming trendy, especially the cuisine of the southwest. In 1984 the late James Beard, the father of American gastronomy, wrote a glowing article praising the delicious dishes served at a New York celebration of Native American cuisine.

Native American ethnic identity is changing. Traditional beliefs and values are often in direct conflict with those of the majority society, and Indians' self-concept has undergone tremendous changes in the process of acculturation. A 1978 study described three transitional adaptations of members of the Chippewa, identified by three different lifestyles; these may serve as a model for the adaptations made by members of other Indian groups (Primeaux & Henderson, 1981). The first stage of adaptation is traditional in which parents and grandparents speak the *Ojibway* language at home, practice the *Midewiwin* religion, and participate in Native American cultural activities such as feasts and *powwows*. The second stage is bicultural. English is the primary language, although some Ojibway is also spoken. Catholicism is the preferred religion, and the family is involved in activities of the majority society. In the third Chippewa lifestyle, the pantraditional stage, the family speaks either English or Ojibway exclusively, practices a religion that is a combination of Indian and Christian beliefs, such as the Native American Church, and is actively involved in activities from both traditional Indian and white societies.

Adaptation of Food Habits

Food habits reflect changes in Indian ethnic identity. Many Indians eat a diet that includes few traditional foods. Others are consciously attempting to revive the foods and dishes of their ancestors.

INGREDIENTS AND COMMON FOODS

When Native Americans were uprooted from their lands and their known food supplies, many immediately became dependent on the foods provided to the reservations. These commodity foods currently include items such as canned and chopped meats, poultry, fruit juices, peanut butter, eggs, evaporated and powdered milk, dried beans, instant potatoes, peas, and string beans. Other sources of food include gardening (reportedly practiced by between 43 and 91 percent of rural Native Americans), fishing, hunting, gathering indigeneous plants, and raising livestock.

Over the years, traditional foods and methods of preparation were lost and substitutions made. For example, beef is a commonly accepted substitute for game among many Indian ethnic groups. Traditional foods comprise less than 25 percent of the daily diet among the Hopi. Older Hopi women lament the fact that younger Hopi are no longer learning how to cook these dishes (Kuhnlein et al., 1979). In a study of Cherokee women (Terry & Bass, 1984), the consumption of traditional foods was found to be directly related to the amount of Indian inheritance of the woman in charge of the food supply in the home. Corn and corn products such as hominy were among the most popular traditional foods; game meat, hickory nuts, raspberries, and winter squash were the least commonly served. Among Cherokee teenagers, traditional items such as fry bread, bean bread (corn bread with pinto beans), and chestnut bread (made from chestnuts and cornmeal) were well-accepted. Although over 80 percent of the adolescents were familiar with typical Cherokee dishes, including native greens and game meat (bear, deer, ground hog, rabbit, raccoon, squirrel, and wild boar), these foods were rarely eaten (Storey et al., 1986).

Navajo women were found to eat traditional foods infrequently, with the exception of fry bread, mutton, and tortillas. Blue cornmeal mush (with ash), hominy, and wild sumac berry pudding were a few of the native dishes consumed occasionally (Wolfe & Sanjur, 1988). Dakota women of all ages take pride in traditional foods but prepare them only when it is convenient or for special occasions. Uncooked meat is still consumed in some nations; it has been noted that some Indians do not care about the temperature of foods (Bass & Wakefield, 1974).

MEAL COMPOSITION AND CYCLE

Little has been reported regarding current Native American meal patterns. It is assumed that three meals per day has become the norm, especially among families without income constraints. One study of Dakota Indians noted that there

A Native American hotel chef, George Crum, is attributed with the invention of potato chips in 1853.

was little variety in daily menus (Bass & Wakefield, 1974). Cereal with milk; fried potatoes; fried eggs, chopped meat, milk; and bread with butter; oatmeal or cornmeal mush; or just bread and butter were eaten for breakfast. Coffee was the most popular beverage. Lunch was the main meal, consisting of bologna sandwiches with potato chips and a carbonated beverage or just fried potatoes. Fried potatoes and chopped meat were eaten for dinner. Similar foods were found to be eaten by Navajo women: fry bread or tortillas, potatoes, eggs, sugar, and coffee were most frequently consumed. Fried foods were preferred for breakfast, and lunch and dinner consisted of one boiled meal and one fried or roasted meal. Fast food restaurants were popular (Wolfe & Sanjur, 1988).

In some homes, special occasions, such as birthdays and specific Native American ceremonies, are celebrated with traditional foods. Other foods are considered appropriate for the holidays of the majority culture. For example, turkey with all the trimmings is served by Dakota Indians for Thanksgiving and Christmas (Bass & Wakefield, 1974).

Nutritional Status

NUTRITIONAL INTAKE

High rates of lactose intolerance have been reported for both Native Americans and Alaska Natives. The occurence among individuals, however, is related to percentage of Indian heritage.

Research on the nutritional status of Native Americans is limited. Severe malnutrition was documented in the 1950s and 1960s, including numerous cases of kwashiorkor and marasmus. Today, low socioeconomic status and lack of transportation, fuel, refrigeration, and running water contribute to an inadequate diet for many Indians. The few studies of what Native Americans now eat suggest that a diet high in refined carbohydrates (starchy and sugary foods) and fat and low in meats, fruits, and vegetables is common. For example, the caloric and protein intake of Alaskan Natives declined over the past 15 to 20 years, as the traditional diet was replaced by processed, canned, and packaged foods that are low in nutrients (Jackson, 1986). Low intake of calcium, iron, phospherous, vitamins A and C, and riboflavin as well as fiber, have been reported. Further, high rates of obesity, heart disease, and cirrhosis of the liver suggest that many other dietary inadequacies exist. Although life expectancy for Native Americans has increased in recent years, it is still six years less than that of the overall U.S. population.

Infant and Maternal Death Rate

The birth rate among Native Americans is nearly 50 percent higher than for the total U.S. population. The infant and maternal death rates are 2.5 times and over 4 times that of the total U.S. population, respectively.

Obesity

Although anthropometric data on the average Native American preschool child show slower overall growth rates than for non-Indian children, a study of Cherokee adolescents found no significant difference in the heights of Indian, black, and white teens. Obesity, however, was more common among Indians. Indians had consistently higher weight-for-height values than black or white adolescents; nearly one-half of the teenage boys and one-third of the girls were obese, as defined by skinfold thickness values above the 85th percentile (Storey et al., 1986). A high incidence of obesity among adult Indians has also been reported. In recent studies, 63 percent of Navajo sampled were over 120 percent of ideal body weight; 60 percent of Seminoles were identified as obese; and 75 percent of Indians from Oklahoma nations averaged 145 percent of ideal body weight (Jackson, 1986). This rate of obesity contradicts the nutritional intake data available, which show the caloric intake of many Indians to be normal or below the recommended dietary allowances. Researchers have suggested that a hereditary metabolic adaptation to a feast-and-famine existence in the past may account for this tendency to gain weight, exacerbated in some cases by a sedentary lifestyle (Bass & Wakefield, 1974).

Diabetes

The incidence of diabetes mellitus, especially among Indians of the Southwest, is estimated to be over three times that of the general population, and the death rate from the disease is twice as high for Indians as for non-Indians. The incidence of diabetes may be associated with the high incidence of obesity.

Heart Disease

The rate of heart disease, although still below that of the total U.S. population, has greatly increased during the past 25 years among Native Americans and is now the leading cause of death. Increases in hypertension, a major risk factor in the development of heart disease, have also been noted. Both chronic conditions may be attributable to dietary changes approximating the diet of the majority culture and high rates of obesity.

Dental Caries

A diet high in simple carbohydrates has led to an increase in dental caries. This problem was virtually unknown among Native Americans before European contact.

Alcoholism

The incidence of alcoholism among Native Americans has dramatically decreased in the last 15 years, but it still remains a significant medical and social problem. High unemployment rates and loss of ethnic identity and self-esteem are frequently cited as reasons for substance abuse among both reservation and urban Indians. Alcoholism accounts for nearly two-thirds of deaths caused by cirrhosis of the liver, and the rate for all alcohol-related deaths is almost six times that of the general U.S. population.

Infectious Diseases

Respiratory infections continue to occur among Native Americans more frequently than among non-Indians, probably because of factors such as malnutrition, overcrowding, and inadequate sanitation. Death rates from tuberculosis, pneumonia, and influenza are much higher than those of the total U.S. population. Gastrointestinal infections, particularly gastroenteritis and bacillary dysentery, are also prevalent.

COUNSELING

Due to the great diversity of Native American ethnic groups, the health practitioner should first become familiar with the traditions of local nations. This is best done through careful questioning of individual Indians and fellow health professionals experienced in caring for Native Americans.

Access to western health care may be limited for some Indians because of low income or inadequate transportation. Others may hold beliefs that cause them to avoid western medical treatment: pregnancy is often considered a healthy state, for example, and Indian women may not seek prenatal care for this reason. Indians' traditional attitudes about time may cause difficulties for health professionals: the importance of finishing a current project or commitment may outweigh that of keeping an appointment with a health provider.

In general, it is important to remember that both verbal and nonverbal communication with Native Americans must take into account cultural traditions. Among the Navajo, the patient should be asked directly for their medical history, as even family members may feel they have no right to speak for another. Many Indians are comfortable with periods of silence in a conversation, using the time to compose their thoughts or to translate responses. A "yes" or "no" response may be considered a complete answer to a question. An Indian may answer "I don't know" if she feels that a question is inappropriate or does not wish to discuss the topic. She may not ask questions during an interview because that would suggest that the health care provider was not communicating clearly. The very concept of a dietary interview may be interpreted by some Indians as interference with their personal autonomy. Although a handshake is customary, a vigorous handshake may be considered a sign of aggressiveness. Direct eye contact may be considered rude, and the health professional should not interpret averted eyes as evidence of disinterest.

An in-depth interview is important to determine not only ethnic identity but also degree of acculturation. Traditional medical beliefs and customs, if practiced, should be acknowledged. Personal dietary preferences are of special importance due to the variety of Native American foods and food habits.

REFERENCES

Bass, M. A. & Wakefield, L. M. 1974. Nutrient intake and food patterns of Indians on Standing Rock Reservation. *Journal of the American Dietetic Association, 64*, 36–41.

Bernardo, S. 1981. *The Ethnic Almanac.* Garden City, N.Y.: Doubleday.

Farkas, C. S. 1986. Ethno-specific communication patterns: Implications for nutrition education. *Journal of Nutrition Education, 18*, 99–103.

Jackson, M. Y. 1986. Nutrition in American Indian health: Past, present, and future. *Journal of the American Dietetic Association, 86*, 1,561–1,565.

Kavasch, B. 1977. *Native Harvests.* New York: Random House.

Keegan, M. 1977. *Pueblo and Navajo Cookery.* Dobbs Ferry, NY: Earth Books.

Kimball, Y., & Anderson, J. 1986. *The Art of American Indian Cooking.* New York, NY: Simon & Schuster.

Kuhnlein, H. V., Calloway, D. H., & Harland, B. F. 1979. Composition of traditional Hopi foods. *Journal of the American Dietetic Association,* *75,* 37–41.

La Farge, O. 1956. *A Pictorial History of the American Indian.* New York: Crown Publishers.

Neithammer, C. 1974. *American Indian Food and Lore.* New York: Macmillan.

Perl, L. 1965. *Red-flannel Hash and Shoo-fly Pie.* Cleveland, OH: World Publishing.

Primeaux, M., & Henderson, G. 1981. American Indian patient care. In *Transcultural Health Care.* G. Henderson & M. Primeaux (Eds.) Menlo Park, CA: Addison-Wesley.

Spicer, E. H. 1980. American Indians. In *The Harvard Encyclopedia of American Ethnic Groups,* S. Thernstrom, A. Orlov, & O. Handlin (Eds.) Cambridge, MA: Belknap Press of the Harvard University Press.

Storey, M., Bass, M. A., & Wakefield, L. M. 1986. Food preferences of Cherokee teenagers in Cherokee, North Carolina. *Ecology of Food and Nutrition, 19,* 51–59.

Storey, M., Tompkins, R. A., Bass, M. A. & Wakefield, L. M. 1986. Anthropometric measurements and dietary intakes of Cherokee Indian teenagers in North Carolina. *Journal of the American Dietetic Association, 86,* 1,555–1,560.

Terry, R. D., & Bass, M. A. 1984. Food practices in an eastern Cherokee township. *Ecology of Food and Nutrition, 14,* 63–70.

Wilson, U. M. 1983. Nursing care of American Indian patients. In *Ethnic Nursing Care,* M. S. Orque, B. Bloch, & L. S. Ahumada Monrroy (Eds.) St. Louis, MO: Mosby.

Wolfe, W. S., Weber, C. W., & Arviso, K. D. 1985. Use and nutrient composition of traditional Navajo foods. *Ecology of Food and Nutrition, 17,* 323–326.

Wolfe, W. S. & Sanjur, D. 1988. Contemporary diet and body weight of Navajo women receiving food assistance: an ethnographic and nutritional investigation. *Journal of the American Dietetic Association, 88,* 822–827.

4

EUROPEANS

The majority of Americans share a common European ancestry. Even within this population, however, there are numerous ethnic and religious groups. The culturally diverse southern, northern, central, and eastern Europeans are represented in the United States in significant numbers. Today, much of the American cuisine reflects the traditional foods and food habits of these earlier settlers to the country; European immigrants started arriving in what is now the United States in the sixteenth century and are still coming today. Each group has brought a unique cuisine that, mixed with indigenous ingredients, blended with other European regional cuisines, and influenced by the cooking of Africans, Asians, and Latinos, created what is now considered the typical American diet. This chapter will discuss the traditional cuisines of northern, southern, and central Europe, the Soviet Union, and Scandinavia and examine their contributions to American foods and food habits. Before discussing individual regions in Europe, a brief history of Europe to the fifteenth century is presented.

EARLY EUROPEAN HISTORY

After the fall of Rome in A.D. 476, warlike tribes fought for control of the empire. By the middle of the sixth century, the former Western Empire of Rome was almost completely occupied by barbarian tribes. The Jutes, Angles, and Saxons set-

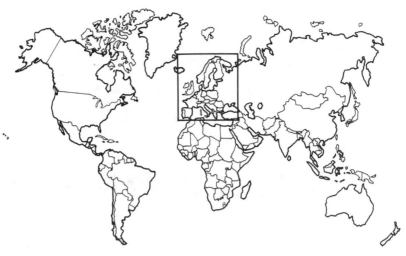

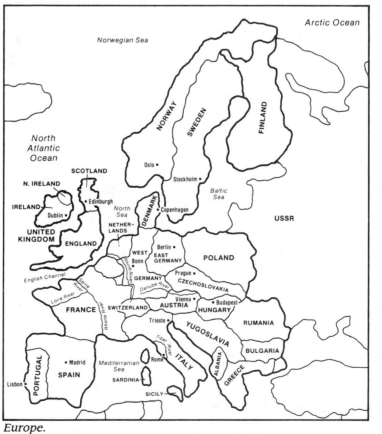

Europe.

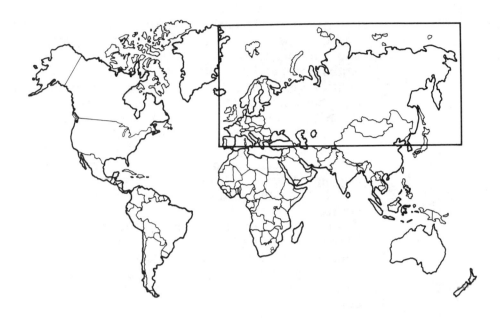

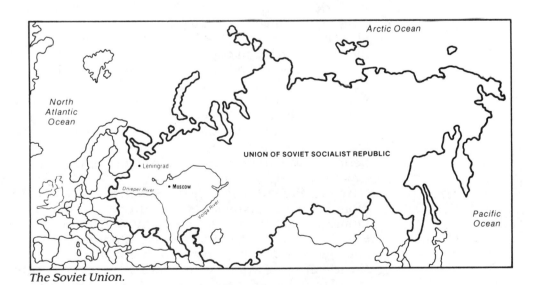

The Soviet Union.

tled in Britain, the Franks and Burgundians inhabited France, and the Ostrogoths invaded Italy. Eastern Europe, in turn, was threatened by the Germans and Huns, as well as by Arabs and Persians. The Celts had dominated western and central Europe before Rome was conquered. In the fifth century they converted to Christianity, as did many other barbarian tribes. However, by then the Celtic foothold in Europe was confined to Ireland, Wales, and Scotland. In the late eighth century, pagan Scandinavians, known as Vikings, attacked western Europe. They eventually settled in Britain, northern France (Normandy), and parts of eastern Europe. The Scandinavians converted to Christianity by the tenth century.

The years between the fifth and fifteen centuries are known as the Middle Ages, or medieval period: the time between the ancient and modern periods. During this time, local feudalism ordered the social and governmental hierarchy. By the eleventh century, trade developed and towns emerged, while politically, the monarchy started to assert centralized authority over individual nobles.

The Crusades, military and religious pilgrimages to the Holy Lands that took place during the eleventh and twelfth centuries, were one factor that helped stimulate trade and exchange of ideas between Europe and the then more civilized East. Beginning in Italy during the fourteenth century, the Renaissance, which means "rebirth," spread to the other countries in Europe. During this period Europe was in transition, moving away from a religious worldview to a more secular, materialistic outlook. Art, music, literature, science, medicine, and technology flourished by enlarging, modifying, and questioning the knowledge handed down from the Middle Ages and antiquity. Roman Catholicism was also undergoing change: during this period the Reformation led to the establishment of the Protestant movement in Christianity (see Chapter 2). European states expanded their influence worldwide through overseas empires. One result of this imperialism was the British establishment of colonies in North America.

By the fifteenth century, the Spanish, French, and English monarchies dominated western Europe, and the Holy Roman Empire of the Germanies ruled central Europe. In the southeast, the Ottoman Turks were well established in the Balkans and were threatening Italy and central Europe.

The nation-of-states in western Europe were continually threatened by other states that attempted to absorb or control them. Endangered states often joined together to fight off the threat and maintain the status quo. Throughout European history, boundaries have been in flux; current national boundaries reflect agreements reached following the last war in Europe, World War II.

NORTHERN EUROPEANS

Great Britain includes the countries of England, Scotland, Wales, and Northern Ireland. Ireland is now a sovereign country. Although quite northern, the Gulf Stream climate is temperate, and the lowlands are arable.

France, the largest nation in western Europe, has been regarded for centuries as the center of Western culture, both politically and in the arts and sciences. Its capital, Paris, is one of the world's most beautiful and famed cities. France contains some of the best farmland in Europe, and three-fifths of its land is under cultivation. It is especially well known for premium wine production.

Traditional foods of northern Europe: Some typical traditional foods in the northern European diet include apples, bacon, beef, cheese, cream, French bread, oatmeal, salt cod, and tripe. (Photo by Laurie Macfee.)

In 1607, people from Great Britain began immigrating to what has become the United States. They brought with them British trade practices and the English language, literature, law, and religion. By the time the United States gained independence from Britain, the British and their descendents constituted half the American population. They produced a culture that remains unmistakably British flavored, even today.

Cultural Perspective

HISTORY OF NORTHERN EUROPE

Great Britain

The ethnic origins of the British are Celtic, Roman, Anglo-Saxon, and Norman. The Angles and Saxons were Germanic tribes that arrived in the British Isles starting in the third century A.D. The Normans invaded and conquered England in the eleventh century and their leader, William of Normandy (northern France), then ruled as William I. William's reign was succeeded by that of the Plantagenets, another French family, whose heirs included Richard the Lionhearted and his brother John. English rulers continued to press their claims to lands in France, which led to the Hundred Years War in the fourteenth century.

In the mid-fifteenth century, rival claims to the English throne triggered the war of the Roses and led to the establishment of the Tudor reign in 1485. Under the Tudor King Henry VIII, Protestantism was established in England as a result of his split with the Roman Catholic Church over his divorce from his first wife and his subsequent marriage to Anne Boleyn. The Tudors continued on the throne through the reign of Elizabeth I, who was succeeded in 1603 by James I, the first Stuart monarch. James was also King of Scotland.

Civil war and revolution rocked England between 1640 and 1660 because of religious and class divisions. Oliver Cromwell ruled England as Lord Protector from 1653 to his death in 1658. The monarchy was reestablished, although weakened, in 1660, but religious intolerance to those not adhering to the Church of England continued. Conflict between Catholicism and Protestantism resulted in the Glorious Revolution of 1689. George I, a German prince, assumed the throne in 1714, and his descendants have ruled Great Britain ever since.

In 1707, Scotland, a Protestant country, joined into a successful union with England. This unification is symbolized by the Scottish cross of St. Andrew and the English cross of St. George on one flag, The Union Jack.

In contrast to the Scots, the Irish, who supported the Catholic cause, have had a bitter existence under English rule. The English presence and control in Ireland had been sporadic for several centuries, but the Irish rebellion of 1641, in which thousands of Protestants were massacred, led Cromwell to retaliate by murdering thousands of Irish Catholics. The resulting war led to a British victory, followed by the imposition of penal laws, which forbade Irish Catholics from voting or being elected to public office, practicing law, studying or teaching at a university, sending their children abroad for education, or practicing their religion. In addition, Irish Catholics could not lease land for longer than 31 years and the land they inherited had to be distributed among all the descendants. The English attempted to secure their rule in Ireland by encouraging lowland Scots, considered to be loyal Protestants, to migrate to northern Ireland, primarily in county Ulster. Ulster rapidly industrialized and became an important textile center.

The oppressive penal laws were eventually repealed in 1829, but repeated crop failure and rising rent for land kept the Irish poor. The majority of Ireland gained independence from England in 1926 and is now governed by a parliamentary democracy. Northern Ireland is still under English control and there is repeated conflict between resident Irish Catholics and Protestants and between both groups and the British army.

During the eighteenth and nineteenth centuries, Britain became a great colonial and maritime power abroad. Even though the American colonies were lost in the Revolutionary War, this loss was balanced by the gain of India. The twentieth century brought a decline in Britain's power; most of its colonies have achieved independence, which has contributed to the slow erosion of its economic base. Today Great Britain is governed by a democratic constitutional monarchy.

The Liberty Bell in Philadelphia cracked when it was rung to celebrate the repeal of the Irish penal laws.

France

France emerged from the Middle Ages as the leading nation-state in Europe. French power and influence expanded under Cardinal Richelieu, minister to Louis XIII (1610–1643). The reign of Louis XIV was the golden era in the history of the French monarchy. The French Revolution (1789) destroyed the monarchy, and the First Republic was established in 1792.

Napoleon, crowned emperor in 1804, dominated European politics for the next decade. He battled, acquired territory, and lost it again repeatedly. After his defeat in 1815 by the combined forces of England, Russia, Austria, Sweden, and Prussia, a short restoration of the French monarchy was followed by the Second Republic (1848–1852) and then the Second Empire (1852–1870) under the nephew of the first Napoleon. His defeat by Prussia in 1870 led to the establishment of the Third Republic.

Although the nation was a victor in World War I, France suffered great human and economic loss. In World War II, France was unprepared for Germany's air and armored attacks. The country fell in June 1940 and was occupied by German forces until liberated by the Allies in 1944. Today, France is governed by a constitutional democracy.

During the nineteenth century France competed with Great Britain in establishing a colonial empire. Since the seventeenth century, the French had been exploring vast areas of America, and by the eighteenth century they had established a territory extending from the Gulf of Mexico to Canada, known as the Louisiana Territory. The United States purchased this land from France in 1803. Most of France's colonies obtained independence by the twentieth century.

HISTORY OF IMMIGRATION TO THE UNITED STATES

Immigration Patterns

Great Britain. The British who immigrated in the seventeenth century settled primarily in New England, Virginia, and Maryland. While many originally came to avoid religious persecution, such as the Puritans in New England and the Catholics in Maryland, most later immigrants earned their passage to America by signing on as indentured servants.

By the eighteenth century, British immigration had slowed. After independence, British immigration to the United States further declined, due to American hostility and disapproval by the British government. However, reported arrivals of Britons in the nineteenth century increased substantially. Early in the century, most immigrants were families from rural areas of southern and western England. In the latter half of the century, the majority of immigrants were from large English towns, many were seasonal unskilled workers who repeatedly returned to Britain.

It is said that there have been Scots in America as long as there have been Europeans on the continent. Over 100 towns and cities in the United States bear Scottish names, and it has been estimated that 1.5 million Scots immigrated to America. Although the majority of Scots came during the eighteenth and nineteenth centuries, 400,000 immigrated between 1921 and 1931, when Scotland suffered a severe economic depression. The Scottish settled over most of the United States and were often professionals or skilled laborers.

Although British immigration did not decline in the early twentieth century, the United States was no longer the country of first choice for those leaving Great Britain. During the Depression of the 1930s, more British people returned to Britain than came to America. After World War II, an increase in immigration was attributable to British war brides returning to the United States with their American husbands. Since the 1970s, British immigration has been constant at about 10,000 persons per year.

Ireland. The first Irish people to immigrate in substantial numbers to the United States were the descendants of Scottish Presbyterians who settled in Northern Ireland in the seventeenth century. Large-scale immigration began in the eighteenth century, and by 1775 there were an estimated 250,000 Scotch-Irish living in the American colonies. Most of the immigration was the result of an economic depression brought on by a textile slump in Ireland.

Initially, the Scotch-Irish settled in Pennsylvania. Before long, the direction of Scotch-Irish immigration was westward to the frontier, first up the Delaware River and then beyond the Susquehanna into the rich farmlands of the Cumberland Valley. The Scotch-Irish played an important role in the settlement of the trans-Allegheny region and eventually clustered around the site of Pittsburgh and in southwestern Pennsylvania. They also settled in the frontier regions of western Maryland, the Shenandoah valley of Virginia, and the backcountry of Georgia.

Irish Catholics started to arrive in the United States by 1820, and their immigration reached an apex between 1840 and 1860, when approximately 2 million arrived. The impetus to leave Ireland was not only religious persecution but also repeated crop failures. The potato blight that destroyed their

St. Patrick's Day parade: The annual St. Patrick's Day parade in front of St. Patrick's Cathedral in New York City. (Courtesy New York Convention and Visitors Bureau.)

principle crop in 1845 resulted in death by starvation to 1 million Irish people.

The Irish Catholics were the first great ethnic minority in American cities, and their early history set the pattern for later minority immigrant groups. They settled in the northeastern cities and were at the bottom of the socioeconomic ladder. While the Scotch-Irish, who were often of relatively high economic standing and Protestant, found it fairly easy to move into mainstream American society, the Irish Catholics were often stereotyped as drunkards, brawlers, and incompetents. The Irish achieved success with painful slowness. For many, their first entry into the American mainstream came by way of city politics.

France. Immigration directly from France has been the smallest yet most constant of that from any European country, and the return rate has been high. Most of the estimated 1 million persons who have immigrated to the United States from France have been middle class, skilled, and have come for economic opportunity. A smaller number came because of religious persecution. Over 12,000 Huguenots, French Protestants, settled in the American colonies in the eighteenth century. They were considered to be excellent skilled workers.

Generally, French people who settled in the United States were eager to assimilate and able to do so because they were economically successful. Few pockets of French culture remain in the United States, with the exception of southern Louisiana, originally a French holding, and northern New England. However, the Frenchness of these areas is probably due more to the influence of French Canadian immigration than direct French immigration.

French Canadians are the descendants of explorers and settlers who came from France, primarily Normandy and Brittany, during the seventeenth century. They established New France in what is today known as Canada. When the English gained control of Canada, many French Canadians moved to the United States, and in some instances they were deported from Canada. Most settled in northern New England, especially Maine, and their descendants are known as Franco-Americans. Others from Acadia (Nova Scotia, New Brunswick, Prince Edward Island, and part of Maine) relocated, sometimes not by choice, to central and southern Louisiana, and their descendants are known as *Cajuns*.

Current Demographics and Socioeconomic Status

British and Irish. The British assimilated into American mainstream society easily. Distinct groups from specific regions of Great Britain can still be found, however. For example, Cornish immigrants of the nineteenth century were often miners, and their descendants are still living in certain old mining regions, such as Grass Valley, California, Butte City, Montana, and the areas around Lake Superior. The Welsh who immigrated in the nineteenth century were miners and millworkers. They settled in the mid-Atlantic and Midwestern states, especially Ohio and Pennsylvania; many were Baptist, Calvinist or Methodists. Remnants of Welsh communities in the United States still celebrate St. David's Day (the feast day of the patron saint of Wales) and the annual festival of the National Gymanfa Ganu Association (an assembly that sings Welsh hymns or folk songs).

Today the Scotch-Irish are widely dispersed and are not easily identifiable. It has been estimated that 1 in every 30 Americans (some 8 million people) is of Scotch-Irish descent. Although Irish Catholics have to some extent assimilated into mainstream American society, they still remain an identifiable ethnic group.

Close to 5 million Irish Catholics have immigrated to the United States, and today there are approximately 16 million Americans who claim to be of Irish descent. Although they started out on a lower economic rung than other older immigrant groups, they are now scattered throughout the occupational structure. In the 1950s, the Irish were over represented as clergymen, fire fighters, and police officers. Today there are disproportionately more in law, medicine, and the sciences. Numerous Irish people have also excelled in the literary arts and in sports, expecially boxing and baseball.

French. It has been estimated that over 1.5 million people of French Canadian descent live in the United States. In Louisiana over 800,000 are of Acadian ancestry. The Cajuns settled in rural and inaccessible areas of southern Louisiana, the bayous, and along the Mississippi River. Primarily farmers, fishermen, and herders, they were self-sufficient and kept to themselves. Today they are still rural but their occupations reflect local economic conditions.

The French Canadians who settled in the New England states were less likely to be farmers; instead, they worked in factories that processed textiles, lumber, and bricks. Since

1950, there has been an increase in the percentage of Franco-Americans holding white collar jobs, but they still lag behind other ethnic groups economically. Compared to the French who immigrated directly from France and assimilated rapidly into American culture, the descendants of French Canadians have clung to their Roman Catholic religion, language, and customs.

Cultural Organizations

Irish Catholics. Once the Irish Catholics had settled into the urban northeast, the predominant organizations that contributed to and often dominated life were the Catholic church, politics (usually in the Democratic Party) and the labor unions.

One of the earliest and most spectacular successes of the Irish in America was in politics, especially in the Democratic Party. The Irish controlled the political machinery in many large cities for decades. Reasons for their achievements have been attributed to their previous experience in Ireland when they campaigned against the English, and to a loyal political body that would vote in a bloc. An Irish politician's supporters could depend on him for help in times of trouble. Lastly, the Irish are said to excel at public speaking, and this has aided their political ascent. Although the influence of the Irish has declined, the majority of Americans of Irish Catholic descent remain politically liberal.

The Irish, concerned over their low wages and poor working conditions, often helped establish worker's unions. By 1900, Irish Americans held the presidencies of over half of the 110 unions in the American Federation of Labor. The Irish still remain important as members and officers in United States labor unions today.

French. In both Louisiana and New England, ethnic revival in the 1970s brought increased awareness of Cajuns and Franco-Americans. The French language is receiving greater emphasis in public schools in Louisiana and New England. There is a renewed interest in Cajun music, humor, and celebrations; Franco-American festivals have been revived. Several organizations dedicated to the preservation of Cajun and Franco-American tradition are the Madawaska Historical Society in Maine, the Council for the Development of French in Louisiana, the Association of Canado-Américaine (ACA), and the Union St. Jean-Baptiste d'Amérique (USJB).

WORLDVIEW

Religion

Irish. Religion is a cornerstone of Irish Catholic society and in the United States it is centered around the parish. Over time, the Catholic church in America came to be dominated by the Irish, often to the resentment of other Catholic immigrants. The church spared no effort to aid its members; it established schools, hospitals, and orphanages across the country. The church helped to bridge the cultural gap for many Irish immigrants, through advice, job placement, and savings clubs and temperance societies. Today religion plays a less important role in Irish Catholic life, although the role of the Irish in the church is still significant.

French. Among French Americans, the Catholic church provided the nucleus of the community, gave it stability, and helped preserve the language and tradition of the people. The church today still plays a central role.

Family Structure

Irish. Many of the characteristics of the Irish family in the nineteenth century persisted into the twentieth century. Irish Catholics tended to marry at a late age, have large families, and divorce rarely. Today, however, most first- and second-generation Irish Catholics are likely to marry outside their group, and with increasing frequency, outside Catholicism.

Traditionally, the father was the breadwinner in the Irish Catholic family, but the mother's position was a strong one. Daughters were often as well-educated as sons. The Irish people's relatively egalitarian attitudes toward sex roles may be responsible for the high concentration of Irish American women in professional jobs and white-collar work.

French. Until the twentieth century, Cajuns lived in rural areas in extended-family households with as many as 10 or 12 children per couple. The whole family worked as a unit, and decisions that affected the group were made jointly by all the adults. Until 1945, many Cajuns were illiterate and spoke only Cajun French. The use of Cajun French was prohibited by the public schools in 1921; as a result, many younger Cajuns today do not speak or understand French. Today the average family size is smaller and there is more marriage outside the community, but Cajuns still retain strong ties to their families.

The Franco-Americans in New England are similar to the Cajuns in that they maintained French traditions; this was not due to isolation, however, but rather to their continued contact with French relatives in Quebec. They had little desire to acculturate. During the 1930s, the bond to Canada weakened because of new laws restricting reentry into the United States and the Depression, which diminished new French Canadian immigration. Today, the descendants of the French Canadians speak French infrequently and often intermarry with outsiders. Family ties are still strong, but as with the Cajuns, family size has decreased. Franco-American women have traditionally had higher status and more authority than their counterparts in France.

Traditional Food Habits

The influence of France on the food habits of Great Britain and Ireland and vice versa has led to many similarities in the cuisines of these countries, although the ingredients of southern French cooking differ in that they are more like those of Mediterranean countries. The influence of these northern European cuisines on American foods and food habits has been extensive.

INGREDIENTS AND COMMON FOODS

Staples and Regional Variations

Great Britain and Ireland. Animal products are of key importance in Great Britain and Ireland. Some form of meat or fish is present at most meals, in addition to eggs, milk, and cheese. In Britain and Ireland, lamb is a commonly eaten meat, as is roast beef, which is often made for Sunday dinner with *Yorkshire pudding* (a popover cooked in meat drippings). Pork is often served as sausages *(bangers)* and bacon. Various game birds are also eaten. The Cultural Food Groups list includes a more complete detailing of ingredients (Table 4.1).

The Irish and British diet also contains a variety of seafood. A well known fast-food item is *fish and chips.* The fish is battered and deep fried, served with fried potatoes, and seasoned with salt and malt vinegar. Fish is often preserved and served as an appetizer or at breakfast. Examples are smoked Scottish salmon and *kippers,* salted and smoked fish.

Dairy products and eggs also play an important role in the diet of the British and Irish. Eggs are traditionally served for

TABLE 4.1. Cultural Food Groups: Northern European

Group	Comments
PROTEIN FOODS	
Milk/milk products	The English and Irish drink milk as a beverage; the French may not.
Meat/poultry/fish/eggs/ legumes	Meat, poultry, or fish is usually the centerpiece of the meal.
	Meats are generally roasted or broiled in Great Britain; also prepared as stews or in pies.
	Smoked, salted, or dried fish is popular in England.
CEREALS/GRAINS	Wheat bread usually accompanies the meal.
	In Britain and Ireland, oatmeal or porridge is common for breakfast.
FRUITS/VEGETABLES	Potatoes are frequently eaten in Ireland.

Common Foods	Adaptations in the United States
Cheese (cow, sheep, and goat milk), cream, milk, sour cream, yogurt.	
Meat: Beef (roasts, variety cuts such as brains, kidneys, liver, sweetbreads, and tripe), horse-meat, lamb, oxtail, tongue, pork, rabbit, snails, veal, venison.	The Irish consume more animal protein.
Poultry and small birds: chicken, duck, goose, partridge, pheasant, pigeon, quail, thrush, turkey.	
Fish and shellfish: anchovies, bass, clams, crab, crayfish, cod, haddock, herring, lobster, mackerel, mullet, mussels, oysters, perch, pike, pompano, salmon, sardines, scallops, shad, shrimp, skate, sole, sturgeon, trout, whiting.	
Eggs: poultry and fish.	
Legumes: split peas, lentils, kidney beans, lima beans.	
Arrowroot starch, barley, hops, oats, rice, rye, taploca, wheat.	Corn and corn products are consumed more.
Fruits: apples, apricots, cherries, currants, gooseberries, grapes (many varieties), lemons, melons, oranges, peaches, pears, plums, prunes, raisins, raspberries, rhubarb, strawberries.	Native and transplanted fruits and vegetables, such as bananas, blueberries, okra, and squash, were added to the diet.
Vegetables: artichokes, asparagus, beets, brussels sprouts, cabbage, carrots, cauliflower, celery, celery root, cucumbers, eggplant, fennel, green beans, green peppers, lettuce (many varieties), leeks, mushrooms (including truffles), olives, onions, parsnips, peas, potatoes, radishes, salsify, scallions, sorrel, spinach, tomatoes, turnips, truffles, watercress.	

TABLE 4.1. Cultural Food Groups: Northern European (*continued*)

Group	Comments
ADDITIONAL FOODS	
Seasonings	
Nuts/seeds	
Beverages	
Fats/oils	
Sweeteners	

A pub, or public house, is a bar that serves beer, wine, hard liquor, and light meals. In contrast to a bar in the United States, the British pub is often the place where friends and family meet to socialize.

breakfast, and cheese is the key ingredient in the traditional *ploughman's lunch* served in pubs. It consists of a piece of cheddar cheese, bread, pickled onions, and a pint of beer. Other cheeses produced in England are the slightly salty and nutty Cheshire, and Stilton, a blue cheese.

Devonshire is known for its rich cream products such as double cream, (which has twice as much butterfat as ordinary cream), and clotted cream, a slightly fermented thickened cream. It is often spread on *scones*, teacakes made with baking powder.

Although not the main focus of the meal, breads, fruits, and vegetables are not overlooked. In Ireland, soda bread, a bread made with baking soda instead of yeast, was tradition-

Common Foods	Adaptations in the United States
Angelica (licorice-flavored plant), bay leaf, capers, chilis, chives, chocolate, chutney, cinnamon, cloves, coffee, cognac, fennel seeds, garlic, ginger, horseradish, juniper berries, mace, marjorum, mint, mustard, nutmeg, oregano, paprika, parsley, pepper (black, white, green, and pink), rosemary, saffron, sage, shallots, sweet basil, tarragon, thyme, vanilla, Worchestershire sauce.	Cajun and Creole cooking are highly spiced. Stews are thickened with *filé* powder (sassafras).
Nuts: almonds (sweet and bitter), chestnuts, filberts (hazelnuts), pecan, walnuts (including black).	
Seeds: sesame.	
Beer (ale, stout, bitter), black and herbal tea (mint, anise, chamomile, etc.), cider, coffee, gin, hot chocolate, liqueurs, port, sherry, whiskey, wine (red, white, champagne, and fruit/vegetable).	
Butter, goose fat, lard, margarine, olive oil, vegetable oil, salt pork.	
Honey, sugar.	Molasses and maple syrup are used as sweeteners.
	Irish Americans use more sugar than members of other groups.

ally made every day to accompany the meal. Wheat flour is commonly used for baking, and oatmeal is eaten as a porridge for breakfast in Scotland, or used in making bread and biscuits throughout Britain and Ireland.

Potatoes, brought to Ireland from the New World in the seventeenth century, are the mainstay of the Irish diet and are found in the British diet as well. Potatoes are found in stews or pies, such as *shepherd's* or *cottage pie,* a meat pie made of leftover ground meat and onions and topped with mashed potatoes. Mashed potatoes are often just referred to as ''mash,'' as in ''bangers and mash'' (sausages and mashed potatoes). Some side dishes made of potatoes are *boxty,* a type of potato pancake, *bubble and squeak,* a dish made of

Colcannon was traditionally served for the harvest dinner and on Halloween in Ireland. For Halloween, coins were wrapped in foil and buried in the dish so the children could find them as they ate.

The Guinness Book of Records was originally published by the family who makes Guinness stout to help settle pub arguments.

Irish whiskey is distilled from mashed, fermented barley. Scotch is a blend of malted whiskey (the barley is germinated before fermentation) and unmalted whiskey.

leftover cabbage and potatoes, chopped and fried together, and *colcannon,* mashed and seasoned boiled white vegetables with onions.

Biscuits, or "bisk-cake," in England can refer to bread, cake, cookies, crackers, or what are known in America as biscuits. Scottish shortbread is an example of a sweet, buttery biscuit.

The most common beverages consumed by adults in Ireland and England are tea, beer, and whiskey. Tea, which has become synonymous with a meal or break in the afternoon, was introduced to England in 1662 by the wife of Charles II. Drunk with most meals and as a refreshment, strong black tea is preferred, served with milk and sugar.

Familiar alcoholic beverages include beer and whiskey. The British and the Irish do not drink the pilsner beer common in the United States. Instead, in Ireland, a favorite is stout, a dark, rich, heavy beer that can provide substantial calories to the diet; in Britain, the pubs usually serve "bitter," a rich amber-colored beer, strongly flavored with hops. Both beers are served at cellar temperature and are naturally carbonated.

Whiskey is made in both Ireland and Scotland but the Irish are usually credited with its invention and name. Other alcoholic drinks popular in Britain are gin, port (a brandy-fortified wine made in Portugal), and sherry (also a fortified wine, from Spain).

France. The cooking of France is divided into classic French cuisine (*haute* or *grande* cuisine) and provincial cooking. Classic French cooking is elegant and formal, mostly prepared in restaurants using the best ingredients from throughout the country. Provincial cuisine is simpler fare made at home featuring fresh regional ingredients.

The ancestors of most French Americans are from two of France's northern provinces, Brittany and Normandy. Brittany, known as Bretagne by the French, is located in the northwest; its shores are washed by the English Channel and the Bay of Biscay. Seafood, simply prepared, is common and the famed Belon oysters are shipped throughout France. It is said that mutton and vegetables from the region have a naturally salty taste because of the salt spray. Apples are the prevalent fruit, and cider is widely exported.

Located along the English Channel and east of Brittany is Normandy, also known for its seafood and apples. *Calvados,* an apple brandy, is thought to be the mother of applejack, an alcoholic apple drink used to clear the palate during meals in Louisiana. Another alcoholic drink produced in the region is *Bènèdictine,* named after the Roman Catholic monks who still make it at the monastery in Fecamp. Normandy is also re-knowned for its dairy products; its butter is considered one of the best in France. *Camembert,* a semisoft cheese with a mild flavor, and *Pont-l'Evque,* a hearty aromatic cheese, are produced in the area. Dishes from Normandy are often pre-pared with rich cream sauces.

The cream used throughout France is slightly fermented until it is thickened. It is called crème fraîche (fresh cream is called fleurette).

Champagne, bordered by the English Channel and Belgium, has a cuisine influenced by the Germanic cultures. Beer is popular, as are sausages, such as *andouille* and *andouillette,* large and small intestines stuffed with pork or lamb stomach. *Charcuterie,* cold meat dishes, such as sausages, *pâtés* and *terrines,* which are often sold in specialty stores, is especially good from this region. Throughout the world, Champagne is probably best known for its naturally carbonated wines. Only sparkling wines produced in this region can be legally called champagne in France.

In the seventeenth century, the method for producing sparkling wine was discovered by the monk Dom Perignon. Today, the champagne bearing his name, Dom Perignon, is considered one of the finest in the world.

The province that borders Germany, Alsace-Lorraine, has been alternately ruled by France and Germany. One of its principal cities is Strasbourg. Many German foods are fa-vored in the region, such as goose, sausages, and sauerkraut. Goose fat is often used for cooking, and one of the specialties of the area is *pâté de fois gras,* pâté made from the enlarged livers of force-fed geese. Another famous dish is *quiche Lor-raine,* a round pastry shell filled with cream, beaten eggs, and bacon. Alsace-Lorraine is a wine-producing area; its wines are similar to the German Rhine wines but are usually not as sweet. Distilled liquors produced in the region are *kirsch,* a cherry brandy, and the brandy *eau de vie de framboise,* made from raspberries.

Pâté is a spread of finely ground, seasoned, and spiced meats. A terrine is commonly made from leftover meats (not ground but cut into small pieces), spices, and jelling substance, then baked in a loaf pan.

Touraine, the province that includes the fertile Loire valley, is located south of Normandy and Brittany. Along the river one can see the beautiful chateaux or palaces built by the French nobility. Known as the "garden of France," Touraine produces some of the finest fruits and vegetables in the coun-try. A dry white wine produced in the area is Vouvray.

The area surrounding the city of Paris, called the Ile-de-France, is the home of classic French cuisine. Some of the finest beef and veal, as well as a variety of fruits and vegeta-bles, is produced in this fertile region. *Brie,* semisoft and mild flavored, is the best-known cheese of the area. Dishes of the Ile-de-France include *lobster à l'américaine,* lobster prepared with tomatoes, shallots, herbs, white wine, and brandy; po-

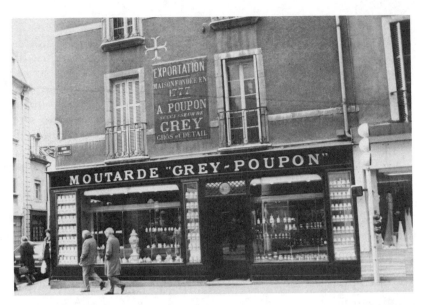

Home of French mustard, Dijon, France.

tage St. Germain, pea soup; *filet de boeuf béarnaise*, filet of beef with a béarnaise sauce; and *crêpes Suzette*, unleavened pancakes seasoned with sugar and orange juice and then flambéed with brandy and orange liquor.

Located southeast of Paris is Burgundy, one of the foremost wine-producing regions of France. Burgundy's robust dishes start to take on the flavor of southern France: they contain garlic and are often prepared with olive oil. Dijon, a principal city, is also the name for the mustards of the region prepared with white wine and herbs. Dishes of the area are *escargot*, snails (raised on grape vines) cooked in a garlic butter and served in the shell; *coq au vin*, rooster or chicken cooked in wine; and *boeuf bourguignon*, a hearty red wine beef stew.

In Burgundy, the red wines are primarily made from the pinot noir grape and the white wines from the chardonnay grape. The great wines of the area are usually named after the villages they are produced in: for example, Gevrey-Chambertin, Vosne-Romanée, and Volnay. *Cassis*, a black currant liquor, is also produced in the region.

The other major wine-producing region of France is Bordeaux, which is also the name of its principal city, known for its hearty cuisine. The term *à la Bordelaise* when applied to food can mean (1) prepared in a seasoned sauce containing red or white wine, marrow, tomatoes, butter and shallots; (2) use of *mirepoix,* finely minced mixture of carrots, onions, and celery, seasoned with bay leaves and thyme; (3) accompanied by *cèpes,* large fleshy mushrooms; or (4) accompanied by an artichoke and potato garnish.

A red Bordeaux wine is full-bodied and made primarily from the cabernet sauvignon grape. (In Great Britain, Bordeaux is called claret.) Among the wines produced are St. Julien, Margaux, Graves, St. Emilion, Pomerol, and Sauternes, a sweet white dessert wine.

Provence, located on the Mediterranean Sea, is a favorite vacation spot because of its warm Riviera beaches. Provence is also known for the large old port city of Marseilles, its perfumes from the city of Grasse, and the internationally known film festival in Cannes.

The cooking of Provence is similar to that of Italy and Spain. Key ingredients are tomatoes, garlic, and olive oil. *A la Provençal* means that a dish contains these three items. Other common food items are seafood from the Mediterranean, eggplant, and zucchini. Popular dishes from the region are *bouillabaisse,* the famed fish stew made with tomatoes, garlic, olive oil, and several types of seafood, seasoned with saffron, and usually served with *rouille,* a hot red pepper sauce; *ratatouille,* tomatoes, eggplant, and zucchini cooked in olive oil; *salade Niçoise,* a salad originating in Nice, containing tuna, tomatoes, olives, lettuce, other raw vegetables, and sometimes hard-boiled eggs; and *pan bagna,* a French bread sandwich slathered with olive oil and containing a variety of ingredients, such as anchovies, tomatoes, green peppers, onions, olives, hard-boiled eggs, and capers.

Cooking Styles

Although the ingredients of the countries on the opposite sides of the English Channel are not substantially different, their cooking styles vary greatly. France's cuisine is admired and imitated around the world, while Britain and Ireland's cuisine is often just described as being hearty.

Great Britain and Ireland. In Britain and Ireland, meat is usually roasted or broiled, depending on the cut, and lightly seasoned with herbs and spices. Strong-flavored condiments, such as Worchestershire sauce (flavored with anchovies, vinegar, soy, garlic, and assorted spices) on roast beef or mint jelly on lamb are often served. Chutneys, highly spiced fruit or vegetable pickles originally from India, are also popular. Leftover meat is finely chopped, then served as a stew, pie, or pudding.

While most Americans think of pies and puddings as being sweet desserts, in Britain and Ireland this is not necessarily the case. A pie is a baked pastry consisting of a mixture of meats, game, fish, and vegetables, or fruit, covered with or enclosed in a crust. A *Cornish pasty* is a small, pillow-shaped pie filled with meat, onions, and potatoes that miners took down in the mines to eat for lunch or dinner. Another well-known British dish is steak and kidney pie.

Pudding is a steamed, boiled, or baked dish that may be based on anything from custards and fruits, to meat and vegetables. An example of a sweet pudding is *plum pudding* which is served traditionally at Christmas. It is a steamed dish of suet, dried and candied fruit, and other ingredients. *Trifle* is a layered dessert made from custard, pound cake, raspberry jam, whipping cream, sherry, and almonds.

France. Classic French cuisine implies a carefully planned meal that balances the texture, color, and flavor of the dishes. Perhaps the soul of French cooking is its sauces, often painstakingly prepared from stocks that are simmered for hours to bring out the flavor of the ingredients. A white stock is made from fish, chicken, or veal, and a brown stock is made from beef or veal.

Sauces are subtlely flavored with natural ingredients, such as vegetables, wine, and herbs. They must never overwhelm the food but rather complement it. The five basic sauces are: *espagnole,* made with brown stock, mirepoix, and *roux; velouté,* made with milk, roux, onions, and spices; *béchamel,* made with white stock and roux; *tomato,* made with white stock, tomatoes, onions, carrots, garlic, butter, and flour; and, *demi-glace,* reduction of espagnole sauce. Examples of classic cold sauces are mayonnaise and *vinaigrette.*

Some common rules in preparing French dishes are (1) never mix sweet and sour flavors in the same dish; (2) never serve sweet sauces over fish; (3) do not under- or overcook food, (4) with the exception of salad and fruit, do not serve uncooked food; (5) always use the freshest, best-tasting ingredients; and (6) wine is an integral part of the meal and must complement the food.

Mincemeat pies, which are traditionally served at Christmas and Thanksgiving in some parts of the United States, were originally made with seasoned ground meat and fruit, but today they are usually made only with dried and candied fruit, nuts, and spices.

Roux is a thickening agent made from flour cooked in butter or other fat drippings.

MEAL COMPOSITION AND CYCLE

Daily Pattern

Great Britain. In Britain, four meals are traditionally served each day: breakfast, lunch, tea, and an evening meal (dinner). In the nineteenth and early twentieth centuries, breakfast was a very substantial meal, consisting of oatmeal; bacon, ham or sausage; eggs (prepared several ways); bread, fried in bacon grease; toast with jam or marmalade; grilled tomatoes or mushrooms; and possibly smoked fish or deviled kidneys. All this was washed down with tea. In Scotland, oatmeal is usually eaten for breakfast, while in England today, packaged breakfast cereals are often eaten during the week and the more extensive breakfast is reserved for weekends and special occasions.

Lunch was originally a hearty meal and still is on Sunday, but during the week it is squeezed in between work hours. It may include a meat pie, fish and chips, or a light meal at the pub with a pint of bitters. Sunday lunch, or the weekday dinner, is much like an American dinner. It consists of meat or fish, vegetable, and starch. The starch is often potatoes or rice, and bread also accompanies the meal. Dessert (often called pudding) follows the main course.

In the late afternoon in Britain and Ireland, most people take a break and have a pot of tea and a light snack. In some areas a "high tea" is served. This can be a substantial meal that includes potted meat, fish, shrimp, ham salad, salmon cakes, fruits, and a selection of cakes and pastries. Children often eat their dinner at tea time.

France. The French eat only three meals a day: breakfast, lunch, and dinner. There is very little snacking between meals. Breakfast, in contrast to the British meal, is very light, consisting of a *croissant* or french bread with butter and jam, and strong coffee with hot milk or hot chocolate. The French breakfast is what is known in the United States as a "continental breakfast."

Lunch is the largest meal of the day, and in many regions of France businesses close at midday for two hours so people can return home to eat. The meal usually starts with an appetizer *(hors d'oeuvre)* such as pâté. The main course is a meat, fish, or egg dish accompanied by a vegetable and bread. If salad is eaten, it is served after the main course. Dessert at home is usually cheese and fruit. In a restaurant, ice cream (more like a fruit sherbert or sorbet), cakes, cus-

Deviled describes a dish prepared with a spicy hot sauce or seasoning.

Potted is a term used by the English to describe fish, meat, poultry, or game pounded with lard or butter into a coarse or smooth pâté, then preserved in jars or pots.

Tea in Great Britain: Tea time in Great Britain typically includes small sandwiches, scones (on second rack of the silver tray), and assorted cookies and pastries. (Courtesy Gossich and Partners.)

tards, and pastries are served in addition to fruit and cheese. Wine is served with the meal, and coffee after the meal.

Special Occasions

Christmas and Easter are the most important Christian holidays celebrated in France, England, and Ireland. Ireland and

France are predominantly Catholic countries and tend to observe all the holy days of obligation and patron saint days. France commemorates the beginning of the French Revolution on July 14, Bastille Day.

Britain and Ireland. The British celebrate Christmas by serving hot punch or mulled wine; roast goose, turkey, or ham; plum pudding and mince pies; and afterwards, port with nuts and dried fruit. The plum pudding is traditionally splashed with brandy, then flamed before serving. Boxing Day, the day after Christmas, is when friends and relatives visit one another.

Foods served at Easter time include hot cross buns and *Shrewsbury simnel.* The cross on the buns is thought to symbolize both sun and fire; the four quarters represent the seasons. Shrewsbury simnel is a rich spice cake topped with 12 decorative balls of marzipan. It is also served on Mother's Day.

Another holiday celebrated throughout Great Britain is New Year's on January 1. The Scottish traditionally eat *haggis* on New Year's Eve. It is a sheep's stomach stuffed with a pudding made of sheep's innards and oatmeal. After it is served, each person drenches his portion with Scotch whiskey before eating.

The Irish customarily eat corned beef and cabbage on St. Patrick's Day, March 17, a tradition followed in the United States as well. St. Patrick is the patron saint of Ireland.

France. In France, the main Christmas meal is served after mass on the night of December 24. Two traditional dishes are a black or white "pudding" (blood or pork sausage), and a goose or turkey with chestnuts. In Provence, the Christmas Eve meal is meatless, usually cod, but the highlight is that it is followed by 13 desserts.

On Shrove Tuesday *(Mardi Gras)* the French feast themselves on pancakes, fritters, waffles, and various biscuits and cakes. During Lent no eggs, fat, or meat are eaten. Dishes served during Lent often contain cod or herring. Cod is also the traditional dish served on Good Friday, and in some regions lentils are eaten to "wash away one's sins." Easter marks the return of the normal diet, and eggs are often served hard boiled (also colored), in omelets, or in breads and pastries. French toast *(soupe dorée* or *croûtes)* is a traditional Easter dish. Also common are pies filled with minced meats.

Traditionally a sprig of holly is placed on top of the Christmas pudding. The holly leaves are supposed to represent Christ's crown of thorns; the red berries, His blood.

Superstition has it in Britain, that when the Christmas pudding is being prepared, each member of the family must take a turn to stir the mixture clockwise (the direction the sun was assumed to rotate around the earth) and make a wish. If a person stirs in the opposite direction he or she is asking for trouble.

"Corn" originally meant "a grain." Before refrigeration, meats were preserved with grains of salt (in a brine solution) by a process called "corning."

Contemporary Food Habits in the United States

ADAPTATION OF FOODS HABITS

Ingredients and Common Foods

British and Irish. Many American dishes have their origins in Great Britain. The Puritans, making do with what they had, made a pudding with cornmeal, milk, molasses, and spices. Today this is called *Indian pudding.* Pumpkin pie is just a custard pie to which the native American squash, pumpkin, is added. *Sally Lunn,* a sweet hot bread made in Virginia, is said to have been sold on the streets of Bath, England, by a young lass who gave them her name. Others claim that the name is a corruption of the French *sol et lune,* a sun and moon cake. *Syllabub,* a milk and wine punch drunk in the American South at Christmastime, is also an English recipe.

La boucherie: *French-speaking Cajuns in Louisiana maintain the hog-butchering traditions of their past. Before the days of refrigeration, everyone in the community helped to clean and butcher a hog and prepare the lard. Participants took home fresh pork cuts and spicy sausages called* boudin. La boucherie *is still a part of many Cajun festivals.* (Courtesy Louisiana Office of Tourism.)

French. French cooking has had less influence on everyday American cooking (except for french fries), but there are probably few cities that don't have a French restaurant (which may or may not be owned by a French immigrant). French Americans adapted their cuisine and meal patterns to the available ingredients and other ethnic cooking styles. The best example of this is found in Louisiana, where the unique *Creole* and *Cajun* cooking developed. Creole cooking is to Cajun cooking as French grande cuisine is to provincial cooking. Some dishes may sound typically French, such as the fish stew, *bouillabaisse,* but it is made with fish from the Gulf of Mexico, not from the Mediterranean. Even the coffee is slightly different, since it is flavored with the indigenous chicory root.

Ingredients for Cajun cooking reflect the environment of Louisiana. Fish and shellfish abound, notably crayfish, crabs, oysters, pompano, redfish, and shrimp to name just a few. Shellfish is commonly eaten raw on the half shell (oysters) or boiled in a spicy mixture. *Gumbo* and *jambalaya* are often made with seafood. Gumbo is a thick, spicy soup made with a variety of seafood, meat, and vegetables. It is thickened with either okra or filé powder and then ladled over rice. Jambalaya, also a highly seasoned stew made with a combination of seafood, meats, and vegetables, was brought to New Orleans by the Spanish. Originally made only with ham *(jambon)* it was later modified. The base for these stews and gravies is roux; however, the Cajun roux is unique in that the flour and fat (usually vegetable oil) are cooked very slowly until the mixture turns brown and has a nutlike aroma and taste.

Other key ingredients in Cajun cooking are rice, which has been grown in Louisiana since the early 1700s, red beans, tomatoes, chayote squash, eggplant, spicy hot sauce, and a variety of pork products. One of the better-known hot sauces, *Tabasco,* is produced in the bayous of southern Louisiana from fermented chili peppers, vinegar, and spices. A deep-fried rice fritter, *calas,* is the Louisiana version of a doughnut. Other rice dishes are *red beans and rice* and *dirty rice.* Dirty rice derives its name from the fact that its ingredients, bits of chicken gizzards and liver, give the rice a brown appearance.

Pecan pralines are a famous New Orleans candy. Pecans are native to Louisiana; pralines are large flat patties made from brown sugar, water or cream, and butter. Another confection eaten often with coffee are *beignets,* round or square

Louis Armstrong, the famous jazz trumpeter, always signed his letters, "Red beans and ricefully yours."

puffed French doughnuts dusted with powdered sugar. French toast or *pain perdu* is another French specialty that was transported to New Orleans and is now familiar to most Americans.

The cuisine of French Americans in New England tends to be traditionally French, but it is influenced by common New England foods and food habits. As with the Cajuns, the main meal of the day has become dinner, instead of lunch. Franco-Americans use more herbs and spices than other New Englanders and take time to prepare the best-tasting food. Traditional French dishes are pork pâté, called *creton* by the Franco-Americans, and the traditional yule log cake *(bûche de Noël)* served at Christmas.

Franco-American cuisine offers numerous soups and stews. One of the most elaborate of the stews, which is also called a pie, is *cipate,* known as *cipaille, si-paille, six-pates,* and "sea pie" in some areas. A typical recipe calls for chicken, pork, veal and beef plus four or five kinds of vegetables layered in a heavy kettle, covered with pie crust. It is slowly cooked after chicken stock has been added through vents in the crust.

Maple syrup is commonly used. One unique breakfast dish is eggs poached in the syrup. Maple syrup is also served over bread dumplings or just plain bread. Franco-Americans appreciate wine and distilled spirits. One unusual combination of both is *caribou,* a mixture of "white whiskey" (a distilled, colorless liquor) and red wine, which is drunk for festive occasions.

Meal Composition and Cycle

British and Irish. American food habits have been greatly influenced by British and Irish immigrants. Meal patterns and composition are very similar to those in Great Britain. Americans eat a hearty breakfast that often includes ham or bacon and eggs. The heart of the evening meal is usually meat that is accompanied by a vegetable and a starch. Bread is served with most meals.

Festive meals also reflect the British influence. A traditional Christmas dinner includes roast turkey or ham, stuffing, and mashed vegetables. For dessert, a pie is customary, often mincemeat.

Two holidays that Americans think of as being typically American, Thanksgiving and Halloween, are actually of British origin. Thanksgiving combined the tradition of an old British harvest festival with the Pilgrims' celebration of a harvest that kept them from starving in their new environment. In Great Britain and Ireland, Halloween, or *All Hallows Eve,* is thought to have originated in ancient times. They believed that on Halloween night ghosts and witches are most likely to wander abroad.

French. In Louisiana, Cajuns have many local festivals, such as the crawfish, rice, and yam festival, but the best-known celebration is in New Orleans: Mardi Gras, Shrove Tuesday, the day preceding Ash Wednesday, the first day of Lent. There are parades, masquerading, and general revelry; the festival reaches its climax at a grand ball before midnight. After this day and night of rich eating and grand merriment, the 40 days of fasting and penitence of Lent begin.

Like the French, Franco-Americans serve meat pies on religious holidays. The special pie for Easter has sliced hard-boiled eggs laid down on the bottom crust, then a layer of cooked meat topped with well-seasoned pork and beef meatballs. For Christmas, *tourtière,* a pie made with simmered seasoned pork, is eaten cold after midnight Mass.

NUTRITIONAL STATUS

The influence of the British and French on American cuisine is undoubtedly one reason the U.S. diet is high in cholesterol and fat and low in fiber and complex carbohydrates. Although few studies have been conducted on the nutritional status of Americans of French, Irish, and British descent, it is assumed they have the same advantages and disadvantages of the general American population.

Nutritional Intake

Irish. One study examined Irish brothers: one group in Ireland, and one group living in the United States (Boston) to determine differences in mortality from coronary heart disease, a third control group of first-generation Irish Americans in the Boston area was also examined (Kushi *et al.,* 1985). Although there was no significantly different relative risk for death from heart disease among the three groups, it was found that their diets varied significantly. The Boston brothers and the first-generation Irish Americans had a higher intake (as a percentage of caloric intake) of animal protein, total fat (more vegetable and less animal), sugar, fiber, and cholesterol, and a lower intake of starch. The Irish brothers had a higher caloric intake than the Boston brothers and the first-generation Irish Americans, yet their relative weight was significantly lower.

Celiac sprue, an intolerance to gluten that results in mal-absorption, appears to be prevalent among the Irish. It has been reported (Stadler 1980) that there is a greater incidence of the disease in Western Ireland (1/303) and Scotland (1/778) than in England (1/6,300) or the United States (1/2,000). It is not known if this tendency is shared by Irish Americans.

It is commonly assumed that there is a high rate of alcoholism among Irish Americans. It has been reported (Greeley, 1972) that they drink more frequently than any other ethnic group, but they are no more likely to be "problem drinkers" than Slavs or Native Americans.

Counseling

Most Americans of British, Irish, or French descent are completely acculturated. Socioeconomic status and religious practice are likely to have greater impact on foods and food habits than country of origin. The in-depth personal interview should reveal any notable ethnically based preferences.

SOUTHERN EUROPEANS

Southern European countries lie along the Mediterranean Sea and include Italy, southern France, Spain, and Portugal. Italy shaped like a boot, sticks out into the Mediterranean and includes the island of Sicily which lies off the boot toe. Italy, is separated from the rest of Europe by the Alps which form its northern border. Spain, located to the west of France (the Pyrenees Mountains forms a natural border between the two countries), occupies the majority of the Iberian peninsula. Portugal sits on the western end of the peninsula, but also includes the Azores, islands located in the Atlantic Ocean. Most of southern Europe enjoys a warm Mediterranean climate except in the cooler mountainous regions.

Immigration to the United States from southern Europe has been considerable, primarily from the poorer regions of southern Italy. Many Americans enjoy Italian cuisine in some form, even those of non-European descent. The foods of Spain and Portugal are similar to those of Italy and France,

Traditional foods of southern Europe: Some foods typical of the traditional southern European diet include almonds, artichokes, basil, cheese, eggplant, garlic, garbanzo beans, olive oil, olives, onions, pasta, prosciutto, *salt cod, sweet bread, and tomatoes.* (Photo by Laurie Macfee.)

because of both the influence of the Greek and Romans in the region and the shared climate, but their preparations differ.

Cultural Perspective

HISTORY OF SOUTHERN EUROPE

At the peak of its empire, Rome occupied and ruled most of Europe, including southern France (Gaul) and the Iberian peninsula. Before the Romans, however, Phoenecians and Greeks had settled all along the Mediterranean coast.

Muslims from north Africa invaded Spain, Portugal, and southern Italy in the eighth century. They introduced Iberia to their Eastern civilization, including their architectural style, art, and technological achievements. Palermo, the capital of Sicily, became a center of learning.

Rome gave the Carthaginian name of Hispania to what is known as Spain today, because of its abundance of rabbits, *sphan.*

Spain and Portugal

The Spanish world "ole,"
used to express excitement
and approval, is thought to
be from the Arabic word for
God, Allah.

The Christians eventually drove the Muslims out of Spain, and the country was unified under the rule of Ferdinand and Isabella in 1492, the same year Columbus discovered the New World. Portugal, also a Christian country, had successfully ousted the Muslims many years before the Spanish did. Both Portugal and Spain became sea powers, and the effects of their colonization of new lands is still evident today, especially in Latin America. In 1497, Portuguese explorer Vasco da Gama successfully navigated an ocean route to the East via the Cape of Good Hope.

Spain became a major European power in the sixteenth century but declined in strength after its navy, the Armada, was defeated by the English in 1588. It eventually lost its colonies in the Americas and its influence in other European countries, notably Italy and the Low Countries. In the twentieth century, Spain's government alternated between dictatorship and democracy. Today it has a parliamentary democracy and a monarch, King Juan Carlos, and is one of poorer nations in Europe.

Portugal's power also steadily declined and by 1820 it had lost most of its major colonies. Portugal was ruled by a dictator from 1928 to 1968. In 1974, revolution resulted in the establishment of a democratic government.

Italy

In Piedmont, the northern
Italian state that borders
France, the dish chicken
Marengo was invented for
Napoleon after he defeated
the Austrians. Legend has it
that because his supply
wagons were far away, the
cooks invented a dish from
locally available ingredients:
chicken, eggs, crayfish,
tomatoes, and garlic.
Napoleon was supposed to
have liked the dish so much
that he insisted it be served
after every battle.

Italy was politically divided from the time of the fall of the Roman empire until 1870. Parts of northern Italy had been ruled by a variety of European countries, including France and Austria, or existed as independent city-states. Southern Italy was ruled at various times by the Muslims, the Normans, and the Spanish. The Catholic church also exerted control over parts of Italy, especially near Rome. Vatican City is still a separate sovereignty.

Today, Italy is a prosperous country that is rapidly becoming industrialized. Its present form of government, consitutional democracy, was established after the defeat of Italy under the fascist dictator Benito Mussolini in World War II.

HISTORY OF IMMIGRATION TO THE UNITED STATES

Immigration Patterns

The majority of immigrants from southern Europe were Italians, who swelled the population of U.S. cities on the eastern seaboard during the late nineteenth and early twentieth centuries. Next in number were the Portuguese, primarily from the Azore Islands. Smaller numbers of Spanish immigrants have been documented.

Italians. According to immigration records, more than 5 million Italians have settled in the United States. The majority came from the poorer southern Italian provinces and Sicily between 1880 and 1920. Although earlier immigrants from northern Italy settled on the west coast of the United States during the gold rush, most of the later immigrants settled in the large industrial cities on the east coast. Several cities still boast Italian neighborhoods such as the North End in Boston and North Beach in San Francisco.

Many Italians came to America for economic reasons; over half of the immigrants, mostly men, returned to their homeland after accumulating money. Peasants in their native land, Italians in the United States often became laborers in skilled or semiskilled professions, especially the building trades and the clothing industry. Immigration from Italy fell sharply after World War I, yet more than one-half million Italians have immigrated since World War II.

Portuguese. Two waves of Portuguese immigrants have arrived in the United States since the early nineteenth century. Early immigrants were primarily from the Azore Islands, and they often located in the whaling ports of New England and Hawaii. The gold rush attracted a great number of Portuguese to the San Francisco bay area. Many of these immigrants came for economic opportunity.

After World War II, a small number of Portuguese from Macao, a Portuguese settlement on the coast of China near Hong Kong, settled in California. They are well-educated and many hold professional jobs. A much more significant number of Portuguese, over 150,000, entered the United States after 1958, again mostly from the Azore Islands following a series of volcanic eruptions that devastated the region. It has been estimated that the Portuguese currently have one of the highest rates of new arrivals among European groups. Since 1970, over 100,000 Portuguese have entered the country.

Spaniards. More than a quarter of a million people from Spain have immigrated to the United States since 1820. However, the majority of the Spanish-speaking population in the United States comes from American acquisition of Spanish territories and the immigration of people from Latin American countries (see Chapter 6 for more detail).

Half the Spanish immigrants to the United States came in the late nineteenth and early twentieth centuries, probably because of depressed economic conditions in Spain. In 1939, after the fall of the second Spanish republic, a small number of refugees immigrated for political reasons. Many of the Spanish immigrants were from the Basque region, located in northeastern Spain on the border with France (there are also French Basques). They came to the United States in the nineteenth century. The Basques are thought to be one of the oldest surviving ethnic groups in Europe; they lived in their homeland before the invasion of the Indo-Europeans around 2000 B.C. Their language, Euskera, is not known to be related to any other language.

Among the Basque it is said that the devil came to the Basque countryside to learn their language, Euskera, so he could ensnare the inhabitants, but after seven years he gave up after learning only two words, *bai* and *ez* ("yes" and "no").

Current Demographics and Socioeconomic Status

Today there are an estimated 21 million Americans of Italian descent, most of whom live in or around major cities. Economically, Italian Americans shared in the general prosperity after World War II, and today most are employed in white-collar jobs or as skilled laborers.

The 1980 census estimated the Portuguese American population to be just over one million. Initially, the Portuguese Americans on the West Coast were farmers and ranchers, but eventually their descendants moved into professional and skilled-labor occupations. On the East Coast, the descendants of the Portuguese who settled in the whaling ports now make up a significant part of the fishing industry.

Unlike the Spaniards, who settled in industrial cities such as New York, and later Tampa, Florida, the Basques settled on the West Coast and became sheepherders. There are between 50,000 and 100,000 Basque Americans living in the West, primarily in small towns and isolated ranches. Today, most Basque descendants are involved in some aspect of animal husbandry or small businesses in rural communities; few have entered the professions. Newer Basque communities now exist in Connecticut and Florida because *jai alai* (a Basque sport) facilities were established there.

Cultural Organizations

One institution that aided the adjustment of early Italian immigrants was the mutual benefit society, which provided a form of health and life insurance during times of crisis. Many of these societies have since merged or disbanded; the largest one existing today is known as the Order of the Sons of Italy in America.

Portuguese cultural organizations, such as social clubs, folklore groups, mutual aid societies, credit unions, Portuguese language newspapers, and radio programs, are closely associated with the Catholic church. Most important are the fraternal benefit societies, the largest ones being the Portuguese Union of the State of California (UPEC) and the Portuguese Continental Union of the United States of America, located in San Leandro, California, and Boston, respectively.

The Basque Americans were slow to form ethnic associations. In 1972, most of the Basque social clubs in the West joined together to form the North American Basque Organization, Inc., in order to foster regional interaction. A resurgence in Basque pride is evident in the National Basque Festival, celebrated annually on the Fourth of July in Nevada since 1964. However, one older and unique Basque institution is the Basque hotel. Throughout the West, these hotels served as mailing addresses for Basque herdsmen and boardinghouses for their wives and children and provided an ethnic haven. To outsiders they were known for their hearty cuisine and friendly family atmosphere.

WORLDVIEW

Almost all the immigrants from Italy, Spain, and Portugal were Roman Catholic, as are their descendants. Traditionally these groups maintain close-knit family groups.

Family

Italians. The social structure of rural villages in southern Italy was based on the family, whose interests and needs molded each individual's attitude toward the state, church, and school. The family was self-reliant and distrusted outsiders. Each member was expected to uphold the family honor and fulfill familial responsibilities. The father was head of the household; he maintained his authority with strict discipline. The mother, although subordinate, controlled the day-to-day activities in the home and was often responsible for the family budget.

Once in America, the children broke free of parental control due to economic necessity: although sons had always been allowed some independence, daughters soon gained their freedom as well, since like their brothers they were expected to work outside the home. Education eventually also changed the family. Early immigrants repeatedly denied their children schooling, sending them to work instead. However, by 1920 education was considered an important stepping-stone for Italian Americans.

Portuguese. Like the Italians, the Portuguese have close family solidarity and have had some success in maintaining the traditional family structure. Sons and daughters often live close to their parents after leaving home, and family members try to care for the sick at home. Men strongly dominate the family, and as a result, some Portuguese women marry outside the group.

Religion

Italians. In Italy, the Roman Catholic church was a part of everyday life. Immigrants to America, however, found the church to be more remote and puritanical, as well as staffed by the Irish. The church responded by establishing national parishes (parishes geared toward one ethnic group by having a priest of that group) which helped immigrants adjust to America. Religious festivals, part of daily religious life in Italy, were transferred to America and some are still celebrated today, such as the Feast of San Gennaro in New York's Little Italy.

Portuguese. The Roman Catholic church also helped ease the Portuguese into the mainstream of American life. Local churches and special parishes often sponsor traditional religious *festas* that include Portuguese foods, dances, and colorful costumes.

Traditional Food Habits

Although the foods of the southern European countries are similar, as detailed in the Cultural Food Groups list (Table 4.2), there are notable differences in preparation and presentation. Many Americans think of Italian cooking as consisting of pizza and spaghetti. In reality, these dishes are only a small part of the regional cuisine of southern Italy, the ancestral homeland of most Italian Americans.

Spanish food is mistakenly equated with the hot and spicy cuisine of Mexico. Although Mexico was a colony of Spain, foods and food habits of the two countries differ substantially. Portugal and Spain have very similar cuisines, but most of the Portuguese immigrants to the United States are from the Azore Islands and the island of Madeira. Their diet was less varied than that of the mainland Portuguese.

INGREDIENTS AND COMMON FOODS

Foreign Influence

Italy. Phoenecians and Greeks, who settled along the Mediterranean coast in ancient times, are thought to have brought the olive tree to Italy and the other Mediterranean countries. In addition, fish stew, known as *bouillabaise* in France and *zuppa di pesce alla marinara* in Italy, may be of Greek origin. The Muslims brought lemons, oranges, sugar cane, rice, and a variety of sweetmeats and spices. *Marzipan,* a sweetened almond paste used extensively in Italian desserts, and rice flavored with saffron, as in the northern Italian dish *risotto alla Milanese,* are both believed to have Muslim origins.

Spain. The Phoenecians, Greeks, and Muslims have influenced Spanish cooking. The Phoenecians are thought to have brought the garbanzo bean to Spain and the Muslim influence is seen in saffron-colored rice and the use of ground nuts to thicken sauces, or in candies and desserts. It was the food of the New World and Asian colonies, however, that shaped Spanish cuisine. Chocolate, vanilla, tomatoes, pimentos, pineapple, white and sweet potatoes, maize (corn), many varieties of squash, and turkey were brought back from the Americas. From India and the Far East came coconuts, bananas, mangoes, sweet oranges, and precious spices, such as pepper, nutmeg, cinnamon, and cloves. The tomato is especially important in southern European cooking.

Staples

Italy. Although the cooking style and ingredients vary from region to region in Italy, some general statements can be made about the differences between the foods of northern

Spaghetti come from the Italian word for string, *spago.*

Rice, brought to Italy by the Muslims, is grown in the fertile Po valley. The Italians eat more rice than any other European people. Thomas Jefferson supposedly smuggled rice out of Italy to the United States, where it was first cultivated in the Carolinas.

TABLE 4.2. Cultural Food Groups: Southern European

Group	Comments
PROTEIN FOODS	
Milk/milk products	Most adults do not drink milk but do eat cheese. Dairy products are often used in desserts. Many adults suffer from lactose intolerance.
Meat/poultry/fish/eggs/ legumes	Small fish, such as sardines, eaten whole, provide substantial dietary calcium.
CEREALS/GRAINS	Bread, pasta or grain products usually accompany the meal.
FRUITS/VEGETABLES	Fruit is often eaten as dessert. Fresh fruits and vegetables are preferred.

Common Foods	Adaptations in the United States
Cheese (cow, sheep, buffalo, goat), milk.	It is assumed that second-and third-generation southern Europeans drink more milk into their adulthood than their ancestors did.
Meat: beef, goat, lamb, pork, veal (and most varietal cuts).	More meat and less fish is eaten than in Europe.
Poultry: chicken, duck, goose, pigeon, turkey, woodcock.	
Fish: anchovies, bream, haddock, halibut, herring, mullet, salmon, trout, tuna, turbot, whiting, dried cod, octopus, squid.	
Shellfish: barnacles, clams, conch, crab, lobster, mussels, scallops, shrimp.	
Eggs: chicken.	
Legumes: broad beans, chick peas, fava and kidney beans, lentils, white beans.	
Cornmeal, rice, wheat (bread, farina, a variety of pastas).	
Fruits: apples, apricots, bananas, cherries, citron, dates, figs, grapefruit, grapes, lemons, medlars, peaches, pears, pineapples, plums (prunes), pomegranates, quinces, oranges, raisins, Seville oranges, tangerines.	First- and second-generation southern Europeans generally eat only fresh fruit and vegetables. Fruit and vegetable consumption tends to reflect general American food habits by the third generation.
Vegetables: arugala, artichokes, asparagus, broccoli, cabbage, cardoon, cauliflower, celery, chicory, cucumber, eggplant, endive, escarole, fava beans, fennel, green beans, lettuce, lima beans, kale, kohlrabi, mushrooms, mustard greens, olives, parsnips, peas, peppers (green and red), pimentoes, potatoes, *radicchio,* swiss chard, tomatoes, turnips, zucchini.	

TABLE 4.2. Cultural Food Groups: Southern European (*continued*)

Group	Comments
ADDITIONAL FOODS	
Seasonings	
Nuts/seeds	
Beverages	
Fats/oils	
Sweeteners	

and southern Italy. Pasta is a common dish throughout Italy, but in the North it is usually made with eggs in the shape of flat ribbons. In the agriculturally poorer South, the pasta is made without eggs, generally in a tubular form, such as macaroni. In the North, pasta (such as *ravioli*) is commonly stuffed with cheese or bits of meat, then topped with a cream sauce, while in the South it is usually served unfilled, with a tomato sauce. Other differences are that northern cuisine uses more butter, dairy products, rice and meat than the South, which is characterized by use of olive oil, little meat, and more beans and vegetables, such as artichokes, eggplants, peppers and tomatoes. Seasonings common to all of Italy are garlic, parsley, and basil.

Spain. The rugged terrain in Spain is suitable for raising small animals and crops, such as grapes and olives. In fact, Spain is the largest producer of olives in the world.

Entrees usually feature eggs, lamb, pork, poultry, or dried, salted fish, called *bacalao*. Sausages, such as the paprika and garlic flavored *chorizo* are common, and seafood is popular in coastal regions. Meats are often combined with vegetables in savory stews. Each region has its own recipe for *paella*, which typically includes saffron-spiced rice topped with

A *tortilla* in Spain is an egg omelet, not the cornmeal flatbread eaten by Mexicans. It is thought that the Spaniards called the Mexican bread by the same name because of its similar shape.

Common Foods	Adaptations in the United States
Basil, bay leaf, black pepper, capers, cayenne pepper, chocolate, chervil, cinnamon, cloves, coriander, cumin, dill, fennel, garlic, leeks, lemon juice, marjoram, mint, mustard, nutmeg, onion, oregano, parsley (Italian and curley leaf), rosemary, saffron, sage, tarragon, thyme, vinegar.	
Almonds, hazelnuts, *pignolis* (pine nuts), walnuts, lupine seeds.	
Coffee, chocolate, liqueurs, port, Madeira, sherry, flavored sodas (e.g. *orzata*), tea and wine.	
Butter, lard, olive oil, vegetable oil.	Decreased use of olive oil.
Honey, sugar.	

chicken, mussels, shrimp, sausage, tomatoes, and peas. *Cocido,* a stew of garbanzo beans, vegetables (such as cabbage, carrots, and potatoes), and meats (often beef, chicken, pork, meatballs and sausages) also varies from area to area, but is always served in three courses. The strained broth with added noodles is eaten first, followed by a plate of the boiled vegetables, and concluded with a plate of cooked meats. Crusty bread is served with the meal.

Garlic and tomatoes flavor many Spanish dishes, for example, *gazpacho,* a refreshing pureed vegetable soup which is usually served cold, and *zarzuela* (meaning "operetta"), a fresh seafood stew. Olive oil is also a common ingredient used in almost all cooking, even deep-frying pastries, such as the cylindrical doughnuts called *churros.* Sauces accompany many dishes. *Ali-oli* is made from garlic pulverized with olive oil, salt, and a little lemon juice. It is served with grilled or boiled meats and fish. Another popular sauce, called *romescu,* is sometimes mixed with ali-oli to taste by each diner at the table. It combines pureed almonds, garlic, paprika, and tomatoes with vinegar and olive oil. Spain's best-known dessert is *flan,* a custard.

Wine usually accompanies the meal, and Spain is probably most famous in the English-speaking world for its sherries.

The name *gazpacho* may have come from the Roman vinegar-and-water drink call *posca,* which was reportedly offered to Christ on the Cross.

Portugal. In addition to the ingredients listed for Spanish cooking, the Portuguese in the Azores and Madeira use cornmeal. It is often mixed with water and baked on flat hearth stones. *Açorda d'azedo,* a dish eaten for breakfast, combines onions, garlic, vinegar, lard, saffron, and the cornbread, all boiled in enough water to moisten the bread. Broad beans and *tremocos,* lupine seeds, are popular. Fish dominates the diet of the Portuguese and they are said to prepare *bacalhau* (dried salt cod) in 125 different ways. Sardines are often grilled or cooked in a tomato and vegetable sauce. *Chouriço,* similar to the Spanish pork sausage, *chorizo,* and *linguiça,* another pork sausage, are often eaten at breakfast. Other typical dishes are *cacoila,* a stew made from pig hearts and liver and served with beans or potatoes; *isca de figado,* beef liver seasoned with vinegar, pepper, and garlic, then fried in olive oil or lard; and *assada no espeto,* meat roasted on a spit. A common soup is *caldo verde,* or green broth, made from kale or cabbage and potatoes. Portuguese sweet breads, *pan doce,* and doughnuts, *malassadas,* are also quite popular.

Regional Variations

Italy. Some of the regional specialties in the northern area around Milan are *risotto,* a creamy rice dish cooked in butter and chicken stock, flavored with *Parmesan* cheese and saffron; *polenta,* cornmeal mush (thought to have been made originally from semolina wheat) often served with cheese or sauce; and *panettone,* a type of fruitcake popular at Christmastime. The cheeses of the region include *gorgonzola,* a tangy, blue-veined cheese made from sheep's milk, and *bel paese,* a soft, mild flavored cheese.

Venice, located on the east coast and known for its romantic canals (although the city actually consists of 120 mud islands), has a cuisine centered around seafood. Its best-known dish is *scampi,* made from large shrimp seasoned with oil, garlic, parsley, and lemon juice. Turin, the capital of the western province of Piedmont is known for its *grissini,* the slender breadsticks popular throughout Italy. Located on the northwest coast of Italy, Genoa is known for its *burrida,* a fish stew containing octopus and squid, and *pesto,* a basil, cheese, and nut paste usually served with pasta, which has recently become popular in the United States.

Moving southward, the city of Bologna is the center of a rich gastronomic region. Pasta specialties of the area include *lasagne verdi al forno,* spinach-flavored lasagne noodles

Bologna is nicknamed "la grossa," (the fat) and is proud of it.

baked in a *ragú* (meat sauce) and white sauce and flavored with Parmesan cheese; and *tortellini*, egg pasta stuffed with bits of meat, cheese, and eggs, served in soup or a rich cream sauce. It is traditionally served on Christmas Eve. A similiar stuffed pasta is *cappelleti*, named for its shape, a "little hat." Other specialties are *mortadella*, a pork sausage; *prosciutto*, a raw, smoked ham served thinly sliced, often as an appetizer with melon or fresh figs; and *Parmesan* cheese, a sharply flavored cow's milk cheese with a finely grained texture.

Florence, the capital of Tuscany, has a long history of culinary expertise. In 1533, Catherine de' Medici (the Medici family ruled Florence) married into the royal family of France. She is often credited with introducing Italian cuisines, at the time the most sophisticated in Europe, to France. Florence is reknown for its green spinach noodles that are served with butter and grated Parmesan cheese. The term *alla Fiorentina* refers to a dish garnished with or containing finely chopped spinach. Tuscany is also famous for its full-bodied red wine, *Chianti*, and its use of chestnuts, which are featured in a cake eaten at Lent called *castagnaccio alla Fiorentina*.

Rome, the capital of Italy, has its own regional cooking and is probably best known for *fettucine Alfredo*, long egg noodles mixed with butter, cream, and grated cheese. Another dish is *saltimbocca*, meaning "jumps in the mouth": thin slices of veal rolled with ham and cooked in butter and Marsala wine. *Gnocchi*, which are dumplings, are eaten throughout Italy, but in Rome they are made out of semolina and baked in the oven. Fried artichokes are popular at Easter time, as is roast baby lamb or kid. *Pecorino romano* is the hard sheep's milk cheese of Rome, similar to Parmesan but with a sharper flavor.

The capital of Campania in southern Italy is Naples, considered the culinary capital of the south. Pasta is the staple food and a favorite way of serving it is simply with oil and garlic, or mixed with beans, as *pasta e fagiole*. Pizza is native to Naples and is said to date back to the sixteenth century. Another form of pizza is *calzone*, which is pizza dough folded over a filling of cheese, ham, or salami, then baked or fried. The area's best-known cheeses are *mozzarella*, an elastic, white cheese originally made from buffalo milk; *provolone*, a firm smoked cheese; and *ricotta*, a soft, white, unsalted cheese made from sheep's milk and often used in desserts.

Sicily and other regions of southern Italy use kid and lamb as their principal meat. Along the coast, fresh fish, such as tuna and sardines, is used extensively; *baccala*, dried salt cod,

Catherine de' Medici's son, Henry III, is said to have introduced the fork to the French court, after he observed it being used in Venice. Although originally from Constantinople, the three-pronged fork was developed in Italy for eating pasta.

The art of making ice cream is thought to have been invented by the Chinese, who brought it to India, where it spread to the Persians and Arabs. The Muslims brought it to Sicily, and it was a Sicilian, Francisco Procopio, who introduced ice cream to Paris in the 1660s. England discovered it soon after, and the skill was brought with the English to America.

is often served on fast days. The North African influence shows up in Sicily in the use of *couscous*, called *cuscus* in Italy, which is commonly served with fish stews.

Southern Italy's cuisine is probably best known for its desserts. Many examples can be found in Italian American bakeries and espresso bars: *cannoli*, crisp deep-fried tubular pastry shells filled with sweetened ricotta cheese, shaved bitter chocolate and citron; *cassata*, a cake composed of spongecake layers with a ricotta filling and a chocolate or almond-flavored sugar frosting; as well as *gelato*, ice cream, and *granita*, flavored ices. *Spumone* is chocolate and vanilla ice cream with a layer of rum-flavored whipped cream containing nuts and fruits. Another popular sweet is *zeppole*, a deep fried doughnut covered with powdered sugar.

Spain. Most Spanish dishes prepared in the United States reflect the cooking of Spain's southern region, with its seafood, abundant fruits and vegetables, and Muslim influence. Central Spain has a more limited diet; roast suckling pig and baby roast lamb are specialties. In the Basque provinces, lamb is the primary meat and charcoaled-grilled lamb is a specialty. Other favored Basque dishes are *bacaloa a la vizcaina*, dried salt cod cooked in a sauce of onions, garlic, pimento, and tomatoes; and *angulas*, tiny eel spawn cooked with olive oil, garlic, and red peppers.

MEAL COMPOSITION AND CYCLE

Daily Patterns

Espresso, which means "made expressly for you," is made from finely ground Italian roast coffee through which water is forced by steam pressure. *Cappuccino* is espresso topped with frothy, steamed milk.

Italy. A traditional Italian breakfast tends to be light, including coffee with milk *(caffe latte)*, tea, or a chocolate drink, accompanied by bread and jam. Lunch is the main meal of the day and may be followed by a nap. It usually starts with *antipasto*, an appetizer course, such as ham, sausages, pickled vegetables, and olives. Next is *minestra* (wet course), usually soup or an *asciutta* (dry course) of pasta, risotto, or gnocchi. The main course is fish, meat, or poultry served with a starchy or green vegetable, followed by a salad. Dessert often consists of fruit and cheese; pastries and ice creams are served on special occasions. Dinner is served at about 7:30 P.M. and is a lighter version of lunch. Wine usually accompanies lunch and dinner. Coffee or espresso is enjoyed after dinner, either at home or in a coffee house. *Marsala*, a sweet dessert wine, may be drunk after dinner, and is often used in the preparation of desserts. One such sweet, now prepared all over Europe, is *zabaglione*, a wine custard.

Spain. By American standards, the Spanish appear to eat all the time. The traditional pattern, four meals a day plus snacks, is spread across the day as follow: a light breakfast at about 8:00 A.M., followed by a midmorning breakfast around 11:00 A.M. and a light snack, *tapas,* at 1:00 P.M.; a three-course lunch at around 2:00 P.M., followed by tea and pastries *(merienda)* between 5:00 and 6:00 P.M. and more tapas at 8:00 P.M.; and finally dinner, three courses, at 10:00 or 11:00 P.M.

Breakfast usually consists of hot coffee or chocolate, toast, or churros, doughnuts fried in hot olive oil. The second breakfast is again coffee and sweet pastries. Tapas, loosely translated as appetizers, are served in bars and cafes and are usually accompanied by a beverage (sherry or wine in the evening). The variety of tapas is tremendous and it is not unusual for more than 20 kinds to be offered on a menu. The evening meal may be skipped if a substantial number of tapas are eaten at night.

The main meal of the day is lunch *(la comida),* which is generally eaten at home and consists of three hefty courses. Dessert is usually cheese and fresh fruit in season. A siesta often follows: many businesses are closed from 1:00–4:00 P.M. Although dinner also includes three courses, they are often lighter dishes consisting of eggs and fish.

Portugal. Portuguese meal patterns are similar to those of Spain, although the evening meal is usually eaten earlier. As in Spain, red wine usually accompanies the meal. Portugal is famous for its sweet, rich wines, port, and Madeira; the latter is often drunk with dessert.

Special Occasions

Italy. Italy celebrates few national holidays, probably because of its divided history. Most *festas* are local and honor a patron saint. Other significant religious holidays are usually observed by families at home, although some cities, such as Venice, have a public pre-Lenten carnival.

Among Italian Americans, it is traditional to serve seven seafood dishes on Christmas Eve. During the Easter holidays, Italian American bakeries sell an Easter bread that has braided into it hard-boiled eggs still in their shells. Special desserts may accompany the holiday meal, such as *pannetone* (fruit cake), *amaretti* (almond macaroons), and *torrone* (nougats) at Christmastime and *cassata* at Easter. Colored,

The word *tapas* means lid, and the first tapas were pieces of bread used to cover wineglasses to keep out the flies. Tapas are differentiated from appetizers in Spain in that they are strictly finger-foods, such as olives, almonds, stuffed mushrooms, mussels, sausage pieces, etc.

Panettone: *The fruit-studded cake called* panettone *is served for holidays and special occasions throughout Italy.* (Courtesy Grossich and Bond, Inc.)

sugar-coated Jordan almonds, which the Italians call *confetti,* meaning "little candies," are served at weddings.

Spain. The most elaborate of Spanish festivals is Holy Week, the week between Palm Sunday and Easter. It is a time of Catholic processions, confections, coffee, chocolate, anisette (licorice flavored), and other liqueurs. Some holiday sweets include *tortas de aceite,* cakes made with olive oil,

Although the Spanish are very fond of chocolate, it is primarily used as a beverage and is not incorporated into confections or desserts.

sesame seeds, and anise; *cortados rellenos de cidra,* small rectangular tarts filled with pureed sweetened squash; *torteras,* large round cakes made with cinnamon and squash and decorated with powdered sugar; and *yemas de San Leandro,* a sweet made by pouring egg yolks through tiny holes into boiling syrup, then cooling it. It is often served with marzipan.

Special dishes are also prepared for Christmas and Easter. The Basques eat a special orange-flavored doughnut on Easter called *causerras,* and roasted chestnuts and *pastel de Navidad,* individual walnut and raisin pies, at Christmas. At New Year's, it is customary for the Spanish and the Portuguese to eat twelve grapes or raisins at the twelve strokes of midnight. It is believed to bring luck for each month of the coming year.

Portugal. In America the Holy Ghost (Spirit) festival is the most popular and colorful social-religious event in the Portuguese community. Although the origins of the event are obscure, it is thought to date back to Isabel (Elizabeth) of Aragon, wife of Portugal's poet king, Dom Diniz (1326). One story is that the festival derives its character from the belief that Isabel was particularly devoted to the Holy Ghost and

The Portuguese Holy Ghost festival: A community banquet featuring Holy Ghost soup and Portugese sweet bread culminates this annual celebration.

that she wanted to give an example of charity in the annual distribution of food to the poor. In the United States, the festival is usually scheduled for a week after Easter and before the end of July and is held at the local church or Hall of the Holy Ghost (IDES Hall). The main event of the festival takes place on the last day, Sunday, with a procession to the church and the crowning of a queen after the service. The donated food, which was originally distributed to needy persons on Sunday afternoon but is now often served at a free community banquet, is blessed by the priest. The most traditional foods at the feast are a Holy Ghost soup of meat, bread, and potatoes and a sweet bread called *massa sovada*.

Also celebrated in the United States is the Feast of the Most Blessed Sacrament, started in New Bedford, Massachusetts, by four Madeirans in gratitude for their salvation from a shipwreck en route to the United States in 1915. Other festivities are associated with the Madeiran cult of Our Lady of the Mount (a shrine on the island of Madeira).

Contemporary Food Habits in the United States

ADAPTATION OF FOOD HABITS

Some diet books now advocate a traditional Mediterranean-style diet to promote weight loss and lessen the risk of heart disease. They recommend a diet high in complex carbohydrates (especially pasta), fresh fruits, and vegetables and low in meats and fats.

It is generally assumed that second-and third-generation Americans of southern European descent have adopted the majority American diet and meal patterns, preserving some traditional dishes for special occasions. These assimilated Americans eat more milk and meat but less fish, fresh produce, and legumes than their ancestors. Olive oil is still used extensively; pasta often remains popular.

NUTRITIONAL STATUS

Nutritional Intake

Little research has been conducted recently on the nutritional intake and status of Americans from southern Europe. It can probably be assumed that they suffer from dietary deficiencies and excesses similar to those of the majority of Americans. However, descendants of southern Europeans may have a higher incidence of lactose intolerance than other European groups.

In a recent study of elderly Portuguese immigrants in Cambridge, Massachusetts, it was found that dinner was the main meal of the day and that the subjects had moderate intake of breads and grains and low intake of fruits, vegetables, and dairy products. Although dairy intake was low, many of the subjects ate sardines, a rich source of calcium. The subjects reported low consumption of sweets and alcohol, although the researcher stated that the Americanized Portuguese diet tends to be high in sugar and fat (Poe, 1986).

Counseling

When interviewing persons of southern European ancestry, the nutritionist should determine the client's degree of acculturation and food preferences. A high rate of illiteracy has been reported in the Portuguese population (40 percent of surveyed elderly persons; 15 percent of recent immigrants). This should be taken into consideration when preparing educational materials.

CENTRAL EUROPEANS AND THE PEOPLE OF THE SOVIET UNION

Central Europe, the countries of East and West Germany, Austria, Hungary, Czechoslovakia, and Poland, stretches from the North and Baltic Seas, south to the Alps, and east to the Soviet Union. Most of the countries share common borders; Austria, Hungary, and Czechoslovakia are situated south of Germany and Poland. The climate of central Europe is harsher and colder than that of southern Europe, but much of the land is agriculturally rich. The Soviet Union extends east to the border with China and the Pacific Ocean. Its vast geography includes the Arctic and parts of the Middle East. Except in its southern republics, the harsh winters of the Soviet Union affect agricultural capacity.

The large number of immigrants from central Europe made significant contributions to the literature, music, and cuisine of the United States. Many central European foods have become standard fare. What would a baseball game be without hot dogs and beer, or a picnic without cole slaw? Croissants originally from Budapest are now a common item at fast-food restaurants. This section will explore the traditional foods and food habits of central Europe and the Soviet Union and their impact on the American diet.

Croissants, according to popular legend, were first produced by the bakers of Budapest who expressed their joy over their city's victory over the Turks in 1683 with a roll in the shape of the Islamic crescent. However, cresent-shaped rolls symbolizing the moon, were made in Europe as early as the eighth century.

Traditional foods of central Europe and the Soviet Union: Some foods typical of the traditional diet of central Europe and the Soviet Union include beets, cabbage, ham, herring, kasha *(buckwheat), potatoes, rye bread, sausages, and sour cream.* (Photo by Laurie Macfee.)

Cultural Perspective

HISTORY OF CENTRAL EUROPE AND THE SOVIET UNION

Germany and the Austrian Empire

Although Germany's influence in the twentieth century and its role in two world wars suggests that it has been a major force in Europe for centuries, it was not until the nineteenth century that Germany became a unified country.

Until the dissolution of the Holy Roman Empire in 1806, Germany was a patchwork of numerous small principalities and free cities stretching from the Netherlands and France to Poland and Czechoslovakia, many of which were prosperous and exerted economic influence throughout Europe. The most powerful state to emerge in the seventeenth and eighteenth centuries was Prussia (eastern Germany) and in 1866 it triumphed militarily over its rival, Austria, resulting in the establishment of a united German nation.

The current boundaries of Austria date only from 1918, and during the past ten centuries the term "Austria" has designated a variety of geographic and political configurations. Although it is a landlocked country of mostly mountainous terrain, Austria is located at the crossroads of Europe and has often been a center of power. The Hapsburgs came to power in the thirteenth century, and from the fifteenth century until the nineteenth, the Holy Roman Emperors were chosen from this dynasty. The land controlled by the Hapsburgs was considerable, including parts of modern-day Germany, Poland, Italy, Yugoslavia, and the Soviet Union, as well as most of Hungary, Czechoslovakia, and Rumania. The Austro-Prussian War of 1866 resulted in the Hungarians gaining control of their internal affairs, but they remained united with Austria in the Austrio-Hungarian Empire.

In the early twentieth century, nationalistic movements grew within the empire and led to the onset of World War I, eventually causing the empire to crumble. In 1918, Poland, Czechoslovakia, and Hungary proclaimed their independence.

Germany, after World War I, became a democratic republic. However, the economic crisis of the postwar years, high unemployment, and inflation resulted in the rise of the National Socialist (Nazi) party. Adolph Hitler became chancellor of Germany in 1933. This turn of events led to World War II. In the early years of the war Germany had great success; it conquered Czechoslovakia, Poland, Denmark, Norway, Belgium, the Netherlands, Luxembourg, France, the Balkan states, and Greece. Hitler attempted to eliminate all those he considered undesirable, such as Jews, dissidents, gypsies, and homosexuals. It has been estimated that over 10 million persons died in concentration camps and by other means. Over 6 million of the dead were Jews.

In May 1945, one month after Hitler committed suicide, Germany agreed to an unconditional surrender to the Allies (the Soviet Union, Great Britain, Free France, and the United States). As a result of the war, the Allies, at the Yalta Conference, divided Germany into two countries, German Federal Republic (West) and German Democratic Republic (East).

Today West Germany and Austria have democratic governments but East Germany, Hungary, and Czechoslovakia are Communist countries under Soviet control. Hungary, in 1956, and Czechoslovakia, in 1968, attempted to revolt against their Communist regimes; both rebellions were put down by the Soviet Union.

It was the assassination of Archduke Francis Ferdinand, heir to the Austrian crown, in Sarajevo (Yugoslavia) in 1914, that precipitated the cataclysm of WWI between the countries of the Three Emperors' League (Austria, Hungary, and Germany) and the Triple Entente (France, England, and Russia).

Poland

Since the seventeenth century Poland's borders have varied considerably. Poland's golden age, in the sixteenth century, was a period when its empire reached from the Baltic to the Black seas and the arts and sciences flourished. By the end of the seventeenth century, Poland was increasingly influenced by its powerful neighbors, Russia, Prussia, and Austria. By 1795, Poland had almost disappeared from the European map because of Russia's expansion. Poland was declared an independent state in 1918 after World War I. In 1939, Germany invaded Poland; after World War II, Poland was declared an independent nation. Today it is a Communist country under Soviet control.

Union of Soviet Socialist Republics

Russia applies to the Russian Empire until 1917, also the Russian Soviet Federated Socialist Republic, largest and most important member of the U.S.S.R. The name is also loosely used to mean the whole of the U.S.S.R.

The early history of the Soviet Union is marked by repeated invasions, by the German Goths in the third century, the Asian Huns in the fourth century, and the Turkish Avars in the sixth century. By the ninth century Slavs had settled in parts of western Russia but were under Turkish control. The first Russian dynasty was founded by the Varangians, who were Scandinavian traders and warriors. They united the Slavs and freed them from the Turks. Vladimir I, a descendant of the Varangians and ruler of Russia, converted the Russians to the Eastern Orthodox Church in A.D. 998. It is said that he preferred the Islamic religion until he discovered that alcohol was forbidden to its followers.

The Mongols (commonly called the Tartars), under Butu Khan, invaded Russia in the thirteenth century, destroyed most of the cities, and established an empire that lasted until 1480. Ultimately the princes of Moscow ended the Tartar rule and later, Ivan the Terrible (1533–1584) was crowned the first *czar*, or emperor.

In 1613 the Romanov dynasty began its rule, which lasted until 1917. Russia in the seventeenth century was still feudal and was not considered a member of the European community. During the reign of Peter I, known as Peter the Great (1689–1725), Russia's government and culture were altered through a program of modernization and rapidly became a European power.

Napolean began his invasion of Russia in 1812 and took Moscow, but his army was nearly destroyed in the freezing winter. Despite other countries' attempts to obtain Russian lands, during the second half of the nineteenth century Russia was able to continue its territorial expansion and industrialization.

In the beginning of the twentieth century, the last czar, Nicholas II, ruled Russia. Lenin, a communist, took control of the government after the February Revolution of 1917. Civil war broke out shortly afterwards and the Soviet regime won in 1920. Poland, Finland, and the Baltic countries became independent states after the civil war and Russia proclaimed itself the Union of Soviet Socialist Republics in 1922. Today the Soviet Union remains a Communist country. In addition, it exerts control over the governments of the countries on its eastern border.

HISTORY OF IMMIGRATION TO THE UNITED STATES

Immigration Patterns

Germans. For almost three centuries Germans have been one of the most significant elements in the U.S. population. In the 1980 census it was estimated that 50 million people identified themselves as of German descent. Germans are also one of the least visible of any American ethnic group.

The earliest German settlement in the American colonies was Germantown, Pennsylvania, founded in 1681. By 1709, large-scale immigration began, primarily from the Palatinate region of southwestern Germany. Most of the immigrants settled in Pennsylvania. The majority were farmers who steadily pushed westward searching for new lands for their expanding families.

Immigration dropped off between 1775 and 1815 but an economic crisis in Europe once again prompted numerous Germans to come to the United States. It is estimated that approximately 5 million Germans immigrated to America between 1820 and 1900. Like the earlier settlers, most were farmers who arrived with their families, although by the end of the century there were increasing numbers of young single people who were agricultural laborers and servants. Many of these settled in the Mississippi, Ohio, and Missouri valleys, the Great Lakes area, or the Midwest. Most Germans avoided settling in the southern United States but there are sizable German settlements in Texas and New Orleans.

A third phase of immigration began after the turn of the century, when approximately 1.5 million Germans came to America. Many were unmarried industrial workers seeking higher pay, and others were the descendants of Germans who had settled in distinct colonies in Russia as early as the sixteenth century. Discrimination and the revolution of 1917 led to their departure. Most of these third-phase immigrants joined growing numbers of second- and third-generation Germans living in urban areas. Cities with considerable German populations were Cleveland, New York, Toledo, Detroit, Chicago, Milwaukee, and St. Louis. Russian Germans, however, tended to settle in rural areas; many settled in Colorado.

During the 1930s, many of the German immigrants were Jewish refugees. After World War II, displaced persons of German descent and East German refugees made up the sizable German immigrant group who settled in the United States.

Poles. Although the Poles have arrived in the United States continuously since 1608, the largest wave of immigration occurred between 1860 and 1914, mostly for economic reasons. The early phase was dominated by Poles (approximately one-half million) from German-ruled areas of Poland (Pomerania and Poznan) or by Poles who worked in western Germany. German Poles often became part of the German or Czech communities or established farming settlements in the Southwest and Midwest.

The number of Polish immigrants from Germany began to decline after 1890, but the slack was taken up by the arrival of Poles (over 2 million) from areas under Russian and Austrian rule. The German Poles left their homeland to become permanent settlers, but the Russian and Austrian Poles came as temporary workers. Although 30 percent returned to Poland, many eventually moved back to the United States permanently. The Austrian and Russian Poles tended to settle in the rapidly developing cities of the middle Atlantic and midwestern states, especially Chicago, Buffalo, and Cleveland.

Polish emigration after World War I was usually not for economic reasons. Most (over a quarter of a million) left because of political dissatisfaction: government instability and dictatorship in the 1920s and 1930s, the German invasion and occupation from 1939 to 1945, and the pro-Soviet Communist government after 1945. Many settled in urban areas in which there were substantial existing Polish populations.

Other Central Europeans. One and one-half million Hungarians, Czechs, and Slovaks have come to the United States, primarily during the late nineteenth and early twentieth centuries for economic and political reasons. Few Austrians have settled permanently in the United States.

Czechs are the most Western branch of the Slavs and their traditional homeland is Bohemia and Moravia, located in the western half of Czechoslovakia; Slovaks, also descendants of Slavic tribes, have formally been considered a distinct nationality and their traditional homeland is Slovakia, the eastern half of Czechoslovakia.

Hungarians who immigrated at the turn of the century were often young, single men who found job opportunities in the expanding industrial workplace. Many worked in the coal mines of eastern Ohio, West Virginia, northern Illinois, and Indiana. Cities that developed large Hungarian populations were primarily located in the Northeast and Midwest. Over 50,000 additional Hungarians entered the United States as refugees after World War II and the 1956 uprising against the Communist government. They first settled in the industrial towns populated by earlier Hungarian immigrants, but many, mostly professionals, soon moved to other cities that offered better jobs.

Czech immigrants initially tended to be farmers or skilled agricultural workers who settled in the states of Nebraska, Wisconsin, Texas, Iowa, and Minnesota, often near the Germans. Later Czech immigrants were skilled laborers; they settled in the urban areas of New York, Cleveland, and especially Chicago.

The majority of the Slovak immigrants were young male agricultural workers. Those who decided to remain in America later sent for their wives and families. The majority settled in the industrial Northeast and Midwest; they labored in coal mines, steel mills, and oil refineries.

Russians. Russian immigrants originally came to Alaska and the West Coast, rather than to the eastern states. Most of their settlements were forts or outposts, used to protect their fur trade and to shelter missionaries. When Russia sold Alaska to the United States in 1867, half the settlers returned home and many of the others moved to California. Subsequent immigration was primarily to the East Coast, although some Russians (Molokans, followers of a religion that had rejected the Russian Eastern Orthodox Church) immigrated to the West Coast in the early twentieth century.

Russians, mainly impoverished peasants seeking a better life, began to arrive in large numbers during the 1880s. A second wave of immigrants came after the 1917 revolution, when more than 2 million people fled the country; 30,000 settled in the United States. After World War II some Soviet refugees emigrated to America. Currently small numbers of Soviet citizens, primarily Jews, are being allowed to leave, and many are emigrating to the United States.

The settlement patterns of Russians are similar to those other immigrants from central Europe. For the later wave of immigrants, the port of entry was New York City. Many re-

Russian is a generic term to describe people of widely varying ethnic and religious backgrounds who came to the U.S. from land that once was Russian, or is now part of the U.S.S.R. Russians include people from Belorussia (White Russians) and the Ukraine as well as Jews, Poles, and Germans.

mained in New York, and others settled in nearby industrial areas that offered employment in the mines and factories.

Current Demographics and Socioeconomic Status

Germans. Germans differ little from the national norms demographically, although they are slightly higher in economic achievement and are generally conservative in attitudinal ratings. Only the Pennsylvania Dutch and the rural-dwelling Germans from Russia who settled in the Midwest retain some aspects of their cultural heritage.

The high degree of German acculturation is attributed to their large numbers, their occupations, and the time of their arrival in the United States. Further, entry of the United States into World War I created a storm of anti-German feeling in America. German-composed music was banned, German-named foods were renamed, German books were burned. As a result, German Americans rapidly assimilated, abandoning the customs still common in other ethnic groups, such as ethnic associations and use of their oral and written language.

Poles. Polish Americans form one of the largest ethnic groups in the United States today. In 1980, it was estimated that there were over 8 million Americans of Polish descent; many still live in the urban areas of the Northeast and upper Midwest in which their ancestors originally settled.

Economically, the third-generation Polish American has moved modestly upward, but the majority of Polish Americans still live just below or solidly at middle-class level. Forty-five percent of the males have white-collar jobs, and 40 percent of working Polish women are semiskilled or unskilled laborers. More recent immigrants usually possess higher occupational skills and educational backgrounds than earlier immigrants.

Other Eastern Europeans. In the 1980 census it was estimated that there were over 1.5 million Hungarian Americans in the United States. Economically, the Hungarians differ little from other central European immigrants. Most live in urban areas and work mostly in white-collar occupations. First- and second-generation Hungarian Americans encouraged their children to become engineers, a science that was respected by the Hungarian aristocracy at the turn of the century.

In 1970 most Czechs lived in cities or rural nonfarm areas;

The word, Dutch, is a corruption of *Deutsch,* meaning German, and has nothing to do with Holland.

statistics show that 450,000 of them grew up in homes where Czech was spoken. Cities and states with large Czech populations are California, Chicago, Iowa, Minnesota, Nebraska, New York City, Texas, and Wisconsin. Occupationally, 9 percent of Czech Americans are still farmers, 18–21 percent are clerical workers, and over 50 percent hold white-collar jobs.

The first two generations of Slovaks grew up in tightly knit communities anchored by work, church, family, and social activities. The third and fourth generations have sought higher education, work in white-collar jobs, and live in the suburbs. The cultural ties are still strong among the later generations of Slovaks, and they have not totally acculturated.

Russians. In 1977, there were approximately 2.78 million Russian Americans living in the United States. They have mostly moved out of the inner-city settlements to the suburbs. Recent Soviet Jewish emigres have also settled in urban areas. Immigrants who have arrived since 1920 have come from relatively high educational and professional backgrounds.

Since World War II, the relations between the Russian American community and American society at large has largely been dependent on the political climate between the United States and the Soviet Union. During the 1950s, anti-Soviet and anti-Communist sentiments in the United States caused many Russian Americans to assume a low profile that hastened their acculturation.

Cultural Organizations

Poles. Polish societies, such as the Polish National Alliance and the Polish Roman Catholic Union (both based in Chicago), were originally set up to aid the newly arrived immigrants. These organizations remain a vital part of Polish American life, supporting cultural preservation and educational projects in the community.

Other Central Europeans. Leisure activities among the first two generations of Slavs revolved around community associations. Many belonged to fraternal lodges that organized dances, plays, and sporting competitions. Lodge membership has dropped off among members of the third and fourth generation.

Many Czechs formed fraternal organizations, often to provide health and life insurance. The Czechoslovak Society, with over 200 lodges, is the oldest existing Czech fraternal benefit society still operating. Children's gymnastic societies, called *sokol*s ("falcon") are also popular. The American Sokol Organization has 70 branches and 9,000 members who particpate in gymnastic classes, cultural activities, summer camps, and ethnic festivals.

WORLDVIEW

Religion

The Amish and Mennonites are referred to as "Plain People"; the more liberal and worldly members of the Lutheran and Reformed Churches are called the "Gay Dutch," "Fancy Dutch," or "Church People."

Germans. The majority of German immigrants were Lutheran; a minority were Roman Catholic. Today the Pennsylvania Dutch and the rural Germans from Russia faithfully maintain their religious heritage. Both groups are primarily Protestant, mostly Lutheran or Mennonite. Mennonites are a religious group derived from the Anabaptist movement, which advocated baptism and church membership for adult believers only. They are noted for their simple lifestyle and rejection of oaths, public office, and military service. The Amish, a strict sect of the Mennonites, follow the Bible literally. They till the soil and shun worldly vanities such as electricity and automobiles.

Poles. Most Polish immigrants were devout Catholics; they quickly established parish churches in the U.S. The Catholic church is still a vital part of the Polish American community, although Polish Americans have been found to marry outside the church more than other Catholics.

Other Central Europeans. Religion is still an important factor in the lives of Slavs. Most are Roman Catholics who attend services regularly. First- and second-generation Slavs usually send their children to parochial schools supported by the ethnic parish.

In Europe most Czechs were Roman Catholics, but one-half to two-thirds of nineteenth century Czech immigrants from rural areas left the church and were considered "freethinkers" who believed in a strong separation of church and state. Subsequent generations now belong to a variety of faiths.

Russians. Except for the Soviet Jews, the primary organization of the Russian American community today is the Russian Orthodox church. Religion has always played a central role in the Russian community, and the Orthodox church has tried to preserve the culture. However, since the largest branch of the Eastern church, officially known as the Orthodox Church in America (formerly the Russian Orthodox

Church Outside Russia), now includes people from other central European countries, the Russian traditions have been de-emphasized.

Family

Poles. Traditionally the Polish American family was patriarchal and the father exerted strong control over the children, especially the daughters. The mother took care of the home, and if the children worked, it was near the father's workplace or home. Since the 1920s, the overwhelming majority of Polish American families have been solely supported by the father's income; wives and children have rarely worked.

Other Central Europeans. Family ties are strong among the Slavs. Parents are respected; they are frequently visited and cared for in their old age. Weddings are still a major event, although they are not celebrated for several days as they were once.

Traditional Food Habits

INGREDIENTS AND COMMON FOODS

Staples and Regional Variations

The regional variations in central European and Russian cuisine are minor. Ingredients in traditional dishes were dictated by what could be grown in the cold, often damp climate.

Common ingredients are potatoes, beans, cabbage and members of the cabbage family, beets, eggs, dairy products, pork, beef, fish from the Baltic Sea and local lakes and rivers, apples, rye, wheat, and barley (see Table 4.3 for the Cultural Food Groups). Foods were often dried, pickled, or fermented for preservation (for example, cucumber pickles, sour cream, and sauerkraut).

Dairy products are eaten daily. Cheeses may be served at any meal, from the fresh, sweet varieties to the strongly-flavored aged types like *Lederkranz* and *Limburger*. Fresh milk is drunk; butter is the preferred cooking fat. Buttermilk, sour cream, and fresh cream are also common ingredients in sauces, soups, stews, and baked products. In Austria and Germany, whipped cream is part of the daily diet, served with coffee or pastries.

Bread is a staple item and there are over 100 different varieties. Because the climate makes wheat harder to grow,

Legend has it that it was the Mongols who showed the Slavs how to broil meat, make yogurt and other fermented dairy products, and to preserve cabbage in salt brine.

In the Germanic regions the shape of the bread is thought to be derived from symbolic offerings to the gods and the ritual cults of the dead. In this way bread took the place of sacrificial beasts. Pretzels may once have been the ancient symbol of the solar cycle.

**TABLE 4.3. Cultural Food Groups: Central European and
Soviet Union**

Group	Comments
PROTEIN FOODS	
Milk/milk products	Dairy items, fresh or fermented, are frequently consumed.
Meat/poultry/fish/eggs/ legumes	Meats are often extended by grinding and stewing.
	Russians tend to eat their meat very well done.
CEREALS/GRAINS	Bread or rolls are commonly served at all meals. Dumplings and *kasha* are also common.
	Numerous cakes, cookies, and pastries are popular.
	Rye flour is commonly used.
FRUITS/VEGETABLES	Potatoes are used extensively, as are all the cold-weather vegetables.
	Fruits and vegetables are often preserved by canning, drying, or pickling.
	Fruit is often added to meat dishes.

Common Foods	Adaptations in the United States
Milk (cow, sheep) fresh and fermented (buttermilk, sour cream, yogurt), cheese, cream.	Milk products still frequently consumed.
Meat: beef, boar, hare, lamb, pork (bacon, ham, pig's feet, head cheese), sausage, variety meats, veal, venison.	Consumption of meat and poultry increased; use of variety meats decreased. Sausages often eaten.
Fish: carp, flounder, frog, haddock, halibut, herring, mackerel, perch, pike, salmon, sardines, shad, shark, smelts, sturgeon, trout.	
Shellfish: crayfish, crab, eel, lobster, oysters, scallops, shrimp, turtle.	
Poultry and small birds: chicken, cornish hen, duck, goose, grouse, partridge, pheasant, quail, squab, turkey.	
Eggs: hens, fish (caviar).	
Legumes: kidney beans, lentils, navy beans, split peas (green and yellow).	
Barley, buckwheat (kasha), corn, millet, oats, potato starch, rice, rye, wheat.	More white bread, less rye and pumpernickel bread is eaten.
Fruits: apples, apricots, blackberries, blueberries, sour cherries, sweet cherries, cranberries, currants, dates, gooseberries, grapefruit, grapes, lemons, lingonberries, melons, oranges, peaches, pears, plums, prunes, quinces, raisins, raspberries, rhubarb, strawberries.	
Vegetables: asparagus, beets, broccoli, brussels sprouts, cabbage (red and green), carrots, cauliflower, celery, celery root, chard, cucumbers, eggplant, endive, green beans, kohlrabi, leeks, lettuce, mushrooms (domestic and wild), olives, onions, parsnips, peas, green peppers, potatoes, radishes, sorrel, spinach, tomatoes, turnips.	

TABLE 4.3. Cultural Food Groups: Central European and Soviet Union (*continued*)

Group	Comments
ADDITIONAL FOODS	
Seasonings	Central Europeans tend to season their dishes with sour-tasting flavors, such as sour cream and vinegar.
Nuts/seeds	Poppy seeds are often used in pastries; caraway seeds flavor cabbage and bread.
Beverages	Central Europeans drink coffee; Russians drink tea.
	Many varieties of beer are produced.
	Hungarians and Austrians tend to drink more wine than other central European people.
Fats/oils	
Sweeteners	

Spätzle are tiny dumplings common in the southern section of central Europe. They are made by forcing the dough through a large spoon with small holes into boiling water. They are usually served as a sidedish.

bread is often made with rye and other grains; thus it is darker in color than bread made from wheat flour. Another common bread-like food in the region is dumplings (called *knedliky* in Czech, *Knödel* in German, and *kletski* in Russian), which can be made with flour or potatoes and with or without yeast. Sometimes they are stuffed with fillings such as liver, bacon, or fruit. Dumplings are usually boiled in water. Related to the dumpling is stuffed pastry dough, which is baked or fried. Typically, it is filled with meat or cabbage. Small individual pastries are called *pirozhki* in Russian, and a large oval pie is known as a *pirog*.

In much of central Europe, pastries are enjoyed each day.

Common Foods	Adaptations in the United States
Allspice, anise, basil, bay leaves, borage, capers, caraway, cardamom, chervil, chives, cinnamon, cloves, curry powder, dill, garlic, ginger, juniper, horseradish, lemon, lovage, mace, marjoram, mint, mustard, paprika, parsley, pepper (black and white), poppy seeds, rosemary, rose water, saffron, sage, savory (summer and winter), tarragon, thyme, vanilla, vinegar, woodruff.	
Nuts: almonds (sweet and bitter), chestnuts, filberts, pecans, walnuts.	
Seeds: poppy seeds, sunflower seeds.	
Beer, hot chocolate, coffee, syrups and juices, fruit brandies, herbal teas, milk, tea, vodka, wine.	Usually only American-style beer is available.
Butter, bacon, chicken fat, flaxseed oil, goose fat, lard, olive oil, salt pork, suet, vegetable oil.	
Honey, sugar (white and brown), molasses.	

They are eaten at coffeehouses in the morning or afternoon, or bought at the local bakery and served as dessert. There are numerous types, such as cheesecakes, coffeecakes, doughnuts, and nut- or fruit-filled individual pastries. Austria is believed to be the home of apple strudel, made from paperthin sheets of dough rolled around cinnamon-spiced apple pieces. Germany is known for *Schwarzwälder Kirschtorte* (Black Forest cake), a rich chocolate cake layered with cherries, whipped cream, and *Kirsch* (cherry liqueur). *Doboschtorte*, a multilayered spongecake with chocolate filling and caramel topping, is a favorite in Hungary.

Next to bread, meat is probably the most important ele-

The dense chocolate cake known as *Sachertorte* was the subject of a seven-year court battle in Vienna over who had the right to claim the original recipe: the Hotel Sacher or Demel's, a famous bakery. The Hotel Sacher won.

Game meats are traditional favorites throughout central Europe. In Germany, the *wildfleisch* season is celebrated in winter. Venison, rabbit, and wild boar are featured in markets and restaurants.

A frankfurter means a sausage from the German city of Frankfurt. There are differing opinions as how the frankfurter was introduced to America, but it soon became a favorite at baseball games. The cartoonist T. A. Dorgan drew a cartoon in which he gave the sausage a tail, legs, and head so that it looked like a dachshund. Since then, the frankfurter has been called a "hot dog."

ment of the diet. Pork is the most popular. In Germany, *Sauerbraten*, or pork roast, is the national dish. *Schnitzel* is a meat cutlet, often lightly breaded and then fried. Ham is served fresh or cured: Poland is famous for its smoked ham, and in Germany, Westphalian ham is lightly smoked, cured and cut into paper-thin slices. Poultry is also well-liked. Germans often eat roast goose, stuffed with onions, apples, and herbs, on holidays. In Russia, chicken is served on special occasions. A famous Russian dish is *chicken Kiev*, breaded fried chicken breasts filled with herbed butter.

In the past, meat was often scarce and expensive; thus many traditional recipes stretched it as far as possible. Dishes common throughout the region are ground meat that has been seasoned, mixed with a binder, such as bread crumbs, milk, or eggs, formed into patties, then fried. In Germany, ground beef (and sometimes pork and veal) is served raw on toast as *steak Tartar*. Ground meat is also used to stuff vegetables (such as stuffed cabbage) or pastry, or is cooked as meatballs. Cut up meat is often served in soups, stews or one-pot dishes. In Germany, a slowly simmered one-pot dish of meat, vegetables, potatoes, or dumplings is called an *Eintopf*. Hungary is known for its *gulyás*, a paprika-spiced stew known as *goulash* in the United States. Sweet Hungarian paprika is ground, dried, red chili peppers to which sugar has been added. Since chilis are a New World food, it is thought the Hungarians used black pepper to season their food before the discovery of the Americas.

Ground meats are also made into sausages. In Germany, there are four basic types of sausage (*Wurst*). *Rohwurst* is cured and smoked by the butcher, and can be eaten as is. *Bruhwurst* is smoked and scalded by the butcher; it may be eaten as is or heated by simmering. *Knockwurst*, which is like a cold cut, may be smoked and is well-cooked by the butcher. *Bratwurst* is sold raw by the butcher and must be pan-fried before eating.

The Polish are famous for *kielbasa*, a garlic-flavored pork sausage. In Austria, sausages are called *wieners*. Two popular sausages in Czechoslovakia are *jaternice*, made from a pork, and *jelita*, a blood sausage, which can be boiled or fried.

Freshwater fish and seafood are also eaten smoked or cured. In Germany, herring is commonly pickled and eaten as a snack or at the main meal. Eel is also popular. In the Soviet Union, smoked salmon and sturgeon are considered delicacies, as is *caviar*, which is fish roe. Caviar, is classified according to its quality and source. *Beluga*, the choicest caviar, is taken from the largest sturgeon, and has the largest eggs; its color varies from black to gray. *Sevruga* and *osetrova*, taken from smaller sturgeon, have smaller eggs and sometimes a darker color. The finest caviar is sieved by hand to remove membranes and is lightly salted. Less choice roes are more heavily salted and pressed into bricks.

In central Europe, the common hot beverage is coffee. In the Soviet Union, strong tea, diluted with hot water from a *samovar*, is drunk instead of coffee. A samovar is a brass urn, which may be very ornate, heated by charcoal inserted in a vertical tube running through the center.

Although southwestern Germany, Austria, and Hungary produce excellent white wine, the two most popular alcoholic drinks of the region are beer and vodka. Czechoslovakia is known for its *pilsner* beer, which is bitter tasting but light in color and body. German beers can be sweet, bitter, weak, or strong, and are typically bottom-fermented (meaning the yeast sinks during brewing). *Lager*, a bottom-fermented beer that is aged for about six weeks, is the most common type. *Bock* beer is the strongest flavored, traditionally made once a year when the brewing tanks are cleaned. *Märzenbier*, a strong beer midway between a pilsner and a bock beer, is served at Oktoberfest (see section on Special Occasions) in Munich.

Malzbier is a German beer (1% alcohol) that is considered appropriate for young children and nursing mothers.

Vodka, which is commonly drunk in Poland and the Soviet Union, is a distilled spirit made from potatoes. It is served ice cold and is often flavored with seasonings, such as lemon or black pepper. In Poland, one vodka, *goldwasser*, contains flakes of pure gold.

MEAL COMPOSTION AND CYCLE

Daily Patterns

Central Europe. Traditionally the people of this region would eat five or six large meals a day, if they could afford it. The poor, and usually the people who worked the land, had fewer meals, which were often meatless. Today modern work schedules have affected the meal pattern, resulting in fewer meals.

In Germany and the countries of central Europe, the first meal of the day is breakfast, which consists of bread served with butter and jam. Sometimes it is accompanied by soft-boiled eggs, cheese, and ham. At midmorning, many people have their second breakfast, which may include coffee and pastries, bread and fruit, or a small sandwich. Lunch is the main meal of the day. Traditionally people ate lunch at home but today they are more likely to go to a cafeteria or restaurant. A proper lunch begins with soup, followed by a fish course, then one or two meat dishes served with vegetables, and perhaps stewed fruit. Dessert is the final course and is usually served with whipped cream. A quicker and lighter lunch may consist of only a stew or a one-pot meal.

A coffee break is taken at midafternoon, if time permits. It typically includes coffee and cake or cookies. The evening meal tends to be light, usually salads and an assortment of pickled or smoked fish, cheese, ham, and sausages eaten with a selection of breads. Guests are usually not invited for dinner but may come for dessert and wine later in the evening.

Soviet Union. In Czarist Russia, the aristocracy ate four complete meals a day; dinner was the largest. The majority of the population never ate as lavishly or as often. One part of the traditional Czarist evening meal, *zakuski* (meaning ''small bites''), is still part of dinner in the Soviet Union today. The meal starts with zakuski, an array of appetizers, which may range from two simple dishes, such as cucumbers in sour cream and pickled herring, to an entire table spread with countless *hors d'oeuvres*. An assortment of zakuski usually includes a variety of small open-faced sandwiches topped with cold smoked fish, anchovies or sardines, cold tongue and pickles, ham, sausages, or salami. Caviar, the most elegant of zakuski, is served with an accompanying plate of chopped hard-boiled eggs and finely minced onions. Other zakuski include marinated or pickled vegetables, hot meat dishes, and eggs served a variety of ways.

The meal that peasants ate after a long day's work is still the basis of a typical dinner in the Soviet Union today. The staples are bread, soup made from beets (*borshch*), cabbage (*shchi*), or fish (*ukha*), and *kasha* (cooked grain, usually buckwheat). Beer brewed from bread, called *kvas*, usually accompanies the meal.

Buckwheat, native to central Asia, is not a true cereal, but is more of a seed.

Special Occasions

The majority of central European holidays have a religious significance, although some traditions date back to pre-Christian times. The two major holidays in the region are Christmas and Easter. Many of the American symbols and activities associated with these holidays, such as the Christmas tree and the Easter egg hunt, were brought to the United States by central European immigrants.

German Christmas tree: This old-fashioned German Christmas tree is decorated with traditional cookies (such as Lebkuchen *and* Pfeffernüsse) *and candy ornaments.* (Courtesy Carris and Associates.)

Germany. Germany is a land of popular festivals: secular, religious, historical, and modern. Nearly all are accompanied by food and drink. Probably the best-known celebration is Munich's Oktoberfest, which lasts for 16 days from late September through early October. Founded in 1810 to celebrate

Marzipan Easter figurines: Marzipan figurines and chocolate eggs on display in a German candy store.

Marzipan, a paste of ground almonds and sugar, is commonly used in desserts and candies.

the marriage of Crown Prince Ludwig of Bavaria, it is now an annual festival.

Advent and Christmas are the holiest seasons in German-speaking countries. The Christmas tree, a remnant of the pagan winter solstice rites, is lit on Christmas Eve when the presents, brought not by Santa Claus but by the Christ Child, are opened. The Christmas tree is not taken down until Epiphany, January 6. A large festive dinner is served on Christmas day, and it is customary for families to visit one another.

Foods served during the Christmas season include carp on Christmas Eve, and roast hare or goose accompanied by apples and nuts on Christmas day. Brightly colored *marzipan* candies in the shape of fruits and animals are traditional Christmas sweets. Other desserts prepared during the season are: spice cakes and cookies (*Pfeffernüsse* and *Lebkuchen*), fruit cakes (*Stollen*), cakes in the shape of a Christmas tree (*Baumkuchen*), and gingerbread houses.

On Easter Sunday, the Easter bunny hides colored eggs in the house and garden for the children to find. Ham and pureed peas are customarily served for Easter dinner. Candy Easter eggs and rabbits are also part of the festivities.

Poland. Christmas and Easter are the two most important holidays in Poland, a predominantly Catholic country. On Easter, the festive table may feature a roast suckling pig, hams, coils of sausages, and roast veal. Always included are painted hard-boiled eggs, grated horseradish, and a Paschal lamb sculptured from butter or white sugar. Before the feasting begins, one of the eggs is shelled, divided, and reverently eaten. The crowning glory of the meal is the *babka*, a rich yeast cake. All the foods are blessed by the priest before being served.

On Christmas Eve, traditionally a fast day, the meal consists of soup, fish, noodle dishes, and pastries. One popular soup, *barszcz Wigilijny*, a cousin to borscht, is made with mushrooms as well as beets. Carp is usually the fish served on Christmas Eve. A rich Christmas cake, *makowiec*, is shaped like a jelly roll and filled with black poppy seeds, honey, raisins, and almonds.

Jelly doughnuts, *paczki*, are eaten on New Year's Eve, while on New Year's Day, *bigos*, "hunter's stew," made with a variety of meats and vegetables (some form of cabbage is required), is washed down with plenty of vodka.

Hungary and Czechoslovakia. At Christmastime the Czechs eat carp four different ways: breaded and fried; baked with dried prunes; cold in aspic; and in a fish soup. The Christmas Eve meal might also include pearl barley soup with mushroom, fruits, and decorated cookies. Christmas dinner may feature giblet soup with noodles, roast goose with dumplings and sauerkraut, braided sweet bread (*vanocka* or *houska*), fruits and nuts, and coffee. *Kolaches*, round yeast buns filled with poppy seeds, dried fruit, or cottage cheese, are served at the Christmas meal and on most festive occasions. For Easter, a baked ham or roasted kid is served with *mazanec* (vanocka dough with raisins and almonds shaped into a round loaf).

The Slovaks break the Advent fast on Christmas Eve by eating *oplatky*, small wafer-like Communion bread spread with honey. The meal may contain wild mushroom soup, cabbage and potato dumplings, stuffed cabbage (*holubjy*), and mashed-potato dumplings covered with butter and cheese (*halusky*). A favorite dessert is *babalky*, pieces of bread, sliced, scalded and drained, then rolled in ground poppy seeds, sugar, or honey. Mulled wine usually accompanies this meal, as do assorted poppy seed and nut pastries and a

In the Polish Easter meal, the dairy products, meats, and pastries symbolize the fertility and renewal of spring, while the horseradish is to remind one of the bitterness and disappointments of life.

One traditional Christmas Eve dish in Poland is *karp po zydowsku*, chilled slices of carp in a sweet-and-sour aspic with raisins and almonds. It is of Jewish origin from the fourteenth century, when Poland was a haven for Jews.

Vanocka, *Czechoslovakian Christmas bread.* (Courtesy Florida State News Bureau.)

variety of fruits. For Easter, the Slovaks prepare *paska*, a dessert in the form of a pyramid containing cheese, cream, butter, eggs, sugar, and candied fruits, decorated with a cross. The meal, blessed by the priest on Holy Saturday, includes ham, sausage (*klobása*), roast duck or goose, horseradish, an Easter cheese called *syrek*, and an imitation cheese ball made from eggs *(hrudka)*.

In Hungary, the most important religious holiday is Easter. Starting before Lent, pancakes are traditionally eaten on Shrove Tuesday; sour eggs and herring salad are served on Ash Wednesday. During Easter week, new spring vegetables are enjoyed, as well as painted Easter eggs. The Good Friday meal may include a wine-flavored soup, stuffed eggs, and baked fish. The biggest and most important meal of the year is the feast of Easter Eve, which consists of a rich chicken soup served with dumplings or noodles, followed by roasted meat (ham, pork, or lamb), then several pickled vegetables, stuffed cabbage rolls, and finally a selection of cakes and pastries served with coffee.

Czechoslovakian kolaches: *Czechoslovakian* kolaches *are prepared for a church bake-off in Texas.* (Courtesy Institute of Texas Cultures at San Antonio.)

The Christmas Eve meal, which is meatless, usually features fish and potatoes. The Christmas Day meal often includes roast turkey, chicken, or goose accompanied by roast potatoes and stuffed cabbage, followed by desserts of brandied fruits or fruit compote and poppy seed and nut cakes.

Soviet Union. Before the 1917 revolution, Russians celebrated a full calendar of religious holidays. Today, on fast days, the religious do not eat any animal products (see Chapter 2 for the fast days in the Eastern Orthodox church). Of all the holidays, the most important is Easter, which replaced a pre-Christian festival that marked the end of the bleak winter season.

The "Butter Festival" (*maslenitas*) precedes the 40 days of Lent. One food eaten during this period is *blini*, buckwheat yeast pancakes. Blini can be served with a variety of toppings such as butter, jam, sour cream, smoked salmon, or caviar. Butter is the traditional topping because it cannot be eaten during Lent.

Traditional foods served on Easter after midnight mass are *pascha*, similar to the Slovak paska but decorated with the letters "XB" ("Christ is risen"); *kulich*, a cake made from a very rich sweet yeast dough baked in a tall cylindrical mold; and red or hand decorated hard-boiled eggs. On Pentecost (Trinity) Sunday (50 days after Easter), kulich left over from Easter is eaten.

Twelve different dishes are served during the Christmas Eve meal. One of the traditional dishes may be *kutia*, wheat grains combined with honey, poppy seeds, and stewed dried fruit. A festive meal is served on Christmas Day.

On New Year's Day, children receive gifts and spicy ginger cakes are eaten. A pretzel-shaped sweet bread, *krendel*, is eaten on wedding anniversaries and name days (saints' day celebrated as birthdays by Eastern Orthodox).

Contemporary Food Habits in the United States

ADAPTATION OF FOOD HABITS

Ingredients and Common Foods

The central European and Russian diet is not significantly different from American fare. The immigrants made few changes in the types of foods they ate after they came to the United States. What did change was the quantity of certain foods. Most central European immigrants were not wealthy in their native lands, and their diets had included meager amounts of meat. After immigrating to the United States, they increased the quantity of meat they ate considerably.

The people of eastern Pennsylvania, where there is a large concentration of German Americans, still eat many traditional German dishes adapted to accommodate available ingredients. Common foods include *scrapple* (also called *ponhaus*), a pork and cornmeal sausage flavored with herbs and cooked in a loaf pan, served for breakfast with syrup; *sticky buns*, little sweet rolls thought to be descended from German cinnamon rolls known as *Schnecken; schnitz un knepp* (apples and dumplings), a one-pot dish made from boiled ham, dried apple slices, and brown sugar, topped with a dumpling dough; *boova shenkel*, beef stew with potato dumplings; *hinkel welschkarn suup*, a rich chicken soup swimming with tender kernels of sugar corn; *apple butter*, a rich fruit spread, very much like a jam; *schmierkaes*, a German cottage cheese; *funnel cake*, a type of doughnut; *shoofly pie*, a molasses pie thought to be descended from a German crumb cake called *Streuselkuchen; fastnachts*, dough-

Funnel cake: *This unusual "doughnut" is made by pouring the batter from a pitcher into hot oil in a swirled pattern. It is a Pennsylvania Dutch specialty.* (Courtesy Pennsylvania Dutch Visitors Bureau.)

nuts, originally prepared and eaten on Shrove Tuesday to use up the fat that could not be eaten during Lent; and *sweets and sours*, sweet-and-sour relishes, such as cole slaw, crabapple jelly, pepper relish, apple butter, and bread-and-butter pickles, served with lunch and dinner.

Much of German cooking has been incorporated into American cuisine. Many foods still have German names, although they are so common in the United States that their source is unrecognized (for example, sauerkraut, pretzels, and frankfurters). Other foods contributed by the Germans are hamburgers, braunschweiger (liver sausage), thuringer (summer sausage), liverwurst, cole slaw, jelly doughnuts, and rye bread. Beer production, especially in Milwaukee, was dominated by the Germans for over 100 years. German immigrants created a lager-style beer that is milder, lighter, and less bitter than typical German beer; it can now be described as American-style beer.

Meal Composition and Cycle

Third- and fourth-generation central European and Russian Americans tend to consume three meals a day (with snacks), and meal composition is similar to that of a typical American meal, although more dairy products and sausages may be eaten. Some traditional foods and ingredients may not be available in areas without large central European or Russian populations.

NUTRITIONAL STATUS

Nutritional Intake and Counseling

Very little has been reported recently on the nutritional intake or status of central European or Russian Americans. In 1984, a Polish study (Kulesza *et al.*) examined the dietary habits of male Poles and Slovaks. They found that 50 percent of the Slovaks ate pork or beef at least four times a week, compared to 10 percent of the Poles; 62 percent of the Poles and 44 percent of the Slovaks drank milk daily. Both groups ate vegetables and fruit frequently.

In a joint study, nutrient intake and its association with high- and low-density lipoproteins in selected American and Soviet subpopulations was reported by the US–USSR Steering Committee for Problem Area I (1984). They found that Soviet men living in Moscow and Leningrad had lower intakes of protein and polyunsaturated and monounsaturated fatty acids, and higher intakes of total carbohydrate, complex carbohydrates, and sucrose than the U.S. sample. The American men had higher polyunsaturated-to-saturated fatty acid ratios. Soviet men consumed on the average 508 mg of cholesterol per day. (The American Heart Association recommends that adults consume fewer than 250 mg of cholesterol per day.)

Based on the results of both studies, it is reasonable to assume that Polish, Slovak, and Russian Americans consume a nutritionally adequate diet but that they may be at risk of developing coronary heart disease. Individual diet and nutritional assessment must be completed through an in-depth interview before any dietary recommendations can be made for Americans of central European and Russian descent.

SCANDINAVIANS

The Scandinavian countries include Sweden, Norway, Denmark, and Finland. With the exception of Denmark, they are located north of the Baltic and North Seas and share common borders with each other and the Soviet Union. Most of the population in Scandinavia is concentrated in the warmer southern regions; the harsher northern areas extend above the Arctic Circle. Norway's weather is more temperate than that of Finland and Sweden because its long western coastline is bathed in the temperate North Atlantic Drift. Denmark juts into the North Sea just north of West Germany and its capital, Copenhagen, is directly opposite from Sweden. The majority of Scandinavian immigrants to the United States arrived in the 1800s.

Cultural Perspective

HISTORY OF THE SCANDINAVIAN COUNTRIES

In the fourteenth century, Margaret of Denmark united the rule of Denmark, Sweden, and Norway (at this time Finland was under the rule of Sweden). Norway virtually ceased to exist as a separate kingdom and was ruled by Danish governors for the following four centuries. Sweden, on the other hand, could not be controlled by Denmark, and King Gustavus I, the founder of the modern Swedish state, came to rule in 1523. Sweden became the dominant Protestant (Lutheran) power of continental Europe in the seventeenth century. Norway and Finland did not become independent nations until the twentieth century: Norway in 1905, and Finland after the Russian revolution of 1917.

All four countries enjoyed economic prosperity and industrial development in this century. During World War II, Germany invaded Denmark and Norway, while Sweden remained neutral and Finland sided with the Germans. The Soviet Union invaded Finland in 1944 and eventually forced the Germans out. After the war, Finland was required to pay the Soviet Union $300 million and to cede disputed territory. Today Denmark, Norway, and Sweden have constitutional monarchies and Finland has an elected democratic government.

HISTORY OF IMMIGRATION TO THE UNITED STATES

It is believed that the Norwegians, long known as seafarers and explorers, first discovered North America and colonized by Norsemen (ancient Scandinavians) as far west as Minnesota in the thirteenth and fourteenth centuries. The docu-

Veal oscar, veal topped with bearnaise sauce, white asparagus, and lobster or crab, is named after Swedish King Oscar II (1872–1907), a renown gourmet.

mented presence of Scandinavians in America dates back to the seventeenth century. Jonas Bronck, a Dane, arrived in 1629 and bought a large tract of land from the Indians that later became known as the Bronx in New York City.

Immigration Patterns

The Scandinavians were responsible for introducing the cast iron stove to Americans. Before the cast iron stove, cooking was done in fireplaces and brick ovens.

The majority of Scandinavians arrived in the United States in the 1800s, led by the Norwegians and the Swedes. During the nineteenth century no other country, except Ireland, contributed as large a proportion of its population to the settlement of North America as Norway. Between 1820 and 1975 approximately 363,000 Norwegians, 1.27 million Swedes, 363,000 Danes, and 300,000 Finns entered the United States.

The vast majority of Scandinavian immigrants entered the United States between 1820 and 1930. Overpopulation was the single most important reason for emigration. The population of all the Scandinavian countries had increased substantially, resulting in economies that could not absorb the unemployed and landless agrarian workers. In Sweden, the problem was magnified by a severe famine in the late 1860s. For the Norwegians, there was the additional lure of freedom that America offered, and the chance to emancipate themselves from the peasant class.

The Scandinavians settled in homogeneous communities. The Norwegians and Swedes often moved to the homestead states of the Midwest, especially Illinois, Minnesota, Michigan, Iowa, and Wisconsin. One-fifth of all Swedish immigrants settled in Minnesota. Pockets of Finns and Danes also settled in this region, but they were fewer in number. Norwegians and Swedes also migrated to the coastal areas of the Northwest, working in the lumber and fishing industries. The shipping industry attracted Norwegians to New York City, where they still live in an ethnic enclave in Brooklyn.

Although Swedes and Norwegians are often associated with the rural communities of the Midwest, by 1890 a third of all Swedes lived in cities and many Norwegians were seeking opportunity in the urban areas. Chicago and Minneapolis still have large Scandinavian populations. The Swedes were particularly prominent in Chicago's construction industry, which was commonly referred to as a Swedish trade guild.

The Danes, in an effort to preserve their ethnicity, developed nearly two dozen rural communities between 1886 and 1935, in which, for a set number of years, land could be sold only to Danes. The best known of these communities are Tyler, Minnesota; Danevang, Texas; Askov, Minnesota; Dagmar, Missouri; and Solvang, California. Today most Danes live in cities, primarily on the East or West Coasts. The largest concentrations of Danes are in the Los Angeles area and in Chicago.

Current Demographics and Socioeconomic Status

According to the 1980 census, there are 1.5 million Danes, 4.3 million Swedes, and 3.4 million Norwegians and their descendants now living in the United States. Most Scandinavians assimilated rapidly into American society, rising from blue-collar to white-collar jobs within a few generations. Many Norwegians and Swedes have continued farming in the Midwest. Danes entered a variety of occupations but they were most prominent in gardening, raising livestock, and dairy farming.

Cultural Organizations

Many Scandinavian ethnic organizations grew out of the need for mutual help or cultural preservation. Although there are hundreds of such organizations at the local and regional level, the larger national ones are The Danish Brotherhood, the American Scandinavian Society, the Sons of Norway, and the Swedish Council of America, which coordinates Swedish American activities.

WORLDVIEW

Religion

The majority of Scandinavians who immigrated to the United States were Lutheran, although each nationality had its own branch of the church. As with other immigrant groups, the church helped to ease the adjustment of recent arrivals and provided ethnic companionship. In this century, many of the Scandinavian and German Lutheran churches joined together to create the American Lutheran Church and the Lutheran Church of America.

Family

The nuclear Scandinavian family was at the center of rural life. The father controlled all family affairs (often to the dissatisfaction of the wife and children). Families were typically large; ten and twelve children were not uncommon. Kinship ties were strong. In America, families were expected to pay the way for relatives remaining in Scandinavia to come to the United States, where they would be given a room, board, and help in finding employment. The family structure was easily maintained in the early homogeneous communities and on isolated farms. The power of the father diminished as the Scandinavian Americans became more integrated in mainstream society.

Traditional Food Habits

In Scandinavia they say "Danes live to eat, Norwegians eat to live, and Swedes eat to drink."

The cooking of Scandinavia is simple and hearty, including the bountiful foods of the sea and making the best use of the limited foods produced on land. Most Scandinavian cooking and food processing reflects preservation methods of previous centuries. Fish was dried, smoked, or pickled, and milk was often fermented or allowed to sour before being drunk. Scandinavians still prepare a large variety of preserved foods and prefer their food salty. Staples of the Scandinavian diet are listed in the Cultural Food Groups list (Table 4.4).

INGREDIENTS AND COMMON FOODS

Staples and Regional Variations

The cooking of Finland is a mix of Swedish and Russian elements, such as *smörgasbords, piroshkis* (meat turnovers), and *blini* (thin pancakes). Vodka is preferred over *aquavit*, the spirit of other Scandinavian countries.

The Scandinavians are probably best known for their use of fish and shellfish, such as salmon, sardines, and shrimp. In Norway, the fish-processing industry is thought to date back to the ninth century. Today Scandinavian dried salt cod is exported all over the world. *Lutefisk* is prepared by soaking the dried cod in a lye solution before cooking. Other fish dishes include salmon marinated in dill, called *gravlax;* smoked salmon, known as *lox;* and the many varieties of preserved herring.

Without fermentation, the Scandinavians would not have been able to store the abundant fresh dairy products produced in the spring and summer. Although they drink milk and cook many of their dishes with cream and butter, they also use considerable quantities of fermented dairy products, such as sour cream, cheese, and buttermilk. Popular Danish cheeses are semifirm, mellow and nutty-tasting *Tybo* (usually encased in red wax); firm and bland *Danbo;* semisoft and slightly acid *Havarti;* rich, soft *Crèma Dania;* and Danish blue cheese.

Common fruits and vegetables are apples, potatoes, cabbage, onions, and beets. A variety of berries and mushrooms are collected from local forests. *Aebleskivers* are round Danish doughnut puffs, sometimes stuffed with fruit preserves. A popular dessert is pancakes served with preserved berries or jam.

Meat, traditionally in limited supply, was stretched by chopping it and combining it with other ingredients. Today the Scandinavians still eat many vegetables, such as onions and cabbage, stuffed with ground pork, veal, or beef. The Swedes are known for their tasty meatballs and the Danes for *fricadeller,* ground pork and veal, breadcrumb and onion patties fried in butter.

Bread is also a staple food item and is often prepared from rye flour (white bread is called French bread in Scandinavia). The Scandinavian breads may or may not be leavened, are often hard, and vary in size and shape. To keep bread for the winter, crusty rye breads with holes punched in them, are hung from the ceilings and dried. A thin round bread called *lefser,* made of potatoes cooked on an ungreased griddle, is usually eaten with butter and sugar and folded up like a handkerchief.

Besides milk and other dairy drinks, common beverages are coffee, beer, and *aquavit.* Aquavit, which means "water of life," is a liquor made from the distillation of potatoes or grain. It may be flavored with an herb, such as caraway, and is served ice cold in a Y-shaped glass. Beer is usually drunk everyday; on occasion, it is drunk with aquavit.

MEAL COMPOSITION AND CYCLE

Daily Patterns

The Scandinavians eat three meals a day, plus a coffee break midmorning, late in the afternoon, or after the evening meal. Breakfast is a hearty meal that may consist of oatmeal porridge, eggs, pastries, cheese, bread, fruit, potatoes, or herring.

Lunch in Denmark is frequently a *smørrebrød,* which means "buttered bread," an open-faced sandwich eaten with a knife and fork. Buttered bread is topped with anything from smoked salmon to sliced boiled potatoes with bacon, cocktail sausages, and tomato slices. A buffet meal in Sweden is the *smörgåsbord* (bread and butter table), a large variety of hot and cold dishes arrayed on a table and traditionally served with aquavit. Ritual dictates the order in which foods are eaten at a smorgasbord. The Swedes start with herring, followed by other fish dishes, such as smoked and fried

One theory about the origin of the *smørrebröd* is it dates back to the time before people used dishes, when rounds of bread were used instead of plates.

TABLE 4.4. Cultural Food Groups: Scandinavian

Group	Comments
PROTEIN FOODS	
Milk/milk products	Dairy products, often fermented, are used extensively.
Meat/poultry/fish/eggs/legumes	Fish is a major source of protein, often preserved by drying, pickling, fermenting, or smoking.
CEREALS/GRAINS	Wheat used less than other grains. Rye used frequently in breads.
FRUITS/VEGETABLES	Fruits with cheese are frequently served for dessert.
	Preserved fruits and pickled vegetables are common.
ADDITIONAL FOODS	
Seasonings	

Common Foods	*Adaptations in the United States*
Milk and cream (cow, goat and reindeer), cheese, sour cream, yogurt.	
Meat: beef, goat, lamb, hare, pork (bacon, ham, sausage), reindeer, veal, venison.	More meat and less fish is consumed.
Fish and shellfish: anchovies, bass, carp, cod, crab, crayfish, eel, flounder, grayling, haddock, halibut, herring, lobster, mackerel, mussels, oysters, perch, pike, plaice, roche, salmon (fresh, smoked, pickled-*gravlax*), sardines, shrimp, sprat, trout, turbot, whitefish.	
Poultry and small birds: chicken, duck, goose, grouse, partridge, pheasant, quail, turkey.	
Eggs: chicken, goose, fish.	
Legumes: split peas (green and yellow), lima beans.	
Barley, cornstarch, oats, rice, rye, tapioca, wheat.	More wheat used, fewer other grains.
Fruits: apples, apricots, blueberries, cherries, cloudberries, currants, lingonberries, oranges, pears, plums, prunes, raisins, raspberries, rhubarb, strawberries.	A greater variety of fruits and vegetables are obtainable in the United States than in Scandinavia, but may not be eaten.
Vegetables: asparagus, beets, cabbage (red and green), carrots, cauliflower, celery, celery root, cucumber, green beans, green peppers, nettles, kohlrabi, leeks, mushrooms (many varieties), onions, parsnips, peas, potatoes, radishes, spinach, tomatoes, yellow and white turnips.	
Allspice, bay leaf, capers, cardamom, chervil, cinnamon, cloves, curry powder, dill, garlic, ginger, horseradish, lemon juice, lemon and orange peel, mace, marjoram, mustard, mustard seed, nutmeg, paprika, parsley, pepper (black, cayenne, white), rose hips, saffron, salt, tarragon, thyme, vanilla, vinegar.	

In Sweden, on the morning of December 13, Saint Lucia's Day, the eldest daughter, wearing a long white dress and a crown of lingonberry greens studded with candles, serves her parents saffron yeast buns and coffee in bed.

TABLE 4.4. Cultural Food Groups: Scandinavian (*continued*)

Group	Comments
Nuts/seeds	
Beverages	
Fats/oils	Butter is often used
Sweeteners	

salmon fins. Next are the meats and salads (pâtés and cold cuts), and the final course before dessert is comprised of hot dishes, such as Swedish meatballs and mushroom omelets.

Dinner is also large, often including an appetizer, soup, entree, vegetables, and dessert. Potatoes are usually served with the evening meal. Desserts, whether they are served after a meal or with the coffee break, are rich but not overly sweet. Most are made with butter and also contain cream or sweetened cheese and the spice cardamom. Coffee is served with the dessert course.

The Scandinavians use almonds or almond paste, marzipan, in desserts, as often as Americans use chocolate. The Danes are best known for their pastries, or, as they call them, *Wienerbrød* (Vienna bread). The pastries were brought to Denmark by Viennese bakers 100 years ago when the Danish bakers went on strike. When the strike was over, the Danes improved the buttery yeast dough by adding jam and other fillings.

Special Occasions

The tradition of serving the two simple foods (rice and fish) for Christmas dates back at least four centuries when the Scandinavians were Catholic and Christmas was a fast, instead of a feast.

December is the darkest month of the year in Scandinavia, and Christmas celebrations are a welcome diversion. The Christmas season lasts from Advent (four weeks before Christmas) until January 13, Saint Canute's Day. However, the climax of the season is on Christmas Eve when the biggest, richest, and most lavish meal of the year is eaten.

Traditional foods eaten on Christmas Eve are rice porridge sprinkled with sugar and cinnamon, and lutefisk served with a white sauce, melted butter, green peas, boiled potatoes, and mustard. Buried in the rice porridge is one blanched almond; the person who receives it will have good fortune in the coming year. Another traditional food served for Christ-

Common Foods	Adaptations in the United States
Almonds, chestnuts, walnuts.	
Coffee, hot chocolate, milk, tea, ale, aquavit, beer, vodka, wine, liqueurs.	
Butter, lard, margarine, salt pork.	
Sugar (white and brown), honey, molasses.	

mas is pork or ham, often accompanied by sauerkraut or red cabbage. In Denmark a goose is preferred.

Dozens of cookies and cakes are prepared for the Christmas season. The cookies are often flavored with ginger and cloves; the Christmas tree may be hung with gingerbread figures. Deep-fried brandy-flavored dough, known as *klejner*, *klener*, or *klenätter*, are also popular. The traditional beverage is *glögg*, a hot alcoholic punch.

Christmas ginger cookies (*pepparkakor*) in Swedish and *pebernødder* in Danish) have become a favorite in Utah. They were brought by Scandinavian Mormon converts and are known as pepper cookies.

Contemporary Food Habits in the United States

ADAPTATION OF FOOD HABITS

The Scandinavians assimilated rapidly into American society, yet their diet did not change significantly. Many of their food habits are similar to the diet of the American majority, such as three large meals a day containing dairy products and animal protein. Since many Scandinavians settled in the Midwest their consumption of fresh seafood declined, but they still eat freshwater fish and prepare dishes from dried salt cod, such as lutefisk.

Scandinavian Americans still eat traditional holiday foods such as rice porridge and lefser. Some Scandinavian foods, such as meatballs and Danish pastries, are commonly eaten by many Americans.

Danish smørrebrød: *Danish* Fontina *and* Havarti *cheeses, ham and salami, are a few of the toppings typical of the open-face sandwiches known in Denmark as* smørrebrød. *(Courtesy Denmark Cheese Association.)*

NUTRITIONAL STATUS

Nutritional Intake and Counseling

Very little has been published on the nutritional status of Americans of Scandinavian descent. It is assumed that since both their traditional diet and the well-accepted typical

Danish Americans in Texas slicing apples, 1915. (Cynthia Thyrsen Preismeyer, Danevang, TX copy from Institute of Texan Cultures at San Antonio.)

American diet is high in cholesterol and fat, Scandinavian Americans may be at increased risk of developing coronary heart disease and other diseases. An in-depth interview should be used to establish the amount and type of foods clients consume.

REFERENCES

Bailey, A. 1969. *The Cooking of the British Isles.* New York: Time-Life Books.

Barer-Stein, T. 1981. *You Eat What You Are: A Study of Ethnic Food Traditions.* Toronto: McClelland & Stewart.

Barron, E. R. 1980. French Canadians. In *Harvard Encyclopedia of American Ethnic Groups.* S. Thernstom (Ed.). Cambridge, MA: Harvard University Press.

Beijbom, U. 1980. Swedes. In *Harvard Encyclopedia of American Ethnic Groups,* S. Thernstom (Ed.) Cambridge, MA: Harvard University Press.

Benkart, P. 1980. Hungarians. In *Harvard Encyclopedia of American Ethnic Groups,* S. Thernstom (Ed.). Cambridge, MA: Harvard University Press.

Berthoff, R. 1980. Welsh. In *Harvard Encyclopedia of American Ethnic Groups.* S. Thernstom (Ed.). Cambridge, MA: Harvard University Press.

Brown, D. 1968. *The Cooking of Scandinavia.* New York: Time-Life Books.

Casas, P. 1983. *The Foods and Wines of Spain.* New York: Knopf.

Cavalli-Sforza, L. T., Strata, A., Barone, A., & Cucrachi, L. 1987. Primary adult lactose malabsorption in Italy: Regional differences in prevalence and relationship to lactose intolerance and milk consumption. *American Journal of Clinical Nutrition 45,* 748–54.

Conzen, K. N. 1980. Germans. In *Harvard Encyclopedia of American Ethnic Groups,* S. Thernstom (Ed.). Cambridge, MA: Harvard University Press.

Crane, B., Christopher, J. B., & Wolff, R. L. 1969. *Civilization in the West.* Englewood Cliffs, NJ: Prentice-Hall.

Donaldson, G. 1980. Scots. In *Harvard Encyclopedia of American Ethnic Groups,* S. Thernstom (Ed.). Cambridge, MA: Harvard University Press.

Douglass, W. A. 1980. Basques. In *Harvard Encyclopedia of American Ethnic Groups.* S. Thernstom (Ed.). Cambridge, MA: Harvard University Press.

Eckstein, E. F. 1983. *Menu Planning* (3rd Ed.). Westport, CT: AVI Publishing.

Erickson, C. J. 1980. English. In *Harvard Encyclopedia of American Ethnic Groups,* S. Thernstom (Ed.). Cambridge, MA: Harvard University Press.

Feibleman, P. S. 1971. *American Cooking: Creole and Acadian.* New York: Time-Life Books.

Feibleman, P. S. 1969. *The Cooking of Spain and Portugal.* New York: Time-Life Books.

Field, M., & Field, F. 1970. *A Quintet of Cuisines.* New York: Time-Life Books.

Fisher, M. F. K. 1969. *The Cooking of Provincial France.* New York: Time-Life Books.

Freeze, K. J. 1980. Czechs. In *Harvard Encyclopedia of American Ethnic Groups,* S. Thernstom (Ed.). Cambridge, MA: Harvard University Press.

Greeley, A. M. 1972. *That Most Distressful Nation: The Taming of the American Irish.* Chicago: Quadrangle Books.

Greene, V. 1980. Poles. In *Harvard Encyclopedia of American Ethnic Groups,* S. Thernstom (Ed.). Cambridge, MA: Harvard University Press.

Hazelton, N. S. 1969. *The Cooking of Germany.* New York: Time-Life Books.

Higonnet, P. L. R. 1980. French. In *Harvard Encyclopedia of American Ethnic Groups,* S. Thernstom (Ed.). Cambridge, MA: Harvard University Press.

Hoglund, A. W. 1980. Finns. In *Harvard Encyclopedia of American Ethnic Groups,* S. Thernstom (Ed.). Cambridge, MA: Harvard University Press.

Jones, M. A. 1980. Scotch-Irish. In *Harvard Encyclopedia of American Ethnic Groups,* S. Thernstom (Ed.). Cambridge, MA: Harvard University Press.

Kinsella, M. 1983. *An Irish Farmhouse Cookbook.* Appletree Press.

Kulesza, W., Rywik, S., Balǎž, V., Budlovsky, I, Marczuk, A. 1984. Prevalence of ischaemic heart disease risk factors in male population aged 45-54 years in Warsaw and Bratislava. *Cor Vasa 26,* 61–71.

Kushi, L. H., Lew, R. A., Stare, F. J., Curtis, R. E., Lozy, M., Bourke, G., Daly, L., Graham, I., Hickey, N., Mulcahy, R., & Kevaney, J. 1985. Diet and 20-year mortality from coronary heart disease: The Ireland–Boston diet–heart study. *New England Journal of Medicine 312,* 811–818.

Le Breton, M. M. 1980. Acadians. In *Harvard Encyclopedia of American Ethnic Groups,* S. Thernstom (Ed.). Cambridge, MA: Harvard University Press.

Leonard, J. N. 1971. *American Cooking: New England.* New York: Time-Life Books.

Magocsi, P. R. 1980. Russians. In *Harvard Encyclopedia of American Ethnic Groups,* S. Thernstom (Ed.). Cambridge, MA: Harvard University Press.

Martin, P. 1981. *The Czech Book: Recipes and Traditions.* Iowa City: Penfield Press.

Munch, P. 1980. Norwegians. In *Harvard Encyclopedia of American Ethnic Groups,* S. Thernstom (Ed.). Cambridge, MA: Harvard University Press.

Nelli, H. S. 1983. *From Immigrants to Ethnics: The Italian American.* Oxford, England: Oxford University Press.

Nelli, H. S. 1980. Italians. In *Harvard Encyclopedia of American Ethnic Groups,* S. Thernstom (Ed.). Cambridge, MA: Harvard University Press.

Pap, L. 1981. *The Portuguese-American.* Boston: Twayne Publishers.

Papashvily, H., & Papashvily, G. 1969. *Russian Cooking.* New York: Time-Life Books.

Parker, A. 1980. Austrians. In *Harvard Encyclopedia of American Ethnic Groups,* S. Thernstom (Ed.). Cambridge, MA: Harvard University Press.

Perl, L. 1965. *Red-Flannel Hash and Shoo-fly Pie.* New York: World Publishing.

Poe, D. M. 1986. *Profile of Portuguese elderly nutrition participants: Demographic characteristics, nutrition knowledge and practices.* Master's Thesis, MGH Institute of Health Professions, Boston, MA.

Rippley, L. V. 1980. Germans from Russia. In *Harvard Encyclopedia of American Ethnic Groups,* S. Thernstom (Ed.). Cambridge, MA: Harvard University Press.

Rogers, A. 1968. *A Basque Story Cook Book.* New York: Scribner's.

Rogers, M. R. 1980. Portuguese. In *Harvard Encyclopedia of American Ethnic Groups,* S. Thernstom (Ed.). Cambridge, MA: Harvard University Press.

Root, W., & De Rochemont, R. 1976. *Eating in America.* New York: Ecco Press.

Root, W. 1966. *The Foods of France.* New York: Vintage Books.

Shenton, J. P., Pellegrini, A. M., Brown, D., & Shenker, I. 1971. *American Cooking: The Melting Pot.* New York: Time-Life Books.

Skårdal, D. B. 1980. Danes. In *Harvard Encyclopedia of American Ethnic Groups,* S. Thernstom (Ed.). Cambridge, MA: Harvard University Press.

Skårdal, D. B. 1974. *The Divided Heart.* Lincoln, NB: University of Nebraska Press.

Stadler, J. 1980. *Genetic component of celiac-sprue.* Presented at the Annual Midwestern Celiac-Sprue Association Conference. Des Moines, IA.

Stolarik, M. M. 1980. Slovaks. In *Harvard Encyclopedia of American Ethnic Groups,* S. Thernstom (Ed.). Cambridge, MA: Harvard University Press.

The US-USSR Steering Committee for Problem Area I: The pathogenesis of atherosclerosis. 1984. Nutrient intake and its association with high-density lipoprotein and low-density lipoprotein cholesterol in selected US-USSR subpopulations. *American Journal of Clinical Nutrition 39,* 942–952.

Visson, L. 1982. *The Complete Russian Cookbook.* Ann Arbor, MI: Ardis.

Wechsberg, J. 1968. *The Cooking of Vienna's Empire.* New York: Time-Life Books.

Wilson, J. 1971. *American Cooking: The Eastern Heartland.* New York: Time-Life Books.

5

BLACK AMERICANS

Black Americans are the largest cultural group in the United States, including nearly 28 million people, almost 12 percent of the total American population. The majority came originally from West Africa, although some have immigrated from the Caribbean and, more recently, from the famine-stricken East African nations.

Black Americans are the only U.S. citizens whose ancestors came by force, not choice. Their long history in America has been characterized by persecution and segregation. At the same time, blacks have contributed greatly to the development of American culture. The languages, music, arts, and cuisine of West Africa have mingled with European influences since the beginnings of the nation to create a unique American cultural mix.

Black Americans live with this difficult dichotomy. They are in many ways a part of the majority culture, because of their early arrival, their large population, and their role in the development of the country. Much of their native West African heritage has been assimilated and their cultural identity results more from their residence in the United States than from their countries of origin. Yet they are often more alienated from American society than other groups.

This chapter discusses black American contributions to U.S. foods and food habits. The historical influence of West African, black slave, and Southern cuisines on current black cuisine is examined.

Traditional black American foods: Some foods typical of the southern black American diet include bacon, black-eyed peas, chayote *squash,* corn, *greens, ham hocks, hot sauce, okra, peanuts, watermelon, and yams.* (Photo by Laurie Macfee.)

CULTURAL PERSPECTIVE

History of West Africa

West Africa borders the Atlantic ocean and includes twenty-five nations south of the Sahara desert from Mauritania in the West, to Angola in the Southwest. Dense equatorial forests and tropical savannas are common through most of the region, although deserts in the northern areas are spreading rapidly.

EARLY CULTURAL CENTERS

Knowledge of early West African history is fragmentary. Archaeological remains of prehistoric cultures in the region indicate that the people lived as hunter-gatherers and produced the most skilled stonework on the continent at that time, which included the development of projectile points. Villages based on an agrarian existence probably didn't spread from North Africa into the area until the Sahara became a desert, around 2500 B.C.

The earliest West African states are thought to have developed next to trade routes established by the Egyptians. The first ruling Kingdom was ancient Ghana, 3rd century A.D., followed by the Mali and Songhai states in the early eleventh century.

ISLAM INFLUENCE

North African traders introduced the Islamic religion to West Africa, where it became widely accepted. Songhai converted to Islam in A.D. 1010, followed by Mali and Ghana. The combined African and Muslim societies resulted in the rise of the Gao, Hausa states, and Kanem-Bornu empires, which, along with Mali, dominated West Africa from the twelfth through sixteenth centuries. Their trade economy was based on gold, slaves, and ivory, which they exchanged for cloth, tools, and weapons. As a result of the trading, a large middle class of merchants evolved during this period.

EUROPEAN DOMINATION

The first European explorers to reach West Africa came from Portugal in the fifteenth century seeking gold and spreading Christianity. Early European settlements in the sixteenth and seventeenth centuries were trade posts in the coastal areas where local Africans would provide them with slaves from the interior regions. With the abolition of slavery in the mid-nineteenth century, the scramble for African natural resources began, and by the early 1900s, most of West Africa was claimed by Belgium, Britain, France, Germany, Italy, Portugal, and Spain. Only Liberia, founded in 1847 by freed black American slaves, remained independent.

INDEPENDENCE

The economic and political changes resulting from World War I, the depression of the 1930s, and World War II, weakened European control over West Africa. Pressure for African representation in their own government increased and was gradually permitted by the Europeans. These African representatives formed movements toward nationalism throughout West Africa. Ghana, formally called the Gold Coast, was the first to achieve independence from Britain in 1957 and

Angola was the last nation to form, when Portugal relinquished control in 1975. Nationhood has not meant economic independence nor political stability in most countries. Even today, frequent changes in government, civil wars, boundary disputes, and poverty are common.

History of Immigration to the United States

The arrival of black indentured servants taken forcefully from West Africa precedes the arrival of the *Mayflower* in America. In 1619, Dutch traders sold 20 West Africans to colonists in Jamestown, an early English settlement. Over 425,000 slaves were subsequently imported legally, ancestors of the majority of black Americans residing in the United States today.

WEST AFRICAN ORIGINS

The institution of slavery was well-established before the first blacks were brought to North America. European slave traders negotiated with West African slave suppliers for their human cargo. Which West Africans became slaves and which sold slaves depended on intertribal conditions.

The European traders kept some records of tribal affiliation, but none of place of origin. It is believed that over half the slaves in the United States came from the coastal areas of what are now Angola and Nigeria. Others came from the regions that are today Senegal, Gambia, Sierra Leone, Liberia, Togo, Ghana, Benin, Gabon, and Zaire. These political identities are relatively recent, however, and the slaves identified with their tribal groups, such as the Ashanti, Bambara, Fulani, Ibo, Malinke, or Yoruba, rather than with a specific country or Africa as a whole.

ENSLAVEMENT

The tribal villages of West Africa were predominantly agricultural. Individuals viewed their existence in relation to the physical and social needs of the group. The extended family and religion were the foundations of tribal culture. It was especially difficult for individuals to be separated from their tribe, because identity was so closely associated with the group.

It is perhaps for this reason that enslaved individuals held on tenaciously to their African traditions. It is thought that African language, ornamentation (such as scarification and

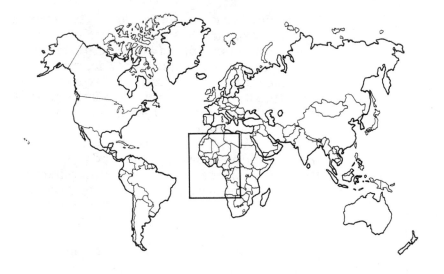

West Africa.

teeth filing), and other traditions were threatening to slave owners. New slaves, usually in small groups from eight to thirty, were often housed at the perimeter of plantations until they became acclimated. They learned English in two or three years through contact with white or Native American indentured servants. When they became sufficiently acculturated, they would be allowed to work in positions closer to the main plantation house.

This initial period of separation allowed slaves to maintain many cultural values despite exposure to slaves from other tribal groups, indentured servants of different ethnic groups, and the majority culture of the white owners. At the same time, frontier farming was sufficiently difficult that slave owners were quite willing to learn from the slaves' agricultural expertise; therefore, intercultural communication was inevitable. Instead of becoming totally acculturated to the ways of the owners, a black Creole, or native-born, culture developed during the early slave period, combining both white and West African influences.

After the end of slave importation in 1807, the black Creole population swelled. By law, slavery was a life-long condition; the children of female slaves were slaves as well. Although most slaves worked on farms and on cotton, tobacco, sugar, rice, and hemp plantations, many others worked in mines and on the railroads. A large number of slaves were found in the cities, doing manual labor and service jobs. It was during this period of rapid growth in the black population that separate racial group identities began to form.

EMANCIPATION

The movement to free the slaves began with the American Revolution. Many of the Northern states banned slavery from the beginning of independence. By the 1830s, there were 300,000 "free persons of color" living in urban areas outside of the Deep South. Tensions between states that supported slavery (the Confederacy) and those that opposed it (the Union) was one factor that led to the Civil War (called the War between the States in the South) in 1861.

In 1862, President Lincoln signed the Emancipation Proclamation. Union victory over the Confederacy gave all blacks living in the United States their freedom in 1865. Some left the South immediately, searching for relatives and a better life. However, most remained in the South, because they lacked the skills needed to begin an independent life; for instance, fewer than 2 percent of former slaves were literate.

After emancipation, former slave owners continued to exploit black labor through tenant farming and sharecropping. Under this system, the black farmer was perpetually in debt to the white landowner. Slowly, as competition for skilled farm labor increased, work conditions for black Americans in the South improved. Literacy rates and political representation increased. At the same time, racial persecution by white supremacists, such as members of the Ku Klux Klan, became more frequent.

At the turn of the twentieth century, depressed conditions in the South and industrial job opportunities in the North prompted over 750,000 black Americans to settle in the Northeast and Midwest. Most were young men, and the majority moved to large metropolitan areas, such as New York, Boston, Chicago, and Philadelphia. The influx of southern blacks was resented by both whites and the small numbers of middle-class blacks who had been well accepted in the northern cities. Laws that established racial segregation were enacted for the first time in the early 1900s, resulting in inner-city black ghettos.

Because of poor economic conditions throughout the country, there was a pause in the black migration north during the Great Depression. The flow increased in the 1940s, and in the following 30 years over 4 million black Americans left the South to settle in other regions of the country. This migration resulted in more than a change in regional demographics. It meant a change from a slow-paced rural lifestyle to a fast-paced, high-pressured, urban industrial existence.

In the 1960s, the movement against the injustices of "separate but equal" laws (which permitted segregation as long as comparable facilities, such as schools, were provided for black Americans) gained momentum under the leadership of blacks such as Martin Luther King, Jr. Violent riots in city ghettos underscored the need for social reform. Civil rights activism resulted in the repeal of many overtly racist practices and passage of compensatory laws and regulations meant to reverse past discrimination, as typified by federal affirmative action requirements.

CURRENT DEMOGRAPHICS

Today, over half of black Americans live in the South, yet according to the 1980 U.S. census fewer than 15 percent live in rural areas. The remaining black population is found predominantly in northeastern and midwestern urban areas. Less than 1 percent of the black population is of Caribbean descent, and even fewer are recent immigrants from Africa.

SOCIOECONOMIC STATUS

Black Americans continue to suffer from the discriminatory practices that began with their enslavement. Their unemployment rate is more than double that of whites; both average income and educational attainment are substantially lower than for whites. In 1985, nearly one-third (31.3%) of black American families lived below the poverty line, and life expectancy for black American males is lower than for any other group in the United States, because of the social problems found in many black communities.

Many blacks feel they are not completely accepted in American society. Blacks isolated in urban ghettos often experience alienation. Frustration, hopelessness, and hostility often result. At the same time, discrimination has promoted ethnic identity amongst blacks, due in part to a shared history of persecution. Although blacks in the United States are geographically, politically, and socioeconomically diverse, there is a strong feeling of ethnic unity, as demonstrated by the black pride movement of recent years.

BLACK AMERICAN ORGANIZATIONS

The major black organizations have been formed to combat racism. They include the National Association for the Advancement of Colored People (NAACP), founded in 1909; the National Urban League, founded in 1911; the Congress of Racial Equality (CORE), which began protest activities in the 1940s; and the Southern Christian Leadership Conference, led by Martin Luther King, Jr., from its beginning in 1957 to his death in 1968. Other black American organizations active today were formed when blacks were barred from joining professional associations, such as the National Medical Association and the National Dental Association.

Worldview

RELIGION

Spirituality was integral to West African tribal society, and indigenous religious affiliations were maintained by slaves despite attempts to convert blacks to Christianity. It was only after American religious groups became involved in the anti-slavery movement that the black Creole community responded with large numbers of conversions.

Religion is as essential to black culture today as it was to the West African society. For many black Americans, the church represents a sanctuary from the trials of daily life. It is a place to meet with other blacks, to share fellowship and hope. Most follow Protestant or fundamentalist religions, although a small percentage are orthodox Muslims who are members of the sect known as the World Community of Al-Islam (see Chapter 2).

FAMILY

The importance of the extended family to black Americans has been maintained since tribal times. It was kinship that defined the form of West African societies. During the early slave period the proportion of men to women was two to one, and the family structure included many unrelated members. As the black Creole population increased, nuclear families were established but often disrupted by the sale or loan of a parent. The extended family provided for dislocated parents and children.

Today, the majority of black American families are headed by women: More than half of black children are born to single mothers and nearly half of those to teenage girls. The family network often includes grandparents, aunts, uncles, sisters, brothers, deacons or preachers, and friends. Such extended kinship still supports and protects individuals, especially children, from the problems of a discriminatory society. The extended family has been found to be equally valued by both wealthy and poor black Americans.

TRADITIONAL FOOD HABITS

What are traditional black foods—foods of West Africans in the seventeenth and eighteenth centuries, foods of the slaves, or foods of the black South since emancipation? Black American cuisine today includes some elements from each of these diets.

TABLE 5.1. Cultural Food Groups: Black American (Southern United States)

Group	Comments
PROTEIN FOODS	
Milk/milk products	Dairy products uncommon in diet (incidence of lactose intolerance estimated at 60–95 percent of the population).
	Milk widely disliked in some studies; well-accepted in others.
	Few cheeses or fermented dairy products eaten.
Meats/poultry/fish/eggs/legumes	Pork most popular, especially variety cuts; fish, small game, poultry also common; veal and lamb infrequently eaten.
	Bean dishes popular.
	Frying, boiling most common preparation methods; stewed dishes preferred thick and "sticky."
	Protein intake high.
CEREALS/GRAINS	Corn primary grain product; wheat flour used in many baked goods.
	Rice used in stew-type dishes.
FRUITS/VEGETABLES	Green leafy vegetables most popular, cooked with ham, salt pork, or bacon, lemon and hot sauce; broth *(pot likker)* also eaten.
	Intake of fresh fruits and vegetables low.
ADDITIONAL FOODS	
Seasonings	Dishes frequently seasoned with hot-pepper sauces.
	Onions and green pepper common flavoring ingredients.
Beverages	
Nuts/seeds	
Fats/oils	

Common Foods	Regional Adaptations in the United States
Milk (consumed mostly in desserts, such as puddings and ice cream), some buttermilk; cheese.	Blacks in urban areas may drink milk more often than rural blacks.
Meat: beef, pork *(chitterlings,* intestines, ham hocks, sausages, variety cuts). *Poultry:* chicken, turkey. *Fish and shellfish:* catfish, crab, crayfish, perch, red snapper, salmon, sardines, shrimp, tuna. *Small game:* frogs, opossum, raccoon, squirrel, turtle. *Eggs:* chicken. *Legumes:* black-eyed peas, kidney beans, peanuts (and peanut butter), pinto beans, red beans.	Pork remains primary protein source; prepackaged sausages and lunch meats popular. Small game rarely consumed. Variety cuts considered to be *soul food* and eaten regardless of socioeconomic status or region. Frying still popular, but more often at evening meal; boiling and baking second most common preparation methods.
Biscuits; corn (corn breads, grits, hominy); pasta; rice.	Store-bought breads often replace biscuits (toasted at breakfast, used for sandwiches at lunch). Cookies (and candy) preferred snacks.
Fruits: apples, bananas, berries, peaches, watermelon. *Vegetables:* beets, broccoli, cabbage, corn, greens (chard, collard, kale, mustard, pokeweed, turnip, etc.), green peas, okra, potatoes, spinach, squash, sweet potatoes, tomatoes, yams.	Fruits eaten according to availability and preference; intake remains low. Green leafy vegetables *(greens),* popular in all regions; other vegetables eaten according to availability and preference, intake remains low.
Filé (sassafras powder), garlic, green peppers, hot-pepper sauce, ham hocks, salt pork or bacon (added to vegetables and stews), lemon juice, onions, salt, pepper. Coffee, fruit drinks, fruit juice, fruit wine, soft drinks, tea. Peanuts, pecans, sesame seeds, walnuts. Butter, lard, meat drippings, vegetable shortening.	

Ingredients and Common Foods

HISTORICAL INFLUENCES

Black foods offer a unique glimpse into the way that a cuisine develops. Even before they were brought to the United States, the food habits of West Africans had changed significantly by the introduction of New World foods, such as cassava *(Manihot esculenta,* a tuber that is also called manioc), chilis, peanuts, pumpkins, and tomatoes, during the fifteenth and sixteenth centuries. The slaves brought a cuisine based on these new foods and native West African foods, such as watermelon, black-eyed peas, okra, sesame, and taro. Adaptations and substitutions were made based on what foods were available. Black cooks added their West African preparation methods to British, French, Spanish, and Native American techniques to produce American Southern cuisine, emphasizing fried, boiled, and roasted dishes using pork, pork fat, corn, sweet potatoes, and local green leafy vegetables.

West African Foods

Knowledge of West African food habits before the nineteenth century is incomplete. It is mostly based on the records of North African, European, and American traders, many of whom considered the local cuisine unhealthy. Most West Africans during the slave era lived in preliterate, agriculturally based tribal groups. There was a heavy dependence on locally grown foods, although some items, such as salt and fish (usually salt-cured), could be traded at the daily markets held through each region.

The staple foods varied in each locality. Corn, millet, and rice were used in the coastal areas and Sierra Leone. Yams were popular in Nigeria (where they are traditionally boiled and pounded into a paste called *fufu).* Cassava (often roasted and ground into a flour known as *gari)* and plantains were the staple foods of the more southern areas of the Congo and Angola. The arid savannah region of West Africa bordering the Sahara desert was too dry for cultivation, so most tribes were pastoral, herding camels, sheep, goats, and cattle. In the north, these animals were eaten; in other regions, local fish and game were eaten. Chickens were also raised, although in many tribes the eggs were frequently traded, not eaten, and the chicken itself was served only as a special dish

Almost every country in West Africa has its own version of hearty *Jollof rice,* believed to be named for the Wolof tribe of Gambia. The rice, seasoned with palm oil, tomato paste, hot peppers, onions, garlic, thyme, and lemon, is topped with chicken and other meats and legumes as well as vegetables typical of the region, such as eggplant, pumpkin, and local leafy green vegetables.

A six-day week is used in many parts of West Africa and is named by many tribes for the regional market that occurs on each day.

Taboos against eating eggs still exist in some regions of West Africa, including the beliefs that they cause difficult childbirth and that they excite children.

A woman in Ghana prepares a meal with the help of her daughter. (Photo by P. Almasy.)

for company. Chicken is still considered a prestigious meat in many tribes.

There were many similarities in tribal cuisine throughout West Africa. Most foods were boiled or fried, then small chunks were dipped in a sauce and eaten by hand. Palm oil was the predominant fat used in cooking, giving many dishes a red hue. Peanut oil, shea oil (from the nuts of the African shea tree), and occasionally coconut oil were used in some regions. The addition of tomatoes, hot peppers, and onions as seasoning was so common that these items were simply referred to as "the ingredients." Most dishes were preferred spicy, thick, and "sticky" (mucilaginous).

Legumes were popular throughout West Africa. Peanuts were especially valued and were eaten raw, boiled, roasted, or ground into meal, flour or paste. Cow peas (*Vigna unguiculata,* neither a standard pea or bean; black-eyed peas are one type of cow pea) were eaten as a substitute for meat, often combined with a staple starch such as corn, yams, or rice. *Bambara groundnuts,* similar to peanuts, were also common. Nuts and seeds were frequently used to flavor and thicken sauces. *Agobono* (or *apon*) *seeds,* cashews, *egusi* (wa-

Okra, when sliced, releases a sticky, milky substance (made mostly of carbohydrate) that thickens liquids and produces a mucilaginous texture in soups, stews, and sauces.

Cow peas were so named by the southern slave owners because they were considered useful only as animal fodder. By the turn of the twentieth century, they were well accepted as human food throughout the South.

Kola nuts are a bitter nut that has twice the caffeine content of coffee. The original recipe for Coca-Cola, invented in 1886, included extracts from cocoa leaves ("coca") and Kola nuts ("cola").

termelon seeds, usually dried and ground), *kola nuts,* and sesame seeds were popular.

A great variety of tropical and subtropical fruits and vegetables were available to the West Africans, but only a few were widely eaten. *Akee* apples, *baobab* (fruit of the baobab tree), guava, lemon, papaya (also called *pawpaw*), pineapple, and watermelon were the most common fruits. Many dishes included coconut milk. In addition to starchy staple roots and the flavoring ingredients of onions, hot peppers, and tomatoes, the most popular vegetables were eggplant, okra, pumpkin, and the leaves from plants such as cassava, sweet potato, and taro (also called *callaloo* or *cocoyam*).

Black Slave Foods

When West African blacks were forcefully taken from their tribes, they were not immediately separated from their accustomed foods. Although conditions on the slave ships were appalling, most slave traders did provide a traditional diet for the tribal members on board. The basic staples of each region, plus salt cod (which was familiar to most West Africans), were fed to the slaves in minimal quantities. Hot peppers were used for seasoning because they were believed to prevent dysentery. It wasn't until the blacks were sold in America that significant changes in their cuisine occurred.

The diet of the field workers was largely dependent on whatever foods the slave owners provided. Salt pork and corn were the most common items. Sometimes rice (instead of corn), salted fish, and molasses were included. Greens, legumes, milk, and sweet potatoes were occasionally added. The foods provided, as well as their amount, were usually contingent upon local availability and agricultural surplus. Hunger was common among the slaves.

A black slave folktale describes the land of Diddy-Wah-Diddy, where roast hogs and chickens run about calling "Eat me!" and there are fritter ponds of oil.

Some slave owners allowed or required their slaves to maintain garden plots or to plant needed vegetables around the periphery of the cotton or tobacco fields. Okra and cow peas from Africa were favored, as well as American cabbage, collard and mustard greens, sweet potatoes, and turnips. Herbs were collected from the surrounding woodlands, and small animals such as opossums, rabbits, raccoons, squirrels, and an occasional wild pig were trapped for supplementary meat. Children would often catch catfish and other freshwater fish.

During the hog slaughtering season in the fall, variety pork cuts, such as *chitterlings* (intestines, also called *chitlins*), *maw* (stomach lining), and hocks, would sometimes be given to slaves. Some slaves were encouraged to raise hogs and chickens. The eggs and the primary pork cuts were usually sold to raise cash for the purchase of luxury foods. Chickens, a prestigious food in West Africa, continued to be reserved for special occasions.

West African cooking methods were adapted to slave conditions. Boiling and frying remained the most popular ways to prepare not only meats but also vegetables and legumes. Bean stews maintained popularity as main dishes. Corn replaced the West African regional staple starches and was prepared in many forms, primarily as cornmeal pudding, *grits* (coarsely ground cornmeal), and *hominy* (hulled, dried corn kernels with the bran and germ removed). Pork fat (lard) replaced palm oil in cooking and was used to fry or flavor everything from breads to greens. Hot-pepper sauces replaced fresh peppers for seasoning. No substitutions were available for the nuts and seeds used in West African recipes, although peanuts remained popular.

Food for the slave field workers had to be portable. One-dish vegetable stews were common, as were fried cakes, such as corn or sweet potato *pone*, and cornmeal cakes baked in the fire on the back of a hoe, called hoecakes. Meals prepared at home after a full day of labor were usually simple.

The black slaves who cooked in the homes of slave owners enjoyed a much more ample and varied diet. They popularized fried chicken and fried fish. They introduced "sticky" vegetable-based stews (thickened with okra or the herb sassafras, which when ground is called *filé* powder), such as the Southern specialty *gumbo z'herbes*, which is nearly identical to a recipe from the Congo. Green leafy vegetables, simply called *greens*, became a separate dish, instead of being added to stews, but they were still cooked for hours and flavored with meat. Ingredients familiar to West Africans were used for pie fillings, such as nuts, beans, and squash.

Foods after Abolition of Slavery

The food traditions of blacks did not change significantly after emancipation, and they differed little from those of white farmers of similar socioeconomic status. One exception was that pork variety cuts and salt pork remained the primary meats for blacks, while whites switched to beef during this period.

In the years following emancipation, chickens were called "preacher's birds" because they were so often served to the preacher when he came for Sunday supper.

Agricultural scientist George Washington Carver conducted extensive culinary experiments with peanuts. He claimed to have discovered over 105 ways of preparing them. He is frequently credited with the discovery of peanut oil and peanut butter, although both had been made in West Africa for centuries before his find.

The nutritional results of such a limited diet were seen in the many cases of pellagra, beri-beri, and "sore-mouth" among the black slaves, caused by deficiencies in vitamin A and many of the B vitamins. Malnourishment also left blacks vulnerable to malaria, yellow fever, cholera, and other diseases common in the southern states.

The phrase "living high on the hog" comes from the post-abolition period, meaning that a family was wealthy enough to eat the primary pork cuts, such as chops and ham.

Black woman feeding white child, circa 1880. (Courtesy Natchez Photographs. Louisiana and Lower Mississippi Valley Collections, LSU Libraries, Louisiana State University.)

STAPLES

The traditional southern black diet that evolved from West African, slave, and post-abolition foods and food habits emphasizes texture before flavor; the West African preference for "sticky" foods continues. Pork, pork products, corn, and greens are still staples. The Cultural Food Groups table (Table 5.1) lists other common southern black foods. (For information regarding the food habits of blacks from the Caribbean, see Chapter 6.)

Pork variety cuts of all types are used. Pig's feet (or knuckles) are eaten roasted or pickled; pig's ears are slowly cooked in water seasoned with herbs and vinegar and then served with gravy. Chitterlings are usually fried, sometimes boiled. Sausages and *head cheese* (a seasoned loaf of meat from the pig's head) make use of smaller pork pieces. Barbecued pork is also common. A whole pig, or just the ribs, are slowly roasted over the fire. Each family has its own recipe for spicy sauce and each has its opinion about whether the pork should be basted in the sauce or the sauce should be ladled over the cooked meat.

Other meats, such as poultry, are also popular. Occasionally the small game that was prevalent during the slave period, such as opossum and raccoon, is eaten. More often the meal includes local fish and shellfish, such as catfish, crab, or crawfish. Frog's legs and turtle are popular in some areas. Meats, poultry, and fish are often combined in thick stews and soups, such as *gumbos* (still made sticky with okra or filé powder), that are eaten with rice. They may also be coated with cornmeal and deep-fried in lard, as in southern-fried chicken and catfish.

The vegetables most characteristic of southern black cuisine are the many varieties of greens. Food was scarce during the Civil War, and most southerners were forced to experiment with indigenous vegetation, in addition to cultivated greens such as chard, collard greens, kale, mustard greens, spinach, and turnip greens. Dockweed, dandelion greens, lamb's quarter, marsh marigold leaves, milkweed, pigweed, pokeweed, and purslane were added as acceptable vegetables. Traditionally, the greens are cooked in water flavored with salt pork, fatback, bacon, or ham, plus hot peppers and lemon. As the water evaporates, the flavors intensify, resulting in a broth called *pot likker*. Both the greens and the liquid are served; hot sauce is offered for those who prefer a spicier dish.

Other common vegetables include black-eyed peas, okra, peas, and tomatoes. Onions and green peppers are frequently used for flavoring. Corn and corn products are as popular in southern black cuisine today as they were during the slave

Fried catfish sandwich.

period. Cornbread and fried hominy are served sliced with butter. Wheat-flour biscuits are also served with butter, or, in some regions, gravy. Dumplings are sometimes added to stews and greens.

Squash is eaten as a vegetable (sometimes stuffed) and as a dessert pie sweetened with molasses. Sweet potatoes are also used both ways. Other common desserts include bread pie (bread pudding), crumb cake, chocolate or caramel cake, fruit cobblers, puddings, and shortcake, as well as sesame seed cookies and candies.

Meal Composition and Cycle

DAILY PATTERNS

Two meals a day were typical in West Africa, one late in the morning and one in the evening. Snacking was common; in poorer tribes snacks would replace the morning meal and only dinner would be served. Food was served family style or, more formally, the men would be served first, then the boys, then the girls, and last, the women. Sometimes men would gather together for a meal without women. Meal times were solemn; people concentrated on the attributes of the food and conversation was minimal.

The West African tradition of frequent snacking continued through the slave period and after emancipation. Meals were often irregular, perhaps due to the variable hours of agricultural labor.

The traditional southern-style meal pattern was adopted as economic conditions for both blacks and whites improved. Breakfast was typically large and leisurely, always including boiled grits and home-made biscuits. In addition, eggs, ham or bacon, and even fried sweet potatoes would be served. Coffee and tea were more common beverages than milk or juice.

Lunch, called dinner, was the main meal of the day. It was eaten at midafternoon and featured a boiled entree, such as legumes or greens with ham, or another stew-type dish. Additional vegetables or a salad may have been served, as well as potatoes and bread or biscuits. Dessert was mandatory and was usually a baked item, not simply fruit. In some homes, a full supper, including meat, vegetables, and potatoes was served in the evening. Poorer agricultural families often ate only two of these hearty meals a day.

Traditionally, black Americans in the South believed that heavy meals would stay with a person. Light meals were considered appropriate for infants and invalids, but were not thought to be a real meal for a healthy individual.

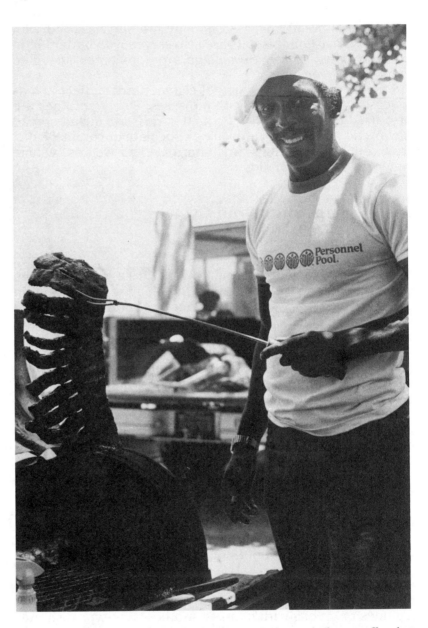

Barbecued ribs at a Juneteenth celebration: Barbecued ribs are offered at this traditional black festival celebrating the emancipation of the slaves.

Today, few southern blacks, or whites, continue this traditional meal pattern in full. The southern-style breakfast might be served just on weekends or holidays, for example. As in the rest of the country, a light lunch has replaced the large dinner on most days, and supper has become the main meal.

SPECIAL OCCASIONS

Sunday dinner had become a large family meal during the slave period, and it continued to be the main meal of the week after emancipation. It was a time to eat and share favorite foods with friends and kin, a time to extend hospitality to neighbors.

Many southern blacks still enjoy a large Sunday dinner. It is usually prepared by the mother of the house, beginning in the early morning. The menu would probably include fried chicken, spareribs, chitterlings, pig's feet (or ears or tail), black-eyed peas or okra, corn, cornbread, greens, potato salad, rice, sweet potato pie, and watermelon. Home-made fruit wines, such as strawberry wine, might also be offered.

Other holiday meals, especially Christmas, feature menus similar to the Sunday meal, but with added dishes and even greater amounts of food. Turkey with cornbread stuffing and baked ham are often the entrees; other vegetable dishes, such as corn pudding, sweet peas, and salads, are typical accompaniments. A profusion of baked goods, including yeast rolls, fruit cakes, pies, and chocolate, caramel, and coconut cake would round out the meal.

Southern black cuisine is particularly well suited to buffet meals and parties. A pan of gumbo, a pot of beans, or a side of barbecued ribs can be stretched to feed many people on festive occasions. Informal parties to celebrate a birthday, or just the fact that it's Saturday night, are still common.

Role of Food in Black Society

Food was central to West African village life. Human fertility, crop fertility, and spiritualism were often interlinked. Many tribes existed at subsistence level yet were generous in sharing available food among tribal members.

In the American South, food has traditionally been a catalyst for social interaction, and southern hospitality is reknowned. Food is lovingly prepared for family and friends. The sharing of food is considered an important factor in the cohesiveness of southern black society.

"Juneteenth" celebrations are held in many black American communities each year with traditional southern cooking commemorating emancipation of the slaves.

Black-eyed peas are eaten on New Year's day in both black and white homes throughout the South to bring a year of good fortune.

In the Dan tribe of Liberia and Ivory Coast, special *wunkirle* spoons in a symbolically female shape are presented to the most generous woman in the village.

West African wunkirle *spoon.* (Private collection with permission.)

Therapeutic Uses of Food

Numerous beliefs about the health implications of certain foods are common among poor black Americans living in the rural South. Some of these dietary concepts were brought to other regions of country during the great migrations.

The conditions known as "high" and "low" blood are one example. High blood (often confused with a diagnosis of high blood pressure) is thought to be caused by excess blood that migrates to one part of the body, typically the head, and is caused by eating excessive amounts of "rich" foods or foods that are red in color (beets, carrots, grape juice, red wine, and red meat, especially pork). Low blood, associated with anemia, is believed to be caused by eating too many astringent and acidic foods (vinegar, lemon juice, garlic, and pickled foods) and not enough red meat.

Some black Americans believe that a mixture of figs and honey will eliminate ringworm and that goat's milk and cabbage juice will cure a stomach infection. In remote rural areas, foods and drinks may be considered the best way to administer a hex. In other areas, eggs and milk may be withheld from sick children to aid in their recovery.

Pica, the practice of eating nonnutritive substances such as clay, chalk, and laundry starch, is one of the most perplexing of all black American food habits. Studies conducted between the 1950s and 1970s determined that pica is most often practiced by black women during pregnancy and the postpartum period (information on pica among other ethnic groups or age groups in the U.S. is limited). It is common in the South, where anywhere from 16 to 57 percent of pregnant black women admit to pica. But pica is also found in other areas of the country where there are large populations of poor blacks. In rural regions, the substance ingested is usually clay. In urban areas, laundry starch is often the first choice, although instances of people who ate large amounts of milk of magnesia, coffee grounds, plaster, ice, and paraffin have also been reported. Many theories about the reasons for pica have been suggested: a nutritional need for minerals, hunger or nausea, a desire for special treatment, and cultural tradition are the most common hypotheses. Reasons for pica reported by rural and urban black women include a craving for clay, and the belief that clay prevents birthmarks or that starch makes the skin of the baby lighter and helps the baby to slip out during delivery (Hunter, 1973).

Geophagy, or clay-eating, is a common practice among men, women and children in West Africa. It is done to alleviate hunger, to soothe the irritation caused by intestinal parasites, for spiritual purposes in connection with the swearing of oaths, and for medical reasons. Active trade in clay processed into tablets and disks can be found at some markets.

CONTEMPORARY FOOD HABITS

Most researchers have noted that the food habits of black Americans today usually reflect their current socioeconomic status, geographic location, and work schedule more than their West African or southern heritage. Even in the South, many traditional foods and meal patterns have been rejected because of the pressures of a fast-paced society.

Adaptation of Food Habits

INGREDIENTS AND COMMON FOODS

Food preferences do not vary greatly between blacks and whites in similar socioeconomic groups living in the same region of the United States. Comparisons show that blacks choose items such as fried chicken, barbecued ribs, corn bread, sweet potato pie, collard greens, and fruit-flavored drinks and juices as favorite foods more often than whites do. In addition, cookies or candy are preferred snack items (versus soft drinks for whites). Black households purchase cereal and bakery products, dairy products, sugar, and other sweets less often than white households, however.

The popularity of *soul food* is notable, considering the similarities between black and white diets. Traditional southern black cuisine was named soul food in the 1960s. Black Americans adopted this cuisine as a symbol of ethnic solidarity, regardless of region or social class. Today, soul food serves as an emblem of identity and a recognition of black history for many black Americans.

MEAL COMPOSITION AND CYCLE

While the ingredients and common foods that black Americans eat reflect geographic location and socioeconomic status, meal composition and cycle have changed more in response to work habits than to other lifestyle factors.

The traditional southern meal pattern of the large breakfast with fried foods, followed by the large dinner with boiled foods and a hearty supper, has given way to the pressures of industrial job schedules. One study (Jerome, 1969) showed that people maintain southern breakfast habits for only eighteen months after migration to the North before they replace them with a meal typically consisting of biscuits or toast, sausage, and coffee. Blacks throughout the country now eat lighter breakfasts and sandwiches at a noontime lunch. Dinner is served after work, and it has become the biggest meal of the day. Snacking throughout the day is still typical among most black Americans. In many households, meal schedules are irregular and family members eat when convenient. It is not unusual for snacks to replace a full meal.

Frying is still one of the most popular methods of preparing food. An increase in consumption of fried dinner items suggests that the traditional method of making breakfast foods has been transferred to evening foods (which were traditionally boiled) when time constraints prevent a large morning meal (Jerome, 1969). Boiling and baking are second to frying in popularity (Wheeler & Haider, 1979). Blacks use convenience foods and fast foods as income permits.

Nutritional Status

The nutritional status of black Americans is difficult to characterize because only a limited number of studies have addressed this population. Most research has shown that black Americans' nutritional intake is associated with socioeconomic status. Poor families of any ethnic group often depend on subsidies such as food stamps, school breakfast and lunch programs, and emergency food programs.

NUTRITIONAL INTAKE

Nutrient deficiencies are prevalent among the large number of black families at or near poverty levels in the United States. The most frequent insufficiencies are of calories, iron, and calcium. There is some question, however, regarding required iron and calcium intake for blacks, based on evidence that blacks have lower hemoglobin levels independent of iron intake and a substantially lower risk of osteoporosis than whites (Kumanyika & Helitzer, 1985). Deficiencies in vitamins A, D, E, C, B-6, niacin, folacin, pantothenic acid, magnesium, and zinc have also been reported. The nutrient density of the diet of poor urban blacks was found to be greater than that of the diet of whites of similar socioeconomic status, suggesting that some nutritional deficiencies may be caused by insufficient food intake, not poor diet (Emmons, 1986). Additionally, laxative use is common and may be a factor in nutritional status.

Many black Americans' diets are low in fruits, vegetables, and whole-grain products, indicating a low intake of fiber. Even as income increases, fresh produce is ignored in favor of increased expenditure on meat and other protein foods. The percentage of calories from animal proteins for blacks is consistently greater than for whites. Sodium intake may be high if convenience foods and fast foods are frequently eaten.

Poor diet, the large number of teenage pregnancies, and inadequate prenatal care result in a greater incidence of prematurity and low-birthweight infants among black Americans than among whites. In 1983, nearly 13 percent of black babies weighed less than 2,500 grams, more than double the percentage for whites. Morbidity and mortality rates for black mothers and their infants are also disproportionately high, due in part to nutritional deficiencies caused by low socioeconomic status.

Black American mothers breastfeed their infants at a lower rate than white mothers. In 1980, 25 percent of blacks breastfed exclusively, compared to 51 percent of whites. Blacks also differ somewhat from whites in what solid foods they feed infants. One study showed that high-sodium foods were more frequently offered to black children than to white children (Schaefer & Kumanyika, 1985).

Obesity is a common problem for black Americans in ado-

It is estimated that 60 percent to 95 percent of adult black Americans are lactose intolerant. Most studies have shown that milk is widely disliked and avoided. Others have noted that milk is consumed by blacks nearly as frequently as by whites.

lescence and adulthood. It is estimated that 48 percent of black women and 30 percent of black men are overweight (compared to 26 percent of white women and 25 percent of white men). Excess weight gain may be attributable to many factors, including socioeconomic status, poor eating habits, genetic predisposition, and a more permissive attitude regarding obesity (Kumanyika, 1987).

Associated with obesity is a high rate of diabetes among blacks, affecting approximately 20 percent of the population. This is three to four times the incidence in the total U.S. population. A higher rate of death due to the disease has also been reported among blacks.

Hypertension is a leading health problem for black Americans. Their incidence of high blood pressure, approximately 28 percent for men and 24 percent for women, is nearly twice that for the white population. Although statistics on the ratio of normotensives to hypertensives by ethnic group are limited, the data suggest that blacks have the highest proportion of hypertensives of any group. Race, obesity, high sodium intake, low potassium intake (due to inadequate consumption of fruits and vegetables), and the pressures of low socioeconomic status may all be contributing factors.

Rates of iron deficiency anemia among black Americans are significantly higher than for whites at every age, regardless of sex or income level, ranging from a low of about 5 percent of 45-to-59-year-olds living above poverty level to a high of nearly 30 percent of persons older than 60 living below poverty level. This incidence remains excessive even after adjustments for differences in hemoglobin distributions are made (Kumanyika & Helitzer, 1985). Hookworm may be a cause in the rural South. Other blood disorders resulting in hemolytic anemia that are prevalent in blacks include sickle-cell disease and glucose-6-phosphate dehydrogenase deficiency.

COUNSELING

Information regarding country or region of origin is necessary in counseling black Americans. People from the Caribbean or Central America are more likely to identify with the foods and food habits of Latinos than with those of American blacks. Religious affiliation may also be important, such as among blacks who practice Islam.

Many blacks have inadequate access to health care. Further, an attitude that fate determines wellness may restrict medical visits.

When counseling black Americans it is important to be direct yet respectful. Attentive listening is more important than eye contact to many blacks, although they may interpret rapid eye aversion as an insult. Reluctance to be close to or touch the client may be viewed as an insult. Some clients may be suspicious or hostile when working with nonblack health care professionals. Such attitudes are rarely directed specifically at the health care worker, however; they are an adaptation to what is perceived as a prejudicial society.

The interviewer may miss nonnutritive food intake during pregnancy unless she solicits information about pica during the interview. Most women who eat clay, laundry starch, or other nonfood items will willingly list the items consumed when asked directly about the habit. The nutritional effects of pica are uncertain. Possible problems include excessive weight gain (from laundry starch), aggravated hypertension (from the sodium in clay), iron deficiency anemia, and hyperkalemia (Kumanyika & Helitzer, 1985).

Traditional health beliefs, such as using diet to cure "high" and "low" blood, may complicate some nutrition counseling. Pregnancy is sometimes considered to be a "high" blood state and pregnant women will avoid red meats. Patients who confuse hypertension with "high" blood may eat astringent foods, which are often high in sodium, to balance the condition.

An in-depth interview is especially important with black American clients. Variability in diet related to region, socioeconomic conditions, and degree of ethnic identity should be considered.

REFERENCES

Anon. 1982. Minorities and high blood pressure. *Dialogues in Hypertension,* 4 (2), 1–8.

Bloch, B. 1983. Nursing care of black patients. In *Ethnic Nursing Care: A Multicultural Approach,* M. S. Orque, B. Bloch, & L. S. Monrroy (Eds.). St. Louis: C. V. Mosby.

Bonham, G. S., & Brock, D. B. 1985. The relationship of diabetes with race, sex, and obesity. *American Journal of Clinical Nutrition, 41,* 776–783.

Burdine, J. N., Chen, M. S., Gottlieb, N. H., Peterson, F. L. & Vacalis, T. D. 1984. The effects of ethnicity, sex, and father's occupation on heart health knowledge and nutrition behavior of school children: The

Texas Youth Health Awareness Survey. *Journal of School Health, 54,* 87–90.

Cussler, M., & Degive, M. L. 1952. *'Twixt the Cup and the Lip.* New York: Twayne Publishers.

Eckstein, E. F. 1983. Foodways of blacks. In *Menu Planning* (3rd ed.). Westport, CT: AVI Publishing.

Emmons, L. 1986. Food procurement and the nutritional adequacy of diets in low-income families. *Journal of the American Dietetic Association, 86,* 1684–1693.

Fabre, J., Baczko, A., Laravoire, P., Dayer, P., & Fox, H. 1983. Arterial hypertension and ethnic factors. *Advances in Nephrology, 12,* 19–39.

Fitzgerald, T. K. 1979. Southern folks' eating habits ain't what they used to be . . . if they ever were. *Nutrition Today, 14,* 16–21.

Gladney, V. M. 1972. *Food practices of some black Americans in Los Angeles county.* Los Angeles: County of Los Angeles Department of Health Services.

Haider, S. Q., & Wheeler, M. 1979. Nutritive intake of black and Hispanic mothers in a Brooklyn ghetto. *Journal of the American Dietetic Association, 25,* 670–673.

Holt, T. 1980. Afro-Americans. In *The Harvard Encyclopedia of American Ethnic Groups,* S. Thernstrom, A. Orlov, & O. Handlin (Eds.). Cambridge, MA: The Belknap Press of Harvard University Press.

Hunter, J. M. 1973. Geophagy in Africa and the United States. *Geographical Review, 63,* 170–195.

Jerome, N. W. 1969. Northern urbanization and food consumption of Southern-born Negroes. *American Journal of Clinical Nutrition, 22,* 1667–1669.

Kumanyika, S. 1987. Obesity in black women. *Epidemiologic Reviews, 9,* 31–50.

Kumanyika, S., & Helitzer, D. L. 1985. Nutritional status and dietary pattern of racial minorities in the United States. In *Report of the Secretary's Task Force on Black and Minority Health* (Vol. II). Washington, DC: U.S. Department of Health and Human Services.

Lackey, C. J. 1982. Pica—pregnancy's etiological mystery. In *Alternative Dietary Practices and Nutritional Abuses in Pregnancy.* Washington DC: National Academy Press.

Leonard, A. R., Jang, V. L., Foerster, S., Igra, A., Ransom, B., & Lambert, C. B. 1981. *Dietary Practices, Ethnicity, and Hypertension: Preliminary Results of the 1979 California Hypertension Survey.* Sacramento: California Department of Health Services.

Mendes, H. 1971. *African Heritage Cookbook.* New York: Macmillan.

Newman, J. M. 1984. *The Melting Pot.* New York: Garland Publishing.

Reiter, A., Boylan, L. M., Driskell, J. & Moak, S. 1987. Vitamin B-12 and folate intakes and plasma levels of black adolescent females. *Journal of the American Dietetic Association, 87,* 1065–1067.

Schaefer, L. J., & Kumanyika, S. K. 1985. Maternal variables related to potentially high sodium infant feeding practices. *Journal of the American Dietetic Association, 85,* 433–438.

Snow, L. F. 1983. Traditional health beliefs and practices among lower-class black Americans. *Western Journal of Medicine, 139,* 820–828.

Thomas, D. N. 1981. Black American patient care. In *Transcultural Health Care,* G. Henderson & M. Primeaux (Eds.). Menlo Park, CA: Addison-Wesley.

Van der Post, L. 1970. *African Cooking.* New York: Time-Life Books.

Walter, E. 1971. The South's great gift of soul food. In *American Cooking: Southern Style.* New York: Time-Life Books.

Wheeler, M., & Haider, S. Q. 1979. Buying and food-preparation patterns of ghetto blacks and Hispanics in Brooklyn. *Journal of the American Dietetic Association, 25,* 560–563.

Wilson. E. G. 1971. *A West African Cookbook.* New York: Avon Books.

Wyant, K. W., & Meiselman, H. L. 1984. Sex and race differences in food preferences of military personnel. *Journal of the American Dietetic Association, 84,* 169–175.

6

LATINOS

L atinos are one of the largest ethnic groups in the United States, representing over 7 percent of the total population. If current growth trends continue, the number of Latinos in America will double within 25 years, and by the middle of the next century they will surpass blacks as the largest American minority group. Yet they are not a single group. Latinos come from throughout Latin America, including Mexico, Puerto Rico, Cuba and other Caribbean countries, Central America, and South America. The majority share Spanish as a common language of origin.

Immigrants from Latin America bring a rich cultural history. The Olmec culture, known for its sophisticated sculpture, existed in southeastern Mexico as early as 1200 B.C. The great Aztec, Mayan, Toltec, and Inca civilizations thrived while Europe was in its dark ages. Their independent mastery of astronomy, architecture, agriculture, and art astonished later explorers.

The influence of the Spanish on Latin American history is nearly as extensive as that of the early native populations. Occupation of Mexico, the Caribbean countries, and the Central and South American countries by various European powers, as well as importation of slave populations from Africa and Asia, has resulted in the multicultural blend seen today throughout the area.

The foods of Mexico typify this heterogeneous society. This chapter will examine Mexico and the food habits of Americans of Mexican descent in depth. The foods of the Caribbean

Traditional Latin American foods: Some foods typical of the traditional Latin American diet include annatto, avocado, bacalao *(salt cod), black beans,* cassava (yuca), *chili peppers,* cilantro, *corn* tortillas, jicama, *papaya, plantains, pinto beans, pork,* tomatillos, *and tomatoes.* (Photo by Laurie Macfee.)

will also be included, focusing on Americans of Puerto Rican and Cuban descent. The cuisines of Central and South America share many similarities with those of Mexico and the Caribbean, especially in ingredients. Some differences are caused by geographical or climatic factors, and food habits may vary slightly. However, fewer than 10 percent of all Latinos in the United States come from Central and South America, and little research on the food habits of immigrants from these areas has been reported.

MEXICANS

Estados Unidos Mexicanos, the United Mexican States, is the northernmost Latin American country. It is over one-fourth the size of the United States with 756,065 square miles of territory. The varied geography includes a large central plateau (6000 to 7000 feet high) surrounded by mountains ex-

Latin and South America.

cept to the north. Coastal plains edge the country along the West and East. The separate Baja peninsula is found in the West and the Yucatán peninsula juts out in the Southeast. Snow-capped volcanos, such as Orizaba, Popocatépetl, Ixtacchiuatl, and El Chichón, and frequent earthquakes also affect the landscape. The climate ranges from arid desert in the northern plains to tropical lowlands in the South.

Almost two-thirds of Mexicans are *mestizos,* that is, of mixed Indian and Spanish ancestry. Thirty percent are native Indians, and about 10 percent are whites of Spanish descent. Spanish is the official language. Only 1.5 percent of Mexicans speak only an Indian language, mostly Nahuatl.

Cultural Perspective

HISTORY OF MEXICO

Current knowledge of Mexican history before Spanish contact is limited. It is believed that nomadic hunting tribes settled in the area around 21,000 B.C. The Olmec civilization emerged about 1200 B.C. in the eastern region of the country. It is not known how long the empire ruled, but by 100 B.C. it had declined for unknown reasons.

The Mayans established another early civilization in southern Mexico at around A.D. 150. During the height of their empire, the Mayans occupied the Yucatán peninsula, as well as parts of what is now Guatemala and Nicaragua, establishing more than 60 cities connected by paved roads. They were conquered by the Spanish in the sixteenth century.

During this time, approximately A.D. 900 to 1200, the Toltecs rose to prominence in the north. They are thought to be the ancestors of the Tenochcas, who later became known as the Aztecs. The Aztecs conquered many of the other Indian tribes in the region and controlled much of what is now Mexico. Their capital city of Tenochtitlan, site of present-day Mexico City, was founded in 1325. The famous emperor Montezuma II ruled from 1502 to 1520.

In 1519, the Spanish explorer Hernán Cortés arrived in Mexico. Cortés conquered the Aztecs in less than two years, and most of Mexico was subjugated to Spanish rule by 1540, when it became the viceroyalty of New Spain. Heavy taxation and land distribution that benefited the Spanish colonists followed.

The movement toward independence grew as the Mexican-born Spanish people, called Creoles, became unhappy with their inferior status among Europeans. However, the original insurrections were led by Catholic priests with an Indian and *mestizo* following. The Creoles eventually joined in the ongoing guerilla war, and under the leadership of Agustín de Itúrbide, independence from Spain was achieved in 1820.

Itúrbide named himself emperor but was soon forced to leave the country after a military coup established a republic. In 1824, a federal constitution was adopted.

The territory of Texas declared independence from Mexico in 1836. In 1845, the United States annexed Texas, and a boundary dispute with Mexico led to war. The Mexican armies suffered repeated defeats, and in 1848 the United States occupied Mexico City. The ensuing Treaty of Guadalupe ceded the area that is now Texas, New Mexico, Arizona, and parts of Colorado, Nevada, and California to the United States.

The liberal Benito Juárez created a new constitution in 1857 to eliminate the unfair laws remaining from the colonial period. This reform was opposed by the conservatives. The liberals won a civil war fought between 1858 and 1861.

In 1862, Mexico was invaded by Britain, France, and Spain on the pretext of nonpayment of debts. After the withdrawal of Britain and Spain, Napoleon III sent the archduke of Austria, Maximilian, to be emperor of Mexico. With the support of the conservatives, Maximilian ruled for three years, but was executed by the liberals under Juárez in 1867.

Dictatorship and Democracy

In 1876, Porfirio Díaz seized power in Mexico and ruled as a dictator for nearly 35 years. He was overthrown in the Mexican Revolution of 1910.

Juárez's reforms had not been completed when Díaz took over. Continued pressure from peasants resulted in a new constitution in 1917. Other reforms were instituted by the leader of the Partido Nacional Revolucionario (in 1946 renamed Partido Revolucionario Institucional: PRI), Lázaro Cárdenas, who was elected president in 1934. A program of modernization was begun by President José López Portillo in 1976. Carlos Salinas de Gortari was elected president in 1988.

HISTORY OF IMMIGRATION TO THE UNITED STATES

Immigration Patterns

Mexican immigration patterns have changed over the years since the Mexican–American War clearly defined the U.S.– Mexican border. Today, Mexicans living in America and their descendants can be classified in the following groups: (1) *Chicanos:* those who are born in the United States (from the descendants of the wealthy Mexican landowners who controlled the area from California to Texas in the eighteenth and early nineteenth centuries to the children of the most recent arrivals), as well as those who have immigrated from Mexico and become U.S. citizens; (2) *braceros:* those who work here legally but remain Mexican citizens; and (3) "undocumented aliens": those who enter the country illegally.

Mexicans lived in what is now the American Southwest for hundreds of years before the United States declared its independence in 1776. Although they welcomed American settlers, they soon found themselves outnumbered and their economic and political control of the region weakened. At the end of the Mexican–American War in 1848, the 75,000 Mexicans living in the ceded territories became U.S. citizens.

Between 1900 and 1935 it is estimated that 10 percent of the Mexican population, approximately one million persons, emigrated north to the United States. Then, during the Depression era, tens of thousands of undocumented aliens, plus those admitted legally under the 1917 contract labor laws, were "repatriated" and sent back to Mexico.

After the Depression, the need for cheap labor increased. The Bracero Program was created to meet this need. Thousands of Mexicans were offered jobs in agriculture and on the railroads. After World War II, the continued need for migrant farm workers encouraged over one million Mexicans to immigrate between 1951 and 1975.

Current Demographics

Economic pressures in Mexico have increased the number of Mexican immigrants entering the United States each year. In general, they are attempting to escape the life-threatening poverty that affects the majority of the populace.

The 1980 U.S. census reported 7.5 million Chicanos and Braceros in this country. This figure may be low because of the ambiguities of the census category "Spanish descent." In

The term *Chicano* came from the Aztec term for Mexicans-*Meshicano.* Chicano replaces the outdated terms Mexicano and Mexican-American.

Ninety percent of documented immigrants from Central and South America before 1980 were white, mostly skilled professionals. It is believed that many additional, undocumented laborers have entered the U.S. illegally.

addition, the census figure does not account for undocumented aliens. Estimates of this population vary from 2 to 5 million.

The majority of Chicanos live in California and Texas. Other states, such as Illinois, Arizona, and New Mexico also host large Chicano populations. Eighty percent of the immigrants from Mexico settle in U.S. cities, such as Los Angeles, San Antonio, and Chicago. Many recent immigrants, legal and illegal, settle in the urban Latino neighborhoods called *barrios.*

Changes in Immigration Patterns

A continuing decline in the Mexican economy may encourage even greater emigration in the near future. Over 61,000 Mexicans entered the United States legally in 1985, the largest group from any country.

However, it is the uncontrolled number of undocumented aliens from Mexico entering the country that concerns U.S. officials. The U.S.–Mexican border is 1,931 miles long, most of it in unpopulated desert regions. Over 1.5 million Mexicans are apprehended each year as they attempt to enter the United States illegally. Some estimates suggest that twice that number may cross successfully.

In an attempt to regain control of illegal immigration, the U.S. Congress enacted the Immigration Reform and Control Act of 1986. The legislation embraces what has become known as the "three-legged stool" concept. The three legs include vastly increased border patrols, sanctions against employers who knowingly hire illegal aliens, and a one-time legalization program for undocumented aliens who have lived in the United States since 1982.

It is unknown how effective the reform act will be in preventing illegal entry into the country or how it will affect immigration patterns. What is certain is that the economic disparities between the two nations will continue to draw Mexicans to the United States.

Socioeconomic Status

Chicanos, Braceros, and undocumented aliens occupy three main socioeconomic classes. There are the migrant farm workers, who maintain a culturally isolated community; the residents of the urban barrios, who are also segregated from much of American society; and a small number of acculturated middle-class Chicanos.

Undocumented aliens tend to move in with family members

who already reside in the United States. Usually this is in a predominantly Latino neighborhood, where they can live inconspicuously among the residents while becoming familiar with the American social and economic systems.

Most Americans of Mexican descent have low socioeconomic status. In 1987, nearly one in every four families (24.7%) fell below the poverty level. This is due in part to a disproportionate number of Chicanos employed in unskilled or semiskilled labor, 25 percent compared to 14 percent for Americans in the majority culture. Less than half of Chicanos graduate from high school, and over 17 percent have less than five years of education.

In contrast to other immigrant groups, women from Central America far outnumber men coming to the U.S. Most are young, and work in the U.S. to help support their families at home.

Cultural Organizations

Most national associations formed by Americans of Mexican descent address political and economic issues. The League of United Latin American Citizens (LULAC) was founded in 1928 to promote better working conditions and job training; it now has chapters throughout the country. The Raza Unido party was begun in the 1970s to increase political influence.

WORLDVIEW

Chicanos, Braceros, and undocumented aliens often live in culturally homogeneous communities. Their ethnic identity is proudly maintained: they speak Spanish and prefer Mexican music and food.

When exposed to the mainstream American society, immigrants from Mexico can be highly adaptive. There are many Chicanos who are completely acculturated. They may speak no Spanish, be future-oriented, and, in fact, consider themselves "white." Others are successfully bicultural. Cross-cultural marriages are becoming more common, especially in the northern United States.

Religion

It is estimated that between 85 percent and 97 percent of Americans of Mexican descent are Catholics. Traditional religious ceremonies, such as baptism, communion, confirmation, marriage, and the novenas (nine days of prayer for the deceased) are important family events (see Chapter 2). Nearly all non-Catholics are Protestants. A strong faith in the will of God influences how immigrants from Mexico perceive their world. Many believe they have no direct control over their own fate.

The Chicano Family

The most important social unit in the Chicano community is the family. In contrast to American majority society, the well-being of the family comes before the needs of the individual.

The Chicano father is the head of the household. He is the primary decision maker and wage earner. In traditional Mexican society, the wife is a homemaker. In America, this role is changing. The Chicana wife often works, in addition to carrying out her household duties, and is likely to be involved in family decisions.

Children are cherished in the Chicano family, and families are usually large. They are taught to share and work together; sibling rivalry is minimal.

When possible, an extended family is the preferred living arrangement. Grandparents are honored and are often involved in child care. Because of space limitations in the United States, however, many elderly Chicanos are living in separate apartments. During periods of hardship, other relatives such as aunts, uncles, and godparents willingly accept the care of children.

Traditional Food Habits

Another New World food is the potato. It is thought to have been first cultivated high in the Andes of Peru and Bolivia, where it was too cold to grow corn. It is a staple in those regions today.

Mexicans are very proud of their culinary heritage. It is a unique blend of native and European foods prepared with Indian (mostly Aztec) and Spanish cooking techniques. There is even some French and Viennese influence from the Maximilian reign. The resulting cuisine is both spicy and sophisticated.

INGREDIENTS AND COMMON FOODS

Many people associate the cooking of Mexico with chilis. Although chilis are used frequently, not all Mexican dishes are hot and spicy. Other New World foods, such as beans, cocoa (from the Aztec word for "bitter"), corn, and tomatoes add equally important flavors to the cuisine. These native ingredients were the basis of Indian cooking throughout Mexico before the arrival of the Spanish.

Aztec Food Traditions

The Aztec empire had an estimated population of 25 million people at its peak in the fifteenth century. About one-quarter of these were an elite class of nobles who were supported by the remaining 75 percent of the Indian slave populace.

The capital city of Tenochtitlan was surrounded by lakes on which were built *chinampas,* rich agricultural fields of mud scooped from the lake bottoms. It is believed that these drought-resistant fields produced enough food to feed 180,000 people annually. The monarchy stored surplus crops. A famine occurring from 1450 to 1454 was mitigated during its first two years by these grain reserves. The Aztecs were also known for their animal husbandry and game protection laws.

Documents from early Spanish expeditions record the enormous variety of foods enjoyed by the Aztec nobility. Over 1,000 dishes are described. Montezuma II reportedly ate up to 30 different foods at a meal, each kept warm on a pottery brazier. These included hot *tortillas* of several types; turkey pie; roast turkey, quail, and duck; fish, lobster, frog, and newt dishes garnished with red, green, or yellow chilis; squash blossoms; and sauces of chilis, tomatoes, squash seeds, or green plums. *Chocolatl,* a hot, unsweetened chocolate drink made from native cocoa beans was the most popular beverage.

Corn was the staple grain. Fruits and vegetables were plentiful, and some small game was available. The one notable deficiency of the Aztec diet was a consistent source of fat or oil.

Spanish Contributions

The Spanish arrived in Mexico with cinnamon, garlic, onions, rice, sugar cane, wheat, and, most importantly, hogs, which added a reliable source of domesticated protein and fat to the native diet. These additions combined with indigenous ingredients to produce the classic flavors and foods of Mexican cuisine, such as corn tortillas with pork; tomato, chili, and onion sauces or *salsas;* rice and beans; and boiled beans fried in lard, known as *frijoles refritos* or, as they are incorrectly called in English, refried beans. The Spanish also introduced the distillation of alcohol to native Mexican fermented beverages; *tequila* and *mescal* were the result.

Staples

The cuisine of Mexico is very diverse, and many inaccessible regions have retained their native diet. Others have held on

Tortillas are the predominant "bread" of Mexico. Traditionally, they are made by hand. The corn kernels are heated in a lime solution until the skins break and separate. The treated kernels, called *nixtamal,* are then pulverized on a stone slab (*metate*). The resulting flour, *masa harina,* is combined with water to make the tortilla dough. Small balls of the dough are patted into round, flat circles, about 6 to 8 inches across. The tortillas are cooked on a griddle (often with a little lard) until soft or crisp, depending on the recipe. They may also be made with wheat flour, which is popular in northern Mexico. (*See* page 214.)

Corn is believed to have been domesticated from now extinct wild varieties in southern Mexico somewhere between 8000 and 7000 B.C. From there, it probably spread south into Central America and north into what is now the United States.

Contrary to the diversity found in Mexican cuisine, the majority of poor Mexicans have little variety in their diet. Some subsist almost entirely on corn, beans, and squash.

TABLE 6.1. Cultural Food Groups: Mexican

Group	Comments
PROTEIN FOODS	
Milk/milk products	Few dairy products used (incidence of lactose intolerance estimated at ⅔ of the population).
	Dairy products are used more in northern Mexico than in other regions.
Meats/poultry/fish/eggs/ legumes	Vegetable protein primary source for majority of rural and urban poor.
	Pork, goat, poultry common meats.
	Beef preferred in northern areas and seafood in coastal regions.
	Meat usually tough. Prepared by marinating, chopping, and grinding (sausages popular), or sliced thinly. Cooked by grilling, frying, stewing, or steaming. Usually mixed with vegetables and cereals.
CEREALS/GRAINS	Corn and rice products used throughout the country; wheat products more common in the north.
	Principal bread is *tortilla*; European-style breads and rolls also popular.
FRUITS/VEGETABLES	Vegetables usually served as part of a dish, not separately.
	Semitropical and tropical fruits popular in most regions (limited availability in north).
ADDITIONAL FOODS	
Seasonings	Food often heavily spiced; 92 varieties of chilis used.
	Regional sauces typical.

Common Foods	Adaptations in the United States
Milk (cow, goat) evaporated milk, hot chocolate; *atole;* unaged cheeses.	Aged cheese used in place of fresh cheese; more milk (usually whole) consumed; ice cream popular.
Meats: beef, goat, pork (including variety cuts). *Poultry:* chicken, turkey. *Fish and seafood: camerones* (shrimp), *huachinango* (red snapper), other firm-fleshed fish. *Eggs:* chicken. *Legumes:* black beans, garbanzo beans (chick peas), pinto beans, kidney beans.	Traditional entrees remain popular. Fewer variety cuts used. Extra income spent on meat.
Corn *(masa harina, pozole, tortillas);* wheat (breads, rolls, *pan dulce,* pasta); rice.	Wheat tortillas used more than corn tortillas; convenience breads used. Increased consumption of baked sweets, such as doughnuts, cake, and cookies. Increased consumption of sugared breakfast cereals.
Fruits: avocados, bananas, *cherimoya,* coconut, *granadilla* (passion fruit), guava, lemons, limes, *mamey,* mangoes, melon, *nopales* (cactus fruit), oranges, papaya, pineapple, plantains, strawberries, sugar cane, *zapote* (fruit of the *sapodilla* tree). *Vegetables:* cactus *(nopalitos),* chilis, corn, *jícama,* onions, peas, potatoes, squashes *(chayote,* pumpkin, summer, etc.), squash blossoms, *tomatillos,* tomatoes, *yuca* (cassava).	Fruit remains popular as dessert and snack item; apples and grapes accepted after familiarization.
Anise, *achiote* (annatto), chilis, *cilantro* (coriander leaves), cinnamon, cumin, cocoa, *epazote,* garlic, mace, onions, vanilla.	

TABLE 6.1. Cultural Food Groups: Mexican (*continued*)

Group	Comments
Nuts/seeds	Seeds often used in flavoring.
Beverages	
Fats/oils	

Menudo is a popular tripe and hominy soup that is believed to have curative properties, especially for hangovers, and is a popular weekend breakfast dish.

to traditional foods and food habits despite Aztec or Spanish domination. The diet of still other areas differs because of the availability of local fruits, vegetables, or meats. This variety makes it difficult to typify Mexican foods in general (see Table 6.1).

Nevertheless, some foods are found, in varying forms, throughout Mexico. One-dish meals are typical, almost always served with warm tortillas. Hearty soups or stews called *caldos* are favorite family dinner entrees. Casseroles, known as *sopas-secas,* using stale tortillas pieces, rice, or macaroni, are also eaten as main dishes.

Stale tortillas can also be broken up and softened in a sauce to make *chilaquiles,* which are served as a side dish or light entree. They can also be soaked in milk overnight, then pureed to make a thick dough. This dough is used to prepare *gordos,* which are fat fried cakes, or *bolitos,* which are added to soup and are similar to dumplings.

Meats are normally prepared over high heat. They are typically grilled, as in *carne asada* (beef strips), or fried, as in *chicharrónes* (fried pork rind). Slow, moist cooking (stewing, braising, etc.) may also be used. These techniques help to tenderize the tough cuts that are generally available, as does marinating, another common preparation method. Nearly all parts of the animal are used, including the variety cuts and organs. Sausage is especially popular, such as spicy pork or beef *chorizo.*

Mexico is famous for its "stuffed" foods, such as *tacos, enchiladas, tamales, quesadillas,* and *burritos.* These are found throughout the country, with regional variations. Tacos are the Mexican equivalent to sandwiches. Tortillas, either soft or crisply fried, are filled with anything from just salsa to meat, vegetables, and sauce. Enchiladas are tortillas softened in lard or sauce, then filled with meat, poultry, seafood, cheese,

Common Foods	Adaptations in the United States
Piñóns (pine nuts), *pepitas* (pumpkin seeds), sesame seeds.	Use of spices depends on availability.
Atole, beer, coffee *(café con leche)*, hot chocolate, soft drinks, *pulque*, *mezcal*, *tequila*, whiskey, wine.	Increased consumption of fruit juices, Kool-Aid, soft drinks, and beverages with caffeine; decrease in use of hard spirits.
Butter, *manteca* (lard).	

or egg mixtures. The tortilla rolls are then baked with a sauce. Tamales are one of the oldest Mexican foods, dating back at least to the Aztec period. A dough made with either *masa harina* (the flour made from corn kernels that have been boiled in a lime solution to remove the skins) or leftover *pozole* (a cereal made with the boiled, lime-treated kernels) is placed in corn husks (in the North), or banana leaves (in the South). The leaves are folded and then baked in hot ashes or steamed over boiling water. The tamale may contain plain dough, be filled with a seasoned meat or vegetable mixture, or be sweetened for a dessert. After cooking, the husk or leaf is unfolded, revealing the aromatic tamale. Quesadillas are tortillas filled with a little cheese, left-over meat, sausage, or vegetable, then folded in half and heated or crisply fried. Burritos are popular in northern Mexico. They are similar to tacos, but large, thin, wheat-flour tortillas are used instead of corn tortillas. The most common filling is beans with salsa.

Beans are ubiquitous in Mexican meals. They are served in some form at nearly every lunch and dinner and are frequently found at breakfast, too. They often comprise the filling in stuffed foods and are a common side dish, such as frijoles refritos.

Vegetables are usually part of the main dish or served as a substantial garnish. Potatoes, greens, tomatoes, and onions are the most common. Chilis are used extensively in seasonings, sauces, and even stuffed, as in *chilis rellenos* and the Independence Day dish *chilis en nogada* [garnished with the colors of the Mexican flag; white sauce, green *cilantro* (coriander leaves), and red pomegranate seeds].

Sugar cane grows well in Mexico, and sweets of all kinds are popular. Dried fruits and vegetables, candied fruits and vegetables, and sugared fruit or nut pastes are eaten alone and used in more complex desserts. The Spanish make many

El Salvador has its own "stuffed" specialty called pupusas. *A tortilla is filled with chiccharones, cheese, or black beans, then topped with another tortilla. The edges are sealed and the pupusa is then fried. They are traditionally served with pickled cabbage. In Argentina, baked turnovers that are stuffed with a savory meat, raisin, and olive mixture, called* empanadas, *are frequently served as a first course in a meal.*

Chili con carne (beans with beef) is not actually a Mexican dish, although there are similar combinations throughout the country. The origins of chili are thought to be in Texas, after the Mexican-American War.

Hand-made tortillas: Tortillas, *made from cornmeal or wheat flour, are the staple bread of Mexico. In this photograph, taken in a* tortilla *factory, the lime-soaked corn kernels are pulverized on a stone* metate. *On the right, a* tortilla *is patted out round by hand.* (Courtesy San Antonio Light Collection copy from Institute of Texas Cultures at San Antonio.)

desserts with eggs, and many of these recipes have been adopted in Mexico. *Flan,* a sweetened egg custard topped with caramelized sugar, is the most common. *Huevos reales* is another popular dessert, made with egg yolks, sugar, sherry, cinnamon, pine nuts, and raisins.

The most common beverage in Mexico is coffee, which is grown in the south. Soft drinks and fresh fruit blended with water and sugar, called *aguas naturales,* are also favored. Adults drink milk infrequently, except in sweetened, flavored beverages such as hot chocolate with cinnamon. The most popular alcoholic beverage in Mexico is beer. The Mexican wine industry is also developing rapidly, in part due to a 1982 ban on the import of foreign wine. Men drink alcoholic beverages at all occasions when they gather socially. In addition to tequila and mescal, whiskey is commonly served at these times.

Regional Variations

Mexican Plains. The northern and west-central regions of Mexico consist of mostly arid plains. The Indians who originally inhabited the area were called Chichimecs by the Aztecs ("sons of the dog") because of their seminomadic lifestyle. It is believed that their diet consisted of corn, beans, squash, greens, potatoes, prickly pear fruit *(nopales),* and young cactus leaves *(nopalitos).* They also hunted small game and ate domesticated turkeys and poultry. When the Mexican Indians mixed with the Indians of the American Southwest, they adopted piñón nuts (also called pine nuts or pignolis), pumpkin, and plums.

The Spanish introduced long-horn cattle to the northern plains, as well as wheat. Today, this is the only region of Mexico where people eat substantial amounts of beef and cheese. A favorite way to prepare beef is to air dry it in thin slices called *cecinas,* an assertive preparation that is similar to American chipped beef but more flavorful. Cecinas can be used in stews or soups; they can be fried or used as fillings for other foods. The most popular Mexican cheeses are unripened. There is *queso blanco,* which is similar to mozzarella, and creamy *queso fresca,* which is similar to ricotta or pot cheese. Wheat is also used in more products in the North than in the South.

Tequila is probably the best known drink of the region. It is made by distilling the fermented sap of the maguey cactus (century plant), which is called *pulque.* Pulque is the sour, mildly alcoholic beverage that was drunk throughout Mexico before the arrival of the Spaniards. The Spaniards, lacking grain, tried their distillation methods on the pulque, producing a rough brew known as mescal. Tequila is the more refined, twice-distilled version of mescal. It is produced in the

One dish that was invented in northern Mexico is Caesar Salad, featuring a tangy dressing of lemon, vinegar, Romano cheese, and raw egg.

Chilis vary enormously in relative hotness. The chemical heat of chili peppers comes from the alkaloid capsaicin, found mostly in the fleshy ribs inside the fruit. It is not known why people enjoy the sting of chili-flavored foods. It is often said that hot foods stimulate the appetite and digestion, perhaps because of irritation of the intestinal linings. It has also been suggested that the body may release pain-killing endorphins in response to the capsaicin, resulting in a comfortable, gratified feeling after a chili-spiced meal.

Achiote is called annatto in the United States. It is made from the seeds of a tropical tree and used sometimes to color cheddar-style cheeses and margarines. Achiote flavors many Guatemalan dishes.

Although insect eating is unappealing to most Americans, insects and spiders are important sources of protein in many areas of the world.

central western state of Jalisco around the towns of Tequila and Tepatitlan from a maguey subspecies *Agave tequiliana.*

Tropical Mexico. Fruits and vegetables are featured foods in the southern coastal regions of Mexico. Tomatoes, green tomatoes called *tomatillos,* 92 varieties of chili peppers, *chayote* squash, onions *jícama* (a sweet, crispy root), sweet and starchy bananas, *mamey* (a type of plum), pineapple, *yuca* (a tuber also called cassava or manioc), and *zapote* (the fruit of the *sapodilla* tree) are just a small sampling of the produce available in this area. Avocados, grown in the tropical climate, vary in size from 2 to 8 inches across, in skin color from light green to black, and in flavor from bland to bitter. Their succulent, smooth flesh is added to soups, stews, and salads. They are most popular in *guacamole,* mashed avocado with onions, tomatoes, chili peppers or powder, and cilantro, the pungent leaf of the coriander plant. It is used as a side dish, a topping, or a filling for tortillas.

Yucatán. The cuisine of the Yucatán peninsula reflects its unique history. It was isolated from the rest of the country by dense, mountainous jungles until modern times. Many of the residents are descendants of the Mayas, the early Indian dynasty of the region. Some of the regional favorites date from this time. For example, one popular preparation method is to steam foods, called *píbil.* Traditionally, food was cooked this way in an outdoor pit, but today it is done more often in a covered pot. Shrimp are a local specialty; the long coastline of the Yucatán along the Gulf of Mexico provides ample seafood. Sauces made with toasted squash seeds or the bright red spice *achiote* are also common to the area.

Southern Mexico. The foods of southern Mexico are similar to those of the Yucatán in that they are more tropical and more Indian-influenced than the foods of other regions. They are reknowned for their complex, spicy sauces that use numerous ingredients such as chilis, nuts, raisins, sesame seeds, spices, even chocolate. These sauces come in many colors, including red, yellow, green and black, and are called *moles,* probably from the Aztec word for sauce with chilis, *molli.* Poultry, goat, and pork are the most popular meats, although some specialties of the region are more unusual, such as *chalupines,* a cricket that is found in the corn fields.

Tropical Latin American fruit. (Courtesy Florida Division of Tourism.)

The foods of Central America are similar to those of tropical and southern Mexico. The staples include beans, chilis, corn, rice, squash, and tomatoes. Bananas, coconut, plantains, and yuca (cassava) are prominent ingredients in the tropical lowlands and along the east coast. Beef is popular in urban areas; pork, in rural regions. Seafood and poultry are common on the coasts.

MEAL COMPOSITION AND CYCLE

Daily Patterns

In families where income is not limited, the preferred meal pattern is four to five daily meals: *desayuno* (breakfast), *almuerzo* (coffee break), *comida* (lunch), *merienda* (late-afternoon snack), and *cena* (dinner). Most meals are eaten at home and served family style. If there are too many people to sit at the table, each one is served individually from the stove.

Desayuno is a filling breakfast, often including tortillas, eggs, meat, beans left over from the previous night, *pan dulce* (sweet bread, pastry, or cake), and fresh fruit. Coffee and hot chocolate are the preferred beverages. Near 11:00 A.M. is almuerzo, which features pan dulce or fruit, served with *café con leche* (coffee with milk).

Comida is traditionally the largest meal of the day, eaten about 1:00 or 2:00 P.M. A complete comida includes six full courses, from soup through dessert. When possible, an afternoon rest period *(siesta)* follows this meal.

Merienda is a light meal of sweet rolls, cake, or cookies eaten around 6:00 P.M. Coffee, hot chocolate, or a warm drink of thin, sugared cornmeal and milk gruel, called *atole*,

Mexican meal: A rural Mexican family enjoys a meal of soup and tortillas. *The diet of the poor in Mexico is limited, often consisting of little more than corn products, beans, and squash.* (Courtesy World Health Organization/ P. Almasy.)

accompanies the sweets. A light supper, *cena,* follows between 8:00 and 10:00 P.M. This meal may be skipped entirely or expanded into a substantial feast on holidays or other formal occasions. Recently, many Mexicans have adopted the American habit of eating a light lunch and a heavy supper, eliminating *merienda* altogether.

Snacking is frequent in urban Mexico; munching occurs from morning to midnight. *Antojitos,* or "little whims," include foods such as *tostados* (called *chalupas* in northern Mexico), fried tortillas topped with shredded lettuce, cheese or meat. Nearly every block offers street-side food vendors, providing everything from fresh fruits to grilled meats. In addition, many neighborhoods feature an open-air market that also offers ready-to-eat foods.

Special Occasions

In Mexico, many foods are associated with holidays. For example, the Fiesta de los Santos Reyes (the Coming of the Three Kings) on January 6 is traditionally celebrated with *rosca de reyes,* a raisin-studded, ring-shaped loaf of bread. Baked inside the bread is a figurine, and the person who receives it is obligated to give a party on February 2.

During Lent, *capirotada* is a popular dessert. Each family has its own recipe for this holiday bread pudding. Another holiday food is bread, decorated with a skull and crossbones *(pan de muerto),* eaten on All Soul's Day (November 2nd) as part of a large feast honoring the deceased. Christmas festivities, called *posadas,* frequently feature *piñatas,* brightly decorated papier-mâché animals and figures that are filled with sweets. Blindfolded children take turns swinging a large stick at the hanging piñata until it breaks and candies fly everywhere. On Christmas Eve, a salad of fruits, nuts, and beets is served. Turkey, tamales, and *arroz con leche* (rice pudding) are special foods eaten at holidays throughout the year.

ROLE OF FOOD IN MEXICAN SOCIETY

In family-centered Mexican society, food-related activities facilitate interactions between family members and help define family roles. Meal planning is usually the responsibility of the wife. Depending on economic status, food is prepared by the wife or by servants supervised by her, since Mexican foods can be laborious to prepare. The final dishes are greatly appreciated by all who partake in the meal, and it is considered an insult not to eat everything that is served.

In rural areas, food sharing is an important social activity, reflecting the Indian worldview. To reject offered food or drink is a severe breach of social conduct.

THERAPEUTIC USES OF FOOD

Some Mexican Indians and peasants practice a hot–cold system of food classification. It is believed to have derived from the Arab system of humoral medicine brought to Mexico by the Spaniards, combined with the native Indian worldview.

On All Saint's Day in Guatemala large groups gather to enjoy *fiambre,* an enormous colorful salad consisting of a variety of vegetables and meats with either a sweet-sour sauce or a sour vinaigrette.

In the city of Oaxaca, thin, fried, anise-spiced cookies called *buñuelos* are eaten at Christmas. They are drenched in syrup and served in crockery bowls, which when empty are smashed on the street for good luck.

Although it has parallels with other systems, such as Asian yin–yang, the Mexican hot–cold theory is applied only to health and diet. It does not encompass social and moral beliefs.

The Mexican hot–cold theory is based on the belief that the world's resources are limited and must remain in balance. People must stay in harmony with the environment. Hot has the connotation of strength; cold, of weakness. When the theory is applied to foods, items can be classified according to proximity to the sun, method of preparation, or how the food is thought to affect the body. Meals balanced between hot and cold foods are considered to be health promoting. Unbalanced meals may cause illness. Thus a typical comida in a rural village would consist of rice (hot), soup (made with hot and cold ingredients), and beans (cold).

Although the hot–cold classification of foods does vary, items generally considered hot are alcohol, aromatic beverages, beef, chilis, corn husks, oils, onions, pork, radishes, and tamales. Cold foods include citrus fruits, dairy products, most fresh vegetables, goat, and tropical fruits. Some foods, such as beans, corn products, rice products, sugary foods, and wheat products, can be classified as either hot or cold depending on how they are prepared.

Illnesses are also believed to be hot or cold and are usually treated with a diet rich in foods of the opposite classification. Certain conditions, such as menstruation and childbirth, are considered to be hot, and some women avoid hot foods at these times.

Food and herbal remedies are also used in some regions. For example, camomile is believed to cure colic, menstrual cramps, anxiety, insomnia, and itching eyes. Garlic is chewed for yeast infections in the mouth, toothache pain, and stomach disorders; boiled peanut broth is used to cure diarrhea; boiled cornsilk is taken for kidney pain; honey and water are given to infants for colic; oregano is used for fever, dry cough, asthma, and amenorrhea; and papaya is thought to help cure digestive ailments, diabetes, asthma, tuberculosis, and intestinal parasites. Sour foods are believed to thin the blood and are avoided by menstruating women because they are thought to increase blood flow; acidic foods may also be shunned because they are said to cause menstrual cramps.

Contemporary Food Habits in the United States

The foods of Mexico have influenced cooking in the American Southwest and California. Tex-Mex cuisine features many modified Mexican dishes, such as chili with beans, tamale pie, and nachos. Chicanos, Braceros, and undocumented aliens living in the United States may eat these and other American foods, or may eat a more traditional diet, depending on length of time in the country, location, income, or other factors.

ADAPTATION OF FOOD HABITS

Many Mexicans in the United States retain their traditional eating patterns. Recent immigrants, those who live near the U.S.–Mexican border, and migrant workers are most likely to continue Mexican food habits.

Mexicans who are well-established in the United States and Chicanos often become more acculturated. In one hospital, it was found that "Mexican" patients overwhelmingly preferred American foods, even when offered traditional Mexican meals (Smith, 1979). In a recent marketing study (Wallendorf & Reilly, 1983), it was noted that Mexican immigrants living in the southwestern United States are more likely to eat a diet with a high intake of red meats, white bread, sugared cereals, caffeine-containing beverages, and soft drinks than their socioeconomic counterparts in Mexico or white neighbors. This suggests that rather than adopting a diet that fell somewhere between the food habits of Mexico and the United States, the Mexican immigrants in the survey accepted the stereotypical American consumption patterns of a decade ago.

Ingredients and Common Foods

Some American foods are accepted in even the most traditional families. Doughnuts, pie, cake, cookies, ice cream, and Popsicles are popular as desserts and snacks. Sugared cereals are becoming more common at breakfast for children, and American cheeses are often used in place of unaged Mexican cheeses.

A preference for sweet or carbonated beverages usually increases in the United States. Soft drinks, Kool Aid, and juices are popular with meals and as snacks. Beer and coffee are

Early researchers were perplexed by the absence of the niacin deficiency disease, pellagra, in the populations that had a corn-based diet in Mexico. Pellagra was common in the southern United States, where corn was also a staple. It was found that when the corn kernels were prepared for masa, the alkaline lime solution used to soften them released the niacin in the corn, which was bound to a protein. The lime is also thought to add calcium to the diet. This is a good example of a traditional food habit that has nutritional benefits.

Mexican foods in America: Mexican foods marketed in the United States include versions of traditional dishes, such as tacos *(upper left, lower left),* enchiladas *(held dish),* quesadillas *(center),* refried beans *(lower right), and* salsa *(center front).* (Courtesy Beatrice/Hunt Wesson.)

also consumed with meals or snacks throughout the day. Whole milk is considered a "superfood" for children, but adults, especially men, consider it to be a juvenile drink. Milk is often flavored with chocolate, eggs, and bananas in a drink called *licuado,* or mixed with coffee or cornmeal to make atole. Many adults reject milk completely, claiming that they are "allergic" to it (it is estimated that two-thirds of Latinos are lactose intolerant).

More acculturated immigrants buy many prepared and convenience foods. Baked goods are usually purchased, including tortillas (often wheat tortillas are chosen over corn), breads, pan dulce, and even special desserts, such as flan. Extra income is usually spent on meats.

Meal Composition and Cycle

Studies of low-income Latinos and Mexican migrant farm workers indicate that for most meals traditional foods are preferred. These include eggs, beans or meat, and tortillas or pan dulce for breakfast; a large lunch of beans, tortillas, and meat, or a soup or stew; and a lighter dinner of tortillas, beans or meat, and rice or potatoes.

As in Mexico, vegetables tend to be served as part of a soup or stew. Fruit remains a typical snack and dessert, especially the familiar varieties such as bananas, oranges, mangoes, guava, pineapple, strawberries, and melon.

Meal patterns of Mexican immigrants change in ways similar to food habits. Recent immigrants, Braceros, and undocumented aliens often eat the traditional large breakfast, large lunch, and small dinner. Chicanos often adopt the American meal pattern of small breakfast, small lunch, and large dinner.

Changes in preparation methods may also occur. Recent immigrants may not know how to use the baking and broiling apparatus on an oven and may continue to fry and grill foods outdoors. Newer immigrants sometimes avoid canned and frozen foods because they do not know how to prepare them. As in Mexico, dishes that require extensive preparation, such as tamales and enchiladas, are saved for Sunday and holiday meals.

In one study (Bruhn & Pangborn, 1971), migrant workers were asked what was the main dish that was served at holidays. No preference was found for Easter; tamales were preferred for Christmas. Turkey with mashed potatoes was the most popular Thanksgiving entree, indicating that this American holiday was adopted along with its traditional foods.

NUTRITIONAL STATUS

Nutritional Intake

It is difficult to determine health statistics on Chicanos, Braceros, and undocumented aliens because they are often grouped with whites or other Latinos in collected data. Information from research on Latinos can be used cautiously, since Mexicans comprise such a large percentage of the total Latino population. Nevertheless, some nutritional problems have been identified in both new and acculturated immigrants from Mexico through studies of Spanish-surnamed patients, especially those residing in the Southwest.

The birth rate among women of Mexican descent who are

The traditional honey-and-water cure for colic may result in infant botulism.

Data from the U.S. Department of Agriculture Nationwide Food Consumption Survey (1977–1978) indicate that the intake of vitamin A for persons with Spanish surnames averages 800–1,600 IU per day (the RDA is 4,000–5,000 IU).

15 to 44 years of age is 114 births per 1,000 women, nearly 90 percent greater than that for white women. Although the incidence of underweight infants and infant mortality are slightly higher than for white infants, the exact figures are unknown. Some researchers suggest that deaths are underreported, due to the illegal immigrant status of parents. Others suggest that a lower than expected neonatal mortality rate for a people of a low socioeconomic level may be due to reproductive efficiency, low rates of smoking and alcohol consumption among women of Mexican descent, and the value placed on parenthood (Markides & Coreil, 1986).

Approximately 20 to 50 percent of Spanish-surnamed women breastfeed their newborn infants, and reported increases in the percentage of women who breastfeed parallel those in the total U.S. population. In one study of migrant farm workers in California, it was found that an infant was less likely to be breastfed after the parents came to the United States, even if the baby was born in Mexico (Kokinos & Dewey, 1986). Breastfed babies are usually weaned from the breast to the bottle. Long-term use of the bottle, with both milk and sweetened liquids (such as Kool Aid, fruit juice, and tea) is sometimes a problem, resulting in iron deficiency anemia and extensive tooth decay among toddlers ("bottle mouth").

In Mexico, the diet of 40 percent of the population fails to meet the minimum standards of the World Health Organization. In the United States, poverty also adversely affects the diet of 30 to 40 percent of the total Latino population. The staple diet of poor migrant farm workers may consist predominantly of beans, rice, tortillas, and salsa. Intake of animal protein and iron may be low, resulting in low hemoglobin levels among young children and pregnant women. However, excessive rates of low iron intake or low blood iron status among Americans of Mexican descent have not been confirmed. Deficiencies of calcium and riboflavin are also common, due to the low consumption of dairy products. Although the traditional Mexican diet has good sources of vitamins A and C, thiamin, niacin, and phosphorus, inadequate income and lack of traditional ingredients may limit intake of these nutrients. These problems may be exacerbated by intestinal infections (the leading cause of death in Mexico), such as amoebic dysentery, especially among new arrivals.

Malnutrition may contribute to other diseases. In the southwestern United States, the mortality rates for pneumonia and influenza are higher for persons with Spanish surnames than for whites. Deaths of Latinos from tuberculosis in New Mexico (1969–1977) and Los Angeles (1972) are nearly double those of whites in those regions.

In contrast to the problem of malnutrition is the prevalence of obesity in persons of Mexican descent, who are two to four times as likely as whites to be overweight (Stern *et al.,* 1983). Cultural ideal weight is greater for Mexicans than for Americans. Many Latina women believe it is normal to gain weight after marriage. Extra weight indicates health and well-being, not only for adults but also for children. Obesity is sometimes perceived as a status symbol.

Several studies have shown that the rate of diabetes mellitus is two to five times higher in persons of Mexican descent than in the white population. It is considered the number one health problem of Chicanos by many health professionals. This high rate is not explained by the incidence of obesity, since it is found in all weight groups, but may be related to percentage of Indian heritage (Markides & Coreil, 1986).

Cavities are more prevalent among Americans of Mexican descent than among other Latinos in the United States. Studies show that nearly one-third of all immigrants from Mexico never receive any dental care.

Counseling

When counseling clients or patients of Mexican descent, it is important to remember that access to health care may be limited, especially for Braceros and undocumented aliens. Income may restrict doctor visits, and transportation to clinics may be unavailable. Further, Spanish-speaking clients may feel uncomfortable with interviews conducted in English. A local folk-healer, called a *curandero,* may be the primary health care provider in some areas.

Health attitudes may also differ from mainstream American medical beliefs. For example, it is considered inappropriate for men to acknowledge illness. People who go on working despite bad health are respected. Individual privacy is highly valued; thus a woman may wish to be treated by a female caregiver and a man by a male caregiver. Within the family unit, the authority of the husband must be respected. Many health-care decisions cannot be made without his approval.

A study of Mexican American families living on the Texas–Mexico border (Yetley, *et al.,* 1981) found that the husband exercised control of the food budget and food purchases. The wife did the actual meal planning, shopping, and preparation.

Women identify strongly with their food-related tasks within the family structure. Because their self-concept and status in the family and community is related to their abilities as a cook and homemaker, nutrition intervention and advice may be perceived as an accusation of inadequacy.

Children are also an important influence on food habits in some households. Those raised in the United States may be the only English-speaking members of the family and may be responsible for translating in the market. It has been found that these children prefer foods that they have seen advertised on television.

Ikeda and Gonzales (1985) studied newly immigrated Latinos in the San Francisco area and found that the importance of the family unit can be used to motivate changes in food habits. Adults unwilling to make changes that would benefit their own health may make those same changes to improve the well-being of their children.

As with all clients, an in-depth interview is crucial in nutrition counseling. Experts in the health care of Latinos recommend that health professionals who often work with Latinos learn Spanish. Familiarity with Spanish medical terminology is the minimum proficiency needed for meaningful interviews.

CARIBBEAN ISLANDERS

Over 1,000 tropical islands in the Caribbean stretch from Florida to Venezuela. They include the Bahamas, the Greater Antilles (Jamaica, Cuba, Hispaniola and Puerto Rico), and the Lesser Antilles. The largest island is Cuba, and the smallest are barely more than exposed rocks. Most were claimed at one time by Spain, Britain, France, the Netherlands, Denmark, or the United States, but now include the independent nations of Antigua/Barbuda, the Bahamas, Barbados, Cuba, Dominica, Dominican Republic, Grenada, Haiti, Jamaica, St. Christopher/Nevis, St. Lucia, St. Vincent/Grenadines, and Trinidad and Tobago, as well as the U.S. territory of Puerto Rico. Many islands, such as the Virgin Islands (U.S.) and Martinique (France) are still under foreign control.

The islands are uniformly scenic. The tropical warmth and torrential rains provide the ideal climate for a lush plant cover that includes numerous edible fruits and vegetables. The native Indians of the Caribbean survived easily on wild foods; later immigrants found the region suitable for imported crops.

The Caribbean islands share a history of domination by foreign powers and political turmoil. Native Indians, Europeans, blacks from Africa, and Asians from China and India have intermarried over the centuries to produce an extremely diverse population.

Cultural Perspective

HISTORY OF THE CARIBBEAN ISLANDS

The original inhabitants of the Caribbean islands are believed to be the prehistoric Cibony Indians. About A.D. 1000, Arawak Indians migrated to the region from South America, followed by the Carib Indians. The Arawaks were an agriculturally based society; the Caribs were hunters and warriors.

When Columbus arrived in the Bahamas in 1492 he believed that he had discovered the East Indies. When this was found to be erroneous, the area became known as the West Indies. During the century following discovery by Europeans, thousands of Spanish settlers arrived in the region searching for riches. The Arawaks were enslaved and eventually exterminated by disease and abuse. The more aggressive Caribs were driven to the remote islands and now exist in only a few small enclaves.

The great natural wealth of the West Indies, especially spices, did not go unnoticed by the other European nations. Pirates from Britain and France regularly attacked the Spanish-occupied ports. Britain, France, the Netherlands, and Denmark established colonies in the Caribbean during the seventeenth century. The Europeans also recognized the region's potential for profitable crops. The Spanish were the first to cultivate sugar cane, although it was the French and British who exploited the crop.

Importation of Labor

The decimated Indian population was not large enough to support the sugar cane plantations that thrived in the West Indies. Fifteen million slaves from Africa were imported to the region from 1518 to 1865 to work in the fields.

Emancipation of the African slaves was granted in the Caribbean during the 1850s and 1860s. This immediately required that a new source of inexpensive labor be found. Indentured servants were brought in from Asia, mostly from India, to support the plantations, particularly on islands where sugar production was a new industry. Established sugar cane–growing islands, such as Puerto Rico, had few Asian immigrants.

Colonial control of the Caribbean islands weakened during the nineteenth century as revolutions led to independence and European interest in the region waned as plantation profits declined. Haiti established the first self-governing nation in 1804. The Dominican Republic separated from Haiti and became an independent country soon after.

The Spanish-American War led to independence for Cuba and ceded Puerto Rico to the United States. The Virgin Islands were purchased by the United States from Denmark in 1917. Cuba, Haiti, and the Dominican Republic remained the only independent Caribbean nations until the early 1960s. Each has been ruled by a succession of dictators. In 1959, revolutionary Fidel Castro established Cuba as a Communist state. Beginning in 1962, other islands slowly gained independence, starting with Jamaica and Trinidad and Tobago. The latest to become a nation was St. Christopher/Nevis in 1983. Puerto Rico has fluctuated between desire for independence and U.S. statehood, and now functions as a commonwealth with an autonomous government that is subject to most federal laws. Citizens of Puerto Rico cannot vote in U.S. elections, nor do they pay federal income tax.

HISTORY OF IMMIGRATION TO THE UNITED STATES

Immigration Patterns

It is estimated that the Latino population in the United States is well over 18 million people. Immigrants from Puerto Rico constitute approximately 14 percent of the total; those from Cuba about 6 percent. Additionally, there are small groups of immigrants from many of the other Caribbean nations; little is known about these other populations after their arrival in the United States.

Puerto Ricans. Puerto Ricans differ from all other people who come to the United States in that they are technically not immigrants. They come to the mainland as U.S. citizens and are free to travel to and from Puerto Rico without restriction. Nearly one-third of the population of Puerto Rico resides on the mainland of the United States, and the number of Puerto Ricans who live in New York City (estimated at 925,000 in the 1980 census) is more than double that living in the largest city in Puerto Rico, San Juan.

Small numbers of political exiles from Puerto Rico arrived in America in the 1800s, but most returned when Puerto Rico became a U.S. possession. Other immigrants arrived when unemployment increased in the depressed agricultural economy of the island during the 1920s and 1930s. It was after World War II that the largest number of Puerto Ricans moved to the mainland. Unlike other immigrants, the Puerto Rican population in the United States is in continual flux. Many Puerto Ricans live alternately between the mainland and the island, depending on economic conditions. In many years, the number of Puerto Ricans leaving the mainland is greater than the number arriving.

Cubans. Cubans have immigrated to the United States since the early nineteenth century. In the early years, the majority were those who found economic conditions unfavorable or who were out of favor with the current government.

The majority of Cubans came to the United States after Fidel Castro overthrew the dictatorship of Fulgencio Batista in 1959. In the three years following the revolution, over 150,000 Cubans arrived in America. Most of these were families from the upper socioeconomic group fleeing the restraints of Communism. Commercial air travel between Cuba and the United States was suspended after the Cuban missile crisis in 1962. Airlifts of immigrants from 1965 to 1973 increased the total number of Cubans in the United States to

Cuban cafeteria, Miami. (Courtesy Metro Dade Department of Tourism.)

nearly 700,000. Due to the political differences between the two countries, most Cubans have not been subject to the usual immigration quotas.

Immigration from Cuba slowed with the end of the airlifts. In 1980, another large group of 110,000 Cubans arrived in Florida in private boats (the Mariel boatlift) seeking asylum. Unlike earlier immigrants, these recent arrivals, called *marielitos,* were mostly poor unskilled laborers. They were often single and black. Today, a trickle of exiles continues to come to the United States. Some arrive by boat and others go through legal immigration channels from a neutral third country.

Current Demographics

The majority of Puerto Ricans coming to the mainland settle in New York City. By 1940, 70,000 Puerto Ricans had moved into East Harlem, which became known both as *El Barrio* and as Spanish Harlem. Over ten times that number now reside in New York City; because Puerto Ricans are a young population, they now comprise nearly one-quarter of the students in the city's public schools. Chicago, Philadelphia, Newark, Miami, San Francisco, and Los Angeles also have Puerto Rican communities.

Americans of Cuban descent prefer to live in the Miami area, which is sometimes called "Little Havana." The climate is similar to that of their homeland, and the Cuban population in the region is the largest in the United States. Efforts to resettle exiles in other areas have been only moderately successful. Many Cubans living in New York City; Jersey City and Newark, New Jersey; Los Angeles; and Chicago choose to move to Miami after gaining job skills. Those Cubans who remain in other cities are most likely to be employed in technical or professional occupations. Nearly all Cubans who live in the United States are urban dwellers.

Socioeconomic Status

Immigrants from the Caribbean vary tremendously in both economic and educational attainment. Among Latinos, Puerto Rican Americans have the highest rate of unemployment and Cuban Americans have the lowest. In 1987, the median annual income of Puerto Ricans in the mainland United States was approximately half that of the U.S. Cuban population, again the lowest and highest among Latinos re-

Immigrants from Central and South America are thought to be comparable socioeconomically to those from Cuba. They attain the highest level of education and income of all Spanish-surnamed Americans.

spectively. It is not known how the arrival of the poor marie-litos will statistically affect the high socioeconomic status of Cuban Americans.

Educational rates for first-generation immigrants from the Caribbean are very similar to those of other Latinos. Nearly half of all adults from Puerto Rico and Cuba did not attend high school. Differences in educational attainment appear with second-generation Americans of Caribbean descent, however. Only 27 percent of Puerto Ricans living on the mainland complete high school; over 50 percent of Cuban Americans graduate from high school.

Socioeconomic differences between Latino groups from the Caribbean are due to many factors. Puerto Ricans living on the mainland are free to travel between the United States and their homeland, and the frequent changes in residence may hamper socioeconomic improvement. Puerto Ricans have also chosen to settle primarily in New York City, where as a new ethnic minority they took over the decayed neigh-borhoods previously occupied by blacks. In general, their low education levels and undeveloped job skills translate into un-employment and low-level employment. In contrast, Cubans in the United States are mostly political refugees who emi-grated out of necessity, not choice. There are a dispropor-tionate number of Cubans in the United States from the upper socioeconomic levels, and although many lost all their ma-terial goods, they brought their upper-class values, including the importance of educational and financial success. Instead of displacing any ethnic minority in Florida, they immigrated in such numbers that they immediately became the dominant ethnic group. This is not to say that there are no well-edu-cated, wealthy Puerto Ricans living on the mainland or poor Cuban Americans. However, circumstances surrounding their immigration have influenced the general socioeco-nomic status of both groups.

WORLDVIEW

Ethnic identity is strongly maintained in both the Puerto Rican and Cuban communities in the United States. Puerto Ricans on the mainland maintain close ties with the island; Cubans feel it is important to retain their heritage because they cannot return. Spanish may be spoken exclusively in the home and used frequently to conduct business within the community.

Religion

The majority of Puerto Ricans and Cubans are Roman Catholics, although many are not faithful followers of the church. The role of the Catholic church has been less important in the Caribbean than in other regions of Latin America. There are a number of other religions in the islands, including Protestantism and Judaism, as well as some folk religions. The best known of these is voodoo, a unique combination of West African tribal rituals with Catholic beliefs and local customs. Saint Patrick is associated with the African snake deity Damballah, for example, and certain rites, such as repeating the Hail Mary, making the sign of the cross, and baptism are practiced in conjunction with ancestor worship, drums, and African dancing. Voodoo originated in Haiti, although very similar Afro-Catholic cults are found on the other islands. In Cuba and Puerto Rico they are called *santeria.*

Family

Puerto Ricans on the mainland and Cuban Americans are similar to other Latino groups in that the family is highly valued (see the section on Mexico). Many live in extended family groups. New immigrants are most likely to settle where their relatives have become established.

Traditional Food Habits

INGREDIENTS AND COMMON FOODS

Caribbean food habits are remarkably similar for an area influenced by so many other cultures. The indigenous Indians, the Spanish, French, British, Dutch, Danes, Africans, Asian Indians, and Chinese have all had an impact on the cuisine. Although each island has its specialties, the basic diet is the same throughout the region.

Native Foods

Columbus likened the West Indies to paradise on earth. The islands are naturally laden with fresh fruits and vegetables that originally came from South America, including the staple cassava (two varieties of tuber, sweet and bitter, that are also known as manioc and yuca; tapioca is a starch product of this plant), avocados, bananas and plantains, some varieties of beans, cashew apples (fruit surrounding the cashew nut), cocoa, coconuts, guavas, malanga (a mild tuber), papayas,

Cassava contains hydrocyanic acid, which is toxic in large amounts. The acid must be leached out and the tuber cooked before it can be eaten safely.

pineapple, soursop (a fruit with a cottonlike consistency), several types of squash (including chayote, called *chocho* or *christophene* in the islands), sweet potatoes, *tanier* (another type of tuber), and tomatoes. Fish and small birds are also plentiful.

As in other Latin American countries, many varieties of chili peppers grow profusely in the West Indies. The native cuisine makes frequent use of these for flavoring, especially in pepper sauces, such as *coui,* a mixture of cassava juice and hot chilis. Other herbs and spices include allspice and annatto.

Because of the abundance of fresh fruits and vegetables year-round, traditionally there was little need for preparation or preservation of foods. Consequently, cooking techniques were underdeveloped in the native populations. Cassava was baked most often in a kind of bread, made from pressed, dried, grated cassava that was fried in a flat loaf. Fish and game were either covered with mud and baked in a pit or grilled over an open fire.

Foreign Influence

The Europeans who settled in the Caribbean were impressed with the abundant supply of native fruits and vegetables. Yet they longed for the accustomed tastes of home. The Spanish brought cattle, goats, hogs, and sheep to the islands, in addition to introducing rice. Plants introduced for trade by the Europeans included breadfruit, coffee, limes, mangoes, oranges, and spices such as nutmeg and mace. The African slaves brought in to work the sugar cane fields cultivated *akee* (a mild, apple-sized fruit), okra, and *taro* (also called *edo* or *dasheen;* both the roots and the leaves are eaten). The demand for Asian ingredients by later immigrants resulted in the introduction of lettuce, cabbage, and tamarind to the Caribbean.

Staples

Beans are eaten throughout the Caribbean; the rice and kidney beans of Puerto Rico are also found in Jamaica and Haiti (where the beans are called peas). In Cuba, black beans are preferred. The beans in all countries are prepared similarly, flavored with lard and salt. Onions, sweet peppers, and tomatoes are added in some variations.

Examples of other foods common throughout the West Indies are found in the Cultural Food Groups list (Table 6.2).

Fruits common in the Caribbean are also found in Central and South America, especially along the coast of the Caribbean. Coconut milk flavors many dishes in Honduras and Belize; the juice of sour oranges is mixed with sweet peppers or mint in many Nicaraguan recipes; and bananas, coconuts, and hot peppers are featured in the spicy, African-influenced cuisine of Bahia, Brazil.

The American word barbecue is probably derived from *barbacoa,* the Arawak word for grilling meats.

Mixtas, a common dish in Guatemala, also reflects a multicultural heritage: Indian, Spanish, and German. A *tortilla* is spread with *guacamole,* then topped with a sausage and pickled cabbage similar to sauerkraut.

The black beans and rice are called *Moros y Cristianos* (Moors and Christians) in Cuba.

TABLE 6.2. Cultural Food Groups: Caribbean Islanders

Group	Comments
PROTEIN FOODS Milk/milk products	Few dairy products used; incidence of lactose intolerance assumed to be high.
	Infants given whole, evaporated, or condensed milk.
Meats/poultry/fish/eggs/legumes	Traditional diet high in vegetable protein, especially rice and legumes; red and kidney beans used by Puerto Ricans, black beans by Cubans.
	Pork and beef used more in Spanish-influenced countries.
	Dried salt cod preferred over fresh fish; some seafood specialties.
	Eggs are a common protein source, especially among the poor.
	Entrees are often fried in lard or olive oil.
CEREALS/GRAINS	Breads of other countries well accepted.
	Fried breads popular.
FRUITS/VEGETABLES	Starchy fruits and vegetables eaten daily; leafy vegetables consumed infrequently.
	Great diversity of tropical fruits available, eaten mostly as snacks and dessert.
	Lime juice used to "cook" (a marinating method called *escabeche*) meats and fish.

Common Foods	Adaptations in the United States
Cow's milk (fresh, condensed, evaporated), *café con leche, café latte);* aged cheeses.	More milk is consumed.
Meats: beef, pork (including intestines, organs, variety cuts), goat.	More meat, poultry, eggs eaten as income increases.
Poultry: chicken, turkey.	Less fresh fish consumed.
Fish and shellfish: bacalao (dried salt cod), barracuda, bonita, butterfish, crab, dolphin, flying fish, gar, grouper, grunts, land crabs, mackerel, mullets, *ostiones* (tree oysters), porgie, salmon, snapper, tarpon, turtle, tuna.	Traditional entrees remain popular.
Eggs: chicken.	
Legumes: black beans, black-eyed peas, garbanzo beans (chick peas), kidney beans, lima beans, peas, red beans, soy beans.	
Cassava bread; cornmeal (fried breads, *surrulitos,* puddings); oatmeal; rice (short-grain); wheat (Asian Indian breads, European breads, pasta).	Short-grain rice still preferred. More wheat breads eaten.
Fruits: acerola cherries, *akee,* avocados, bananas and plantains, breadfruit, *caimito* (star apple), cashew apple, citron, coconut, cocoplum, custard apple, gooseberries, *granadilla* (passion fruit), grapefruit, guava, *guanábana* (soursop) kumquats, lemons, limes, *mamey,* mangoes, oranges, papayas, pineapple, pomarrosa, pomegranates, raisins, *sapodilla,* sugar cane, tamarind.	Temperate fruits substituted for tropical fruits when latter unavailable. More fresh fruit eaten. Starchy fruits and vegetables still frequently consumed. Low intake of leafy vegetables often continues.
Vegetables: arracacha (Peruvian carrot), arrowroot, black-eyed peas, broccoli, cabbage, *calabaza* (green pumpkin), *callaloo* (malanga or taro leaves), cassava (*yuca,* manioc), chilis, corn, cucumbers, eggplant, green beans, lettuce, *malangas,* okra, onions, palm hearts, peppers, potatoes, radishes, spinach, squashes (*chayote,* summer, and winter), sweet potatoes, *taniers,* taro *(edo, dasheen),* tomatoes, yams.	

TABLE 6.2. Cultural Food Groups: Caribbean Islanders (*continued*)

Group	Comments
ADDITIONAL FOODS	
Seasonings	Chili-based sauces often used to flavor foods.
Beverages	
Fats/oils	
Sweeteners	

Black beans are also popular throughout Central and South America. In Brazil, the national dish is *feijoada completa*, a lavish dish of black beans garnished with bacon, beef, dried beef, pork, smoked tongue, and sausage. It is served with seasoned rice, sliced oranges, toasted cassava meal, and vegetables, such as kale.

Pickled fish is thought to have originated in Peru, where scallops or cubes of raw fish are marinated in salted lemon or lime juice mixed with chilis and garlic until the fish becomes "cooked"; that is, opaque and flaky. It is called *ceviche* and can be found in some variation throughout Latin America.

They include Indian foods such as cassava bread, chili pepper sauces, and pepper pot (a meat stew made with the boiled juice of the cassava called *cassarep*). European dishes, such as *escabeche* (pickled fish, seafood, or poultry), *morcillas* (a type of blood sausage), and fried corn cakes, are popular in most Caribbean countries. Foods from Africa found throughout the region include *callaloo* (a dish of taro or malanga greens cooked with okra), salt cod fritters (called *bacalaitos* in Puerto Rico, these cakes have a different name on nearly every island, from *arcat de marue* to "stamp and go"), *foofoo* (okra and plantain), and *coocoo* (cornmeal-and-okra bread). Dishes from Asia are also common on many islands, although they are better known in the areas where cheap labor was most needed: the French-, British-, and Dutch-dominated islands (few Asians immigrated to Puerto Rico or Hispanola). Curried dishes, called *kerry* in the Dutch-influenced islands and *colombo* on the French-influenced islands, and variations of pilaf are considered to be Caribbean foods. Chinese cuisine is also popular and Chinese-owned restaurants are ubiquitous.

The most popular beverage in the Caribbean is coffee. It is often mixed with milk and is drunk at meals, as a snack, and even as dessert, flavored with orange rind, cinnamon,

Common Foods	*Adaptations in the United States*
Anise, annatto, bay leaf, chives, *cilantro* (coriander leaves), cinnamon, *coui* (chilis mixed with cassava juice), garlic, mace, nutmeg, onions, parsley, scallions, *sofrito* (fried onions with garlic, sweet peppers, tomatoes and cilantro, from Puerto Rico), thyme.	
Beer, coffee *(café con leche)*, soft drinks, milk, rum.	Fruit juice and soft drink consumption may increase.
Butter in French-influenced countries; coconut oil; *ghee* (Asian Indian clarified butter); lard in Spanish-influenced countries; olive oil.	
Sugar cane products, such as raw and unrefined sugar and molasses.	

whipped cream, coconut cream, or rum. Some of the most expensive coffee in the world is produced in the Blue Mountains of Jamaica, where the cool, moderately rainy climate is ideal for coffee cultivation. Most of the rich beans are exported to England and Italy, although small amounts can be found in the United States.

The most important beverage in the Caribbean, at least historically, is the spirit distilled from fermented molasses: rum. This alcoholic drink is believed to have originated on the island of Barbados in the early 1600s as a byproduct of sugar cane processing. Molasses is the liquid that remains after the syrup from the sugar cane has been crystallized to make sugar. It is fermented, naturally or with the addition of yeast, then distilled to make a clear, high-proof alcoholic beverage. Rum can be bottled immediately or aged in oak casks from a few months to 25 years. Caramel is added to achieve the desired color. Nearly every island produces its own variety of rum.

The molasses produced in the West Indies was crucial to the development of the region during the seventeenth and eighteenth centuries. The Caribbean islands were one corner of the infamous slave triangle, formed when molasses was

Many well-known mixed drinks were developed in the Caribbean with rum. Planter's punch is an adaptation of the recipe from India for *panch* (lime juice, sweetening, spirit, water, and spices), and was probably invented by the British in the 18th century. Daiquiris, a popular mix of lime juice, sugar and rum was created in the 1890s and named after a Cuban town. The *cuba libre* (rum and coke with a slice of lemon) is popular throughout the Caribbean and Central America.

shipped to New England for distillation into rum, rum was shipped to Africa and exchanged for slaves, and slaves were shipped to the West Indies to work in the sugar cane fields.

Regional Variations

Despite the similarities in foods throughout the West Indies, most islands have their own specialties. Jamaica is known for its spicy vegetable soup called pepper pot and for "pickapeppa" sauce (a sweet mango sauce or a hot pepper sauce); Haiti for its banana-stuffed chicken dish called *poulet rôti à la créole;* the Dominican Republic for *sancocho,* a pork intestine stew; Curaçao for its orange-flavored liqueur of the same name; Dominica for its "mountain chicken," a large, tasty frog; and Barbados for its unusual seafood dishes made with flying fish, green turtles, and sea urchins.

Puerto Rico. In addition to rice and kidney beans, the Puerto Rican cuisine is notable for its use of *sofrito,* a combination of onions, garlic, cilantro, sweet chilis, and tomatoes that is lightly fried in lard colored with annatto seeds. Sofrito serves as a base for many dishes, as well as an all-purpose sauce. More pork, beef, and goat is eaten in Puerto Rico than in most Caribbean countries. Plantains are stuffed with spicy beef mixtures or *chicharrones* (fried pork rind). Land crabs and *ostiones,* a type of oyster that grows on the roots of mangrove trees, are popular, but the fish most commonly eaten is dried salt cod, called *bacalao.* It is soaked and drained before use to remove some of the salt and is added to numerous dishes. Starchy vegetables, such as potatoes and plantains, are eaten almost daily, but leafy green vegetables are uncommon.

Cuba. Cuba is unique in the West Indies in the use of black beans in its cuisine. In addition to black beans and rice, black bean soup is very popular. *Picadillo* is a type of beef hash that is flavored with traditional Spanish ingredients of olives and raisins, as well as Caribbean tomatoes and hot chilis. It is served with fried plantains or boiled rice, or topped with fried eggs. Another specialty is *chicharrones de pollo,* small pieces of chicken that are marinated in lime juice and soy sauce, breaded, then fried in lard. As in Puerto Rico, starchy vegetables are preferred over leafy green vegetable side dishes.

MEAL COMPOSITION AND CYCLE

The most typical aspect of a Caribbean meal is its emphasis on starchy vegetables with some meat, poultry, or fish. Meats are frequently fried. Leafy vegetables are often an ingredient in soups, stews, and stuffed foods; fruits are enjoyed fresh, frequently as snacks and dessert.

What dishes are served often depends on the ethnic heritage of the preparer. A poor native Indian may eat mostly cassava, tomatoes, and chilis with a bit of meat or fish at every meal. An Asian Indian may serve typically Indian meals adapted to Caribbean ingredients, such as a curried dish garnished with coconut, rice, fried plantains, and pineapple. Most menus, however, consist of a multicultural mix, such as European blood sausage and *accra,* West African–style fritters made from the meal of soybeans or black-eyed peas. The list of dishes served at a meal on a French-influenced island may be identical to that on a Spanish-influenced island, yet the two meals will taste different because butter was used for cooking the former and lard the latter.

Daily Patterns

Breakfast usually consists of coffee with milk and bread. Eggs are the most common addition if money permits, then cereals and fruits. Urban residents are more likely to skip breakfast than are people in rural households.

Rice and beans with meat, if affordable, is the most popular lunch. In rural regions, a starchy vegetable such as potatoes, plantain, breadfruit, taniers, taro, or yams, with salt cod is also common. Meats, milk, and salad vegetables are extra items added to the basic foods whenever possible.

Dinner is similar to lunch. Rice and beans provide the core of the meal, with meats, vegetables, and milk added when available. In upper-income households, the meal may consist of three or four different dishes.

Milk and coffee with milk (*café con leche*) are the preferred beverages. Soft drinks and beer are also popular. Ice cream and pastries are popular desserts to those who can afford them. Snacking is frequent among some groups, especially children. Fruits, sweetened fruit juices poured over shaved ice, and coffee with milk are common.

Typical Cuban meal: This meal includes savory picadillo *(right), black beans and rice, bread, and Spanish-style custard* (flan) *for dessert. (Courtesy Florida News Bureau.)*

Special Occasions

The early European dominance in the West Indies resulted in an emphasis on Christian holidays. Christmas is important, especially in the Spanish-influenced islands that are predominantly Catholic. In Puerto Rico, *pasteles* are prepared to celebrate Christmas. Similar to Mexican *tamales*, *pasteles* are a savory meat mixture surrounded by cornmeal or mashed plantains, wrapped in plantain leaves, and steamed. Carolers traditionally stop at houses late at night to request hot *pasteles* from the occupants.

Other holidays reflect the multicultural history of the islands. *Carnival* is celebrated in some Caribbean countries, such as Trinidad and Tobago, and is similar to Mardi Gras in the United States. The pre-Lent festivities feature parades of dancing celebrants; many are elaborately costumed as traditional European or African figures. Food booths that line the parade route provide a day-and-night supply of carnival treats. Fried Asian Indian fritters are particularly popular.

Examples of nonreligious events include the day-long birthday open house on Curaçao for friends, relatives, and acquaintances. Thanksgiving is observed in Puerto Rico. Turkey, stuffed with a Spanish-style meat filling, is the main course.

On Good Friday in Trinidad and Tobago, the white of an egg is added to warm water and the future is predicted by its shape.

THERAPEUTIC USES OF FOOD

Some Caribbean Islanders practice the Latin American hot–cold classification of foods (see the previous section on Mexico), especially during pregnancy, which is considered a hot condition. Foods may also be categorized as being "heavy" or "light," which may determine when and in what combination they are eaten. As with most other beliefs in the region, however, these food classification systems are usually combined with other ideas about health and illness. The curative methods of some Puerto Rican practitioners, for example, are related more to African healing beliefs than to the Arab–Spanish humoral medicine. It is an informal system, and the healer is often an older woman member of the household who is familiar with the use of herbs, amulets, and charms, rather than a healer by profession. In Cuba, most indigenous health belief systems have given way to socialized medical care.

Raw rum was believed to cure many types of diseases and injuries in the 17th and 18th centuries. As late as 1892, a physician prescribed Cuban rum for the six-year-old future King of Spain when he suffered from fever. The royal family was so impressed by his quick recuperation that they granted the maker of the rum, the Bacardi family, the right to use the Spanish coat of arms on their label.

Contemporary Food Habits in the United States

ADAPTATION OF FOOD HABITS

Traditional food habits are easily maintained in the self-sustaining immigrant communities of Spanish Harlem in New

York and Little Havana in Miami. Ingredients for Caribbean cuisine are readily available through Puerto Rican and Cuban American grocery stores. Cubans, for example, consider drinking strong coffee as one way in which they maintain their ethnic identity; by contrast, Americans drink "weak" coffee (Pasquali, 1985). Changes do occur, however, as immigrants settle into culturally mixed communities and children grow up as Americans.

One study compared the diet of three groups of women from Puerto Rico: (1) those living in New York (forward migrants); (2) those who had lived on the mainland but later returned to the island (return migrants); and (3) those who never lived on the mainland (nonmigrants). It was found that nonmigrants and return migrants ate more starchy vegetables, sugar, and sweetened foods than did forward migrants. Forward migrants ate a greater variety of foods, including more beef, eggs, bread, fresh fruit, and leafy green vegetables. Puerto Rican women who had lived on the mainland quickly reverted to their traditional food habits when they returned to the island (Immink *et al.*, 1983).

Ingredients and Common Foods

Research on the eating patterns of Caribbean immigrants in the United States is scanty. It is thought that rice, beans, starchy vegetables, sofrito, and bacalao remain the basis of the daily diet of many Puerto Ricans who live on the mainland. Poultry is used when possible, and egg intake decreases. Because of Cuban Americans' greater discretionary income, their diet usually includes additional foods, such as more pork and beef. Recent poorer immigrants from Cuba, including the marielitos, are more restricted in what foods they purchase, however, and may follow a diet that is closer to the subsistence-level Puerto Rican regimen.

A study of Puerto Rican teenagers in New York found that, consistent with traditional food habits, there is little diversity of food items in their diet (Duyff *et al.*, 1975). In another study, adult Puerto Rican women living on the mainland ate a greater variety of foods than those residing on the island, including more fresh fruit, juices, leafy vegetables, bread, eggs, and beef (Immink *et al.*, 1983).

According to marketing studies, Caribbean Islanders accept some American foods, especially convenience items, and purchase frozen and dehydrated products when they can afford to. The proportion of meat in the diet increases on the

In a study of elderly Cubans living in the United States, it was found that convenience items were sometimes used to prepare traditional foods: aluminum foil in place of banana leaves for *tamales* and packaged crescent rolls for *pastele* dough (Pasquali, 1985).

mainland, as does the consumption of milk and soft drinks. Intake of leafy vegetables continues to be low. Local fruits often replace the tropical fruits of Puerto Rico.

Meal Composition and Cycle

The meals of Puerto Ricans residing on the mainland are similar to those of people on the island, with a few changes. A light breakfast of bread and coffee may be followed by a light lunch of rice and beans or a starchy vegetable, with or without bacalao. Often this traditional midday meal becomes a sandwich and soft drink, however. A late dinner consists of rice, beans, starchy vegetable, meat, if available, or soup. Many researchers have reported an increase in the amount of snacking between meals, mostly of high-calorie foods with little nutritional value.

One study (Haider & Wheeler, 1979) reported that many low-income Latina women living in New York did not plan menus far in advance and that this hampered their ability to add variety to their diets. It was found that food shopping serves as a social occasion for many of the women and is one of the few opportunities they have to get out of the house; thus they may go to the grocery store more often than is really necessary. The investigators reported that nearly half of the women questioned preferred to fry main dishes. Boiling was the second-choice method, baking third. Broiling food was a distant fourth choice. The researchers note that in many low-income households the oven or broiler element may not work, restricting food preparation methods to frying and boiling.

NUTRITIONAL STATUS

Nutritional Intake

There is even less information on the nutritional status of Caribbean immigrants to the United States than on Chicanos (see the section on Mexico). The few studies available suggest several health trends in these immigrants that have important nutritional implications.

Although the birth rate for Puerto Ricans is lower than for Americans of Mexican descent, it is still higher than for the non-Latino population. Additionally, nearly 10 percent of Puerto Rican infants born on the mainland are of low birthweight. This undoubtedly contributes to the high infant mortality rate: among Puerto Ricans in New York, the infant mortality rate is reported to be 70 percent higher than that of the total population.

Breastfeeding is reportedly uncommon among Puerto Rican and Cuban women in the United States. Those few who start breastfeeding may switch to bottle feeding after two to four weeks. Whole milk, condensed milk, and evaporated milk are frequently fed to infants, as are juices. Solid food is typically introduced at a young age (Kumanyika & Helitzer, 1985). Observation of other Caribbean islanders suggests that breastfeeding may be prevalent, however (Gupta, 1987).

When the traditional Caribbean diet is limited because of low income, it inevitably results in low intake of many vitamins and minerals. The emphasis on carbohydrates and vegetable protein with a low consumption of leafy vegetables and fruit provides inadequate intake of calories, vitamins A and C, iron, and calcium. A study indicated that the only foods consumed by at least half of recent Cuban immigrants were eggs, rice, bread, legumes, lard and oils, sugar, and crackers (Gordon, 1982). Of the same group, 79 to 100 percent reported never eating leafy green vegetables or fresh fruits. Anthropometric measurements and physical observation suggested that 20 percent of the children under 15 years old showed signs of malnutrition, 37 percent of the men and 17 percent of the women had adipose tissue measurements consistent with adult marasmus, and 12 percent of the immigrants suffered from anemia.

Research on Latinas in New York (Haider & Wheeler, 1979) showed that although calorie, iron, and calcium intake was low, 29 percent were found to be overweight. It was postulated that nonreported high-calorie snack items and a sedentary lifestyle contributed to the extra weight.

In another study, Puerto Rican women living in New York (Immink *et al.*, 1983) were found to consume more calories, calcium, iron, vitamins A and C, and riboflavin than those residing in Puerto Rico, approaching or exceeding the recommended dietary allowance for those nutrients. Obesity was found to be less prevalent among women on the mainland than those in Puerto Rico. The researchers could not explain why obesity rates were lower in the women with greater overall calorie intake.

Many native Puerto Ricans suffer from parasitic diseases, including dysentery, malaria, hookworm, filariasis, and schistosomiasis. It is believed that 60 percent of the rural population in Cuba is infected with parasites. These conditions contribute to general poor health and nutritional deficiencies among poorer immigrants.

Lactose intolerance is believed to be a problem among Caribbean populations, although estimated incidence has not been reported.

The incidence of dental caries among Caribbean immigrants is similar to that of other Latino groups. Among recent Cuban immigrants, children had the lowest rate (25 percent), adults over 65 the highest rate (50 percent). Cuban men were found to have a higher rate of caries, 73 percent, than Puerto Rican men, 62 percent (Gordon, 1982).

Counseling

Counseling Americans of Caribbean descent is similar to counseling other Latino clients and patients (see the previous section on Mexico). Access to medical care may be limited, health beliefs may differ from those of the provider, and language problems may make interviews difficult.

Although an immigrant from the Caribbean may be of African, Asian, European, or Indian descent, the island of origin is as important in determining diet as ethnic identity. A black from Puerto Rico, for example, is more likely to eat Latino foods than just African dishes or soul food.

A study that modified the food behavior of low-income Latinas and black women in New York (Wheeler & Haider, 1979) recommended that significant attention be placed on the client's socioeconomic status. Diet therapy for a poor Puerto Rican immigrant is likely to require a different approach than that for a wealthy Cuban immigrant within the context of the basic Caribbean cuisine.

Researchers have reported that 92 percent of Puerto Rican teenage girls obtain nutrition information from their mothers, 51 percent from home economics classes, 43 percent from health professionals, and 37 percent from friends (Duyff et al., 1975). These data suggest that, as in Chicano households, the mother is the primary source of food and nutrition beliefs and must be respected by the health professional as an expert in her role.

An in-depth interview should be conducted with each client of Caribbean descent to establish country of origin, ethnic identity, and length of stay in the United States. The client's degree of acculturation, socioeconomic status, and personal food preferences should also be determined.

REFERENCES

Barer-Stein, T. 1979. *You Eat What You Are.* Toronto: McClelland and Stewart.
Bruhn, C. M., & Pangborn, R. M. 1971. Food habits of migrant workers in California. *Journal of the American Dietetic Association, 59,* 347–355.

Bullough, V., & Bullough, B. 1981. The Spanish-speaking minority groups. In *Health Care for the Other Americans.* New York: Springer.

Cortez, C. E. 1980. Mexicans. In *The Harvard Encyclopedia of American Ethnic Groups,* S. Thernstrom, A. Orlov and O. Handlin (Eds.). Cambridge, MA: The Belknap Press of Harvard University Press.

Cravioto, R., Lockhart, E. E. Anderson, R. K., Miranda, F., & Harris, R. S. 1945. Composition of typical Mexican foods. *Journal of Nutrition, 29,* 317–329.

Duyff, R. L., Sanjur, D., & Nelson, H. V. 1975. Food behavior and related factors of Puerto Rican teenagers. *Journal of Nutrition Education, 7,* 99–103.

Eckstein, E. F. 1983. Foodways of Chicanos. In *Menu Planning* (3rd ed.). Westport, CT: AVI Publishing.

Eckstein, E. F. 1983. Foodways of Puerto Ricans and Cubans living in the United States. In *Menu Planning* (3rd ed.). Westport, CT: AVI Publishing.

Fernandez, N. A., Burgos, J. C., Asenjo, C. F., & Rosa, I. 1971. Nutritional status of the Puerto Rican population: Master sample survey. *American Journal of Clinical Nutrition, 24,* 952–965.

Fitzpatrick, J. P. 1980. Puerto Ricans. In *The Harvard Encyclopedia of American Ethnic Groups,* S. Thernstrom, A. Orlov and O. Handlin (Eds.). Cambridge, MA: The Belknap Press of Harvard University Press.

Gabriel, A., Gabriel, K. R., & Lawrence, R. A. 1986. Cultural values and biomedical knowledge: Choices in infant feeding. *Social Science and Medicine, 23,* 501–509.

Gladney, V. M. 1966. *Food practices of Mexican-Americans in Los Angeles County.* Los Angeles: Los Angeles County Health Department.

Gordon, A. M. 1982. Nutritional status of Cuban refugees: A field study on the health and nutrition of refugees processed at Opa Locka, Florida. *American Journal of Clinical Nutrition, 35,* 582–590.

Gupta, R. 1987. *Caribbean Prenatal Nutrition Project* (extended abstract). Dorchester, MA: The Codman Square Health Center.

Haider, M. & Wheeler, M. 1979. Nutritive intake of black and Hispanic mothers in a Brooklyn ghetto. *Journal of the American Dietetic Association, 75,* 670–673.

Harris, M. 1985. *Good to Eat: Riddles of Food and Culture.* New York: Simon and Schuster.

Ikeda, J. & Gonzalez, M. M. 1986. *Food Habits of Hispanics Newly Migrated to the San Francisco Bay Area* (abstract). Oakland, CA Dietetic Association Annual Meeting.

Immink, M. D. C., Sanjur, D., & Burgos, M. 1983. Nutritional consequences of U.S. migration patterns among Puerto Rican women. *Ecology of Food and Nutrition, 13,* 139–148.

Ingham, J. M. 1970. On Mexican folk medicine. *American Anthropologist, 72,* 76–87.

Kennedy, D. 1975. *The Tortilla Book.* New York: Harper & Row.

Knapp, J. A., Haffner, S. M., Young, E. A., Hazuda, H. P., Gardner, L. & Stern, P. 1985. Dietary intakes of essential nutrients among Mexican-Americans and Anglo-Americans: The San Antonio Heart Study. *American Journal of Clinical Nutrition, 42,* 307–316.

Kokinos, M., & Dewey, K. G. 1986. Infant feeding practices of migrant Mexican-American families in Northern California. *Ecology of Food and Nutrition, 18,* 209–220.

Kumanyika, S., & Helitzer, D. L. 1985. Nutritional status and dietary pattern of racial minorities in the United States. In *Report of the Secre-*

tary's Task Force on Black and Minority Health (Vol. II). Washington, DC: U.S. Department of Health and Human Services.

Leonard, J. N. 1968. *Latin American Cooking.* New York: Time-Life Books.

Markides, K. S. & Coriel, J. 1986. The health of Hispanics in the southwestern United States: An epidemiological paradox. *Public Health Reports, 101,* 253–263.

Marks, C. 1985. *False Tongues and Sunday Bread: a Guatemalan and Mayan Cookbook.* New York: M. Evans.

McGee, H. 1984. *On Food and Cooking: The Science and Lore of the Kitchen.* New York: Charles Scribner's Sons.

Messer, E. 1981. Hot/cold classification: Theoretical and practical implications of a Mexican study. *Social Sciences and Medicine, 158,* 133–145.

Monrroy, L. S. 1983. Nursing care of Raza/Latina patients. In *Ethnic Nursing Care: A Multicultural Approach,* M. S. Orque, B. Bloch, & L. S. Monrroy (Eds.). St. Louis: C. V. Mosby.

Newman, J. M. 1986. Hispanic-Americans. In *Melting Pot: An Annotated Bibliography and Guide to Food and Nutrition Information for Ethnic Groups in America.* New York: Garland Publishing.

Pasquali, E. A. 1985. The impact of acculturation on the eating habits of elderly immigrants: A Cuban example. *Journal of Nutrition for the Elderly, 5,* 27–36.

Perez, L. 1980. Cubans. In *The Harvard Encyclopedia of American Ethnic Groups.* S. Thernstrom, A. Orlov and O. Handlin (Eds.). Cambridge, MA: The Belknap Press of Harvard University Press.

Sanjur, D. 1982. *Social and Cultural Perspectives in Nutrition.* Englewood Cliffs, NJ: Prentice-Hall.

Smith, L. 1979. Mexican-American views of Anglo medical and dietetic practices. *Journal of the American Dietetic Association, 74,* 463–464.

Stern, M. P., Gaskell, S. P., Hazuda, H. P., Gardner, L. I., & Haffner, S. M. 1983. Does obesity explain excess prevalence of diabetes among Mexican-Americans? Results of the San Antonio Heart Study. *Diabetologia, 24,* 272–277.

Wallendorf, M., & Reilly, M. D. 1983. Ethnic migration, assimilation, and consumption. *Journal of Consumer Research, 10,* 292–302.

Wheeler, M., & Haider, S. Q. 1979. Buying and food preparation patterns of ghetto blacks and Hispanics in Brooklyn. *Journal of the American Dietetic Association, 75,* 560–563.

Windham, C. T., Wyse, B. W., & Hansen, R. G. 1983. Nutrient density in diets in the USDA Nationwide Food Consumption Survey, 1977–78: Impact of socioeconomic status on dietary density. *Journal of the American Dietetic Association, 82,* 28–34.

Wolfe, L. 1970. *The Cooking of the Caribbean Islands.* New York: Time-Life Books.

Yetley, E. A., Yetley, M. J. & Aguirre, B. 1981. Family role structure and food-related roles in Mexican-American families. *Journal of Nutrition Education, 13* (Supplement No. 1), S96–S101.

7

ASIANS

A sia, one of the largest continents, is thought to have been named by the Greeks, who divided the world into two parts: "Europe" and "Asia." It includes China, Japan, Democratic People's Republic of Korea (North Korea), Republic of Korea (South Korea), Mongolian People's Republic, and the countries of Southeast Asia, stretching from the cool northern borders with Europe to the tropical islands of the Pacific.

Immigrants from China, Japan, and the Philippines have been coming to the United States since the 1800s. Many settled on the West Coast, where the majority of their descendants still live. Small numbers of Koreans began to come following the Korean War in 1953 and more recently, refugees from Vietnam and Cambodia have arrived, also settling primarily on the West Coast. This chapter will discuss the traditional cuisines of the Chinese, Japanese, Filipinos, and Vietnamese and examine changes they have made in their foods and food habits in the United States.

CHINA

Chinese civilization is over 4,000 years old. The name *China* is probably derived from that of a dynasty that ruled in the third century B.C. China's land mass is approximately half the size of the continental United States, yet its population is

248

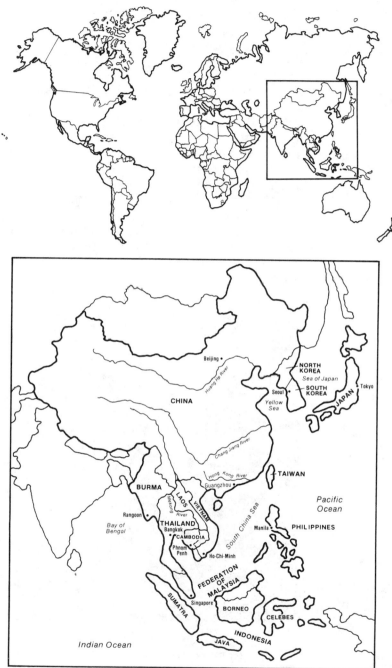

Asia

over four times as large, with numerous ethnic and racial groups.

China's landscape is dominated by the valleys of two great rivers, the Huang (Yellow) river in the North and the Chang Jiang (Yangtze) in the South. The climate is monsoonal in nature, with most of China's rainfall occurring in the spring and summer months.

The northern plain through which the Huang River flows is agriculturally very fertile. However, the area is cold and sometimes the severe winter results in a growing season of only 4 to 6 months. In the South, the Chang Jiang River starts in Tibet, traverses the southern provinces and eventually empties into the China Sea near the city of Shanghai. South of the mouth of the Yangtze delta is a rugged and mountainous coastline off of which is located the islands of Hong Kong and Taiwan. The southern provinces are warmer, wetter and have a growing season that is longer (6 to 9 months) than in the North.

Traditional foods of China: Some foods typical of the traditional Chinese diet include bitter melon, bok choy, *Chinese eggplant, ginger root, long beans, lotus root, mushrooms, oyster sauce, pork, rice, shrimp, soy sauce, and water chestnuts.* (Photo by Laurie Macfee.)

Cultural Perspective

HISTORY OF CHINA

China's history is generally divided into periods named for the dynasties under which it was ruled. One of the earliest dynasties is thought to be that of Hsia (2205–1766 B.C.?), but it is uncertain if it actually existed. The Chou dynasty (1122–256 B.C.) may have been the first to unify China, although it was really only a collection of states with unstable borders. It extended as far south as the Chang Jiang valley and north to the Huang River. Several schools of philosophy were established during the Chou dynasty that influenced China for centuries, such as, Confucianism and Taoism, as well as the concepts of *yin* and *yang*. It is believed that the philosopher Confucius lived from 551 to 479 B.C.; Lao Tzu, the founder of Taoism, may have been his contemporary.

The Ch'in dynasty (221–206 B.C.) preceded the next great dynasty, Han (206 B.C.–A.D. 220), which further expanded the borders and unified China. During this period Confucianism became the leading philosophy of the state; its texts were studied in schools and the basis of the civil service examination. An important event during the Han dynasty was the introduction of Buddhism to China; it would later become one of the primary religions of the region.

Following the collapse of the Han dynasty, the period of the "Three Kingdoms," when China was divided into three major regions is considered the most romantic time in Chinese history. During this time of political upheaval, as well as under subsequent rulers, Buddhism spread through most of China, and Japan and Korea were brought into the sphere of China's cultural influence. By A.D. 589, China was once again unified under the Sui dynasty, and a short while later under the T'ang dynasty.

During the T'ang dynasty (A.D. 618–907), China's poetry and art attained high levels of sophistication and Buddhism reached its apex. The T'ang dynasty also pushed China's border outward to control Tibet, Mongolia, and southern Manchuria. Under the Sung dynasty (A.D. 960–1127), China was unable to fight off Mongol invaders, and by 1279 it became part of the Mongolian empire (A.D. 1280–1368) that stretched from Europe to India and Korea. Through the Mongols, Islam was introduced to China, and there are still Muslims in China today.

People from northern China often call themselves the "people of Han."

People from southern China often call themselves the "people of T'ang."

The most famous European traveler to China during the reign of the Mongols was Marco Polo, who is said to have brought back Chinese noodles to the Italians. However, the Italians claim to have eaten wheat noodles long before Marco Polo's travels.

The Ming dynasty (A.D. 1368–1644) once again put China under Chinese rule, but it was the Manchus, from Manchuria, who established the subsequent Ch'ing dynasty (A.D. 1644–1911) that lasted into the twentieth century. At its height, this dynasty ruled over more territory than any previous government, and in the seventeenth century China was one of the most prosperous nations on earth. The dynasty started to crumble in the nineteenth century and by the twentieth century it was replaced by a republic founded by Sun Yat-sen.

Japan occupied most of China during World War II, and after Japan's defeat China continued to be ruled by the Kuomintang or Nationalist Party. In 1949, the Communists under Mao Zedong ousted the Nationalists, who now occupy the island of Taiwan. Today China is known as the People's Republic of China. Taiwan is known as the Republic of China.

HISTORY OF IMMIGRATION TO THE UNITED STATES

Immigration Patterns

The first major Chinese immigration to the United States occurred in the early 1850s when the Chinese joined in the gold rush and came to California. In fact, many Chinese still refer to America as the "Land of the Golden Mountain." As mining became less lucrative, the Chinese opened their own businesses, such as laundries and restaurants, but also worked for others. The Central Pacific Railroad, which joined the Union Pacific as the first cross-country line, was built primarily by 10,000 Chinese workers.

By 1870 there were 63,000 Chinese, mostly male, in the United States, nearly all on the West Coast. It is estimated that another 120,000 Chinese entered the United States during the following decade. By 1880 the Chinese immigration slowed to a trickle due to exclusion laws directed against Asians. Chinese also immigrated to Hawaii, and when the islands were annexed by the United States in 1898, approximately 25,000 Chinese were living there.

Most early Chinese immigrants were from the Guangdong province of China, usually referred to as Canton. Most of these young men had no intention of staying: they came to make their fortune and then return to China and their families. Most married before coming to the United States, and more than half returned to China. In each city where the Chinese settled they usually lived within a small geographical area known as Chinatown. There the Chinese could live their life, socially and culturally, as if they were in the villages of their youth. Not until 1943 could Chinese become naturalized U.S. citizens.

Current Demographics and Socioeconomic Status

When the exclusion laws were repealed in 1943, people from many Asian countries once again entered the United States. Immigrants who have arrived since World War II are usually not from Canton. They are urban dwellers from other regions and are generally better educated than earlier immigrants. They often reside in Hong Kong or Taiwan before coming to the United States.

Today it is estimated that there are over 812,000 Chinese living in the United States, over half of whom are native-born Americans. After World War II many native-born Chinese Americans moved out of their Chinatowns; thus members of the second and third generations have much less knowledge of their Chinese heritage than their ancestors. Chinese Americans are better educated and have higher incomes than the average U.S. citizen. One-fourth work as scientists or other professionals. Most live in cities on the West Coast or in Hawaii, and sizable Chinese populations are found in the met-

Early immigrants and their descendants as well as many current immigrants from Hong Kong speak Cantonese, a Chinese dialect difficult for immigrants who speak Mandarin to understand.

Chinatown, New York City: Mott Street, the main thoroughfare in New York's Chinatown, is lined with Chinese markets and restaurants. (Courtesy New York Convention and Visitors Bureau.)

ropolitan areas of the Midwest and East Coast. As a result of recent immigration, New York City has one of the largest Chinatowns in the United States. Foreign-born Chinese, many of whom live in Chinatowns, may be less educated and earn less than native-born Chinese Americans.

Cultural Organizations

The early Chinese immigrants rapidly developed organizations that helped regulate or govern their lives. Many of these organizations provided jobs, acted as credit unions, resolved differences among their members, and acted as liaisons with the non-Chinese community.

The primary association for the Chinese is their family and clan. Clan associations were formed among people with the same last name. It has been estimated that there are only 438 last names in China, and everyone with the same surname is believed to be descended from the same ancestors. Chinese Americans also belong to associations that represent the district in China in which they or their family originated.

The Chinese Benevolent Association represents all Chinese organizations, and each city with a considerable Chinese population usually has such an association. In the past, the Chinese Benevolent Association was a powerful institution that oversaw business transactions, arbitrated disputes, and was the unofficial voice of the Chinese community. Today its functions are primarily ceremonial.

District and clan associations have become less important as the Chinese have grown more acculturated. Government social agencies have taken over many of the associations' functions, and communal organizations have little meaning for the newer immigrants from Hong Kong and Taiwan. However, the Chinese American Citizens Alliance, a nationwide organization, still attempts to fight against discrimination directed against the Chinese.

WORLDVIEW

Religion

Chinese religious practices are often eclectic, a combination of animism, polytheism, Confucianism, Buddhism, Taoism, and, today, Christianity. Many early Chinese immigrants were not formally schooled in any religion; instead, beliefs and practices were passed orally from generation to generation. Chinese family structure and beliefs in the importance of the clan and reverence for ancestors are closely linked with religious heritage.

Early Religion. The ancient faith of China was probably a mixture of ancestor worship and respect for the forces of nature and the heavenly bodies. The supreme power was either Tien (Heaven) or Shang Ti (the Supreme Ruler or the Ruler Above). One gained favor with the spirits by the correct performance of ceremonies. These beliefs and practices were later incorporated into subsequent Chinese religions.

Confucianism. Confucius was a sage, one of many who gave order to Chinese society by defining the ways in which people should live and work together. Confucianism incorporated the ceremonies of earlier religions; its cornerstones are:

1. Fatherly love and filial piety in the son. That is, children are expected to obey their parents and adults are expected to take care of their children.
2. Tolerance in the eldest brother and humility in younger.
3. Proper behavior by the husband and submission by the wife.
4. Respect for one's elders and compassion in adults.
5. Allegiance to rulers and benevolence by leaders.

Inherent in these relationships is the ideal of social reciprocity, which means that one should treat others as one would wish to be treated. To enhance harmony in the family and in society as a whole, one must exercise self-restraint. One must never lose face—one's favorable name and position—because that would defame the family name. Many of these values influence Chinese behavior today.

Ceremonies for the dead are a prominent Chinese religious practice. The dead are supposed to depend upon the living for the conditions of their existence after death. In turn, the dead can influence the lives of the living.

Taoism. The Taoist believes, like the Confucianist, that heaven and humanity function in unison and can achieve harmony, but under Taoism people must subordinate themselves to nature's way. That is, in nature there exist two interacting and opposite forces or principles, the *yang* (masculine, positive, bright, steadfast, warm, hard, and dry; sometimes referred to as *Shen*) and the *yin* ((feminine, negative, dark, cold, wet, mysterious, and secret; also called *Kwei*). Everything contains both *yin* and *yang,* and a balance between them is necessary for harmony, which occurs when Tao, the way of nature, is allowed to take its course, rather than being impeded by human willfulness. Taoism advocates the simple life, communion with nature, and the avoidance of extremes.

Buddhism. Buddhism flourished during the T'ang dynasty but then suffered a slow decline. The Mahayana sect dominated in China, cross-fertilizing with traditional Chinese beliefs and resulting in a unique Chinese form of Buddhism. Ten schools of Buddhism flourished in China at one time, but only four were left by the twentieth century. The two dominant schools in China are Ch'an (Zen Buddhism in Japan) and Pure Land.

Family

Confucius's teachings about correct relationships are still important for many Chinese American families, even if they adopted Christianity. Children are expected to be quiet and submissive and respect their elders. Harmony in the family is the ideal, so children are taught not to fight or cry. Showing emotion is discouraged. Chinese parents may be very strict, and children are enjoined not to dishonor the family. Many of these ideas conflict with American ideals of equal rights and freedom of speech and can lead to conflict in the Chinese home.

Traditional Food Habits

It is said about the Cantonese that they will eat anything with four legs except a table and anything with wings except an airplane.

The Chinese eat a wide variety of foods and avoid very few. Perhaps this developed out of necessity, since China has long been plagued with recurrent famine caused by too much or too little rainfall. Chinese cuisine largely reflects the food habits and preferences of the Han people, the largest ethnic group in China, but not to the exclusion of other ethnic groups' cuisines. For example, Beijing has a large Muslim population, whose restaurants serve lamb, kid (baby goat), horse meat, and donkey, but no pork. Foreigners have also introduced ingredients that have been incorporated into local cuisines. Some foods now common in China, but not indigenous, are tomatoes, potatoes, and chili peppers.

INGREDIENTS AND COMMON FOODS

Staples

Traditional Chinese foods are listed in Table 7.1, Cultural Food Groups. In China, few dairy products, whether fresh or fermented, are eaten. Rice, the staple food of southern China, is used throughout Asia and is believed to have originated in India. There are approximately 7,000 different forms of the grain, but the Chinese prefer a polished white long-grain variety that is not sticky and remains firm after cooking. Sticky glutinous rice is used occasionally, mainly in sweet dishes. Although it is usually steamed, rice can also be made into a porridge called *congee,* eaten for breakfast or as a late-night snack, with meat or fish added for flavor. Congee is also fed to people who are ill. Rice flour is used to make rice sticks, which can be boiled or fried in hot oil.

Wheat is also common throughout China, although it is used more often in the North than the South. It is popular as noodles, dumplings pancakes, and steamed bread. Thin, square wheat-flour wrappers are used to make steamed or fried *egg rolls* (or *spring rolls*) with a meat, vegetable, or mixed filling, and *wontons* (in which the wrapper is folded over the filling) served either fried or in soup.

The Chinese eat a variety of animal protein foods. Although they eat all kinds of meat, fish, and poultry, they eat less at any one meal than is customary in the West.

In China, soybeans are known as the poor man's cow, since they are made into products that resemble milk and cheese. Soybeans are transformed into an amazing array of food products that are indispensable in Chinese cooking:

Soy sauce, cooked soybeans first fermented and then processed into sauce. The Cantonese prefer light soy sauce in some dishes over the darker, more opaque kind used by the Japanese and in some Chinese cooking.

Soy milk, soaked soy beans first pureed, then filtered, and then boiled to produce a white milklike drink.

Bean curd, or *tofu,* made by boiling soy milk and then adding gypsum, which causes it to curdle. The excess liquid is pressed from the curd, producing a firm, bland, custardlike product.

Black beans, cooked fermented soybeans preserved with salt and ginger. Black beans are usually used as a seasoning.

Hoisin sauce, a thick, brownish-red sweet–sour sauce that

The Chinese, like most Asians, wash rice before cooking.

The custom of throwing rice at newlyweds is thought to come from China, where rice is a symbol of fertility.

The Chinese prefer the dark meat of poultry, because they consider it tastier and more tender than white meat.

TABLE 7.1. Cultural Food Groups: Chinese

Group	Comments
PROTEIN FOODS Milk/milk products	Dairy products are not routinely used in China. Many Chinese are lactose intolerant.
	Traditional alternative sources of calcium are *tofu,* calcium-fortified soy milk, small bones in fish and poultry, and dishes in which bones have been dissolved.
Meat/poultry/fish/eggs/ legumes	Few protein-rich foods that are not eaten.
	Beef and pork are usually cut into bite-sized pieces before cooking. Fish is preferred fresh and is often prepared whole and divided into portions at the table.
	Preservation by salting and drying is common.
	Shrimp and legumes are made into pastes.
CEREALS/GRAINS	Wheat is the primary staple in the North, white rice in the South.
	Fan (cereal or grain) is the primary item of the meal; *t'sai* (vegetables and meat or seafood) makes it tastier.
	Rice is washed before cooking.
FRUITS/VEGETABLES	Vegetables are usually cut into bite-sized pieces before cooking.
	Slightly unripe fruit is often served as a dessert.
	Both fresh fruits and vegetables are preferred; seasonal variation dictates the type of produce used.

Common Foods	Adaptations in the United States
Cow's milk, buffalo milk.	Most Chinese, even the elderly, consume dairy products, especially milk and ice cream. Some alternative sources of calcium may no longer be used.
Meat: Beef and lamb (brains, heart, kidneys, liver, tongue, tripe, oxtails); pork (bacon, ham, roasts, pig's feet, sausage, ears). *Poultry:* chicken, duck, quail, rice birds, squab. *Fish:* bluegill, carp, catfish, cod, dace, fish tripe, herring, king fish, mandarin fish, minnow, mullet, perch, red snapper, river bass, salmon, pea bass, sea bream, sea perch, shad, sole, sturgeon, tuna. *Eggs:* chicken, duck, quail, fresh and preserved. *Shellfish and other seafood:* abalone, clams, conch, crab, jellyfish, lobster, mussels, oysters, periwinkles, prawns, sea cucumbers (sea slugs), shark's fin, shrimp, squid, turtle, *wawa* fish (salamander). *Legumes:* broad beans, cowpeas, horse beans, mung beans, red beans, red kidney beans, split peas, soy beans, white beans, bean paste.	
Corn, buckwheat, millet, rice, sorghum, tapioca, wheat.	Chinese Americans eat less *fan* and more *t'sai.* The primary staple remains rice, but more wheat bread is eaten.
Fruits: apples, bananas, custard apples, coconut, dates, dragon's eyes, figs, golden melon, grapes, kumquats, lily seed, lime, litchi, mango, muskmelon, oranges, papaya, passion fruit, peaches, persimmons, pineapples, plums (fresh and preserved), pomegranates, pomelos, tangerines, watermelon.	

TABLE 7.1. Cultural Food Groups: Chinese (*continued*)

Group	Comments
	Many vegetables are pickled or preserved. Fruits are often dried or preserved.
ADDITIONAL FOODS Seasonings	
Nuts/seeds	
Beverages	In northern China, the beverage accompanying the meal may be soup. In the South it is tea.

Common Foods	*Adaptations in the United States*
Vegetables; amaranth, asparagus, bamboo shoots, banana squash, bean sprouts, bitter melon, broccoli, cauliflower, celery, cabbage *(bok choi* and *napa),* chili peppers, Chinese long beans and mustard, chrysanthemum greens, cucumbers, eggplant, flat beans, melon (bitter, fuzzy, and winter), garlic, ginger root, green peppers, kohlrabi, leeks, lettuce, lily blossoms, lily root, lotus root and stems, dried and fresh mushrooms (black, button, cloud ear, wood ear, stone ear, elm ear, yellow ear, cassia ear, snow ear, monkey's head), mustard root, okra, olives, onions (yellow, scallions, shallots), parsnip, peas, potato, pumpkin, seaweed (agar), snow peas, spinach, squashes *(nangua* and *luffa),* taro, tea melon, tomatoes, turnips, vegetable sponge, water chestnuts, watercress, wax beans, winter melon, yams, yam beans.	
Anise, bird's nest, chili sauce, Chinese parsley (fresh coriander), cinnamon, cloves, cumin, curry powder, five-spice powder (anise, star anise, clove, cinnamon or cassia, Szechuan pepper), fennel, fish sauce, garlic, ginger, golden needles (lily flowers), green onions, hot mustard, mace, monosodium glutamate (MSG), mustard seed, nutmeg, oyster sauce, parsley, pastes *(hoisin,* sweet flour, brown bean, Szechuan hot beans, sesame seed, shrimp), pepper (black, chili, red, and Szechuan), red dates, sesame seeds (black and white), star anise, tangerine skin, turmeric, soy sauce (light and dark), vinegar.	Many Chinese restaurants use MSG, but it is not usually used in the home.
Almonds, apricot kernels, areca nuts, betel nuts, cashews, chestnuts, peanuts, walnuts; sesame seeds, watermelon seeds.	
Beer, distilled alcoholic spirits, soup broth, tea.	

TABLE 7.1. Cultural Food Groups: Chinese (continued)

Group	Comments
Beverages (continued)	Alcoholic drinks, usually called wines, are not made from fruit. They are either beers or distilled spirits made from starches.
Fats/oils	Traditionally, lard was used if it could be afforded. In recent years, soy, peanut, or corn oil is more commonly used.
Sweeteners	Traditionally, sugar was not used in large quantities; many desserts were made with bean pastes.

is a combination of fermented soybeans, flour, sugar, water, spices, garlic, and chili, often used in Cantonese cooking.

Oyster sauce, a thick brown sauce made from oysters, soybeans, and brine, is also used in Cantonese dishes.

Traditionally, people cooked with lard if they could afford it. In recent years, soy, peanut, or corn oil is more common. Until recently, sugar was not used in large quantities; many desserts were made with bean pastes. Fruit is often served for dessert, but it is frequently eaten slightly unripe or even salted.

Hot soup or tea is the beverage that usually accompanies a meal. Tea, used in China for over 2,000 years, was first cultivated in the Chang Jiang valley and was introduced to western Europe in the seventeenth century. There are three general types of tea: green, black (red), and oolong (black dragon). Green tea is the dried, tender leaves of the tea plant. It brews a yellow, slightly astringent drink. Black tea consists of toasted, fermented leaves that have a black color; it makes a reddish drink. Black tea is commonly drunk in Europe and America. Oolong tea is made from partially fermented leaves.

Chinese alcoholic drinks are usually called wines, but they are not made from fruit. They are either beers or distilled alcohol made from starches. A few examples are bamboo-leaf green (95 proof), *fen* (130 proof), *hua diao* (yellow wine), *mou tai* (110 proof), and red rice wine.

Most Chinese food is cooked; very little raw food, except fruit, is eaten. Cooked foods may be eaten cold. Common

In China, tea is used to officially consummate a marriage when the new parents-in-law formally accept the cup of tea offered by the bride. If the intended groom dies before the marriage, the bride-to-be is said to have "spilled her tea."

Common Foods	Adaptations in the United States
Bacon fat, butter, lard, corn oil, peanut oil, sesame oil, soybean oil, suet. Honey, maltose syrup, table sugar (brown and white).	Sugar consumption has increased, mainly because of consumption of soft drinks, candy, and American desserts.

cooking methods are stir-frying, steaming, deep-fat frying, simmering, and roasting. In stir-frying, foods are cut into uniform, bite-sized pieces and quickly cooked in a *wok* in which oil has been heated. Food can also be steamed in the wok. Bamboo containers, perforated on the bottom, are stacked in a wok containing boiling water and fitted with a domed cover. Roasted food is usually bought from a commercial shop, not prepared in the home.

The Chinese usually strive to obtain the freshest ingredients for their meals, and in most U.S. Chinatowns it is common to find markets that sell live animals and fish. However, because of seasonal availability and geographical distances, many Chinese foods are preserved by drying or pickling.

Regional Variations

China is usually divided into five culinary regions characterized by flavor or into two areas (northern and southern) based on climate and the availability of foodstuffs.

Northern. This area includes the Shandong and Honan regions of Chinese cooking. The Shandong area (Beijing is sometimes included in this area, sometimes it is considered a third division of northern cooking) is famous for *Peking duck* and *mu shu pork,* both of which are eaten wrapped in Mandarin wheat pancakes topped with hoisin. Honan, south of Beijing, is known for its sweet-sour freshwater fish, made from whole carp caught in the Huang River. Much of the North is bordered by Mongolia, whose people eat mainly

A wok *is a hemispherical shell made out of metal, usually iron or steel; some in the U.S. have nonstick coatings. In the United States the* wok *is placed on a burner and held steady by a metal ring.*

mutton. Grilling or barbecueing is a common way of preparing meat in this area.

Northern China has a cool climate, limiting the amount and type of food produced. In general, its staples are millet, and soybeans. Winter vegetables are common, such as cabbage and onions. A delicacy from this area is braised bear paw. Hot clear soup is the beverage that usually accompanies a meal.

Southern. Southern China is divided into three culinary areas: Sichuan (Szechwan)-Hunan, Yunnan, and Cantonese. Szechwan-Hunan dishes are distinguished by their use of chilis, garlic, and the Szechwan pepper, *fagara.* Characteristic dishes include *hot and sour soup, camphor- and tea-smoked duck,* and an oily walnut paste and sugar dessert that may be related to the nut halvah of the Middle East. Yunnan cooking is distinctive in its use of dairy products, such as yogurt, fried milk curd, and cheese. Dishes are often hot and spicy, and some of the best ham and head cheese in China is found in this area.

Cantonese cooking is probably the most familiar to Americans, because the majority of Chinese restaurants in the United States serve Cantonese-style food. It is characterized by stir-fried dishes, seafood (fresh and dried or salted), and the use of vegetable oil instead of lard. The Cantonese are known for *dim sum* ("small bites," such as steamed or fried dumplings stuffed with meat or seafood) that are served with tea. Tea is the beverage served with meals.

The staple foods of the South are rice and soybeans. As in the North, a variety of vegetables from the cabbage family are used, as well as garlic, melon, onions, peas, potatoes, squashes, tomatoes, and a range of rootlike crops, such as taro, water chestnuts, and lotus root. Southern cooking uses mushrooms of many types to enhance the flavor of the foods and produces an abundance of fruits and nuts. Originally from China, many of them are now cultivated in other parts of the world, such as oranges, oriental persimmons, peaches, and tangerines. Fish, both fresh- and salt-water, is popular. Also important are poultry and eggs. Pork is the preferred meat.

MEAL COMPOSITION AND CYCLE

Daily Patterns

The Chinese customarily eat three meals a day, plus numerous snacks. Breakfast often includes the hot rice porridge

In southern China, people greet each other by asking "Have you had rice today?" instead of "How are you?"

congee, and in southern China it may be seasoned with small amounts of meat or fish. In northern China hot steamed bread, dumplings, or noodles are served for breakfast. In urban areas lunch is a smaller version of dinner; soup, a rice or wheat dish, vegetables, and fish or meat.

Although the Chinese are receptive to all types of food, the composition of a meal is governed by specific rules: a balance between yin and yang foods and the proper amounts of *fan* and *ts'ai*. Fan includes all foods made from grains, such as steamed rice, noodles, porridge, pancakes, or dumplings, which are served in a separate bowl to each diner. Ts'ai includes cooked meats and vegetables, which are shared from bowls set in the center of the table. Fan is the primary item in a meal; ts'ai only helps people eat the grain by making the meal more tasty. A meal is not complete unless it contains fan, but it does not have to contain ts'ai. At a banquet, the opposite is true. An elaborate meal must contain ts'ai, but the fan is often served as an afterthought and may not be eaten.

Etiquette

The traditional eating utensils are chopsticks and a porcelain spoon used for soup. Teacups are always made out of porcelain, as are rice bowls. At a meal, all diners should take equal amounts of the ts'ai dishes, and younger diners wait to eat until their elders have started. It is considered bad manners to eat rice with the bowl resting on the table; instead, it should be raised to the mouth.

Chopsticks are long narrow stick-like implements usually made of bamboo, ivory, or plastic and are held between the thumb and index finger.

Special Occasions

Traditionally, the Chinese week did not include a day of rest. Consequently, there were numerous feasts to break up the continuous work days. Chinese festival days do not fall on the same day each year since their calendar is lunar. The most important festival is New Year's, which can fall anytime from the end of January to the end of February. Traditionally, the New Year was a time to settle old debts and to honor ancestors, parents, and elders.

The New Year holiday season begins on the evening of the twenty-third day of the last lunar month of the year. At that time the Kitchen God, whose picture hangs in the kitchen and who sees and hears everything in the house, flies upward to make his annual report on the family to the Jade Emperor. To ensure that his report will be good, the family smears his lips

According to the Chinese, a child is one year old at birth and becomes two years old after the New Year.

The traditional dragon dance and firecrackers, part of the New Year's celebration, inhibit the less desirable *yin* element and promote the *yang* force. Red, the color of the *yang* force, is much used during the New Year's season.

with honey before they burn his picture. A new picture of the Kitchen God is placed in the kitchen on New Year's Eve.

Food preparation must be completed on New Year's Eve, since knives cannot be used on the first day of the year because they might "cut luck." Deep-fried dumplings, made from glutinous rice and filled with sweetmeats, and steamed turnip-and-rice-flour puddings are usually included in the New Year's day meal. During the New Year festivities, only good omens are permitted and unlucky-sounding words are not uttered. Foods that sound like lucky words, such as tangerine (good fortune), fish (surplus), chicken (good fortune), chestnuts (profit), and tofu (*fu* means riches) are eaten.

Friends and relatives visit each other during the first ten days of the new year, and good wishes, presents, and food are exchanged. Children receive money in tiny red envelopes. Traditionally, the Feast of Lanterns, the fifteenth day of the first month, ends the New Year's season and is marked by the dragon dancing in the streets and the explosion of firecrackers.

Ch'ing Ming, the chief spring festival, falls 106 days after the winter solstice. Families customarily go to the cemetery and tend the graves of their relatives. Food is symbolically fed to the dead, then later eaten by the family.

The Moon Festival occurs at the end of September on a full moon (fifteenth day of the eighth lunar month). Since the moon is a yin symbol, this festival was traditionally for women, but today it also symbolizes the togetherness of the family. It is sometimes called the harvest festival or moon's birthday. Large round cakes filled with spices, nuts, and fruit are typically eaten during this festival and are called *moon cakes.*

THERAPEUTIC USES OF FOOD

During the first month after birth, it is traditionally believed that women should avoid "wind" (a noxious vapor found in wind, cold weather and cold water) that enters the body, causing illness. This is accomplished by consuming pig's feet cooked with ginger and vinegar or chicken cooked with rice wine.

The Chinese believe that food is critical for bodily harmony. Health is maintained by eating the proper balance of yin and yang foods. In general, yang (hot) foods are stronger, richer, and spicier. Strong alcoholic drinks and rich feast foods with a high fat content are the hottest. Cold foods (yin) are bland, low in calories, and often consist of vegetables and herbs. Hot foods should be eaten in the winter, by postpartum women (especially during the first month), and for tiredness. Cool foods should be eaten in the summer, for dry lips, and to relieve irritability. Some food processing can make foods hotter or colder by the infusion or removal of heat. Which

Vegetable vendor, Chinatown, San Francisco. (Photo by Pat Goyan.)

foods are considered yin or yang tends to vary from region to region.

Diseases are also classified as hot (yang) and cold (yin). "Hot" diseases, such as measles and sore throats, are treated with cool foods; "cold" diseases, such as anemia, with warm foods. It is believed that as one gets older the body cools off and more hot foods should be eaten. Extra care should be taken with children's diets, because they are more susceptible to imbalance.

The Chinese use numerous herbs to treat diseases, and there are herb shops in most U.S. Chinatowns.

Contemporary Food Habits in the United States

ADAPTATION OF FOOD HABITS

Generally, changes in eating habits correlate with increasing length of stay in the United States. Dinner remains the most traditionally Chinese meal, whereas breakfast, lunch, and snacks tend to become more Americanized.

Ingredients and Common Foods

Most Chinese Americans use several Chinese foods, such as rice, soybeans and their products, and tea. They also use dairy products, sugar, meat, poultry, and coffee in larger amounts. Sugar intake has increased, mainly through consumption of soft drinks, candy, and pastries.

Meal Composition

A survey reported that elderly Chinese people living in northern California still eat an almost traditional diet (Chau *et al.,* 1987). Their lunches and dinners consisted mainly of Chinese-style foods; their breakfasts varied. Those with higher educational levels consumed more American foods. Approximately half of the respondents attempted to balance hot and cold foods.

NUTRITIONAL STATUS

Nutritional Intake

The traditional Chinese diet is low in fat and dairy products and high in carbohydrates and sodium. As the number of generations living in the United States increases, the diet becomes more like the majority American diet: higher in fat, protein, simple sugar, and cholesterol, and lower in complex carbohydrates.

Chinese Americans often continue to avoid fresh dairy products, because of lactose intolerance. Alternative calcium sources are soy bean curd, soy milk, if fortified with calcium, and a condiment made from vinegar in which bones have been dissolved. Unfortunately, some traditional dishes that were alternative sources of calcium may no longer be eaten.

It is generally assumed that Chinese people eat a diet high in sodium, contributing to hypertension. Results of a preliminary report on dietary practices, ethnicity, and hypertension showed that the Chinese had a lower sodium intake than whites but had similar rates of hypertension (Leonard *et al.,* 1981).

Counseling

Elderly or less acculturated Chinese American clients may show deference to authority by means of acceptance and submission. They may not ask questions or challenge the health provider's advice, but they may then go ahead and follow their own health practices. In counseling clients who have traditional beliefs about health and illness, it is useful to find out what they think are the causes of their illness. When explaining treatment procedures, it is helpful to relate the

One food taboo among older Chinese in America is the belief that eating crabs and persimmons together is poisonous because they represent extreme hot and cold foods.

treatment rationale to the patient's understanding of the illness. Practices such as yin and yang may affect health care if dietary advice is in conflict with traditional cures. It is important to conduct an in-depth interview with Chinese clients to determine what customary cultural beliefs they maintain and to what degree they are acculturated.

JAPANESE

The islands of Japan are strung out off the coast of East Asia and have approximately the same latitude and range of climate as the East Coast of the United States. The capital of Japan is Tokyo and is located on the island of Honshu. Today, Japan is a prosperous country of 121 million people that has overcome the limitations of a mountainous geography, a rugged coastline, and few mineral resources. Perhaps Japan's

Traditional foods of Japan: Some typical foods in the traditional Japanese diet include azuki beans, agar-agar, daikon, *dried sardines, Japanese eggplant, Japanese pickles,* nori *(seaweed),* shitake *mushrooms, short-grain rice, shrimp, soy sauce, and wheat noodles. (Photo by Laurie Mac-fee.)*

greatest natural resource is the sea, which provides it with one of the richest fishing grounds in the world.

Cultural Perspective

HISTORY OF JAPAN

Today it is thought that the earliest inhabitants of Japan were the Ainu, a proto-Caucasoid people. They were culturally and racially absorbed by immigrants from the mainland of Asia. Early Japanese society was organized into a number of hereditary clan units that were unified in the fifth or sixth century A.D. under the authority of the Yamato emperors.

Japan is sometimes referred to as the daughter of Chinese civilization. Contact between the two peoples dates back at least to the first century A.D. However, it was in the sixth century that Japan began to absorb China's knowledge of science, art, agriculture, and cooking. It was also during this period that Buddhism and Confucianism were introduced into Japan. Although the Japanese borrowed much from Chinese culture, by the tenth and eleventh centuries Japanese culture had developed a distinctive character.

By the twelfth century, the emperor became a figurehead without political or economic power. Japan had become a feudal society whose central figure was the aristocratic fighting man (knight) on horseback, managing and defending an estate in allegiance to court families or central monasteries. Although the imperial family still nominally ruled, real power was held by *shoguns* who controlled loose associations of knights by longstanding ties of friendship and loyalty.

Through the fourteenth and fifteenth centuries, warriors who had won strong local followings assumed the role of feudal lords and became increasingly powerful. They later became known as *daimyo,* and their importance grew with the rapid expansion of the Japanese economy. By the fifteenth century, Japan was an important trading partner in the East China Sea.

Larger and stronger daimyo took over weaker daimyo until, by the end of the sixteenth century, a single powerful overlord ruled Japan, Tokugawa Ieyasu. He created a political system that endured for almost 250 years. He again took the title of shogun and ruled the daimyo through strong military power and close supervision. He also controlled all cities and ports.

Tokugawa adopted the social theories of Confucianism and created a hierarchy of four social classes: the warrior/administrator, the peasant, the artisan, and the merchant. The warrior aristocrats, called *samurai,* were the most prestigious; merchants were the lowest class. A fifth social class also existed unofficially. They were the *eta,* which means "much filth," whose jobs involved killing or handling dead animals. Although Buddhism had become the dominant religion of the masses, Confucianism had become the strongest intellectual and ethical force in Japan.

Before Tokugawa came to power, Christianity had been introduced to Japan by Portugese traders. The Jesuit missionary St. Francis Xavier had lived in Japan from 1549 to 1551 and had won converts. However, in 1587 Tokugawa expelled the Christian missionaries and banned the practice of Christianity in Japan. His successors later banned all foreign contact with Japan, and only the Dutch were allowed a trading mission in the port of Nagasaki.

Isolated, both politically and socially, Japan remained unchanged from the sixteenth century to the middle of the nineteenth century. The Japanese people became accustomed to rigid patterns of conduct, they looked to their superiors for leadership, and they followed orders without question. Eventually, Japan was pressured into change by the western powers' desire to establish contact and trade. It was the U.S. government that forced the door open after Commodore Perry steamed into Tokyo Bay in 1853.

In 1868 the Tokugawa regime fell and the office of shogun was abolished. In its place, a new central government revolutionized the military and social structure of Japan, ending the old feudal order. The Meiji restoration and its rulers brought Japan into the twentieth century and made the nation a world power.

In the 1930s, Japan swung violently back to authoritarian rule at home and military expansion abroad. Japan dominated Korea and large areas of northern China, and by 1941 the military controlled the Japanese government. On December 7, 1941, they bombed Pearl Harbor in Hawaii, which brought the United States into World War II. Japan lost the war, but not until the United States had carried out the first and only wartime use of atomic bombs at Hiroshima and Nagasaki. Democratic rule was established after the war. Today, Japan is a prosperous country and a leading economic power.

HISTORY OF IMMIGRATION TO THE UNITED STATES

Immigration Patterns

Among Japanese Americans, first-generation immigrants born in Japan are called *Issei*, the second generation, born in the United States, are called *Nisei*, the third generation *Sansei*, and the fourth *Yonsei*.

Significant Japanese immigration to the United States occurred after 1890 during the Meiji era. The immigrants were mostly young men with four to six years of education from the rural southern provinces of Japan. Most came for economic opportunities and many eventually returned to Japan. They settled primarily in Hawaii and on the West Coast of the United States and often worked in agriculture, on the railroads, and in canneries.

Like the Chinese before them, the Japanese immigrants opened small businesses to provide services for their countrymen. In contrast to the Chinese, many Japanese became farmers, ran plant nurseries, and were employed as gardeners. Most Japanese women came to the United States as "picture brides": their marriages were arranged by professional matchmakers and they were married by proxy in Japan. They did not usually meet their husbands until they debarked from the ship in the United States.

Discrimination against the Japanese was commonplace. The *Issei* were classified as aliens who were ineligible to become naturalized U.S. citizens and thus were not allowed to own land in California (California Alien Land Bill, 1913). Many bought land in their children's names, since they were Americans by birth. In 1907 the Japanese government informally agreed to limit the number of emigrants, and in 1924 the Japanese Exclusion Act halted Japanese immigration completely.

World War II heightened the prejudice against the Japanese on the West Coast. After Japan attacked Pearl Harbor, all West Coast Japanese, even if they were U.S. citizens, were "evacuated" to war relocation camps and many remained there for the duration of the war. Nevertheless, many *Nisei* volunteered for combat duty and fought in Europe.

Current Demographics and Socioeconomic Status

After the war, most Japanese Americans resettled on the West Coast and the majority of the discriminatory laws were repealed or ruled unconstitutional. Today approximately 716,000 Japanese Americans live in the United States, 70 percent of whom live in California or Hawaii.

Japantown, San Francisco. (Photo by Pat Goyan.)

Many West Coast cities have a section of town called Little Tokyo or Japantown and many older Japanese still live in these homogeneous neighborhoods. Most Japantowns contain Japanese restaurants, grocery stores, other small businesses run by Japanese, and Chinese churches or Buddhist temples.

Today, most Japanese live in urban areas; their family incomes are above the national average. Of the *Sansei,* many of whom were born in the relocation camps, 88 percent have attended college and most hold professional jobs.

Cultural Organizations

The roots of the Japanese community in America lie in Japan. It is from Japan that the Issei learned the ideals of putting family and community interests ahead of one's personal needs. Mutual assistance groups rapidly developed in the United States to help new immigrants acclimate themselves to a new culture. Later the community institutions helped fight against discrimination.

One of the first organizations founded by the Issei was the Japanese Association. It helped to regulate internal community affairs and served as a liaison with the outside community. It usually had a close working relationship with the local Japanese consul, since Issei were Japanese citizens. Another important organization was the *kenjinkais (ken)* or prefectural organization. Like the Chinese, the Japanese often belong to a group of families that immigrated from the same area in Japan and thus share customs and speak the same dialect. Today, both organizations are supported by donations and jointly sponsor the local annual Japanese picnic, which usually occurs in the summer.

A later organization was the Japanese-American Citizen's League (JACL). It was formed to serve the needs of the Nisei, represent the Japanese American community, and fight discrimination. Today it is still a strong organization, but for many Japanese its image was tarnished during World War II when it aided the U.S. government in evacuating the West Coast Japanese.

WORLDVIEW

Religion

Early Japanese immigrants usually joined a Buddhist temple (Pure Land sect) or a Christian church after arriving in America. The church frequently provided employment and an opportunity to learn English. Shintoism, the indigenous religion of Japan, does not have a formal organization, but its beliefs are a fundamental part of Japanese culture.

The Shinto view is that humans are inherently good. Evil is caused by pollution or filthiness, physical as well as spiritual, and goodness is associated with purity. Evil can be removed through ritual purification.

Shinto deities, called *kami,* represent any form of existence (human, animal, plant, or geological) that evokes a sense of awe and are worshiped at their shrines. Many kami represent the power of productivity and fertility. Worship of the kami, either privately at home or communally at the shrine, gives ritual expression to a sense of awe and thankfulness. Prayers are also said for divine favors and blessings, as well as for avoidance of misfortunes and accidents.

Family

Up until World War II, the structure of the Japanese American family had its roots in Japan and was similar to that of the Chinese, due to the strong influence of Confucianism. In addition, the rigid pattern of conduct that evolved in Japan during the sixteenth century resulted in the following practices among the Issei and their descendants:

1. *KōKō.* Filial piety defines the relationship between parents and children, between siblings, and between individuals and their community and rulers. (See the section on Confucianism in the first part of this chapter for further explanation.) One outcome is that the Issei expect their children to care for them in their old age.

2. *Gaman.* The Japanese believe it is virtuous to suppress emotions. The practice of self-control is paramount.

3. *Haji.* Individuals should not bring shame on themselves, their families, or their communities. This Japanese cultural concept exerts strong social control.

4. *Enryo.* There is no equivalent word in English, but the Japanese believe it is important to be polite, and to show respect, deference, self-effacement, humility, and hesitation. Thus many older or less acculturated Japanese Americans are neither aggressive nor assertive.

The internment of Japanese Americans during World War II brought about many changes in family structure, and many people believe that it accelerated acculturation into the majority American society after the war. In the camps, very low wages were paid and the pay was the same for everyone; thus the father could no longer be the primary wage earner. Additionally, the camps were run democratically, but positions could be held only by American citizens, so the younger generation held positions of authority. The camps also allowed the Japanese to work in a wider range of jobs than those available to them on the outside. After their internment, the Nisei no longer had to follow the few occupations of their parents.

Traditional Food Habits

Japanese foodstuffs and cooking and eating utensils are very similar to those of the Chinese, due to the strong influence China had on Japan from the sixth century. In addition, some of the concepts of yin and yang are present in the use of herbal medicines and food combinations. Yet Japanese food preparation and presentation is unique. The Japanese reverence for harmony within the body and community and with nature has resulted in a cuisine that offers numerous ways to prepare a limited number of foods. Each ingredient is to be

TABLE 7.2. Cultural Food Groups: Japanese

Group	Comments
PROTEIN	
Milk/milk products	Japanese cooking does not utilize significant amounts of dairy products. Many Japanese are lactose intolerant. Soybean products, seaweed, and small bony fish are alternative calcium sources.
Meat/poultry/fish/eggs/ legumes	Soy bean products and a wide variety of fish and shellfish (fresh, frozen, dried, smoked) are the primary protein sources in the Japanese diet. Fish and shellfish are often eaten raw.
	Chicken is used more often than beef; price is probably the limiting factor in meat consumption.
CEREALS/GRAINS	Short-grain rice is the primary staple of the diet and is eaten with every meal. It used to be coated in talc and is still washed before cooking.
	Wheat is often eaten in the form of noodles, such as *udon* and *soba*.
FRUITS/VEGETABLES	Fresh fruits and vegetables are the most desirable; usually eaten only in season.
	Fresh fruit was the traditional dessert.
	Many fruits and vegetables are preserved, dried, or pickled.

Common Foods	Adaptations in the United States
Milk, butter, ice cream	First-generation Japanese Americans drink little milk and eat few dairy products. Subsequent generations eat more dairy foods.
Meat: beef, deer, lamb, pork, rabbit, veal. *Poultry:* capon, chicken, duck, goose, partridge, pheasant, quail, thrush, turkey. *Fish:* blowfish, bonita, bream, carp, cod, cuttlefish, eel, flounder, herring, mackerel, porgy, octopus, red snapper, salmon, sardines, shark, sillago, snipefish, squid, swordfish, trout, tuna, turbot, yellowtail, whale. *Shellfish:* abalone, *ayu,* clams, crab, earshell, lobster, mussels, oysters, sea urchin roe, scallops, shrimp, snails. *Legumes:* black beans, red beans, lima beans, soy beans.	Dried fish and fish cakes are available in the United States, but some varieties of fresh fish are not. Japanese Americans eat more poultry and meat than fish.
Wheat, rice, buckwheat, and millet.	Rice is still an important staple in the diet and is usually eaten at dinner.
Fruits: apples, apricots, bananas, cherries, dates, figs, grapefruits *(yuzu),* kumquats, lemons, limes, grapes, loquats, melons, oranges, pears, pear apples, peaches, persimmons, plums (fresh and pickled), pineapples, strawberries, summer mandarin *(mikan).* *Vegetables:* artichokes, asparagus, bamboo shoots, beans, bean sprouts, broccoli, brussels sprouts, beets, burdock root *(gobo),* cabbage (several varieties), carrots, chickweed, onions, chrysanthemum, eggplant (long, slender variety), ferns, ginger and pickled ginger *(beni shoga),* green onions, green peppers, gourd	Fewer fruits and vegetables are eaten; freshness is less critical.

TABLE 7.2. Cultural Food Groups: Japanese (*continued*)

Group	Comments
ADDITIONAL FOODS	
Seasonings	Sugar, *shoyu,* and vinegar are a basic seasoning mixture. *Shoyu* and *mirin* can vary in strength; amounts used will vary according to taste.
Nuts/seeds	
Beverages	Green tea is the preferred beverage with meals; coffee or black tea are drunk with western-style foods. *Saki* or beer is often served with dinner.
Fats/oils	The traditional Japanese diet is low in fat and cholesterol.
Sweeteners	

seen, tasted, and relished. The Japanese also place an emphasis on the appearance of the meal so that the visual appeal reflects the harmony among the foods and the environment. For example, a summer meal may be served on glass dishes so that the meal looks cooler, while a September meal may include the autumn colors of reds and golds.

Common Foods	Adaptations in the United States
(*Kanpyo,* dried gourd shavings), leeks, lettuce, lotus root, mushrooms (*shiitaki, matsutake, nameko),* okra, peas, potatoes (noodles made from potato starch also called cellophane noodles: *harusame),* pumpkins, sweet potatoes, radishes, rhubarb, seaweed, sorrel, spinach, snow peas, taro, tomatoes, turnips, squash, watercress, yams.	
Alum, anise, bean paste *(miso),* caraway, chives, *dashi,* fish paste, garlic, ginger, mint, *mirin,* MSG, mustard, red pepper, *sake,* seaweed, sesame seeds, *shoyu,* sugar, thyme, vinegar (rice), *wasabi* (green horseradish).	
Chestnut, gingko nuts, peanuts, walnuts; poppy (black and white), sesame seeds.	
Carbonated beverages, beer, coffee, gin, tea (black and green), *sake,* scotch.	Japanese Americans drink less tea and more milk, coffee, and carbonated beverages.
Butter, cottonseed oil, olive oil, peanut oil, sesame seed oil, vegetable oil.	Japanese Americans consume more fats and oils because of increased use of western foods and cooking methods.
Honey, sugar.	Increased use of sugar, sweet desserts.

INGREDIENTS AND COMMON FOODS

Japan's mountainous terrain and limited arable land have contributed historically to a less-than-abundant food supply. Even today, much of Japan's food supply is imported.

Staples and Regional Variations

The basic foods of the Japanese diet are listed in Table 7.2. Several key ingredients were borrowed from China, including

Japanese sushi *chef.* (Courtesy Benihana of Tokyo, Inc.)

Gohan means cooked rice and is also the word for meal since rice has traditionally been the primary food in the Japanese diet.

Red rice, made by steaming rice and red azuki beans together, is often eaten on happy occasions (birthdays, weddings, and holidays), because red is considered a joyous and lucky color.

soybeans, rice, and tea. Rice *(gohan)* is the main staple, and it is eaten with almost every meal. In contrast to the Chinese, the Japanese prefer a short-grain rice that contains more starch and is stickier after cooking. Rice mixed with a rice vinegar *(su)* is called *sushi* and is often served with sliced raw fish.

Soybean products are an important component of Japanese cuisine. Tofu (bean curd), soy sauce *(shoyu)*, and fermented bean paste *(miso)* are just a few. *Teriyaki* sauce ("shining broil") is made from soy sauce and *mirin*, a sweet rice wine. Sugar, shoyu, and vinegar are a basic seasoning mixture. Shoyu and mirin can vary in strength, and the amounts used depend on personal taste.

Green tea is served with most meals. Tea was originally used in a devotional ceremony in Zen Buddhism. The ritual was raised to a fine art by Japanese tea masters; as a result, they also set the standards for behavior in Japanese society. Today the tea ceremony *(kaiseki)* and the accompanying food remain a cultural ideal that reflects the search for harmony with nature and within one's self. It is also serves as a form of entertainment. The tea that is used for the ceremony is not the common leaf tea that is usually used for meals, but rather a blend of ground dry tea or a tea powder. Hot water is added to the tea and the mixture is whipped together using a hand-made whisk, resulting in a frothy green drink.

Japanese cooking does not use many dairy foods. Soybean products and a wide variety of fish and shellfish (fresh, dried, or smoked) are the primary protein sources. Fish and shellfish are often eaten raw. Beef and poultry are also popular but are very expensive. Only small amounts of meat, poultry, or fish are added to the vegetables in traditional Japanese recipes.

Fresh fruits and vegetables are the most desirable and are eaten only when in season. Pickled vegetables are available year round and are eaten extensively. Fresh fruit is the traditional dessert.

The Japanese use a large amount of seaweed and algae in their cooking for seasoning, as a wrapping, or in salads and soups. There are many types: *nori* is a paper-thin sheet of algae that is rolled around rice and other ingredients. *Kombu* is a vital ingredient in *dashi*, or soup stock. *Wakame* and *hijiki* are used primarily in soups and salads. *Aonoriko* is powdered green seaweed used as a seasoning agent.

Cooking style varies from region to region in Japan. Kyoto is known for its vegetarian specialties, Osaka and Tokyo for seafood. Nagasaki's cooking has been greatly influenced by the Chinese.

MEAL COMPOSITION AND CYCLE

Daily Pattern

Traditionally, the Japanese eat three meals a day plus a snack called *oyatsu*. Breakfast usually starts with a salty sour plum (*umeboshi*), followed by rice garnished with nori, soup (*misoshiru*), and pickled vegetables. Some families may have an egg with their rice.

Lunch is simple and may consist only of rice combined with leftovers from the night before. Sometimes hot tea or dashi is added to the rice mixture (*chazuke*) and eaten with chopsticks. Many people prefer to have rice or wheat noodles cooked or served with meats, poultry, or fish, and vegetables.

Dinner must always include three dishes: rice, soup, and *tsukemono* (pickled vegetables). The main dish usually consists of fish or shellfish, either broiled, steamed, or deep-fried. Snacks usually consist of several kinds of sweets, rice crackers, or fruit. Traditional Japanese confections include *mochigashi* (rice cakes with sweet bean paste), *manju* (dumplings), and *yokan* (sweet bean jelly).

The cuisine of Korea reflects its location between China and Japan. Barbecued beef and spicy pickled vegetables, such as *kim chee*, are specialties. Short-grain rice, noodles, seafood, and soybean products are common, and chilis, garlic (large amounts), ginger, green onions, and sesame seeds season many dishes. Woks are used for cooking and chopsticks are used for eating.

Kombu sounds like the word for happiness, and Japanese guests often bring their hostess a gift box of it.

Misoshiru is a thick soup made from *miso* (a paste of fermented soy beans and rice) and *dashi* (a soup stock made from dried seaweed and bonita fish). *Misoshiru* is not eaten with a spoon but drunk straight from the bowl.

Sukiyaki is a simmered beef dish usually prepared at the table. The word actually means "broiled on the blade of the plow," and it has been speculated that the dish was originally prepared by hunters who cooked their prey on whatever was handy, such as a metal plow. However, modern *sukiyaki* is misnamed, since *yaki* means broiled and *sukiyaki* is a simmered dish *(nimono)* that is served at the table *(nabemono)* in one pot.

Green tea is served after all meals except when western-style food is eaten; then coffee or black tea is served. Beer or *sake* (rice wine) may be served with dinner. Japanese dishes are modified for children, since it is believed that adult recipes are too spicy for them.

The Japanese tend not to serve meals by courses. Instead, all the dishes are presented at the same time, with each food in its own bowl or plate. The soup, however, is usually served last or near the end of the meal. Traditionally, desserts were not common in Japan; meals usually ended with fruit.

Ingredients in Japanese dishes are usually cut into small pieces if the food is not naturally easy to eat with chopsticks. Recipes are classified by the way in which the food is prepared: *suimono*, clear soups; *yakimono*, broiled food; *nimono*, foods boiled in seasoned liquids; *mushimono*, steamed foods; *agimono*, fried foods; *sashimi*, sliced raw fish; *namasu*, salad; *aemono*, mixed foods in dressing; *sunomono*, vinegared salad; *chameshi*, rice cooked with other ingredients; *nabimono*, food cooked at the table and one-pot cooking; and tsukemono, soaked things or pickles. *Tempura* is lightly battered deep-fried shrimp and assorted vegetables. The Portuguese introduced this dish to Japan in the sixteenth century but now it is a uniquely Japanese dish.

Obon *festival, San Jose, California: Dancing and traditional foods are featured at this annual Buddhist festival.*

Special Occasions

In Japan there are numerous festivals associated with the harvesting of specific crops, or with local Shinto shrines or Buddhist temples. The most important and largest holiday in Japan and for Japanese Americans is New Year's. Like the Chinese, the Japanese traditionally settle all debts before the New Year, and food is prepared beforehand so that no knives or cooking will interfere with the seven-day celebration. The Japanese celebrate New Year's on the first day of January. The New Year's foods consist of 10 to 20 meticulously prepared dishes served in a special set of nesting boxes. Each dish symbolizes a specific value, such as happiness, prosperity, wealth, long life, wisdom, and diligence.

An important New Year's food is *mochi*, a rice cake made by pounding hot, steamed rice into a sticky dough. Another special food is *ozoni*, a soup cooked with mochi, vegetables, fish cakes, and chicken or eggs. A special rice wine called *otoso* is drunk, and it is thought to prevent disease in the coming year.

Japanese Buddhist temples usually hold an Obon festival in the second or third week of July to appreciate the living, honor the dead, and comfort the bereaved. Food and dancing are a traditional part of the holiday.

THERAPEUTIC USES OF FOOD

Belief in yin and yang is not as prevalent among the Japanese as it is among the Chinese, but traditionally it is believed that certain foods have harmful or beneficial effects. Among older Japanese Americans certain combinations of foods, such as eel and pickled plums, watermelon and crab, or cherries and milk, are thought to cause illness. Pickled plums and hot tea, which are customarily eaten for breakfast, are used to prevent constipation. Pickled plums and rice porridge are thought to be easily digested and well-tolerated after one recovers from an illness.

There is an old Japanese saying that if you eat something that you have not tasted before, your life will be prolonged by 75 days.

Contemporary Food Habits in the United States

ADAPTATIONS OF FOOD HABITS

In general, second-generation Japanese Americans eat a typical American diet, but they eat more rice and use more soy sauce than non-Asians. Traditional foods are prepared for special occasions. Third- and fourth-generation Japanese Americans appear to be totally acculturated to American foodways. Even in Japan, a westernized diet is increasingly followed. Bread and butter are becoming dietary staples, and consumption of milk and eggs is increasing.

NUTRITIONAL STATUS

Nutritional Intake

The traditional Japanese diet is low in fat and cholesterol. Most cooking fats are polyunsaturated and butter is rarely used. As expected, younger Japanese Americans consume a more typically American diet. Unfortunately, the change in diet may contribute to increased incidence of several diseases. According to epidemiological studies, mainland Japanese Americans have a higher risk of developing colon cancer and heart disease than the Japanese in Hawaii or Japan. It has been postulated that the increase is caused by diet, since it is correlated to a higher intake of cholesterol and animal fat and a lower intake of dietary fiber (Marmot & Syme, 1976; Wenkam & Wolff, 1970).

Elderly Japanese Americans may have a low intake of calcium and iron because of limited consumption of dairy products and red meat. The Japanese have a high incidence of lactose intolerance. Although seaweed, tofu, and small bony fish contain calcium, they may not be eaten in adequate amounts to provide sufficient intake. Traditional diets tend to be high in sodium from soy sauce, dashi, miso, monosodium glutamate (MSG), and pickled vegetables.

Counseling

It is important not to address older Japanese Americans (Issei and some Nisei) by their first names, since this is considered an insult. Japanese Americans will also feel insulted if they are ordered to do anything that they feel requires only an explanation.

Japanese Americans believe that the health care provider is a knowledgeable authority figure who will meet their needs without their assistance. Thus, they may not ask questions. In providing health education to older Japanese Americans, an in-depth interview should be done to establish whether they were born in the United States and their degree of acculturation. The provider should not criticize the client's health habits, since this may lead to embarrassment and loss of effective communication.

SOUTHEAST ASIANS

Southeast Asia is a tropical region south of China and east of India whose lands straddle the equator. It includes the countries of Burma, Thailand, Laos, Kampuchea (Cambodia), Vietnam, Malaysia, Brunei, Indonesia, Singapore and the Philippines. The countries are similar in climate, flora, and fauna. Fertile deltas and river valleys are commonly separated by rugged mountains. Somewhat over half of the region is on the Asian mainland and the rest is made up of the thousands of islands that are part of Indonesia and the Philippines.

This section discusses the Southeast Asian countries whose people have immigrated in substantial numbers to the United States: the Philippines, Vietnam, Cambodia, and Laos.

Traditional foods of Southeast Asia: Some foods typical of the diet of Southeast Asians include coconut, dried anchovies, dried mango, French bread, lemon grass, lime, nuoc mam, *pineapple, pork,* rau muong, *rice, rice paper, rice sticks, taro root, and water chestnuts.* (Photo by Laurie Macfee.)

Cultural Perspective

HISTORY OF SOUTHEAST ASIA

Much of the history of Southeast Asia includes long periods of foreign domination or repeated conflicts between the nations of the area. National boundaries were first defined by the western nations during the nineteenth century. The conflicts between Vietnam and Thailand have continuously influenced the politics and independence of their neighbors, Laos and Cambodia, and still do today.

Vietnam

Vietnam, which hugs the eastern coastline of the region, borders China in the North and Cambodia and Laos on the West. The two most fertile areas of the country are along the Red River in the North and in the Mekong River delta region in the South. The two major cities of the country are located within these regions; Hanoi is in the North and Ho Chi Minh City (Saigon) is in the South.

The original inhabitants of Vietnam are thought to have been Austro-Negroid migrants who were pushed south by Mongolian tribes who were in turn overcome by the Chinese (207 B.C.). The Chinese ruled Vietnam for 1,000 years (111 B.C.–A.D. 939). Vietnam adopted the Chinese system of government (Confucianism), religious beliefs (Taoism and Buddhism), and many of their agricultural and cooking practices. However, the Vietnamese have their own unique culture and language and they resented Chinese rule.

Successive Vietnamese dynasties ruled after the Chinese were driven out. During the 1860s, the French responded to attacks on Catholic Vietnamese and French Catholic missionaries by seizing the southern provinces and created the French colony of Cochinchina. By the 1880s, the remaining Vietnamese court fell, relinquishing complete control of North (Tonkin), Central (Annam) and South Vietnam to the French, who dominated the country, except during a period of Japanese occupation during World War II, until 1954. After a bloody war with the Vietnamese, who followed the Communist leader Ho Chi Minh, the French withdrew their forces and the country was divided between the North and South. With the aid of the United States, South Vietnam resisted reunification with the North, but after the United States pulled out of Vietnam in 1975 the Saigon government fell, and the country was reunified under a Communist government.

Cambodia

Cambodia, sandwiched between Vietnam, Laos, Thailand, and the Gulf of Thailand, was known as the Funan empire in the first century A.D. In the fourth century, an Indian Brahmin introduced Hindu customs, legal code, and alphabet to the region. The Khmer invaded from the North in the sixth century, and their empire ruled until the 1400s. In the twelfth century the Khmer nation gained control of a rival nation, Champa, which today is the southern province of Vietnam. As the power of the Khmer nation declined, Thailand encroached on the western border and Vietnam expanded on the eastern side.

In 1864, Cambodia became a colony of the French and did not gain independence until 1955. In 1970, Prince Norodum Sihanouk was removed from office as chief of state and a military premier was appointed. The Khmer Rouge, a Communist regime led by Pol Pot, later took over the government. As a result of their efforts to "reeducate the masses," it is estimated that over 3 million Cambodians were killed. The armies of Vietnam have since removed the Khmer Rouge government and set up a puppet government that is essentially ruled from Vietnam. The country is now called Democratic Kampuchea. Rebels living on the border of Thailand and Kampuchea continue to battle the current government.

Laos

The people of Laos are thought to be descendants of southwestern Chinese and Thais. Several distinct tribes exist in Laos, including the Tai, Lao Theung (a diverse group of peoples who are descendants of earlier groups that arrived before the Thai tribes), and the Hmong and Yao, mountain dwellers who are more recent migrants (1850s) from southern China. At one time or another Laos has been dominated by each of its neighbors. It too became a French colony, in 1893, and with Cambodia and Vietnam became known as French Indochina. Laos gained independence from France in 1953, but in 1975 a Communist government (Pathet Laos), strongly influenced by Vietnam, overthrew the government and currently rules the country.

The Philippines

The Philippines is an archipelago of 7,100 islands located on the eastern edge of Southeast Asia. Located off the coast of

The Philippines were named after King Philip II of Spain. In the past, Spanish was widely spoken in the Philippines, but today the official language is Filipino, formerly Tagalog. It is spoken by approximately 25 percent of the population; Ilocano is spoken by 15 percent of Filipinos, and Visayan by 44 percent.

Vietnam and south of Taiwan the Philippine islands form a nation, approximately 1000 miles long. Manila, the trade center of the Philippines, is located on the largest island, Luzon.

The original inhabitants (Aetas) of the Philippines, who were short and had Negroid features, were pushed into remote mountainous areas by successive waves of peoples from Asia, beginning with the Indonesians and followed by the Malays. Culturally, except for some Moslem influence in the southern islands, the Philippines has been strongly influenced by the Spanish, who dominated the country by the sixteenth century. The Philippines adopted their religion, Roman Catholicism, and many Spanish food habits.

At the conclusion of the Spanish–American War in 1898, the Philippines became a protectorate of the United States. Starting in the nineteenth century, numerous Chinese emigrated to the Philippines, and many entered into local trade. The term Filipino, which originally meant a person of Spanish descent who was born in the Philippines, eventually came to mean the people of the country, who were a blend of the indigenous population, the Spanish, and the Chinese. During World War II, the Philippines was occupied by the Japanese, but soon after the Japanese surrender, the Philippines declared its independence on July 4, 1946.

Corruption, low morale, inflation, and political and economic problems have plagued the country for several decades. More recently, Ferdinand Marcos was ousted from the presidency in 1986, and the government is now headed by Corazon Aquino.

HISTORY OF IMMIGRATION TO THE UNITED STATES

Immigration Patterns

The majority of mainland Southeast Asians who have immigrated to the United States have come since the 1970s because of the military conflict in the area. In 1975, when South Vietnam fell to the North, 60,000 Vietnamese left the country with the assistance of the United States. Another 70,000 managed to flee on their own. Most of these refugees were either employed by the United States or were members of the upper classes. The latter group immigrated in intact family groups and were able to bring their property with them.

From 1975 to 1977, another wave of Vietnamese left for political or economic reasons. Many of these "boat people" lost their families and what little money they had. The third phase of immigration started in 1978, when increasing numbers of ethnic Chinese living in Vietnam fled the country. This wave of immigration was accelerated by the Chinese invasion of northern Vietnam in 1979. These second boat people left with no financial resources, and many lost family members escaping in unseaworthy vessels that were easy prey for pirates. After rescue, the boat people often lived for several months, even years, in refugee camps in various Southeast Asian countries before immigrating to the United States.

Immigration from Cambodia and Laos is similar in that political conflict in the 1970s resulted in substantial numbers of refugees who eventually settled in camps along the Thai border. Of those who have immigrated to the United States, length of stay in the camps and the conditions of the camps themselves varied considerably.

Substantial immigration from the Philippines to the United States started in 1898 after the country became a U.S. territory. Approximately 113,000 young male Filipinos traveled to the Hawaiian Islands between 1909 and 1930 to work in the sugar cane fields. Many of these immigrants later moved to the U.S. mainland. These early immigrants were considered U.S. nationals and carried U.S. passports, but they were not allowed to become citizens or own land. Most were uneducated peasant laborers from the island of Illocos. Since they were not allowed to bring their wives or families, social and political clubs replaced the family as the primary social structure. In 1934, the immigration of Filipinos slowed as a result of Asian exclusion laws. After World War II it became legal for Filipinos to become U.S. citizens, and the number of immigrants increased. A substantial increase in Filipinos emigrating to the United States was seen after 1965, when the U.S. immigration laws were changed. Two-thirds of the Filipinos who immigrated after World War II qualified for entrance as professional or technical workers.

Current Demographics

Over 450,000 Vietnamese have entered the United States since 1975. Many were sponsored by American agencies or organizations, which provided food, clothing, and shelter until the Vietnamese could become self-supporting. Many Vietnamese later relocated in the western and Gulf states, probably because the climate is similar to that of Vietnam. It is estimated that over 35,000 Cambodians and 75,000 Laotians have entered the country since 1975. Approximately one-half million Filipinos live in the United States; the majority reside on the West Coast or in Hawaii.

Socioeconomic Status

Vietnamese in the United States live primarily in urban areas. Many are young and live in an extended family, which may include aunts, uncles, and cousins. The first wave of Vietnamese immigrants were well educated, could speak English, and had held white-collar jobs in Vietnam. Many of them had to accept blue-collar jobs initially and could not support their extended families. The boat people were even less prepared for life in the United States, because they often had no English-language skills, were illiterate, had less job training, and did not have support from an extended family. In general, most Vietnamese are presently at the lower end of the socioeconomic spectrum.

Although more recent immigrants from the Philippines are better educated than those who arrived earlier, their education or professional experience is often not recognized in the United States, forcing them to accept blue-collar jobs. Nevertheless, this group is economically better off than previous immigrants, of whom most of those still alive are now poor elderly single men. Some of these older men did marry late in life, however, and when they died they often left their young wives with several young children and inadequate financial resources.

Less information is available on other Southeast Asian immigrants, but it is generally assumed that most refugees from Cambodia and Laos are in a weak economic position, dependent on a wide variety of government services.

Cultural Organizations

Compared to the the Japanese and the Chinese, Southeast Asians have fewer organizations to serve their needs, perhaps because they have been in the country a relatively short time. In some areas, the social-support organizations are loosely formed around the Buddhist temple or Catholic church. There are not yet any statewide or national groups.

The Filipinos have numerous regional associations, but they have not coalesced into a state or national group, perhaps because there are considerable regional and language differences in the Philippines which may prevent Filipinos from joining U.S. Filipino associations. The Agricultural

Workers Organizing Committee, composed primarily of Filipino farm workers, joined with the Chicano organization, the National Farmworkers Association, led by Cesar Chavez, to initiate the successful grape strike in Delano, California, in 1965.

WORLDVIEW

Family

Southeast Asians place a high value on the family, respect for elders, and interdependence among family members. Behavior that would bring shame to the family's honor is avoided, as is direct expression of conflict. Social acceptance and smooth interpersonal relationships are emphasized. Traditionally, the Southeast Asians live in extended families, with up to three or four generations living together; this remains common among immigrant families in the United States.

Breakdown of traditional family structure has been reported among both Vietnamese and Cambodian refugees. Children are often the first to learn English, and acculturate more easily than their parents, causing value conflicts and loss of respect for elders. Further, the male head of the household may be unable to support his family on his wages alone, and his wife may be forced to work, eroding his authority. The role of the elderly is also changing: old age is esteemed in Southeast Asia, but in the United States older relatives are often isolated from their peers and even younger family members. Language and transportation problems are prevalent.

Religion

Theravada Buddhism is the predominant religion in Cambodia and Laos. About half the Hmong population is now Christian as a result of French and American missionary work in Laos. The other half practice ancestor worship. Ninety percent of the Vietnamese are also Buddhist, but of the Mahayana sect, as a result of Chinese influence. Some Vietnamese are Roman Catholics, resulting from the French occupation; most Filipinos are also Roman Catholic, as a result of Spanish influence.

Religious affiliations influence the worldview of Southeast Asians. Filipinos, especially the elderly, believe that those who lead a good life on earth will be rewarded with life after death. Human misfortunes are violating the will of God. One should accept one's fate, because supernatural forces control the world. Time and providence will ultimately solve all problems.

Buddhists believe that a person's present life reflects his past lives and also predetermines his own and his descendants' future lives. They consider themselves as a part of a greater force in the universe. Many Southeast Asians believe that spirits and deities control the universe and that the spirits of their ancestors dwell in their homes to protect them. Ancestor worship is most common among mainland Southeast Asians.

Traditional Food Habits

The cuisines of Southeast Asia share many similarities in ingredients, but food preparation methods and meal patterns reflect the foreign cultures that have influenced the individual countries. For example, the Vietnamese often serve cream-filled French pastries for dessert, whereas Filipinos frequently have milk-based custard flan. As in China and Japan, the staple foods are rice (primarily long grain), soybean products, and tea. A meal is not considered complete unless rice is included. Instead of soy sauce, however, Southeast Asians often season their food with strongly flavored fermented fish sauces and fish pastes.

Filipinos say that a young person should never sing in front of the stove or they will marry old maids or widowers.

There are three central themes in Filipino cooking: One, never cook any food by itself; two, fry with garlic in olive oil or lard; three, the food should have a sour-cool taste. *Adobo*, for example, is a stew that consists of chicken, pork, and sometimes fish and shellfish, first fried with garlic in lard and then seasoned with vinegar. Filipinos use a clay pot in the shape of a wok to fry, but they tend to leave the food in longer than the Chinese and allow it to absorb more fat.

It is generally accepted that ingredients are similar in all the mainland Southeast Asian countries but that meal patterns and recipes vary. The French introduced and popularized such items as strong coffee, pastries, asparagus, French bread, and meat pâtés. The Chinese influence, seen mainly in Vietnam, resulted in the use of chopsticks; stir-frying in the wok; serving long-grain rice separately at the meal, rather than mixed with other ingredients; and the concept of yin and yang foods for the treatment and prevention of disease.

INGREDIENTS AND COMMON FOODS

Staples

Filipino. The common foods of the Philippines are listed in the Cultural Food Groups table (Table 7.3). The Filipinos drink *caraboa* (water buffalo) milk and use it to make one of the few native cheeses in Asia. Because of U.S. influence in the Philippines, many western dairy products are available, but cow's milk is not commonly used. Evaporated milk is a common ingredient in *leche flan*, a custard, and in *halo-halo*, a liquid dessert that is served in a glass but is eaten with a spoon, consisting of shaved ice and coconut milk mixed with mung beans, boiled nipa-palm seeds, corn kernels, pineapple jelly, as well as other ingredients. Ingredients for halo-halo can be bought premixed.

Rice is the staple of the diet, and the long-grain variety accompanies the meal either steamed or fried. (Usually only left-over rice is fried.) The short-grain, glutinous rice is often used for sweet desserts, such as *puto*, a sweet, fluffy cake made from glutinous rice, sugar, and sometimes coconut milk. A common bread, *pan de sol*, is made from rice flour. Noodles are also used extensively. *Pancit*, a noodle made from rice, wheat, or mung beans, is mixed with cooked

In the Philippines, noodles known as rice sticks are called *bijon*, egg noodles are *canton*, and mung bean threads are *sotanghon*.

Filipino lumpia *on* pancit.

TABLE 7.3. Cultural Food Groups: Filipino

Group	Comments
PROTEIN FOODS Milk/milk products	Filipinos make one of the few native cheeses in Asia, from *carabao* (water buffalo) milk.
	U.S. influence has resulted in the availability of many western dairy products.
	Many Filipinos may be lactose intolerant.
	In desserts, coconut milk is frequently used in place of cow's milk.
Meat/poultry/fish/eggs/ legumes	The amount of protein food consumed by a family usually depends on economic status.
	Many small dried salt fish are called *dilis* or *daing.*
CEREALS/GRAINS	Rice is the main staple and is usually eaten at every meal.
FRUITS/VEGETABLES	

Common Foods	Adaptations in the United States
Evaporated and fresh milk (goat or carabao), white cheese.	Consumption of milk and other dairy products has increased.
Meat: beef, goat, pork, monkey, variety meats (liver, kidney, stomach, tripe), rabbits. *Poultry and small birds:* chicken, duck, pigeon, sparrow. *Fish and shellfish:* anchovies, bonita, carp, catfish, crab, crayfish, cuttlefish, ladyfish, mackerel, milkfish, mussels, prawns, rock oyster, salt cod, sardines, sea urchins, shrimp, sole, squid, swordfish, tuna. *Eggs:* chicken, fish. *Legumes:* black beans, black-eyed peas, chick peas, lentils, lima beans, mung beans, red beans, soy beans, white kidney beans.	Consumption of fish has decreased; intake of meat, poultry, and eggs has increased.
Corn, oatmeal, rice (long and short grain, flour, noodles), wheat flour (bread and noodles).	Rice is not usually eaten at breakfast.
Fruits: apples, avocados, bananas (100 varieties), banana blossoms, breadfruit, *calamansi* (lime), citrus fruit, coconut, durian, grapes, guava, litchi, mangoes, melons, pomelo, papaya, pears, persimmons *(chicos)* pineapples, plums, pomegranates, rhubarb, star fruit, strawberries, sugar cane, tamarind, watermelon. *Vegetables:* bamboo shoots, bean sprouts, beets, bitter melon, cabbage, carrots, cashew nut leaves, cassava, cauliflower, celery, Chinese celery, heart of palm, eggplant, endive, garlic, green beans, green papaya, green pep-	

TABLE 7.3. Cultural Food Groups: Filipino (*continued*)

Group	Comments
ADDITIONAL FOODS	
Seasonings	Food is spicy, but the variety of spices used is limited.
Nuts/seeds	
Fats/oils	
Beverages	
Sweeteners	

chicken, ham, shrimp, or pork in a soy- and garlic-flavored sauce.

The amount of meat, poultry, or fish a family eats depends on economic status. Pork, chicken, and fish are popular. Milkfish *(bangus)* is the national fish of the Philippines. Many small dried salt fish are called *dilis* or *daing.* Some common Filipino dishes are the following:

Dinu-guan, a stew consisting of diced pork, chicken, or entrails cooked in pig's blood and seasoned with vinegar and hot green chilis.

Sinigang, a soup of fish or meat cooked in water with sour fruits, tomatoes, and vegetables.

Ukoy, a vegetable-and-shrimp fritter eaten as an appetizer.

Chicken relleño, a whole chicken stuffed with boiled eggs, pork, sausage, and spices.

Common Foods	Adaptations in the United States
pers, hyacinth bean, leeks, lettuce, long green beans, mushrooms, nettles, okra, onions, leaf fern, parsley, pigeon peas, potatoes, pumpkins, purslane, radish, safflower, snow peas, spinach, spineless amaranth, sponge gourd, squash blossoms, winter and summer squashes, sugar palm shoot, swamp cabbage, sweet potatoes, taro leaves and roots, tomatoes, turnips, yams, waterchestnuts, watercress, winged beans.	
Atchuete (annatto), bagoong, garlic, hot pepper, lemon grass, turmeric, vinegar, patis, seaweed, soy sauce.	
Betel nuts, cashews, peanuts, pili nuts.	
Coconut oil, lard, vegetable oil.	
Soy milk, cocoa, coffee with milk, tea.	Chocolate milk substituted for soy milk.
Brown and white sugar, coconut, honey.	

Puchero, a beef, chicken, and vegetable stew with an eggplant sauce.
Kari-kari, beef and oxtails cooked in a sauce of string beans and ground peanuts, seasoned with bagoong, a fermented fish paste.
Lechon, roasted whole pig, served on special occasions.

A common seasoning, used instead of salt and found throughout Southeast Asia, is fermented fish paste or sauce. In the Philippines, the paste is called bagoong and tastes somewhat like anchovies, although it can be made from a variety of fish or shellfish. Patis is the transparent amber sauce.

A principal food in many Pacific islands is the coconut, and it is widely used in Filipino cooking. It takes approximately one year for a coconut to mature, but if picked at six months

The name coconut comes from the Spanish who thought the "nut" had the face of a clown (coco).

In the Philippines it is considered good luck if one cleanly splits open a coconut without jagged edges.

the soft, jellylike coconut meat can be eaten with a spoon and is a popular delicacy.

The coconut plant provides several food products, including beverages, cooking liquids, and even a vegetable. The sweet, clear liquid found in young coconuts is the juice or water. It is drunk but is not used in cooking. Coconut cream, which is used for cooking along with coconut milk, is the first liquid extracted from grated mature coconut meat. After the cream is removed, coconut milk is made by adding water to the meat and then squeezing the mixture. Coconut milk is used primarily in delicacies. Coconut-palm blossom sap can be fermented to produce a powerful alcoholic drink called *tuba* in the Philippines. Heart of palm, sometimes called palmetto cabbage, is the firm, greenish inner core of the tree; it is used as a vegetable. Bananas, durian (a large, strong-smelling, sweet fruit with a creamy texture), and pineapples are also popular.

Vietnamese and Mainland Southeast Asians. The common foods of mainland Southeast Asians are listed in the Cultural Food Groups table (7.4). Like other Asians, the people of mainland Southeast Asia do not use appreciable amounts of dairy products. However, soy milk is a common beverage.

In Vietnam, more fish and shellfish is eaten than meat and poultry. However, pork is preferred over beef. Soy products are common. Vietnamese Buddhists eat tofu (soybean curd), on the first, fifteenth, and last day of the lunar month, when no meat is allowed.

Laotians tend to use glutenous rice more than long-grain rice.

Rice, both long and short grain, is one of the main staples. Rice products, such as noodles (sticks), paper, and flour, are used extensively. In Vietnam, rice paper is used as egg roll or wonton wrappers. In the dish *cha gio,* the moistened paper is wrapped around a variety of meats, fish, vegetables, and herbs and then deep fried. Often the rice paper is filled with meat, fresh herbs, and vegetables at the table. These dishes are commonly seasoned with a sauce made from fermented fish called *naoc mam.* Also used in cooking, naoc mam is a salty condiment that is often used instead of soy sauce. It can be transformed into a hot sauce, *nuoc cham,* with the addition of ground chili, vinegar, sugar, garlic, and citrus-fruit juice.

In Cambodia and Laos, fermented fish is called *prahoc* and *padek,* and fish sauce *tuk-trey* and *nam pa,* respectively.

The Vietnamese serve many uncooked vegetables, often in the form of salads and pickles. A special-occasion dish is shredded chicken and cabbage salad, *goi go.* Many fresh herbs and spices, including basil, fresh coriander, chili peppers, garlic, ginger, lemon grass, and mint, give their food its distinctive flavor and add color to many dishes. Grilled lemon grass beef, *bo nuong xa,* is usually served at summer picnics and is always found at parties and celebrations. Due to the influence of the French, the Vietnamese also eat asparagus, green beans *(haricots),* and potatoes.

MEAL COMPOSITION AND CYCLE

Daily Pattern

Filipino. The traditional meal pattern in the Philippines consists of three meals a day with two *meriendas* or "snack breaks," one in midmorning and one in late afternoon. Breakfast may be garlic fried rice with dried fish or sausage, plus hot coffee or hot chocolate. Lunch and dinner may be similar, but both usually include rice, some fish or fish paste, meat, if affordable, a vegetable, and fruit or a sweet. The snacks may consist of substantial amounts of food, such as fritters, sweets, fruits, *lumpia* (the Filipino version of the egg roll), or almost anything else except rice.

Vietnamese and Other Mainland Southeast Asians. The Vietnamese eat three meals per day and optional snacks. A traditional breakfast may consist of soup with rice noodles, meat, bean sprouts, and greens; boiled egg with meat and pickled vegetables on French bread; and either rice and left-over meat or boiled sweet potatoes with chopped roasted peanuts. Lunch and dinner include rice, fish or meat, a vegetable dish, and a clear soup with vegetables or meat. Snacks may include clear soup, fruit, or pastries. Southeast Asians do not associate particular foods with breakfast, lunch, or dinner; thus a variety of foods may be eaten at any meal. Hot water and tea are generally drunk with the meal, but coffee with sugar and condensed milk may be drunk after the meal or with snacks.

In Vietnam, food is commonly stir-fried, simmered, or boiled. Soup may accompany every meal; it is often eaten in restaurants that specialize in *pho,* a delicate beef and noodle soup, to which bean sprouts, herbs, and other seasonings are added immediately before serving. *Mien ga* is a chicken noodle soup served in a similar manner.

Special Occasions

Filipino. In the predominantly Catholic Philippines, religious festivals and Saints' days are numerous (see Chapter

TABLE 7.4. Cultural Food Groups: Mainland Southeast

Group	Comments
PROTEIN FOODS	
Milk/milk products	Most Southeast Asians do not drink milk and may be lactose intolerant.
	Sweetened condensed milk is used in coffee; whipping cream is used in pastries.
	Many use soy and coconut milk.
Meat/poultry/fish/eggs/ legumes	The traditional Southeast Asian diet is low in protein.
	Fish, pork, and poultry are common; most parts of the animal are used (brains, heart, lungs, spleen).
CEREALS/GRAINS	Rice is the staple grain and is usually eaten with every meal.
	French bread is commonly eaten.
FRUITS/VEGETABLES	The Vietnamese eat a considerable amount of fruit and vegetables, fresh and cooked.
	Fruit is often eaten for dessert or as a snack.

Common Foods	Adaptations in the United States
Sweetened condensed milk, whipping cream.	It is expected that younger Southeast Asians will increase their use of most dairy products.
Meat: beef, lamb, pork. *Poultry and small birds:* chicken, duck, quail, pigeon, sparrow. *Eggs:* chicken, duck, fish. *Fish and shellfish:* almost all varieties of fresh- and saltwater sea food, fresh and dried. *Legumes:* chick peas, lentils, mung beans (black and red), soy beans and soy bean products (*tofu,* soy milk, bean sprouts).	Meat, lamb, and eggs are eaten more; fish, shellfish, and duck are eaten less because of price.
Arrowroot, cornstarch, rice (long and short grain, sticks, noodles), tapioca, wheat (French bread, cakes, and pastries).	Intake of baked goods increases.
Fruits: apples, bananas, cantaloupe, coconut, custard apple, dates, durian, figs, grapefruit, guava, jackfruit, jujube, lemon, lime, litchi, longans, mandarin orange, mango, orange, papaya, peach, pear, persimmon, pineapple, plum, pomegranates, pomelo, raisins, rambutan, *sapodilla,* star fruit, soursop, strawberries, tamarind, watermelon.	Use of fruits and vegetables is dependent on availability and price. It is expected that use of fruits and vegetables will decline.
Vegetables: artichokes, asparagus, bamboo shoots, banana leaves, beans (yard-long and string), bitter melon, breadfruit, broccoli (Chinese and domestic), cabbage (domestic, Chinese, savoy and Napa), calabash, carrot, cassava, cauliflower, celery (domestic and Chinese), Chinese chard, Chinese radish *(daikon),* chrysanthemum, corn, cucumber, eggplant (domestic and Thai), leeks, lotus root, luffa, matrimony vine, mushrooms (many varieties), mustard (Chinese, greens), okra (domestic, lady finger), peas, peppers, potato,	

TABLE 7.4. Cultural Food Groups: Mainland Southeast Asians (*continued*)

Group	Comments
ADDITIONAL FOODS	
Seasonings	Fish sauce as well as soy sauce is often used.
Nuts/seeds	
Beverages	Drunk after the meal or with snacks or desserts.
Fats/oils	
Sweeteners	Sweets are luxury foods.

2). On all special occasions it is customary to serve plenty of food buffet-style. There are numerous practices and customs associated with Easter, whose observances begin on Ash Wednesday. One is that young children are awakened late on Easter Eve to partake of special meat dishes, such as adobo and dinu-guan, in the belief that if they do not do so, they will become deaf.

The Filipinos claim to have the longest Christmas season in the world, from December 16 to January 6. The midnight mass celebrated on Christmas Eve is usually followed by the traditional *"media noche,"* a midnight supper of fiesta foods such as roast ham, sweet potatoes, banana-flower salad, and

Common Foods	Adaptations in the United States
pumpkin (flowers, leaves), spinach (Chinese, Indian, domestic), squash *(chayote, luffa)*, sweet potatoes (tubers, leaves), taro (root, stalk, leaf, shoots), tomatoes, turnips, water lily greens, water chestnut, wax gourd, winged beans, yams.	
Allspice, alum, findweed, black pepper, borax, cayenne pepper, chives, coconut milk, fresh coriander, curry powder, fennel, galanga root, garlic, ginger, chili pepper, lemon grass, lemon juice, lily flowers, lotus seed, mint, monosodium glutamate, *nuoc mam*, paprika, saffron, star anise, cinnamon, tamarind juice, and vinegar.	
Almonds, cashews, chestnuts, macadamia nuts, peanuts, pili nuts, walnuts; locust seeds, pumpkin seeds, sesame seeds, watermelon seeds.	
Coffee, tea, sweetened soybean milk, a wide variety of fruit and bean drinks, hot water, hot soup.	Increased use of carbonated drinks.
Bacon, butter, lard, margarine, peanut oil, vegetable oil.	The Vietnamese have increased their use of butter and margarine.
Cane sugar, candy.	The use of sweetened products has increased in the United States.

niaga, a dish made of boiled meat, onions, and vegetables whose name means "good life." Other specialties eaten during the Christmas season are *puto bumbong,* a rice-flour delicacy cooked in a whistling bamboo kettle, and *bibingka,* a sweet roll cooked in a clay pan over hot coals.

A midnight mass is also held on New Year's Eve, but many Filipinos attend parties to celebrate the holiday instead. Again, a midnight supper consisting of fiesta foods is traditional. There is also a superstition that if one eats seven grapes in succession as the clock strikes midnight, one will have good luck in the coming year. For birthdays pancit is eaten to ensure a "long life."

Snack vendor, Vietnam. (Courtesy World Health Organization/P. Almasy.)

Vietnamese and Other Mainland Southeast Asians. Of all Vietnamese holidays, Tet, the New Year's celebration, is the most important. It is observed at the end of the lunar year (end of January or beginning of February), just after the rice

Vietnamese restaurants, San Francisco.

Cambodians celebrate the New Year later in the spring than the Vietnamese. During the three-day festival, prayers and special foods, such as fried coconut and fried bananas rolled in coconut, are left for the New Year angel, who is waiting to descend with either blessings or ill will.

harvest. In Vietnam, the first Tet ritual is an observance at the family gravesites. Offerings of cake, chicken, tea, rice, and alcohol, as well as money, are made at the graves, then the family picnics on the offerings.

The second ritual, held on the twenty-third day of the twelfth lunar month, is to celebrate the departure of the Spirit of the Hearth, Ong Tao. He is represented by three stones on which the cooking pots are placed and honored by a small altar. Like the Chinese Kitchen God, Ong Tao returns to the celestial realm each year and reports on the family's behavior. After the family makes an offering to symbolize his departure, they share a feast including glutenous rice cakes and a very sweet soybean soup. One week later, the family celebrates Ong Tao's return to their hearth. The following day is the first day of Tet. Guests (especially those with favorable names, such as *Tho,* meaning longevity) are entertained with tea, rice alcohol, red-dyed watermelon seeds, candied fruits, and vegetables. Special dishes prepared for the week-long celebration include *banh chung,* glutenous rice cakes filled with meat and beans and boiled in banana leaves, squid soup, stir-fried young seasonal vegetables, pork with lotus root, and sometimes a special shark fin soup. Traditionally, the Vietnamese did not commemorate birthdays but rather honored their ancestors on the anniversary of their death with a special celebration and meal. In the United States, it is now more common to celebrate birthdays.

THERAPEUTIC USE OF FOODS

Filipino

When the Spanish came to the Philippines, they brought the hot—cold theory of medicine adopted from the Arabs (for more explanation, see Chapter 4 on Latin America). Foods are classified as being hot or cold based on their innate qualities, not on their spiciness or temperature. It has been suggested that the reason Filipino dishes contain so many ingredients is that they help blend and balance the hot and cold foods within the meal.

Filipino folklore states that when women are pregnant, eating eggplant before delivery of the baby will cause a difficult labor.

Vietnamese and Other Mainland Southeast Asians

Many Vietnamese follow the Chinese yin—yang theory of disease and disease treatment. They also believe that ingestion of specific organ meats will benefit the like internal organs. For example, consumption of liver will produce a stronger

The Vietnamese believe that a diet high in salt is good for pregnant women.

liver. Some Vietnamese believe that eating gelatinous tiger bones (produced by prolonged cooking) will make them strong.

Contemporary Food Habits in the United States

ADAPTATION OF FOOD HABITS

Filipinos

Filipinos in the United States are able to obtain some traditional foodstuffs without much difficulty, although many of the familiar fresh fruits and vegetables are not often available. Most Filipinos still eat rice every day, but not with every meal, and their diets tend to contain a greater variety of foods, more meat, and less fish than they did in the Philippines. Meriendas tend not to be eaten as often.

Vietnamese and Other Mainland Southeast Asians

A recent study (Tong, 1986) conducted in Washington, D.C., found that 30 percent of the 50 Vietnamese households surveyed had changed their eating habits since coming to the United States. Although most continued to eat rice at least once a day, they were eating more bread or instant noodles at lunch and more cereal at breakfast. Respondents reported eating more meat and poultry and less fish and shellfish than in Vietnam, mainly because of cost. Pork and pork products were still preferred to beef. They also reported fewer bananas and more oranges, fruit juices, and soft drinks. These findings are similar to those reported in a survey conducted in the 1970s among Vietnamese living in northern Florida (Crane & Green, 1980).

NUTRITIONAL STATUS

Nutritional Intake

Filipino. The traditional Filipino diet is higher in total fat, saturated fat, and cholesterol than most Asian diets. Urban Filipinos living in the United States tend to have even higher intakes of these dietary components. They often suffer from conditions that result from nutritional excess, such as renal and cardiovascular disease, possibly caused by hypercholesterolemia and hypertension. Both conditions may be influenced by the large amounts of sodium in many traditional condiments and by a diet high in cholesterol and saturated fat.

Filipinos also suffer from more diabetes mellitus, hyperuricemia, and glucose 6-phosphate dehydrogenase deficiency than white Americans. It should be noted that alpha thalassemia (hemoglobin H disease) is also prevalent among Filipinos and results in a hypochromic microcytic anemia, especially during an infection or when oxidant drugs are taken.

Although Filipinos consume more milk and cheese than other Asians, it is assumed that many are lactose intolerant and that calcium intake may therefore be limited. Dried fish, fish sauce, and fish paste may provide calcium, but amounts may vary depending on the source and quality of the product.

Betel nuts may be chewed by older men, resulting in stained teeth.

Vietnamese and Other Mainland Southeast Asians. Food intake data suggests that the Vietnamese immigrant's intake of calcium is low, although this observation needs to be verified, since fish sauces and other traditional foods may contain sufficient calcium. Vietnamese have been reported to be lactose intolerant. Their iron intake may also be marginal. Certain conditions common among recent immigrants from Southeast Asia may compromise their nutritional status. These include: (1) tuberculosis, usually the inactive form; (2) intestinal parasites, which can contribute to anemias, fatigue, and weight loss; (3) malaria; (4) renal disease, whose contributing factor is the presence of hepatitis B surface antigens; and (5) dental problems, caused by chronic malnutrition and, in the United States, excessive consumption of sweets. Previous malnutrition also contributes to the prevalence of microcytic anemia and to short stature in recent immigrants.

Normally, the Vietnamese consider their children to be one year old at birth; with each Tet (New Year's) celebration, a child becomes one year older. This is important to remember when plotting growth curves. However, some Vietnamese parents may report their children as being younger than they are in order to enroll them in lower school grades. This allows the children to catch up in their schooling.

Recent immigrants have been reported to have a high incidence of low birthweight infants, as a result of poor maternal weight gain during pregnancy. Traditionally, Southeast

Asians gained less weight during pregnancy in order to have an easier birth. In one study, it was found that the birthweight of babies of less recent Southeast Asians are close to the U.S. average (3.34 kg); these groups are thought to have benefited from medical and nutritional care (Davis *et al.*, 1982).

Counseling

Filipino. The health provider should not address elderly Filipinos by their first names, as this is disrespectful. They may not make direct eye contact, which is used only to express sexuality or anger, and their responses may be both formal and modest, because the health care provider is considered an authority figure. In addition, because Filipinos often avoid direct expression of disagreement and situations in which self-esteem is lost, the health care provider should be sensitive in discussing certain topics, such as socioeconomic background.

Because of Filipinos' strong family orientation, relatives play a significant role in a patient's treatment and recovery. For most effective treatment, the provider should discuss diet modifications with family members as well as with the patient. The in-depth interview should be used to determine the patient's degree of acculturation and resulting food habits.

Vietnamese and Other Mainland Southeast Asians. The Vietnamese place a high value on social harmony; both Confucian and Buddhist belief systems encourage modesty. The clinician should be aware that the patient will be agreeable to avoid disharmony or to please the questioner. In addition, since the family is the fundamental social unit, a health-care decision may be made by the family, not just by the patient.

Proper form and appearance are important to the Vietnamese. In addition, certain nonverbal forms of communication should be observed: (1) the head is considered sacred, and it is impolite to pat the head of an adult or child; (2) the feet are the lowest part of the body; thus it is impolite to point with the foot or show the bottoms of one's shoes; and (3) it is impolite to signal by using an upturned index finger, since this is how dogs are called.

An in-depth interview is critical to determine the patient's country of origin (a patient may be offended if grouped with all other Southeast Asians), length of time in the United States and any immediate health problems. Degree of acculturation and personal food preferences should also be noted.

When conducting diet interviews, it should be remembered that Vietnamese may not distingish between fruit juice and fruit flavored soda.

REFERENCES

Barer-Stein, T. 1981. *You Eat What You Are: A Study of Ethnic Food Traditions.* Toronto: McClelland and Stewart.

Chang, K. C. (Ed.). 1977. *Food in Chinese Culture: Anthropological and Historical Perspectives.* New Haven, CT: Yale University Press.

Chau, P. P., Lee, H. S., Tseng, R., & Downes, N. J. 1987. *Dietary habits, health beliefs, and health-related food practices among Chinese elderly: A pilot study.* Master's project. Department of Nutrition and Food Science, San Jose State University, San Jose, CA.

Chen, P. K., Chen, T. C., & Tseng, R. 1983. *Everything You Want to Know about Chinese Cooking.* Woodbury, NY: Barron's.

Chen-Louis, T. 1983. Nursing Care of Chinese-American patients. In *Ethnic Nursing Care: A Multicultural Approach*, M. S. Orque, B. Block & L. S. Monrroy (Eds.). St. Louis: C. V. Mosby.

Crane, N. T., & Green, N. R. 1980. Food habits and food preferences of Vietnamese refugees living in northern Florida. *Journal of American Dietetic Association, 76,* 591–593.

Davis, J. M., Goldenring, J., McChesney, M., & Medina, A. 1982. Pregnancy outcomes of Indochinese refugees, Santa Clara County, California. *American Journal of Public Health, 72,* 742–743.

Eckstein, E. F. 1983. *Menu Planning* (3rd ed.). Westport, CT: AVI Publishing.

Grivetti, L. E., & Paquette, B. 1978. Nontraditional ethnic choices among first-generation Chinese in California. *Journal of Nutrition Education,10,* 109–112.

Hahn, E. 1968. *The Cooking of China.* New York: Time-Life Books.

Hashizume, S., & Takano, J. 1983. Nursing care of Japanese-American patients. In *Ethnic Nursing Care: A Multicultural Approach*, M. S. Orque, B. Block, and L. A. Monrroy (Eds.). St. Louis: C. V. Mosby.

Hosokawa, B. 1969. *Nisei: The Quiet American.* New York: William Morrow.

Ichiro, H., Fujio, I., Tsuneya, W., & Keiichi, Y. 1972. *Japanese Religion.* Palo Alto, CA: Kodansha International.

Joya, M. 1955. *Quaint Customs and Manners of Japan* (Vol. IV). Tokyo: Tokyo News Service.

Kitano, H. H. 1976. *Japanese Americans: The Evolution of a Subculture* (2nd ed.). Englewood Cliffs, NJ: Prentice-Hall.

Latourette, K. S. 1964. *The Chinese: Their History and Culture* (4th ed.). New York: Macmillan.

Lee, C. 1965. *Chinatown, U.S.A.* Garden City, NY: Doubleday.

Lee, R. H. 1960. *The Chinese in the United States of America.* Hong Kong: Hong Kong University Press.

Leonard, A. R., Jang, V. L., Foester, S., Igra, A., Ransom, B., & Lambert, C. B. 1981. *Dietary Practices, Ethnicity and Hypertension: Preliminary Results of the 1979 California Hypertension Survey.* Sacramento, CA: California Department of Health Services.

Marmot, M. G., & Syme, S. L. 1976. Acculturation and coronary heart disease in Japanese Americans. *American Journal of Epidemiology, 104,* 225–247.

Nguyen, M. D. 1985. Culture shock: A review of Vietnamese culture and its concepts of health and disease. *Western Journal of Medicine, 142,* 409–412.

Orque, M. S. 1983. Nursing care of South Vietnamese patients. In *Ethnic Nursing Care: A Multicultural Approach*, M. S. Orque, B. Block, and L. S. Monrroy (Eds.). St. Louis: C. V. Mosby.

Reischauer, E. O. 1974. *Japan: The Story of a Nation.* New York: Alfred A. Knopf.

Steinberg, R. 1970. *Pacific and Southeast Asian Cooking.* New York: Time-Life Books.

Steinberg, R. 1969. *The Cooking of Japan.* New York: Time-Life Books.

Tate, D. J. M. 1979. *The Making of Modern South-East Asia* (Vols I & II). Oxford: Oxford University Press.

Tong, A. 1986. Food habits of Vietnamese immigrants. *Family Economic Review, 2,* 28–30.

U.S. Department of Agriculture, Food and Nutrition Service. 1980. *Nutrition Education and the Use of WIC Foods.* Pub. No. FNS-227. Washington, D.C.

Wenkam, N. S., & Wolff, R. J. 1970. A half century of changing food habits among Japanese in Hawaii. *Journal of American Dietetic Association, 57,* 29–32.

Zeigler, V. S., Sucher, K. S., and Downes, N.J. 1986. Southeast Asian Renal Exchange List. Master's project. Department of Nutrition and Food Science, San Jose State University, San Jose, CA.

8

THE PEOPLE OF GREECE AND THE MIDDLE EAST

Greece and the countries of the Middle East are considered the cradle of western civilization and democracy. The Middle East is geographically situated between Africa, Europe, and Asia. It has traditionally been a cultural crossroad; ideas and products of the region, including food, have influenced all western societies. Many immigrants from the Middle East have come to the United States in search of economic opportunity and political stability. Most retain a strong ethnic identity in the United States, exhibited in their religious faith and in their maintenance of many traditional food habits. This chapter will examine the cuisine of the Middle East, its role in the culture, and the changes that have occurred in the United States.

CULTURAL PERSPECTIVE

The countries of the Middle East include Egypt, Iran, Iraq, Israel, Jordan, Lebanon, Saudi Arabia, Syria, Turkey, and the other countries of the Arabian peninsula. Although Greece is considered a European country, its cuisine resembles that of the Middle East; the geography and climate are also similar. Greece dominated or greatly influenced its Middle Eastern neighbors in ancient times, and in turn was conquered and ruled by the Turkish Ottoman Empire for four centuries in the modern era. Although Armenia no longer exists as an inde-

Other countries whose cuisine has been greatly influenced by the Middle East and Greece are the Balkan states (Yugoslavia, Albania, Romania, and Bulgaria) and the countries of North Africa (Tunisia, Libya, Morocco, and Algeria).

312

*Traditional foods of Greece and the Middle East: Some foods typically in-
cluded in the diet of people in Greece and the Middle East include almonds,
chick-peas (garbanzo beans),* couscous, *cracked wheat, dates, eggplant,
feta cheese, figs,* filo dough, *garlic, lamb, lemon, olives,* pita bread, *and
yogurt.* (Photo by Laurie Macfee.)

pendent state in the Middle East, Armenians also have similar
food habits.

Geographically, most of the area is considered sandy and
arid, but distinct units of arable land exist along the sea
coasts and in some plains and valleys, such as the Fertile
Crescent (a plain in Iraq fed by the Euphrates and Tigris Rivers), and the Nile River valley of Egypt.

History of Greece and the Middle East

Two centers of political power developed in the Middle East
long before the birth of Christ: one in Egypt and the other in
Mesopotamia (Iraq). Egypt was ruled by a succession of
kings, called pharaohs, from approximately 4000 to 1200 B.C.
They are known today for their monuments, pyramids, palaces, and temples. Agriculture, masonry, glass making, and
metal smelting may all have developed in Egypt. In Mesopotamia, the city of Babylon became the capital of the Hammur-

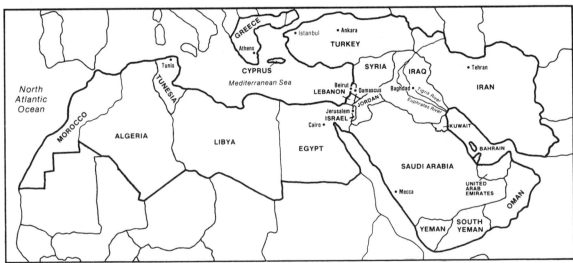

Greece and the Middle East.

abi dynasty (1728–1686 B.C.). The Hammurabi were later overthrown by the Hittites (1800–1200 B.C.), who were the first to use horses in warfare, and who dominated the area now known as Turkey, Lebanon, Syria, and Iraq. They were eventually deposed by the Assyrians from the city of Assur. By the seventh century B.C., the Assyrian empire included most of the Middle East, exluding Persia (Iran). The next power to dominate the Middle East was the Persian empire (550 B.C), which ruled until the rise of Alexander the Great from Macedonia (Greece).

In ancient times, Greece was divided into independent, mutually competitive city-states. They were ultimately united by Alexander in 335 B.C. Alexander extended his empire until he controlled the area that today includes Egypt, Turkey, Lebanon, Israel, Syria, Iraq, and Iran. Although Alexander's empire did not last long after his death (323 B.C.), Greek cultural influence in these areas remains to this day.

The Romans were the next power to dominate the Middle East. Trading and manufacturing flourished under their rule, and many merchants grew rich from trade between Europe, Asia, and East Africa. In addition to the movement of material goods, religious ideas, especially Christianity, spread throughout the Roman empire. In A.D. 324 the emperor Constantine, who had become a Christian, chose the ancient city of Byzantium to be his new capital, later renamed Constantinople in his honor (now called Istanbul, Turkey).

As Constantinople rose in power to become the center of the Byzantine empire, Rome weakened. It was sacked in A.D. 475 by Germanic barbarian tribes. The Byzantine empire, which included Greece, was Greek in language and religion (Eastern Orthodox). It ruled what is now Turkey for centuries, but its dominance over the rest of the Middle East waned by the 600s, due in part to conflicts with a powerful Persian dynasty, the Sasanid empire (226–651).

The rise of Islam in the Arabian peninsula in the seventh century radically changed the course of history in the Middle East (see Chapter 2). It ended the dominance of Greco-Roman politics and culture, introduced a new monotheistic religion, and spread a new language, Arabic, which is still spoken today in most Middle Eastern countries.

After Islam had become established in the Arabian peninsula, primarily by military conquest, its influence continued to expand. Muslims conquered most of the Middle East (except Constantinople), North Africa, Sicily, Spain, Portugal, and western India by the early eighth century, and in the pro-

An Arab is commonly defined as a person who speaks Arabic; the term does not refer to any particular religious belief. Persons from Iran speak Farsi and call themselves Persians, not Arabs.

cess, converted many of the inhabitants of these areas to Islam. The height of Islamic rule came under the two great caliphal dynasties, the Umayyads and Abbasids, from 685 to 945. During this time Islam attained its greatest literary and scientific achievements; the Arabs were both feared and courted by the Europeans and the Chinese.

Between the tenth and thirteenth centuries, the Islamic community declined in power as a result of conflict among the various Islamic religious sects, rebellion in previously conquered nations (Spain and Portugal), and outside attacks by Asian Turks, Mongols and the European Christian Crusaders.

The invading Turks adopted the Islamic religion and eventually settled in the area now known as Turkey. They rose to power and toppled the weakened Byzantine empire. By the fifteenth century, the Turkish Ottoman empire controlled Greece, the other Balkan states, Yugoslavia, Albania, and Bulgaria, and part of Hungary. By the sixteenth century it also dominated Egypt, Syria, Lebanon, Israel, and parts of Saudi Arabia, Iraq, and North Africa.

Although the Ottoman empire existed into the twentieth century, by the early eighteenth century the West (Europe, Russia, and later the United States) achieved and maintained military, political, and economic superiority in the Middle East. By 1920, France ruled Morocco, Algeria, Tunisia, and Syria (Syria then included the area now called Lebanon). Britain governed Egypt, Sudan, Palestine (Israel), Transjordan (Jordan), Iraq, and parts of the Arabian peninsula.

Greece became a sovereign nation in 1832, but its resentment against Turkish rule is still evident in the continuous conflict over the now independent island of Cyprus. Iran, although influenced by the West, remained an independent nation and today is an Islamic republic. The remaining Arab nations gained their independence after World War II. Israel was established as a Jewish nation in 1948.

History of Immigration to the United States

IMMIGRATION PATTERNS

Immigration from Greece and the Middle East has occurred in two waves. The first lasted from the late 1800s to the 1920s, when the restrictive Immigration Act of 1924 was imposed; the second wave started after World War II and has not yet ended.

Both the early Greek and Arab immigrants were from rural agricultural areas, and they came to America primarily for economic opportunities. The Arabs were mainly Christians from the area that is today Lebanon.

Immigration from Greece and the Middle East after World War II reflected political unrest in the area. In Greece, a bitter civil war from 1946 to 1949, and a military coup in 1967, resulted in numerous refugees who sought asylum in the United States. A high percentage of immigrants from Jordan, Egypt, Lebanon, Iraq, and Syria were Palestinian refugees who initially fled Israel when it was declared a state to settle in refugee camps. Many later immigrated to the United States after Israel won the 1967 war against neighboring Arab countries. Political unrest in Iran led to a large exodus of Persians after 1976. In addition, many Arabs who were sent to the United States for education and training remained for economic reasons.

CURRENT DEMOGRAPHICS AND SOCIOECONOMIC STATUS

Early Greek and Arab immigrants did not turn to the land for a living but preferred to live in urban areas. The Arabs often became peddlers and later opened family businesses, usually dry goods or grocery stores. Many recent Arab immigrants are well-educated professionals. The Greeks settled primarily in the northeastern and north central states, such as Massachusetts, as well as in California and Florida. Many sought economic independence by opening small businesses, especially restaurants. Recent Greek immigrants are mostly professionals and skilled laborers.

Greek Americans estimate their population in the United States to be between 1.3 and 1.5 million. It has been estimated that one million Arabs live in the United States as a result of the first wave of immigration and that another quarter million Arabs have entered since World War II.

CULTURAL ORGANIZATIONS

In addition to the Greek Orthodox Church, the American Hellenic Educational Progressive Association (AHEPA) is one of the largest national organizations of Greek Americans. Before the 1967 Arab–Israeli War, the early and late Arab immigrant groups tended not to associate with each other; after 1967, perceived American hostility toward Arabs drew the

Half a million Armenian Americans are thought to currently live in the U.S. The dominant religion among Armenian Americans is the Armenian Apostolic Church which is similar to Eastern Orthodoxy and Roman Catholicism, but is independent of Constantinople and Rome.

two groups closer together. The aims of the National Association of Arab Americans, founded in 1972 by American-born businessmen and professionals of Arab descent, and the Association of Arab-American University Graduates, is to correct misinformation about Arabs, improve the image of the Arab American, and influence American Middle East policy.

Worldview

RELIGION

The ethnicity of first- and second-generation Greek Americans was affirmed mostly by language and religion. Today, most Greek Americans speak English but still belong to the Greek Orthodox church. Early Arab immigrants were primarily Christians belonging to the Eastern Orthodox, Maronite, or Melkite church, whereas most later immigrants have been Muslims.

FAMILY

Traditionally, both Greek and Arab cultures center around a strong patriarchal extended family whose honor and status must be maintained. The family demands conformity and subordination of individual will and interest, but in return the members of the family are protected and can identify with the family's honor and status.

One of the first effects of immigration to the United States was the breakdown of the extended family and reduction in the father's authority, although filial respect was retained. Further, women were gradually freed from some Middle Eastern customs, such as veils for Muslim women. Family ties are still very strong among Greeks and Arabs, and it is still common for elderly parents to live with the family.

TRADITIONAL FOOD HABITS

The tall white hat usually worn by professional chefs is thought to have originated with Eastern Orthodox priests who wear tall black hats.

Certain common foods in Greece and the Middle East, such as wheat, olives, and dates, are indigenous to the whole region. Yet most countries in the area claim one dish or another prepared in all the countries to be their own invention. It is doubtful if the source of any Middle Eastern dish will ever be known, since the political and economic history of the region has resulted in very similar foods and food habits.

Middle Eastern market. (Courtesy World Health Organization/P. Merchez.)

Ingredients and Common Foods

STAPLES

The common ingredients used in Greek and Middle Eastern cooking are listed in the Cultural Food Groups table (Table 8.1). Numerous food items, such as wheat, rice, legumes, and lamb, are common to most of the countries.

Wheat, thought to have been cultivated first in this region, is usually eaten as leavened bread in Greece and flat leavened bread in the Arabic countries. One example of an Arabic bread is the flat round bread with a hollow center called *pita*. Bread traditionally accompanied every Greek and Middle Eastern meal.

Besides bread, wheat dough is also used to make pastry for pies. They are prepared in a variety of sizes and may contain meat, cheese, eggs, or vegetables. For desserts they are usually filled with nuts and covered in a thick sugar and honey syrup. Pie pastry, flaky pastry, paper-thin pastry called *filo*, and bread dough can all be used. An example of a meat- or cheese-filled pastry that can be served hot or cold is *sanbu-*

TABLE 8.1. Cultural Food Groups: Greek and Middle Eastern

Group	Comments
PROTEIN FOODS	
Milk/milk products	Most dairy products are consumed in fermented form (yogurt, cheese). Whole milk is used in desserts, especially puddings.
	High incidence of lactose intolerance.
Meat/poultry/fish/eggs/ legumes	Pork is eaten only by Christians; not by Muslims and Jews.
	Jews do not eat shellfish. In Egypt, fish is generally not eaten with dairy products.
	Dried as well as fresh fish is used throughout the region.
CEREALS/GRAINS	Some form of wheat or rice usually accompanies the meal in Greece and the countries of the Middle East.
FRUITS/VEGETABLES	Fruits are eaten for dessert or as snacks. Fresh fruit and vegetables are preferred, but if they are not available, fruits are served as jams and compotes and vegetables as pickles. Eggplant is very popular.
	Vegetables are sometimes stuffed with rice or a meat mixture.
ADDITIONAL FOODS	
Seasonings	Numerous spices and herbs are used.
	Lemons are often used for flavoring.

Common Foods	Adaptations in the United States
Cheese (goat's, sheep's, and cow's), milk (goat's, sheep's, and cow's), yogurt.	More cow's milk and less sheep's and goat's milk is drunk. Ice cream is popular. *Feta* is the most common Middle Eastern cheese available in the United States.
Meat: beef, kid, lamb, pork, rabbit, veal, some varietal cuts. *Poultry:* chicken, duck, pigeon, turkey. *Fish and shellfish:* anchovies, bass, clams, cod, crab, crayfish, flounder, frog legs, lobster, halibut, mackerel, mullet, mussels, oysters, redfish, salmon, sardines, shrimp. *Eggs:* poultry and fish. *Legumes:* black beans, chick-peas, fava (broad) beans, horse beans, lentils, navy beans, red beans.	Lamb is still very popular. More beef and fewer legumes are eaten.
Bread (wheat, barley, corn, millet), barley, corn, cornstarch, farina, oatmeal, pasta, rice (long grain and *basmati*), wheat *(bulgur couscous)*.	Bread and grains eaten at most meals. *Pita* bread is commonly available.
Fruits: apples, apricots, avocado, cherries, currants, dates, figs, grapes, lemons, limes, melons (most varieties), oranges, peaches, pears, plums, pomegranates, raisins, strawberries, tangerines.	Fewer fruits and vegetables are consumed. Olives still popular.
Vegetables: artichokes, asparagus, beets, broad beans, broccoli, brussels sprouts, cabbage, corn, cauliflower, carrots, celeriac, celery, cucumbers, eggplant, grape leaves, greens, green beans, green peppers, leeks, lettuce, mushrooms, okra, olives, onions, parsley (flat-leaf), peas, pimientos, potatoes, spinach, squashes, tomatoes, turnips, zucchini.	
Allspice, anise, basil, bay leaf, caraway seed, cardamom, chervil, chives, chocolate, cinnamon, cloves, coriander, cumin, dill, fen-	

TABLE 8.1. Cultural Food Groups: Greek and Middle Eastern (*continued*)

Group	Comments
Nuts/Seeds	Ground nuts are often used to thicken soups and stews.
Beverages	Coffee and tea are often flavored with cardamom or mint, respectively. Aperitifs are often anise-flavored.
Fats/oils	Olive oil is generally used in dishes that are to be eaten cold. For most deep frying, corn or nut oil is used; olive oil is preferred for deep frying fish.
Sweeteners	Coffee is heavily sweetened. Dessert syrups are flavored with honey or rose water.

The traditional recipe for *sanbusak dough* calls for one coffee cup of oil, one coffee cup of melted butter, one coffee cup of warm water, and one teaspoon of salt. Flour is then worked into the mixture until it is stiff.

sak. Traditionally half-moon shaped and three inches long, it is popular in Syria, Lebanon, and Egypt. *Bisteeva* (*pastilla*), Filo dough filled with a cinnamon-scented chicken mixture, is a specialty in Morocco. Throughout the Middle East and Greece the dessert made with filo dough, *baklava*, is served at every party. No cafe or bakery would be without it. Baklava contains numerous alternating sheets of filo dough and nut filling and is bathed in a sweet syrup flavored with honey, brandy, or rose water. It is frequently cut into diamond shapes.

Cracked wheat is also used in a number of Middle Eastern dishes. *Couscous,* cracked, uncooked wheat granules (often of semolina), is steamed and served with stews and broths in North African countries, while in Lebanon, cracked wheat (*burghul* or *bulgur*) is made into *tabouli*, a salad containing

Common Foods	Adaptations in the United States
nel, fenugreek seeds, garlic, ginger, gum arabic and mastic, lavender, linden blossoms, mace, marjoram, mint, mustard, nasturtium flowers, nutmeg, orange blossoms or water, oregano, paprika, parsley, pepper (red and black), rose petals and water, rosemary, **saffron**, sage, savory, sorrel, sumac, tarragon, thyme, turmeric, vinegar.	
Almonds, cashews, hazelnuts, peanuts, pine nuts, pistachios, walnuts; poppy, pumpkin, sunflower, sesame seeds.	
Coffee, date palm juice, fruit juices, tea and herbal infusions, yogurt drinks, wine, brandy, aperitifs.	
Butter (often clarified), olive oil, sesame oil, various nut and vegetable oils.	Olive oil is still popular.
Honey and sugar.	

onions, parsley, mint, and a variety of fresh vegetables. *Kibbeh*, one of the national dishes of Lebanon and Syria, is a mixture of fine cracked wheat, grated onion, and ground lamb pounded into a paste. This mixture can be eaten raw, fried, or grilled, and with a great deal of dexterity it can be made into a hollow shell, then filled with a meat mixture and deep fried.

In addition to wheat, rice is also a staple item in Greek and Middle Eastern cuisine. The long-grain variety is used to make *pilaf*, a dish that commonly accompanies meat. The rice is first sauteed in butter or oil in which chopped onions have been browned. It is then steamed in chicken or beef broth. Occasionally saffron or turmeric is added to give the dish a deep yellow color. *Polo* is the Iranian version of pilaf, but a final step in its preparation produces a rice with a crunchy brown crust. A more fragrant variety of rice, *basmati*, is used in Iran to make the national dish, *chelo kebab*, which is thin pieces of marinated charcoal-broiled lamb served over rice (*chelo*).

A large variety of legumes are another important ingredient in Middle Eastern cooking. Cooked pureed chick-peas (garbanzo beans) are the base for the salad called *hummus*, which is often used as an appetizer or as a dip. Ground chick-peas or fava beans are sometimes formed into small balls, then fried, and served as a main course (*ta'amia*) or in a pita bread with raw vegetables (*falafal*). The national dish of Egypt is *ful medames*, cooked brown beans, seasoned with oil, lemon and garlic, sprinkled with parsley, and served with hard-boiled eggs.

Fruits, many first cultivated in the region, are eaten for dessert or as snacks. Fresh fruits and vegetables are preferred, but if they are not available fruits are served as jams and compotes and the vegetables as pickles. Lemons are often used for flavoring. Although many vegetables are used, eggplant is the most popular. A common cooking method for vegetables (the Greek term is *yiachni*; the Arabic word is *yakhini*) is to combine them with tomatoes or tomato paste and sauteed onions, together with a small amount of water, then cook until the vegetables are soft and very little liquid remains. Vegetables are also eaten raw, mixed together in a salad. Eggplant and other vegetables are sometimes stuffed with rice or a meat mixture. A delicacy favored throughout the region is stuffed grape leaves, *dolmas*.

The olive tree contributes in many ways to Greek and Middle Eastern cooking. Olives prepared in the Middle Eastern way have a much stronger taste than American olives; they often accompany the meal or are served as an appetizer. There are three basic types of olives in Greece and the Middle East. Black olives are ripe when picked, are small, round, and wrinkled, and taste slightly bitter and salty. Green olives are picked unripe, having an oblong shape, firm flesh, smooth skin, and tart flavor. Greek *kalamata* olives are large, oblong, with soft flesh and smooth purplish skin; they are considered the most delicious.

The olive is also a source of oil, which is frequently used in food preparation, although both Greeks and Arabs also use clarified butter (*samana*) and most vegetable oils and margarine. Olive oil is generally used in dishes that are to be eaten cold. For most deep frying, corn or nut oil is used, but olive oil is preferred for deep frying fish.

Many people in the area are lactose intolerant, so fresh

Athens is named after the Greek goddess Athena, because she gave the city the olive tree.

milk is not widely consumed in Greece or the Middle East, although it is used in dessert puddings. Dairy products are usually fermented (yogurt or cheese). Yogurt is often eaten as a side dish and is served plain (unsweetened) or mixed with cucumbers or other vegetables. It is even diluted to make a refreshing drink. Cheese is usually made from goat's or sheep's milk. The most widely used Middle Eastern cheese is the Greek *feta*, which is a salty, white, moist cheese that crumbles easily. Another is *kaseri*, a firm, white, aged cheese, mild in flavor and similar to Italian provolone.

Almost all meats and seafoods are eaten in Greece and the Middle East, with the exception of pork in the Muslim countries and pork and shellfish among observant Jews in Israel. However, lamb is the most widely used meat. Grilling, frying, grinding, and stewing are the common ways of preparing meat in the region. A popular dish is *shish kebab*, marinated pieces of meat threaded on to skewers with pieces of raw tomatoes, onions, and sweet peppers and then grilled over a fire. *Souvlaki* is very thin slices of lamb layered onto a rotisserie (resulting in one roast), grilled, then carved and served. A whole roasted lamb or sheep is a festive dish prepared for parties, festivals, and family gatherings.

Numerous spices and herbs are used in Middle Eastern seasoning as a result of a once thriving spice trade with India, Africa, and Asia. Common spices, and herbs are dill, garlic, mint, cinnamon, oregano, parsley, and pepper. Sumac, ground berries from a nontoxic variety of the plant, is sprinkled over salads to give a slightly astringent flavor.

Ground nuts are often used to thicken soups and stews. Sesame seeds are crushed to make a thick sauce, *tahini*, which is used as an ingredient in Arabic cooking and in a sweet dessert paste known as *halvah*.

Although observant Muslims do not drink alcohol, aperitifs are available in the region. Several are anise flavored; depending on the country, they are called *raki* (Turkey), *arak*, or *ouzo* (Greece). Spirits are distilled from dates, potatoes, plums, molasses, wine, and grain. Greece also produces wine and brandy. *Retsina* is a white wine with a resinous flavor; *metaxia* is an orange-flavored brandy.

REGIONAL VARIATIONS

There are two schools of thought about the number of regional cooking areas in the Middle East. One identifies three culinary areas: Greek/Turkish, Iranian, and Arabic. The other makes five divisions: Greek/Turkish, Arabic, North African,

Many people from the Middle East and the Mediterranean area are unable to digest the milk sugar, lactose.

Yogurt is actually the Turkish name for this fermented milk product. In Syria and Lebanon it is called *laban*, in Egypt *laban zabadi*, and in Iran *mast*.

In Egypt, fish is generally not eaten with dairy products.

The Arabs were the first to mix *gum arabic* with sugar to produce chewing gum. The Greeks chewed on *mastic*, a licorice-flavored gum; it is the source for the word, masticate.

Iranian, and Israeli. Certainly every region has some unique recipes and cooking methods, but the similarity in cuisine throughout the region is striking. Israel probably has the most different foods and food habits, because its cuisine blends the indigenous Middle Eastern cooking with that of many immigrant groups (Russians, Germans, Austrians, and Eastern Europeans) who have settled in the area since the turn of the century. Further, many of Israel's citizens adhere to the kosher laws of the Jewish religion (see Chapter 2 for more information on Jewish dietary practices).

Meal Composition and Cycle

DAILY PATTERN

People in Greece and the other Middle Eastern countries eat three meals per day. The main meal is at midday, and in the hotter climates, a short nap follows. Dinner is lighter and is served in the cooler evening hours. In addition, a wide variety of bite-sized snacks, *mezze*, are available in cafés and served at home throughout the day for friends and relatives, either as appetizers or as a meal in themselves.

In Greece, the traditional breakfast may consist of a slice or two of bread with white cheese, olives, or jam, with coffee or tea. The main meal, eaten at around 2:00 P.M., might include a meat stew, meat balls, or vegetables stuffed with chopped meat or baked beans, accompanied by a salad of raw seasonal vegetables, yogurt or cheese, and fruit as dessert. Roasted or baked whole meats are served on weekends, accompanied by cooked vegetables, salad, and dessert.

In the other Middle Eastern countries, coffee or tea is often served first for breakfast, followed by a light meal that might include cheeses, eggs, jam and bread, and plain yogurt. Lunch is the main meal of the day, served between noon and 2:00 P.M. It may consist of a meat and vegetable stew, accompanied by rice and bread. Supper is light, like breakfast, but it may also include sandwiches.

Throughout Greece and the Middle East, coffee and tea are the common beverages drunk after the meal. They are frequently flavored with cardamom or mint, respectively. Coffee is also served in cafes. The drink is traditionally made in a long-handled metal *briki*, producing a strong, thick, and often sweet brew that is served in small cylindrical cups.

At happy occasions, the coffee should always be sweet, while at funerals it should be bitter, without any sugar added.

Preparing Middle Eastern coffee: The coffee of Greece and the Middle East is brewed in a long-handled briki. It is strong, thick, sweet, and often flavored with cardamom.

ETIQUETTE

Throughout the Middle East, hospitality is a duty and food plays an important part in it. Guests, even uninvited ones, should be made to feel welcome and are offered food and drink. Even if they refuse at first, they must eventually accept, since refusal is considered an insult. Invited guests bring a gift, often candy or other sweets, and the host must open it immediately and offer them some.

"Give the guest food to eat even though you yourself are starving" is an Arabic saying.

One is obligated to feed a guest, but which pieces of certain foods the guest is given, and in what order the food is served, expresses the recipient's status. Status is based on sex, age, family, and social rank. For example, a dignitary or head of the family is served the best portion first. In some areas, it is customary for women to eat separately from men.

Guests are traditionally entertained in a separate room before the meal, at which time scented water is provided so they may wash their hands. The dining table might be a large round metal tray, resting on a stool or platform, and the diners sit around it on cushions. In Iran, food is traditionally served on a rug. The meal is set out in several bowls placed on the table or rug and then shared by the diners. After the meal, the guests leave the table, wash their hands, and then have coffee or tea.

Several rules of etiquette apply to eating. One should always wash one's hands before eating; eat with three fingers (usually on the right hand); and lick the fingers after eating. It is considered polite to continue eating until everyone else is finished, because if one person stops eating the others will feel compelled to stop too. Only pleasant and joyful things are discussed at the meal, and one must compliment the host and hostess.

SPECIAL OCCASIONS

In Greece and the Middle Eastern countries, food plays an important role in the celebration of special occasions (often religious) and in the observance of certain events, such as weddings and births.

In the Eastern Orthodox church, there are several feast and fast days (see Chapter 2). The most important religious holiday for the Greeks is Easter. Immediately after midnight mass on Holy Saturday, the family shares the first post-Lenten meal. It traditionally begins with red-dyed Easter eggs and continues with *mayeritsa*, a soup made of the lamb's innards,

Assorted Greek pastries.

perhaps flavored with *avgolemono*, a tart egg and lemon sauce used throughout the Middle East. The Easter Sunday meal usually consists of roast lamb, pilaf, accompanying vegetables, cheese, yogurt, and a special Easter bread. Dessert usually includes sweet pastries made with filo dough and *koulourakia*, a traditional Greek sweet bread cookie, sometimes shaped into a hairpin twist or wreath or coiled in the shape of a snake (which the pagan Greeks worshipped for its healing powers).

There are feasts and fasts connected with Islamic religious observances. Traditional festive foods vary from country to country. *Iftar* is the meal that breaks the fast during Ramadan, the month in which Muslims fast from sunrise to sunset. The meal usually starts with a beverage, preferably water, followed by an odd number of dates and coffee or tea. A larger meal, served after prayers, often includes a soup, and most dishes are moist and hearty. It is common to dine with relatives and neighbors. Regular items eaten during Ramadan include soups, fruit juices, fresh or dried fruit, and *kataif*, a sweet stuffed pancake. The dawn meal is usually light, and salty foods are avoided since water is not allowed during the fast.

In Iran, the traditional meal for Nau Roz, the holiday that

The sweet and spicy bread which Greek women bake for Sundays, holidays, and religious festivals is known as *tsoureki*. For New Year's Day it is called *vasilopitta* and is baked with money inside. Whoever receives the piece containing the coin will have good luck for the coming year. The bread called *christopsomo*, "Christ's bread," is served at Christmas (decorated with a cross) and on Easter (topped with dyed red eggs known as *lambropsomo*).

In Greece and the Middle East, sweetened almonds (Jordan almonds) are served at weddings to ensure sweetness. Greeks also serve them at baptisms.

marks the spring equinox, must include seven foods that start with the letter "s." The number seven probably relates to the seven days of the week or the seven planets of the ancient solar system. On the thirteenth day of Nau Roz it is customary to have a picnic.

Therapeutic Uses of Food

Arabs have been reported to believe that illness can be caused by hot-cold shifts in food, food deprivation, and damp weather (Meleis, 1981). The temperature of the food (not spiciness) can cause a shift in the body from hot to cold, or vice versa, and it is believed that the digestive system must have time to adjust to one extreme temperature before a food of the opposite temperature can be introduced. Extreme shifts are thought to cause headaches, colds, and flu. Food deprivation is also believed to cause illness, and poor appetite is regarded as a disease in itself or as a generalized complaint signifying that one's life is not as it should be. Little has been reported about the therapeutic use of food in Greece.

CONTEMPORARY FOOD HABITS IN THE UNITED STATES

Adaptation of Food Habits

There is limited information on the adaptation of Greek and Arab diets in the United States. It is assumed that, as in other immigrant groups, increasing length of stay is correlated with Americanization of the diet, with traditional dishes prepared and eaten only for special occasions.

INGREDIENTS AND COMMON FOODS

It has been reported that Greek Americans still use olive oil extensively, although they use less of it than their immigrant relatives (Valassi, 1962). Salads still accompany the meal, and fruit is often served for dessert. Vegetables are prepared in the traditional manner. Lamb is still very popular; for special occasions roasted leg of lamb is substituted for the whole animal. Consumption of beef and pork has increased, whereas consumption of legumes has decreased. Cereal and grain consumption among Greek Americans is still high, and bread, rice, or cereal products are usually included in every meal. Greek Americans consume more milk than their immigrant parents, and ice cream is very popular.

MEAL COMPOSITION AND CYCLE

Greek Americans still maintain traditional meal patterns, but the main meal of the day is now dinner (Valassi, 1962). They prefer an American-type breakfast and lunch, but dinner is more traditional. However, they have adapted Greek recipes to make them less time consuming to prepare and to include fewer fats and spices.

Nutritional Status

NUTRITIONAL INTAKE

Very little has been reported on the nutritional composition of the Greek American or Arab American diet. However, one aspect of their diet has recently received considerable media attention because of its possible link to prevention of cardiovascular disease. Traditional Greek and Middle Eastern diets contain more monounsaturated fatty acids (primarily from olive oil) than American diets (Fordyce *et al.*, 1983); a diet high in monounsaturated fatty acids has been correlated with lower readings of resting blood pressure (William *et al.*, 1987).

COUNSELING

Arab Americans place a high value on western medicine and have considerable respect for authority figures. However, they may expect the provider to make decisions for them and be responsible for the consequences. Arab Americans also resist disclosing information about themselves and their families to strangers, and they may not question the advice given them because of shyness, respect for authority, or fear of rejection. In addition, Arab Americans do not expect personal care from health professionals; they expect effective cure. In their view, the more intrusive the medical procedure, the more effective the treatment (Meleis, 1981).

The health provider may have to assess and give advice about a medical or dietary problem without the client requesting the information. If the provider does not repeat the offer to help, the client may believe that the provider is indifferent. Body movement, such as touch (only allowed between members of the same sex), posture, and eye contact, is important in enhancing communication. Therefore, Arab Americans tend to be more receptive to verbal than to written information.

Older Greek Americans should be asked if they use certain foods or herbs for self-treatment. The in-depth interview should be used to determine country of origin, degree of acculturation, and religious faith. Information on traditional health care beliefs that are still practiced should be elicited.

REFERENCES

Fordyce, J. K., Christakis, G., Kafatos, A., Duncan, R., & Cassady, J. 1983. Adipose tissue fatty acid composition of adolescents in a U.S.–Greece cross-cultural study of coronary heart disease risk factors. *Journal of Chronic Diseases, 36*, 481–486.

Hitti, P. K. 1961. *The Near East History.* New York: D. Van Nostrand.

Meleis, A. I. 1981. The Arab American in the health care system. *American Journal of Nursing, 81*, 1180–1183.

Naff, A. 1980. Arabs. In *Harvard Encyclopedia of American Ethnic Groups,* S. Thernstrom (Ed.). Cambridge, MA: Harvard University Press.

Nickles, H. G. 1969. *Middle Eastern Cooking.* New York: Time-Life Books.

Perl, L. 1967. *Rice, Spice and Bitter Oranges: Mediterranean Food Festivals.* New York: World Publishing.

Roden, C. 1974. *A Book of Middle Eastern Food.* New York: Vintage.

Scourby, A. 1984. *The Greek Americans.* Boston: Twayne.

Valassi, K. 1962. Food habits of Greek Americans. *American Journal of Clinical Nutrition, 11*, 240–248.

William, P. T., Fortman, S. P., Terry, R. B., Garay, S. C., Vranizan, K. M., Ellsworth, N., & Wood, P. D. 1987. Association of dietary fat, regional adiposity and blood pressure in men. *Journal of the American Medical Association, 257*, 3251–3256.

Yianilos, T. K. 1970. *The Complete Greek Cookbook.* New York: Funk and Wagnalls.

9

Asian Indians

I ndia is a culturally complex country with a population of
750 million people, three times that of the United States.
The sophisticated civilization dates back to 2500 B.C. and is
the source of some of the most influential religions, art, architecture and widespread foods in the world. The subconti-
nent contains the fertile Indus and Ganges river basins, and
parts of the Himalaya mountain range, and it varies in climate
from extensive desert regions to jungle forests to the world's
largest mountain glaciers.

The people of India are as diverse as its geography and
climate. People from virtually every racial and religious group
have migrated to or invaded India at some time in history,
and each group brought its own language and customs. As
these different races and religions intermingled, other cultures were created. One result is that there are currently 15
separate languages recognized by the Indian government;
there are an estimated 700 dialects.

More than 500,000 Asian Indians live in the United States
today. They represent numerous racial and religious groups,
yet many share high educational levels and socioeconomic
status. This chapter examines traditional Indian foods and
food habits, as well as the dietary changes that occur when
Asian Indians come to the United States.

Traditional foods of India: Some foods typical of the traditional Indian diet include basmati *rice, broccoli, coconut, cucumber, eggplant,* ghee, *herbs and spices (black pepper, cardamon, chilis, fresh coriander, cloves, coriander, cumin, garlic, ginger root, mint, mustard seeds, nutmeg, tamarind, and turmeric), lentils, peas, plantains, and yogurt.* (Photo by Laurie Macfee.)

CULTURAL PERSPECTIVE

History of India

EARLY URBANIZATION

The earliest civilization in India arose in the Indus valley around 2500 B.C. The largest city, Mohenjo-Daro, was a commercial trade center based on advanced metal, pottery, and cotton fabric crafts.

Sometime between 1500 and 1200 B.C., Aryan peoples from Persia (now Iran) began to settle first in bordering Afghanistan, then in the Ganges valley. The early invaders overwhelmed the descendants of the Mohenjo-Daro culture, who are known as Dravidians. The combination of the Aryan and Dravidian cultures laid the foundation for Indian society, including the development of Hinduism and Sanskrit (the official language of India for over 2000 years).

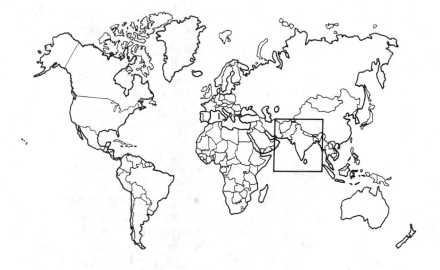

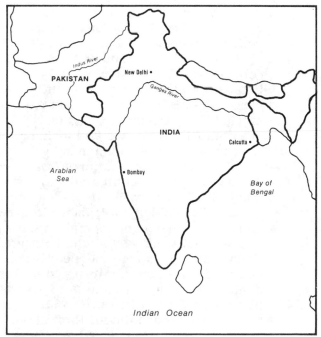

India.

The first Hindu empire was established under Chandra-gupta Maurya, who ousted Alexander the Great (from Greece) from Northern India in 320 B.C. He founded the Maurya dynasty, unifying two-thirds of the Indian peninsula. His grandson, Ashoka, was influential in the spread of Buddhism in the third century B.C.

The dissolution of the Mauryan dynasty in 185 B.C. resulted in numerous small regional governments. Northern India was unified again 500 years later with the formation of the Gupta empire. Invasions from groups such as the White Huns terminated Gupta rule around A.D. 470.

Beginning in the tenth century, India was subjected to numerous waves of Muslim invaders from Mongolia and Afghanistan. A sultanate was established in Delhi and was extended in the fourteenth century throughout northern India. The Moghul (from the Persian word for Mongolian) empire was established in 1526 by Babar the Moghul; it was strengthened by his successors, including Akbar the Great. The Hindu rule of Vijayanagar in southern India coincided with the Moghul empire.

European contact with India began in 1497 with the arrival of Vasco de Gama from Portugal. The Dutch, French, and British were soon competing with the Portuguese for trade with India. The British East India Company rose to prominence, monopolizing European trade and subduing the Moghuls in 1757. The Hindus in central and south India were conquered in 1818. Rule passed from the British East India Company to the British government in 1858, following the massacre of British citizens in the Indian mutiny (the Sepoy rebellion of the Bengal Army) of 1857. British India was divided into 16 provinces and included numerous states that were under British dominion but governed by Indian princes.

In 1885 the Indian National Congress was formed by Indians who were discontented with British hegemony. It was followed in 1906 by the founding of the All-Indian Muslim League. Opposition to British rule grew after World War I, and a program of noncooperation was begun in 1920 by Mohandas (Mahatma) K. Gandhi. Pressure from the Indian nationalists for complete independence and from the Muslim League for a separate Muslim state resulted in granting of limited powers in 1919 and 1935. As total independence was negotiated with Britain in 1946, savage rioting erupted between Muslims and Hindus throughout northern India. When unity could not be achieved, a compromise establishing the independent nations of Pakistan (predominantly Muslim) and

India (predominantly Hindu) was accepted in 1947. Violence continued during the following year as Hindus fled Pakistan and Muslims from throughout India immigrated to Pakistan.

Jawaharlal Nehru was elected the first prime minister of the democratic republic of India. Border disputes have occurred with both China, in 1962, and Pakistan, in 1965 and 1971. Nehru's daughter, Indira Gandhi, was elected prime minister in 1967. A short war with Pakistan in 1971 resulted in the formation of the nation of Bangladesh out of eastern Pakistan. Gandhi remained in power until her assassination in 1984 by members of the Sikh religion as retribution for purported government repressions. Her son, Rajiv Gandhi, was elected her successor in 1985.

History of Immigration to the United States

Given the complexity of Indian culture, it is not surprising that the Asian Indian immigrants to the United States differ from other immigrant groups in several ways. Most importantly, the majority of Indians arriving in America are not escaping political or economic pressures in their homeland. Since 1965, when the national quota system was temporarily dropped from U.S. immigration laws, most Asian Indian immigrants have been from the upper socioeconomic classes. They were somewhat acculturated at the time of arrival, fluent in English, and acquainted with many western habits.

IMMIGRATION PATTERNS

The first immigrants to the United States from India were members of the Sikh religion, who arrived on the West Coast in the early twentieth century. They faced overt discrimination and persecution. Newspapers warned of the "Hindoo invasion," and anti–Asian Indian feelings brought about expulsion of Indians from Washington logging communities and riots in 1907 in California. Although such extreme bigotry lessened after a time, the Indian immigrant population remained small until after World War II.

Relaxed immigration laws encouraged Asian Indians, especially professionals, to come to America in the 1960s and 1970s. In general, economic and social adjustment is these immigrants' highest priority. They are a strong, self-reliant community and do not like to be identified with other ethnic groups.

Recent changes in Asian Indian immigration patterns may

change this typically high degree of acculturation. Indians coming to America today are more likely to be from rural towns and villages. They are less educated and less westernized than previous Indian immigrants. There are also fewer professionals among them. Most recently arrived Indians are self-employed in jobs that serve their Indian immigrant community, such as restaurateurs, importers, and travel agents.

As a result of this change in the Asian Indian immigrant profile, newcomers now identify more with their immediate ethnic subgroup community than with the wider, pan-Indian community. Their adjustment to American culture is more difficult. The religion, language, and social class of each cultural subgroup retain greater importance for recent immigrants than for previous immigrants from India.

CURRENT DEMOGRAPHICS

Today, Asian Indians are one of the fastest-growing immigrant groups in the United States. Their population increased 20 percent between 1980 and 1984, from 400,000 to 500,000. They have settled throughout the United States, especially in the metropolitan areas of California and New York, as well as in Illinois, Maryland, Massachusetts, Michigan, Ohio, Pennsylvania, and Texas. There are also several Asian Indian communities in the agricultural regions of California.

SOCIOECONOMIC STATUS

The relative affluence of Americans of Asian Indian descent is due to the large percentage of highly educated immigrants. Over two-thirds were employed in professional occupations in India, such as college professors, engineers, physicians, and scientists. It is not known how current changes in immigration patterns will affect this socioeconomic position.

Many Asian Indians come to the United States alone to continue their educations. They are either unmarried or have left their spouses and children in India. It is not uncommon for the families to join the student in America after he or she has become financially established.

CULTURAL ORGANIZATIONS

Four major national organizations were established in the 1970s to promote and protect Asian Indian interests in the United States. They are Associations of Indians in America

(AIA), the National Federation of Indian Associations, the Indian American Forum for Political Education, and the National Association of Americans of Asian Indian Descent. These organizations are also actively involved in improving relations between the United States and India. Many communities also support smaller organizations that offer classes in Indian culture or sponsor events.

Worldview

A reverence for all life, called *ahimsa*, is fundamental to Indian ideology. It is reflected in the religions native to India, as well as in the vegetarian diet that many Indians follow.

THE SACRED COW

The best-known example of ahimsa in the western world is the sacredness of the cow in India. It is difficult for most Americans to understand the logic of not eating beef when so many people in India exist on a subsistence level.

Anthropologists suggest that prohibitions against cow slaughter serve several economic and ecologic purposes in India. Over 80 percent of the Indian population lives in rural areas, and most of these people make their living by farming. Cows produce the primary power source in this agricultural society: oxen. Animal power is absolutely essential to grow the food each rural family requires. Tractors, and the fuels required to run them, are much too expensive for the average Indian farmer. Another source of energy produced by cows in India is dung which is used as clean, slow-burning cooking fuel. Since India has limited fossil fuel and forest resources, manure energy is important to both the Indian economy and the environment.

In addition to energy and power, cows provide dung for fertilizer and milk for the dairy products essential to Indian vegetarian cuisine. Finally, even a dead cow serves a purpose in India. The poor often survive through the sale of leather products crafted from salvaged hides and the consumption of needed protein gathered from carrion.

THE CASTE SYSTEM

The traditional Indian caste system, which influences the social structure of many Asian Indian groups, is the Hindu method of ordering an individual's role in society. A more encompassing term is *jati*, which is the system used to organize all aspects of Hindu life, including actions, places, things, and symbols, not just people.

Caste categories are hereditary. There are four main castes: the *brahmins* (priests), *kshatriyas* (soldiers), *vaisyas* (merchants or farmers), and the *sudras* (serfs). These castes are divided into over 1,000 subcastes. Existing outside the caste system are those individuals who are considered so impure that they were called "untouchables." Although the laws discriminating against untouchability were repealed in 1949, this group of the desperately poor continues to occupy the lowest stratum in Indian society.

The caste system has permeated Indian society despite the fact that it is an exclusively Hindu classification system. Americans of Asian Indian descent often continue to proudly identify with their caste. Most come from the upper castes of brahmins and kshatriyas.

RELIGION

The influence of religion on Indian culture is all-encompassing. Every aspect of life and death is affected not only by individual religious affiliation but also by the Hindu ideology that permeates Indian society.

Hinduism

Nearly 85 percent of Indians are Hindus. Hinduism is an ancient faith, believed to have developed in India between 2000 and 1500 B.C. from the Aryan hymns and prayers known as the Vedas mixed with elements from traditional Dravidian religion (see Chapter 2 for more information about Hinduism and the other major Indian religions).

Islam

Today the Islamic religion is second only to Hinduism in number of followers. One in every nine Indians in a Muslim. Islam was brought to India by traders from Persia, and it expanded with the Muslim invasions of the northern regions beginning about A.D. 1000. The Islamic Moghul empire dominated the country for nearly 800 years. The influence of Islam is seen today mostly in northern India.

Buddhism

Buddhism developed as a protestant revolt against Hinduism. Its founder, known as Gautama Buddha, lived in India during

Although the early Hindus practiced many dietary restrictions, it was the enormous popularity of Buddhism that spread vegetarianism throughout India. People again ate meat for a brief period when the influence of Buddhism declined. Gradually, the orthodox disciples of Hinduism adopted a vegetarian diet, and vegetarianism became widely accepted. The elimination of meat from the diet is consistent with the concept of ahimsa.

the fifth century B.C. Although it is a popular religion in other parts of Asia, Buddhism is followed by fewer than one percent of Indians today.

Jainism

This branch of Hinduism developed at about the time Buddhism emerged. The Jains believe that all living things have souls. They wear masks to prevent breathing in insects and sweep a path in front of them to prevent stepping on any animals. Orthodox Jains are strict vegetarians. Approximately 2 percent of Indians are Jains.

Sikhism

The Sikh religion is best known for its military fraternity, although most Sikhs in India are farmers. Male Sikhs wear a turban and follow the "five K's": uncut hair (*kes*), a comb worn in the hair (*kanga*), short pants (*kaccha*), a steel bracelet worn on the right wrist (*kada*), and use of a special saber (*kirpan*). Each has a spiritual meaning. For example, the short pants symbolize self-restraint, the bracelet obedience, and the comb purity of mind.

Although Sikhs are only two percent of the population of India, it is estimated that they comprise nearly one-third of all Asian Indians living in California.

Syrian Christians

One form of Christianity emerged when the Syrians who migrated to the Malabar coast of southwest India in A.D. 345 intermarried with native people. Syrian Christians do not observe Hindu dietary laws, but they do participate in the caste system. Their agricultural community is operated with farm laborers who can be described as serfs.

Goan Christians

Another Christian community developed at the former Portuguese colony of Goa, farther north on the Southwest Coast. Approximately half of the citizens are Catholic, and the city is dedicated to St. Catherine.

Zoroastrianism

Over 1,200 years ago, the Parsis fled from Persia to northern India. The religion they brought is known as Zoroastrianism, an ancient faith that venerates Ahur Mazda, the god of fire. The Parsis are the most westernized of all Indians.

Animism

The oldest religions in India are those practiced by the small tribal populations that live in isolated regions of the Himalayas. They worship spirits associated with natural phenomena, a religious practice known as animism. In the past they have practiced such varied social customs as polyandry (having more than one husband) and headhunting.

Indian Sects in the United States

There are many Indian and non-Indian followers of Indian religions in the United States. For the most part, their membership remains small (see Chapter 2).

FAMILY

The husband is the head of the household in the traditional Indian family. The wife usually does not work outside the home and is expected to perform all duties related to housekeeping and child care. She obtains help in these responsibilities from the extended family and, in some homes, from servants. If the wife does hold a job, she can depend on the help of relatives. Children are expected to show respect for their elders. The careers and spouses of children, especially daughters, are often chosen by their parents.

Strains in the traditional family structure often occur in the United States. Asian Indian women are more likely to work in America than in their homeland, yet they lack the support system of an extended family. Children who grew up in the United States usually insist on making their own career choices. They may also pick their own spouses or even decide not to marry. Some Indians, especially women raised in India, find it difficult to adjust to these changes. More men than women choose to become U.S. citizens.

TRADITIONAL FOOD HABITS

It is difficult to generalize about Indian cuisine because of the diverse geography and population of the country. Foods vary North to South, East to West, region to region, and between religious and caste groups.

Ingredients and Common Foods

STAPLES

Few foods are eaten throughout all of India. Rice is the most commonly consumed. The average Indian eats one-half pound of it each day. This amount, however, varies considerably from region to region. Fruits and vegetables predominate in the mostly vegetarian cooking, but the types and ways in which they are prepared also depends on local customs. Dairy foods are also important in most areas. Fermented milk products such as yogurt are found throughout most of the country, as is the cooking fat *ghee,* pure, clarified butter (since this butter, known as *usli ghee*, is too expensive for daily use in many homes, vegetable shortening, also called ghee, is often used instead). Beyond these generalities, the staples of the Indian diet are best classified by region.

The greatest division in diet is seen between northern and southern India. Northern cuisine is characterized by the use of wheat, tea, a large number of eggs, garlic, dried or pickled fruits and vegetables, and use of dry *masalas* (spice mixtures which are fresh and "wet," or dried) that are distinctively aromatic rather than hot. These foods are typical of a cooler climate, where wheat grows better than rice and fruits, vegetables, herbs, and spices are available only seasonally. Boiling, stewing, and frying are the most common form of cooking.

In the South, steaming is the preferred method of food preparation. Rice, coffee, fresh pickles (some of which are known as chutney), *pachadi* (seasoned yogurt side dishes that are called *raytas* in northern India), "wet" masalas that are spicy hot, and fresh fruits, vegetables, herbs, and spices are fundamental to the cuisine. Again, these foods reflect the regional agricultural conditions.

Most southern Indians are strict vegetarians; they use some milk products but avoid eggs. Pork is eaten in some communities in the West, beef is eaten in many areas of the North, and fish and poultry are eaten in a few eastern regions. The Cultural Food Groups list is found in Table 9.1.

REGIONAL VARIATIONS

Northern India

In the North, rice may be served as a pilaf. Saffron rice with seasoned chicken, lamb, or beef, called *biryani* is also popu-

The word curry is believed to be the English adaptation of a southern Indian word for sauce, *kari*. Curry powder is not a single spice, but rather a complex blend of spices that varies according to the dish and the cook. The closest Indian equivalent is *garam masala*, a fragrant mixture of ground spices, usually containing cardamom, cumin, coriander, cloves, and cinnamon. In addition, other spices, such as pepper, chilis, fenugreek, fennel, mace, saffron, and turmeric, may be included.

Rice cultivation: Rice is the staple grain of India. It is estimated that nearly 1,000 varieties are grown. (Courtesy United Nations/John Isaac.)

lar, as are skewered pieces of broiled or grilled meats, known as *kababs*. Northern specialties include *korma*, a curried lamb dish with a nut-and-yogurt-thickened sauce, and masala chicken. Bread, which is called *roti* in India, is eaten daily. Examples include whole-wheat flatbreads, such as *chapatis*, which are cooked on a griddle without oil, or *puris*, which are fried. *Paratha*, another fried roti, is used as a wrapping for spiced vegetable fillings. A spicy lamb, potato, or vegetable stuffing is used in the deep-fried turnovers called *samosas*.

Chicken biryani. (Courtesy Raga Restaurant, New York, NY Taj Group of Hotels.)

Milk desserts are favored, such as carrot pudding (*gajar halva*) and rice pudding with cardamom, called *kheer*.

In northwestern India and in Pakistan, a special cylindrical clay oven called a *tandoor* is used. It is heated with charcoal. *Tandoori* cooking is identified particularly with lamb and chicken dishes, although the leavened bread known as *naan* is also typically baked in a tandoor.

Coastal India

The coastal regions offer a number of seafood specialties, including curried shrimp, crab, and clam dishes. Fish is prepared in a variety of ways, including frying, steaming, boiling, currying, and stuffing with herbs. Bombay, located on the West Coast, boasts a dried salted fish, which is thin, bony, and strongly flavored, known as *Bombay duck*.

Southern India

The vegetarian menus of the South feature numerous steamed and fried rice dishes. Rice is even served puffed, as in a snack called *bhelpuri*. Other grains such as semolina are

TABLE 9.1. Cultural Food Groups: Asian Indian

Group	Comments
PROTEIN FOODS 　Milk/milk products	In general, milk is considered a beverage for children. Fermented dairy products popular.
Meats/poultry/fish/eggs/ 　legumes	Sophisticated vegetarian cuisine; legumes primary protein source. Eighteen varieties of beans, peas, and lentils commonly used. Collectively, legumes called *pulses.* Chick-peas and lentils known as *dals.* Legumes are typically prepared whole or pureed, or used as flour to prepare baked, steamed, or fried breads and pastries.
CEREALS/GRAINS	Over 1,000 varieties of rice cultivated. Wheat used mostly in the North; rice in the South. Most breads *(roti)* unleavened.
FRUITS/VEGETABLES	Over 100 types of fruit and 200 types of vegetables commonly used. Fruits and vegetables may be used in fresh or preserved pickles, called *rayta* (northern), *pachadi* (southern), or chutney.

Common Foods	Adaptations in the United States
Fresh cow's, buffalo's, ass's milk; evaporated milk; fermented milk products (yogurt, *lassi*); fresh curds very popular; milk-based desserts, such as *kheer, khir, kulfi, barfi;* butter, especially clarified *(usli ghee).*	More cheese consumed, ice cream popular.
Meats: beef, goat, mutton, pork. *Poultry:* chicken, duck. *Fish and seafood:* Bombay duck, clams, crab, carp, herring, mackerel, mullet, pomfret, sardines, shrimp, turtle. *Eggs:* chicken. *Legumes:* beans (kidney, mung, etc.), chick-peas, lentils (many varieties and colors), peas (black-eyed, green).	Consumption of legumes decreases; meat intake increases. Meat may be added to traditional vegetarian dishes. Fast foods popular.
Rice (steamed, boiled, fried, puffed), wheat, buckwheat, millet.	Use of American-style breads in place of *roti.*
Fruit: apples, avocados, bananas (several types), coconut, dates, figs, grapes, guava, jackfruit, limes, litchis, loquats, mangoes, melon, *nongus* (fruit of the palmyra), oranges, papaya, peaches, pears, persimmons *(chicos),* pineapple, pomegranate, pomelos, raisins, starfruit, strawberries, sugar cane, tangerines, watermelon.	Decreased variety of fruits and vegetables available; decreased vegetable intake. More fruit juice consumed. Salad is well accepted. Use of canned and frozen produce increases.
Vegetables: agathi flowers, artichokes, amaranth, banana rhizome, bamboo shoots, beets (leaves and root), bitter melon, brussels sprouts, cabbage, carrots, cauliflower, corn, collard greens *(haak),* cucumbers, eggplant, lettuce, lotus root, manioc (tapioca), mushrooms, mustard greens, okra, onions, parsnips, plantain flowers, potatoes, radishes, (four types, leaves and roots), rhubarb, sago palm, spinach, squash, sweet potatoes (leaves and roots), tomatoes, tur-	

TABLE 9.1. Cultural Food Groups: Asian Indian *(continued)*

Group	Comments
ADDITIONAL FOODS	
Seasonings	Aromatic (northern) and hot (southern) combinations of fresh or dried spices and herbs accentuate or complement food flavors.
Nuts/seeds	Nuts and seeds of all types popular. Used to thicken *korma* sauces.
Beverages	Tea common in the North; coffee in the South. Coffee houses are favored meeting places.
Fats/oils	
Sweeteners	

also popular, cooked as a cereal known as *uppama*, which may include vegetables. Chick-peas and lentils *(dals)*, accompany nearly every meal in the form of a spiced puree known as *sambar* or a thin, crisply fried *roti* called *pappadams*. Fermented lentil flour is used at breakfast for *idli*, which are steamed cakes, and for *dosas*, which are spicy fried pancakes. Fresh milk curds are also served for breakfast. Highly spiced vegetable curries, such as *aviyal*, include such southern ingredients as bananas, bitter melons, coconut, green mango, and jackfruit seeds, in addition to potatoes, cauliflower, and eggplant. Refreshing yogurt-based pachadi and spicy pickled fruits and vegetables, such as chutney, accompany the main course. Deep-fried salty foods are favored snacks, as are deep-fried sweets, such as the syrup-soaked pretzels called *jalebis*.

Common Foods	Adaptations in the United States
nips, yams, water chestnuts, water lilies.	
Ajwain (carob seeds), *amchoor* (dried ground mango), asafetida (a powdered resin), bay leaf, cardamom (two types) chilis, fresh coriander, cinnamon, cloves, coconut, coriander seeds, cumin, dill, fennel, fenugreek, garlic, *kewra* (essence of screwpine flowers), limes, lemon, mace, mint, mustard, nutmeg, pepper (black and red), poppy seeds, rose water, saffron, tamarind (a type of bean), turmeric.	Spice use dependent on availability.
Almonds, betel nuts and leaves, cashews, peanuts, pistachios, sunflower seeds, walnuts.	*Paan* tray may be limited to betel nuts and spices.
Coffee, tea, water flavored with fruit syrups, spices, or herbs; alcoholic beverages such as fermented fruit syrups, rice wines, beer.	Increased consumption of soft drinks and coffee. Alcoholic beverages widely accepted (women may abstain).
Coconut oil, *ghee,* mustard oil, peanut oil, sesame seed oil.	Purchased *ghee* often made from vegetable oil instead of butter.
Sugar cane, *jaggery* (unrefined palm sugar), molasses.	Candy and sweets enjoyed, but not overconsumed.

RELIGIOUS VARIATIONS

In addition to region, religious affiliation may greatly influence diet in India. Indian cuisine, in general, reflects the food habits of the religious majority, the Hindus. Other religious groups have varying dietary practices, yet their cooking is Indian in flavor. Muslims, for example, avoid all pork and pork products but are not vegetarians. Orthodox Jains, even though they are vegetarians, avoid eating root vegetables, because insects might be killed when the tubers are harvested. They also refuse to eat any blood-colored foods. Sikh cuisine is noted for its use of wheat, corn, and sugar. The Syrian Christians are renowned for their beef (tenderized by grating or marinating), duck, and wild boar dishes. Goan Christians are unique in Indian cooking for their use of pork.

Samosas. (Courtesy Raga Restaurant, New York, NY Taj International Hotels.)

They make western-style sausages and have such specialties as a vinegar-basted hog's head stuffed with vegetables and herbs. The Parsis blend Indian and Persian elements in their cuisine, exemplified by dishes such as *dhansak*, an entree combining lamb, tripe, lentils, and vegetables.

Meal Composition and Cycle

DAILY PATTERNS

Although meal patterns vary throughout the country, most people eat two meals a day, almost always at home.

Early risers drink rich coffee or tea made with milk and sugar. Breakfast, served between 9:00 and 11:00 A.M., consists of rice or roti, a pickled fruit or vegetable, and a sambar or cooked cereal. Tea or coffee is served at 4:00 or 5:00 in the afternoon, with breads, rice dishes, and salty or sweet snacks. The evening meal, which is the main meal of the day, is eaten between 7:00 and 9:00 P.M.

Texture, color, and balance of seasoning are all important factors in an Indian meal. A typical menu includes at least one rice dish, a curried vegetable, legume or meat dish, a vegetable legume side dish, a baked or fried roti, a fruit or vegetable pickle, and a yogurt *rayta* or pachadi. Sometimes a dessert is served, usually fruit. The meal concludes with the passing of the *paan* tray. Paan is a combination of betel nuts and spices, such as anise seed, cardamom, and fennel, wrapped in large, heart-shaped betel leaves, and secured with a clove. It is chewed to freshen the breath and aid digestion.

A clear distinction is made between meals and snacks. Many Indian languages have specific words to define each form of eating. In southern India, the word *tiffin* is used to distinguish a snack from a meal. The coffee or tea drunk before breakfast or in the late afternoon is considered tiffin. A meal is not a meal unless the traditional staples prepared in the traditional manner, such as boiled rice in south India, or roti, in north India, are served. This means that no matter how substantial the snack, and some include more food than a meal, it is still called tiffin. Milk-based sweets, such as the cardamom- and saffron-spiced *khir*, the Indian ice cream called *kulfi*, and the candy *barfi*, are popular snacks, as are

It is illegal to bring betel nut leaves into the United States. There is even an underground trade in paan obtained in Canada and other countries.

Street vendor, Calcutta: Fried foods are popular snacks in India. (Courtesy World Health Organization/P. Almasy.)

salty foods. A snack may also include a cooling beverage, such as the sweetened, diluted yogurt drink *lassi,* or a fruit juice called *shurbut.*

ETIQUETTE

The most important aspect of Indian manners is that food is eaten with the hands. Food is served in small individual bowls from serving trays called *thalis.* The thalis may be silver or brass, with matching bowls. Originally, the thalis were simply banana leaves and the bowls were earthenware; these are still used today in some rural areas or when disposable trays and bowls are desired.

Rules of etiquette are important for food that is eaten by hand and prepared with little or no means of refrigeration. Food spoilage and contamination are problems, especially in the warmer regions of the country. Cleanliness is imperative, and many Indian manners clearly support this need.

Early Aryan rules of etiquette promoted healthy food preparation. They included the following: everyone must clean

Traditional Indian thali: *A traditional silver* thali *(individual serving tray), featuring a selection of* roti *(breads), fruit and vegetable pickles, such as chutneys, and yogurt-based* pachadi *or* rayta. *(Courtesy Raga Restaurant, New York, NY Taj Group of Hotels.)*

their hands, feet, and mouth before and after eating, both morning and evening; servants who worked with food had to shave their beards and heads, cut their nails, and bathe before entering the kitchen; food that was cooked the previous night, that turned sour, or that was cooked twice must be discarded; all grains, vegetables, and meat had to be thoroughly washed before cooking.

During the Buddhist period, other rules were added. Dating from 300 B.C., they recommended that one should not talk with food in one's mouth; stuff one's mouth full of food; shake one's hands while eating, as one would scatter rice all over; put one's tongue out while eating; make hissing sounds while eating; or lick one's finger or bowl, or accept a drinking cup with hands that are soiled with food. Finally, everyone should start eating at the same time.

Other etiquette rules state that food should be discarded if it comes in contact with the hem of one's gown, if it has been touched by animals, or if it is contaminated by insect or rodent droppings. Traditionally, Indians never serve themselves (especially after their hand is soiled from eating), never offer food from their plates to another person, and never save leftovers.

Such manners are essential to maintaining sanitary conditions in rural homes. These rules of etiquette may be practiced in even the most westernized families, however, and they remain important symbols of the Indian relationship with food.

As in other cultures where the hands are used instead of utensils, it is considered an unforgiveable breach of good manners to eat with the left hand. One eats with the right hand and takes care of all other personal needs with the left hand.

SPECIAL OCCASIONS

Another aspect of Indian culture that affects daily diet is the concept of feasting and fasting. As with other Indian food habits, feasting and fasting activities are complex and vary greatly from person to person and group to group. No occasion passes in India without some special food observance: regional holidays, community celebrations, and personal events such as births, weddings, funerals, and illness. A devout Hindu may feast or fast nearly every day of the year (see Chapter 2).

Feasting

Feasts serve as a method of food distribution throughout the community. They are generally observed by presenting large amounts of everyday foods and sweets of all kinds to the

Another holiday, *Janmashtami* (also known as *Gokul Ashtami*), commemorates the birth of Krishna. As a boy, Krishna and his friends would steal butter and curds that were hung high in earthen pots. Part of the festival recreates this mischief, as boys form human pyramids in an attempt to break elevated clay pots full of curds.

appropriate holy figure; all members of the community then eat the food. Feasts may be the only time that the poor get enough to eat.

Some foods are associated with certain concepts. Rice and bananas symbolize fertility, for example. Betel leaves represent auspiciousness; ghee, purity; salt, hospitality and pleasantness; mango, hospitality and auspiciousness; betel nuts and coconuts, hospitality, sacredness, and auspiciousness.

Most festivals are Hindu in origin, and though many are nationwide, each is celebrated differently according to the region. *Holi* is a spectacular holiday in the North, featuring reenactments of Krishna's life, fireworks, and colored powders and waters. Celebrants snack at bazaar booths. *Dussehra* is a ten-day holiday observed in both the North and South. A special dish is prepared each day, and every day that dish is added to those prepared the previous days, culminating in an enormous feast on the last evening, following a torchlight parade of ornamented elephants. *Divali,* the "feast of lights," is the New Year's holiday celebrated everywhere with gifts of sweets.

Non-Hindu harvest festivals also feature feasts. They are dedicated to wheat in the North and rice in the South. At the three-day rice festival in Pongal, dishes made from the newly harvested rice are ceremonially "fed" to the local cows. The ten-day festival of *Onam* in Kerali culminates with a feast served by the local women, including 30 to 40 dishes ranging from fiery curries to foods sweetened with a combination of molasses, milk, and sugar.

Fasting

Fasting is also associated with special occasions in India. It accompanies both religious and personal events.

The decorative red or yellow dot that Indian women apply to their foreheads represents prosperity or joy. It is omitted during fast days.

An orthodox Hindu may fast more days a week than not. But the term "fast" includes many different food restrictions in India, from avoidance of a single food item to complete abstinence from food. One might adopt a completely vegetarian diet for the day, or eat foods believed to be spiritually "purer," such as those cooked in milk (see the section on purity and pollution). Individuals rarely suffer from hunger because of fasting in India. In fact, more food may be consumed on fast days than on a nonfast day.

Role of Food in Indian Society

The importance of food in Indian culture goes far beyond mere sustenance. A quote from the ancient Sanskrit scriptures states *"Annam Brahma"*: "Food is God." In a society that traditionally experienced frequent famines and chronic malnutrition, food is venerated. Complex traditions have developed around when, how, and why foods are prepared, served, and eaten.

Purity and Pollution

Many Hindu dietary customs are meant to lead to purity of mind and spirit. Pollution is the opposite of purity, and polluted foods should be avoided or ameliorated. To be pure is to be free of pollution. The Hindu classification system of jati is used to evaluate the relative spiritual purity of all foodstuffs. Purity is determined by the ingredients, how they are prepared, who prepares them, and how they are served. Some foods, such as milk, are inherently pure. Raw foods that are naturally protected by a husk or a peel are less susceptible to pollution. Fried foods (*pakka* foods) are more pure than baked, boiled, or steamed foods (*kaccha* foods), especially if they are fried in ghee. Food that is served in brass dishes is also less vulnerable to pollution than is food in clay dishes. Some foods, such as alcohol and meat, are *jhuta*, meaning that they are innately polluted.

Traditionally, only foods cooked and served by a member of an equal or superior caste could be consumed by any Hindu. Only members of the same caste will eat together. Untouched leftovers can be given to a member of a lower caste, such as servants, but polluted leftovers are eaten only by scavengers of the lowest caste.

People adhere to these commensal rules to various degrees, however. An orthodox Hindu would attempt to follow them at all times. A more modern Hindu might adhere to them only during holy services and holidays. Most westernized Indians eat in restaurants and use convenience products in cooking, ignoring how and by whom the food was prepared.

The consumption of jhuta foods also varies among Hindus. Historically, laborers and warriors were allowed to eat meat to help keep up their strength. Some brahmin subcastes permit consumption of impure foods that happen to be plentiful in their region, such as fish (referred to as "fruit of the sea")

Pakka (meaning "cooked") foods are those that are fried or fat-basted during preparation, preferably in *ghee*. Pakka foods, due to their high degree of purity, are not subject to as many restrictions as impure foods.

Kaccha (meaning "undercooked") foods are those that are boiled in water, baked or roasted. *Kaccha* foods are subject to more pollution than *pakka* foods, and must therefore be treated carefully during serving and consumption.

Jhuta foods are those that are inherently polluted. All leftovers, unless completely untouched by the eater or by other food that has been eaten, are considered *jhuta*. Those foods that are innately polluted vary according to degree of orthodoxy and sect. The term *jhuta* is also used for garbage and offal.

in the coastal areas, and lamb in the North. Other sects are so rigid that even inadvertent intake of polluted food results in spiritual disaster. Members of the International Society for Krishna Consciousness believe that if they accidentally eat a prohibited animal food, they will lose human form in their next life and assume the form of an animal that is the prey of the animal they ate.

INDIAN WOMEN AND FOOD

A Hindu woman is considered impure during her menses, and is prohibited from cooking or touching any food that is to be consumed by others.

The kitchen is considered sacred in many Hindu homes. The purity is maintained through several customs related to early Aryan manners. Traditionally, no one can enter the kitchen with shoes on; younger children with questionable sanitation habits are prohibited from entering; and all who come in must bathe and put on clean clothes first.

The Aryan diet used to keep the bodily humors in balance recommended consumption of cooling foods, such as vegetables, in the summer; venison during the rainy season; and hard-to-digest foods during the winter. In addition, food was divided into six tastes: sweet, acid, salt, pungent, astringent and bitter. It was considered important to keep these flavors in balance in the diet.

The role of women in food preparation is extremely important throughout Indian culture. Feeding the family is an Indian woman's primary household duty. She is responsible for overseeing the procurement, storage, preparation, and serving of all foods. Because arranged marriages are common, training in kitchen management is considered essential for a Hindu woman in obtaining good marriage offers.

It is generally believed that a woman cannot be completely substituted for in the kitchen, for she imparts a special sweetness to food. If the wife is unable to perform food-related duties, a daughter or daughter-in-law may substitute. If servants help in meal preparation, it is still important for the woman of the house to serve the food directly from the *chula*, or stove, to the table. This often requires many trips. Traditionally the wife serves the men and guests first, then the children.

Therapeutic Uses of Food

There is a rich history of medicinal uses of food in India. The early Aryans wrote extensively on health and nutrition. Their medical system was based on the belief that the body consisted of five humors, and that if these humors were kept in balance through a regulated lifestyle, including diet, a person would never suffer illness.

Today, only a few of the Aryan therapeutic uses of food remain common. Lentil and peas, for example, are cooked with ginger, asafetida, mint, or dill to reduce flatulence. In northern India, garlic is thought to excite undesired passions, and may therefore be avoided. It is widely believed that a highly spiced diet is necessary in the tropical Indian climate to stimulate the liver.

One food habit that may result in ill health is the common practice of disguising otherwise undrinkable water with flavorful herbs and spices. Cholera, dysentery, and typhoid are endemic in many regions.

CONTEMPORARY FOOD HABITS IN THE UNITED STATES

Adaptation of Food Habits

Americans of Asian Indian descent are often westernized before arrival in the United States. They usually speak English fluently and have been exposed to American and European lifestyles in India. Yet even the most acculturated Asian Indian Americans continue some traditional food habits. The recent influx of Indian immigrants from rural regions will undoubtedly influence how native diets are adapted to American foodways.

INGREDIENTS AND COMMON FOODS

Very little research has been conducted on the food habits of Asian Indians in the United States. One study of Indians in Pennsylvania suggested that acculturation takes place in two phases (Gupta, 1976). Typically, the first lasts for two to three years, often while the immigrant is a student. Interaction with mainstream American society may be limited at this period. The Indian immigrant prefers to associate with members of the same caste, regional, or linguistic group; his experience with American foods often include only fast foods. Male Indian students are often unable to cook and may rely heavily on purchased meals. Many Indian immigrants will eat hamburgers, because of their availability and low cost.

Sometime during the next ten years, Indians who stay in the United States longer than four years enter the second phase of acculturation. They are usually employed by American businesses and are raising families. They keep their social interactions with Americans separate from those with other Asian Indian Americans. They might serve meat and alcohol to American guests, for example, and vegetarian dishes to Indian guests.

A study of Indians living in Cincinnati found several changes in the types of foods they ate (Karim *et al.,* 1986). Foods that subjects used frequently in India but that were in only "low moderate" use in the United States were ghee, yogurt, dal, roti, rice dishes, and tea. Foods that were in "low moderate" use in India but frequent use in the United States were fruit juice, canned or frozen vegetables, American bread, dry cereals, cheese and cheese dishes and soft drinks; coffee consumption also increased.

Variables that affect acculturation include sex (men tend to change their food habits more readily than women because women are the traditional food preparers in Indian society); age (children raised in the United States prefer American foods); marital status (single unmarried men are the most acculturated, married men with families in India next, and married men with families here in the U.S. least accultur-ated); caste (depending on whether caste members used meat or alcohol in India) and region (Indians from the South and rural areas are stricter vegetarians than those from the North or the cities).

A majority of Americans of Asian Indian descent make an effort to obtain traditional food products. Many markets in the United States specialize in Indian canned and packaged food products, including spices. These stores often provide mail orders. Fresh foods are more difficult to find. Some fruits and vegetables can be bought at Asian specialty markets, and Indian bakeries featuring sweets and tiffin items have opened in some areas. In Cincinnati, 100 percent of Indians inter-viewed reported that their traditional foods were available (Karim et al., 1986).

VEGETARIANISM AND NONVEGETARIANISM

Indian vegetarians sometimes become nonvegetarians when living in America. In one study, one-third of those who were vegetarians in India became nonvegetarians in the United States (Karim et al., 1986).

Three types of nonvegetarian Asian Indian Americans have been identified: (1) "eggetarians," or those who eat eggs only; (2) semi-vegetarians, who eat meat, poultry, and fish at restaurants and on social occasions, but not in their own homes; and (3) full nonvegetarians, who eat meat, poultry, and fish at any time (Gupta, 1976). Indian vegetarians may pass through all these phases in becoming nonvegetarians. Egg eating begins soon after arrival in the United States, pro-gressing to chicken and finally beef. It is estimated that non-vegetarian Indians take between two months and one year to accept beef. It may take vegetarian Indians seven years to complete the transition to beef consumption.

As yet, the reasons vegetarians become nonvegetarians have not been stated conclusively. It has been suggested that vegetarianism may lose its social and cultural significance in the United States. Data regarding the influence of factors such as sex, income, region of origin in India, and length of stay in America have been contradictory.

Asian Indians who are practicing Muslims rarely begin eating pork in the United States. They may drive long distances to purchase kosher meats, which also satisfy traditional Moslem dietary restrictions.

MEAL COMPOSITION AND CYCLE

Asian Indians' eating patterns may become more irregular in the United States, possibly because of the pressures of a faster-paced lifestyle. Breakfast is the meal most commonly omitted. People reportedly snack between once and three times a day (Karim *et al.*, 1986).

Many Americans of Asian Indian descent eat American foods for breakfast and lunch. Traditional Indian evening meals are preferred, if native foods and spices are available. Yet dinners at home may also be influenced by U.S. food habits in that more meat may be eaten and American breads served in place of roti.

Nutritional Status

NUTRITIONAL INTAKE

There is little specific information about the Asian Indian community, perhaps because most Indian immigrants have come from the higher socioeconomic levels. They more often suffer from the effects of nutritional overconsumption than inadequacy. One researcher has commented that young Asian Indian Americans, especially students, may rely heavily on fast-food and restaurant meals and are thus susceptible to the same nutritional problems common to most American youth (Eckstein, 1983).

The arrival of Indians from poor, rural regions may result in nutritional deficiency problems (it is estimated that 17 percent of the Indian population suffers from moderate to severe malnutrition). These immigrants are also the ones most likely to practice traditional food habits the longest after coming to the United States. It has been found that Asian Indians who live in Great Britain and follow vegetarian diets have marginal intakes of protein, iron, and vitamin B-12. A recent study suggests that although zinc deficiency may not be a problem among vegetarian Asian Indian women living in India, bioavailability may be impaired when they come to the United States if these women add significant amounts of dairy products to their diet (Ellis *et al.*, 1987). Nutritional adequacy may be compromised if traditional food habits are maintained despite inadequate food sources: if native spices and foods are not available or are too costly, the diet may be poor.

COUNSELING

Concepts of western medicine are familiar to most Asian Indians. Native cures and home remedies do not usually conflict with American health practices.

An in-depth interview should be used to establish the client's religious affiliation and degree of adherence, length of residency in the United States and degree of acculturation, and vegetarian or nonvegetarian preferences.

REFERENCES

Bindra, G. S., & Gibson, R. S. 1986. Iron status of predominantly lacto-ovo vegetarian East Indian immigrants to Canada: A model approach. *American Journal of Clinical Nutrition, 44,* 643–52.

Carstairs, G. M. 1979. *Daru* and *bhang:* cultural factors in the choice of intoxicant. In *Beliefs, Behaviors, and Alcoholic Beverages,* M. Marshall (Ed.). Ann Arbor, MI: University of Michigan Press.

Chakravarty, I. 1972. *Saga of Indian Food: A Historical and Cultural Survey.* New Delhi, India: Sterling Publishers.

Devi Dasi, K., & Devi Dasi, S. 1973. *The Hari Krishna Cookbook.* Los Angeles: Bhahtivedanta Book Trust.

Eckstein, E. R. 1983. Foodways of Indians and other orientals in the U.S. In *Menu Planning* (3rd ed.). Westport, CT: AVI Publishing.

Ellis, R., Kelsay, J. L., Reynolds, R. D., Morris, E. R., Moser, P. B., & Frazier, C. W. 1987. Phytate:zinc and phytate x calcium:zinc millimolar ratios in self-selected diets of Americans, Asian Indians, and Nepalese. *Journal of the American Dietetic Association, 87,* 1043–1047.

Farb, P., & Armelagos, G. 1980. *Consuming Passions.* New York: Washington Square Press.

Goody, J. 1982. The high and the low: Culinary culture in Asia and Europe. In *Cooking, Cuisine and Class.* Cambridge, England: Cambridge University Press.

Gupta, S. P. 1976. Changes in food habits of Asian Indians in the United States: A case study. *Sociology and Social Research, 60,* 87–99.

Harris, M. 1974. *Cows, Pigs, Wars, and Witches.* New York: Random House.

Ho, G. P., Nolan, F. L., & Dodds, M. L. 1966. Adaptation to American dietary patterns by students from oriental countries. *Journal of Home Economics, 58,* 277–280.

Jaffrey, M. 1975. *Invitation to Indian Cooking.* New York: Vintage Books.

Jensen, J. M. 1980. East Indians. In *Harvard Encyclopedia of American Ethnic Groups,* S. Thernstrom, A. Orlov, and O. Handlin (Eds.). Cambridge, MA: The Belknap Press of Harvard University Press.

Karim, N., Bloch, D. S., Falciglia, G., & Murthy, L. 1986. Modifications of food consumption patterns reported by people from India, living in Cincinnati, Ohio. *Ecology of Food and Nutrition, 19,* 11–18.

Katone-Apte, J. 1975. Dietary aspects of acculturation: Meals, feasts and fasts in a minority community in South Asia. In *Gastronomy: The Anthropology of Food Habits,* M. L. Arnott (Ed.). The Hague: Mouton Publishers.

Khare, R. S. 1976. *The Hindu Hearth and Home.* Durham, NC: Carolina Academic Press.

Newman, J. M. 1986. *The Melting Pot: An Annotated Bibliography and Guide to Food and Nutrition Information for Ethnic Groups in America.* New York: Garland Publishing.

Rau, S. R. 1969. *The Cooking of India.* New York: Time-Life Books.

Singer, E. A. 1984. Conversion through foodways acculturation: The meaning of eating in an American Hindu sect. In *Ethnic and Regional Foodways in the United States,* L. K. Brown and K. Mussel (Eds.). Knoxville, TN: University of Tennessee Press.

ADDITIONAL REFERENCES ON FOOD AND CULTURE

In many ways, a book like this poses more questions than it answers. Our knowledge of cultural foods is neither balanced nor complete. Many interested readers are undoubtedly asking why there is so little research on adaptations of food habits in the United States or why there is virtually no information available on some minority populations. As stated in the Preface, only the major American cultural groups were presented in this book. And although the authors reviewed numerous resources, the resulting text is undeniably inadequate in some areas. Thus, the most urgent question is, "Where to go from here?"

Classes, seminars, association memberships, research, and client interaction are all useful ways to learn more about food habits. Dietitians' knowledge of cultural food habits has been shown to improve with both classroom and experiential education (Kittler *et al.,* 1986). Within the nutrition community, many departments of dietetics and home economics offer courses in food and culture. Professional nutrition, dietetics, and home economics associations occasionally sponsor seminars on general topics in food habits as well as on culturally specific food habits. Other fields, such as medical anthropology, feature related classes.

Associations that specialize in cultural foods are few and for the most part directed towards other disciplines. Groups such as the West Coast Network for Nutrition and Anthropology, the Culinary Historians of Boston, and the Culinary Historians of New York are knowledgeable sources of information about food habits. A recently formed national organization, the Association for the Study of Food in Society, promises an exciting interdisciplinary approach to the study of food and culture.

Publications that feature research on food habits are also limited. The journals *Ecology of Food and Nutrition* and *Food and Foodways* are the most prominent; the professional nutrition journals also print articles on the topic. Anthropology, history, home economics, geography, medicine, nursing, public health, psychology, and sociology journals are sometimes good sources of data on food and culture. Even newsletters, such as *Foodtalk*, can provide useful information.

There are many books on food and culture from the numerous fields which have contributed to research on food habits. Cookbooks and other popular literature frequently include anecdotal information of interest. Some of the many references available follow.

Ultimately, the practicing nutritionist or dietitian may learn more from patients and clients than from other sources. They are often good sources of information on culturally based food habits, although the data may apply only to the individual rather than to the whole culture and acculturation may influence personal dietary preferences. Nevertheless, accumulated experience with a minority population can be an important adjunct to printed research.

The authors encourage nutritionists and dietitians to undertake and publish studies on food and culture to expand the limited knowledge in the topic. We also hope that all health professionals will share their experiences with minority patients and clients through associations and publications. Such research and communication will help us all to become more culturally sensitive and thus more effective health care providers and educators.

REFERENCES

Kittler, P., Sucher, K., & Tseng, R. Y. 1986. Cultural foods education: An exploratory study of dietitians and Plan IV programs in California. *Journal of the American Dietetic Association, 86,* 1705–1708.

Books and Bibliographies

Barèr-Stein, T. 1979. *You Eat What You Are.* Toronto: McClelland and Stewart.
Bryant, C. A., Courtney, A., Markesbery, B. A., & Dewalt, K. M. 1985. *The

Cultural Feast: An Introduction to Food and Society. St. Paul, MN: West Publishing

Claiborne, C. 1985. *Craig Claiborne's The New York Times Food Encyclopedia.* New York: Times Books.

Cole, K. W. 1985. *Minority Organizations: a National Directory.* Garrett Park, MD: Garrett Park Press.

Farb, P., & Armelagos, G. 1980. *Consuming Passions: The Anthropology of Eating.* New York: Washington Square Press.

Fieldhouse, P. 1986. *Food and Nutrition: Customs and Culture.* London: Croom Helm.

Fitzgerald, T. K. (Ed.). 1977. *Nutrition and Anthropology in Action.* Amsterdam: Van Gorcum.

Freedman, R. L. 1981. *Human Food Uses: A Cross-Cultural Comprehensive Annotated Bibliography.* Westport, CN: Greenwood Press.

Harris, M. 1985. *Good to Eat: Riddles of Food and Culture.* New York: Simon and Schuster.

Jerome, N. W., Kandel, R. F., & Pelto, G. H. (Eds.) 1980. *Nutritional Anthropology: Contemporary Approaches to Diet and Culture.* Pleasantville, NY: Redgrave Publishing.

Lankevich, G. J. 1981. *Ethnic America.* London: Oceana Publications.

Lowenberg, M. E., Todhunter, E. M., Wilson, E. D., Feeney, M. C., Savage, J. R., & Lubawski, J. L. 1979. *Food and People* (3rd ed.). New York: John Wiley & Sons.

Macdonald, D. 1983. *Resources on Food, Nutrition and Culture.* Nutrition Information Service, Ryerson Polytechnic Institute Library, Toronto.

Mariani, J. F. 1983. *Dictionary of American Food and Drink.* New Haven, CT: Ticknor & Fields.

McGee, H. 1984. *On Food and Cooking: The Science and Lore of the Kitchen.* New York: Charles Scribner's Sons.

Montagne, P. 1977. *The New Larousse Gastronomique.* New York: Crown Publishers.

National Agricultural Library. 1988. *Diet, Race & Ethnicity in the U.S.: Research and reference materials 1979–1987.* (NAL-BIBL. QB 88-29), Beltsville, MD.

National Research Council. 1945. *The Problem of Changing Food Habits.* National Research Council Bulletin 108, Washington, D.C.

Newman, J. M. 1986. *Melting Pot: An Annotated Bibliography and Guide to Food and Nutrition Information for Ethnic Groups in America.* New York: Garland Publishing.

Nichter, M., Nichter, M. 1981. *An Anthropological Approach to Nutrition Education.* Newton, MA: International Nutrition Communication Service.

Root, W., & Rochemont, R. 1976. *Eating in America.* New York: Ecco Press.

Sanjur, D. 1982. *Social and Cultural Perspectives in Nutrition.* Englewood Cliffs, NJ: Prentice-Hall.

Simoons, F. J. 1961. *Eat Not This Flesh.* Madison: University of Wisconsin Press.

Tannahill, R. 1973. *Food in History.* New York: Stein & Day.

Thernstrom, S., Orlov, A., Handlin, O. (Eds.). 1980. *Harvard Encyclopedia of American Ethnic Groups.* Cambridge, MA: The Belknap Press of Harvard University Press.

USDA/USDHHS. 1986. *Cross-Cultural Counseling: A Guide for Nutrition and Health Counselors.* United States Department of Agriculture FNS-250, U.S. Government Printing Office 1987-720-484-1302/60133.

Von Welanetz, D., & Von Welanetz, P. 1982. *The Von Welanetz Guide to Ethnic Ingredients.* Los Angeles: J. P. Tarcher.

Wilson, C. S. (Ed.). 1979. *Food: Custom and Nurture. An Annotated Bibliography on Sociocultural and Biocultural Aspects of Nutrition.* Journal of Nutrition Education, *11*, Supplement 1, 212–261.

Cookbooks

AMERICAN

Feibleman, P. S. 1971. *American Cooking: Creole and Acadian.* New York: Time-Life Books.
Jones, E. 1981. *American Food: The Gastronomic Story* (2d ed.). New York: Vintage Books.
Leonard, J. N. 1971. *American Cooking: New England.* New York: Time-Life Books.
Shenton, J. P., Pellegrini, A. M., Brown, D., & Shender, I. 1971. *American Cooking: The Melting Pot.* New York: Time-Life Books.
Tastes of Liberty: A Celebration of Our Great Ethnic Cooking. 1985. Chateau Ste. Michells, WA.
Walter, E. 1971. *American Cooking: Southern Style.* New York: Time-Life Books.
Wilson, J. 1971. *American Cooking: The Eastern Heartland.* New York: Time-Life Books.

ASIAN INDIAN

Jaffrey, M. 1973. *An Invitation to Indian Cooking.* New York: Vintage Books.
Rau, S. R. 1969. *The Cooking of India.* New York: Time-Life Books.
Sahni, J. 1985. *Classic Indian Vegetarian and Grain Cooking.* New York: William Morrow.

BLACK

Kaiser, I. Y. 1968. *Soul Food Cookery.* New York: Pitman Publishing Co.
Mendes, H. 1971. *African Heritage Cookbook.* New York: Macmillan.
Van der Post, L. 1970. *African Cooking.* New York: Time-Life Books.
Wilson, E. G. 1971. *A West African Cookbook.* New York: Avon Books.

CARIBBEAN

Wolfe, L. 1970. *Cooking of the Caribbean Islands.* New York: Time-Life Books.
Kaufman, W. I. (Ed.). 1964. *Recipes from the Caribbean and Latin America.* New York: Dell.

CHINESE

Chang, W. W. 1973. *An Encyclopedia of Chinese Food and Cooking.* New York: Crown Publishers.
Chen, P. K., Chen, T. C., & Tseng, R. 1983. *Everything You Want to Know about Chinese Cooking.* Woodbury, NY: Barron's.

Hahn, E. 1968. *The Cooking of China.* New York: Time-Life Books.
Simmond, N. 1983. *Classic Chinese Cuisine.* Boston, MA: Houghton Mifflin Co.

EASTERN EUROPEAN

Hazelton, N. S. 1969. *The Cooking of Germany.* New York: Time-Life Books.
Martin, P. 1981. *The Czech Book: Recipes and Traditions.* Iowa City: Penfield Press.
Papashvily, H., & Papashvily, G. 1969. *Russian Cooking.* New York: Time-Life Books.
Visson, L. 1982. *The Complete Russian Cookbook.* Ann Arbor, MI: Ardis.
Wechsberg, J. 1968. *The Cooking of Vienna's Empire.* New York: Time-Life Books.

JAPANESE

Omae, K., & Tachibana, Y. 1981. *The Book of Sushi.* Tokyo: Kodansha International.
Ortiz, E. L., & Endo, M. 1976. *The Complete Book of Japanese Cooking.* New York: M. Evans.
Steinberg, R. 1969. *The Cooking of Japan.* New York: Time-Life Books.

JEWISH

David, S. 1984. *The Sephardic Kosher Kitchen.* Jerusalem: Keter Publishing House.
Ross, E. 1984. *The Complete International Jewish Cookbook.* London: Robson Books.

MEXICAN

Bayless, R. 1987. *Authentic Mexican.* New York: William Morrow.
Kennedy, D. 1972. *The Cuisines of Mexico.* New York: Harper and Row.
Leonard, J. N. 1970. *Latin American Cooking.* New York: Time-Life Books.
Rexach, N. L. 1985. *The Hispanic American Cookbook.* Secaucus, NJ: Lyle Stuart.

MIDDLE EASTERN

Dosti, R. 1982. *Middle Eastern Cooking.* Tucson, AZ: HP Books.
Khalil, N. E. 1980. *Egyptian Cuisine.* Washington, D.C.: Worldwide Graphics.
Najmieh, B. 1986. *Food of Life: A Book of Ancient Persian and Modern Iranian Cooking and Ceremonies.* Washington, D.C.: Mage.
Nickles, H. G. 1969. *Middle Eastern Cooking.* New York: Time-Life Books.
Rodin, C. 1968. *A Book of Middle Eastern Food.* New York: Vintage Books.
Yianilos, T. K. 1970. *The Complete Greek Cookbook.* New York: Funk and Wagnalls.

NATIVE AMERICAN

Keegan, M. 1977. *Pueblo and Navajo Cookery.* Dobbs Ferry, NY: Earth Books.
Kimball, Y., & Anderson, J. 1986. *The Art of American Indian Cooking.* Garden City, NY: Doubleday.
Neithammer, C. 1974. *American Indian Food and Lore.* New York: A Fireside Book, Simon and Schuster.

NORTHERN EUROPEAN

Bailey, A. 1969. *The Cooking of the British Isles.* New York: Time-Life Books.
Claiborne, C. 1970. *Classic French Cooking.* New York: Time-Life Books.
Child, J., Bertholle, L., & Beck, S. 1961. *Mastering the Art of French Cooking* (Vol. I). New York: Alfred A. Knopf.
Child, J., & Beck, S. 1970. *Mastering the Art of French Cooking* (Vol. II). New York: Alfred A. Knopf.
Fisher, M. F. K. 1969. *The Cooking of Provincial France.* New York: Time-Life Books.
FitzGibbon, T. 1983. *Irish Traditional Food.* New York: St. Martin's Press.

SCANDINAVIAN

Brown, D. 1968. *The Cooking of Scandinavia.* New York: Time-Life Books.
Hazelton, N. S. 1987. *Classic Scandinavian Cooking.* New York: Charles Scribner's Sons.

SOUTHERN EUROPEAN

Anderson, J. 1986. *The Food of Portugal.* New York: William Morrow & Co., Inc.
Casas, P. 1983. *The Foods and Wines of Spain.* New York: Alfred A. Knopf.
Field, C. 1985. *The Italian Baker.* New York: Harper and Row.
Feibleman, P. S. 1969. *The Cooking of Spain and Portugal.* New York: Time-Life Books.
Rogers, A. 1968. *A Basque Story Cookbook.* New York: Charles Scribner's Sons.
Root, W. 1968. *The Cooking of Italy.* New York: Time-Life Books.

SOUTHEAST ASIAN

Alejandro, R. 1982. *The Philippine Cookbook.* New York: Coward-McCann.
Nhu Huong Miller, J. 1980. *Vietnamese Cookery.* Rutland, VT: Charles E. Tuttle Co.
Ngo, B., & Zimmerman, G. 1979. *The Classic Cuisine of Vietnam.* Woodbury, NY: Charles E. Tuttle.
Sing, P. 1981. *Traditional Recipes of Laos.* London: Prospect Books.
Steinberg, R. 1970. *Pacific and Southeast Asian Cooking.* New York: Time-Life Books.

Food Composition Tables

Some of these tables are now out of print but may be available through university and college libraries. Foreign food composition tables may be difficult to use, for the following reasons: (1) a given food may have several names within a cultural region, and (2) several different foods used within a cultural region may have the same name.

Caribbean Food and Nutrition Institute. 1974. *Food Composition Tables for Use in the English-Speaking Caribbean.* University of the West Indies, Kingston, Jamaica.

Department of Nutrition of the Chinese Academy of Sciences. 1981. *Table of Food Composition.* S. M. Yu (Trans.) Department of Nutrition of the Chinese Academy of Sciences, Beijing.

De Reguero, L. C., & De Santiago, S. M. R. 1981. *Tabla de Composicion de Alimentos de USA en Puerto Rico.* University of Puerto Rico, San Juan.

Food Research and Industry Development Institute. 1971. *Table of Taiwan Food Composition.* Food Research and Industry Development, Hsinchu, Taiwan.

Gopalan, C., Rama-Sastri, B. V., & Balasubramanian, S. C. 1971. *Nutritive Value of Indian Foods.* National Institute of Nutrition, Hyderbad.

Jardin, C. 1967. *List of Foods Used in Africa.* Nutrition Division of the FAO of the United Nations, Rome, Italy.

Leung, W. T. W., Brisson, F., & Jardin, C. 1968. *Food Composition Table for Use in Africa.* Nutrition Division of the FAO of the United Nations, Rome, Italy.

Leung, W. T. W., & Chang, F. H. 1972. *Food Composition Table for Use in East Asia.* National Institutes of Health, Bethesda, MD.

Leung, W. T. W., & Flores, M. 1961. *Food Composition Tables for Use in Latin America.* Nutrition Division of the FAO of the United Nations, Rome, Italy.

Leung, W. T. W., Pecot, R. K., & Watt, B. K. *Composition of Foods Used in Far Eastern Countries.* USDA Handbook 32, Washington, D.C.

National Institute of Science and Technology. 1968. *Food Composition Table Recommended for Use in the Philippines* (3rd ed.). National Institute of Science and Technology of the Philippines, Manila.

Pellett, P., & Shadarevian, S. 1970. *Food Composition Tables for Use in the Middle East.* American University of Beirut, Beirut, Lebanon.

Polacci, W., McHargue, J. S., & Perloff, B. P. 1962. *Food Composition Tables for the Near East.* Her Majesty's Stationery Office, London.

United States Department of Agriculture. 1976–. *Composition of Foods.* USDA Handbook 8.

U.S. Interdepartmental Committee on Nutrition for National Defense. 1961. *Food Composition Table for Use in Latin America.* Interdepartmental Committee on Nutrition for National Defense, Bethesda, MD.

INDEX

Accra, 239
Acculturation, 5
Achiote. *See* Annatto.
Açorda d'azedo, 124
Acorns, 71
Adobo, 292, 303
Advent, 150, 151, 164
Aebleskivers, 161
Aemono, 282
Age calculation,
  Chinese, 265
  Vietnamese, 308
Agimono, 282
Agobono (apon) seeds, 184
Aguas naturales, 215
Ahimsa, 42, 45, 339
Akee apples, 184, 233
Akutok, 70
Alaskan natives, 69. *See also*
  Native Americans.
Alcohol, prohibitions against,
  27, 35, 36, 40, 45, 355,
  357
Alcoholism,
  Irish, 112
  Native Americans, 78
Aleuts, 69. *See also* Native
  Americans.
Ali-oli, 123
All Saints' Day, 219
All Souls' Day, 219
Almonds, 164, 329
Almuerzo, 217
Alpha thalassemia, Filipinos, 308
Amaretti, 127
American diet, 1, 3, 17–18

American Indians. *See* Native
  Americans.
Anchovies, 103, 285
Andouille (andouillette), 101
Angulas (eel), 126
Animism, 342
Anise, 351
Annatto, *201,* 216, 238
Antipasto, 126
Antojitos, 218
Aonoriko, 281
Apache Indians, 68. *See also*
  Native Americans.
Appetizers, 14. *See also*
  individual appetizers; meal
  composition and cycle of
  each group.
Apple butter, 154
Apples, 58, 100, 141, 160, *167*
  cider, 100
Apple strudel, 145
Aquavit, 161
Arabs, 315. *See also* Greeks/
  Middle Easterners; Middle
  East.
Arak, 325
Arapaho Indians, 66. *See also*
  Native Americans.
Arcat de marue, 236
Armenians, 317. *See also*
  Greeks/Middle Easterners.
Arroz con leche, 219
Artichokes, 113, 122
  fried, 125
Asafetida, therapeutic use of,
  356

Asciutta, 126
Asia, *249*
Asian Indians, 333–361. *See also*
  India.
  adaptation of food habits in
    U.S., 357–359
    vegetarianism, 358–359
  ahimsa (reverence for life), 339
  caste system, 339–340
  counseling, 360
  cultural food groups table,
    346–349
  cultural organizations, 338–
    339
  current demographics in U.S.,
    338
  etiquette, 352–353
  family, 342
  fasting, 354
  feasting, 353–354
  food habits,
    contemporary in U.S., 357–
     360
    traditional, 342–357
  immigration to U.S. of, 337–
    338
  malnutrition, 359
  meal composition and cycle,
    350–354
  nutritional intake in U.S., 359–
    360
  pollution of food, 355–356
  purity of food, 355–356
  religion, 340–342
  role of food in society, 355–
    356

Asian Indians (*cont.*)
  socioeconomic status in U.S., 338
  special occasions, 353–354
  staples, 343
    regional variations, 343–349
    religious variations, 349–350
  therapeutic use of food, 356–357
  women and food, 356
  zinc deficiency, 360
Asians, 248–311. *See also* Chinese; Japanese; Koreans; Southeast Asians.
Asparagus, 292, 299
Assada no espeto, 124
Atchuete. *See* Annatto.
Atole, 217, 222
Austria, history of, 132–133
Austrians. *See also* Central Europeans; Austria.
  immigration to U.S. of, 136
Avgolemono, 329
Avocados, *201*, 216
Azuki beans, *269*, 280

Babalky, 151
Babka, 151
Bacalaitos (arcat de marue, stamp and go), 236
Bacalao, 122, *201*, 238
Bacalao, a la vizcaina, 126
Bacalhau, 124
Baccalà, 125
Bagoong, 297
Baklava, 322
Bambara groundnuts, 184
Bamboo-leaf green, 262
Bananas. *See* Plantains.
Bangers, 95
  and mash, 99
Bangus (milkfish), 296
Banh chung, 306
Baobab, 184
Barbecued foods, 187, *191*, 233, 281
Barfi, 351
Barszcz Wigilijny, 151
Basil, 122, 298
Basmati rice, 324, *334*
Basques, 116, 117
  foods, 126, 129
Bastille Day, 107
Baumkuchen, 150
Bean bread, 75
Bean curd (tofu), 14, 257, 280, 298
Beans, 51, 59, 208
  azuki, *269*, 280
  black, 233, 236, *240*

Boston baked, 60
  fava, 324
  green, 299
  jellied, 281
  kidney, 233
  mung, 293
  paste, 262
  paste (miso), 280
  red, 109
  refried, 209
  and rice, 109, 233, *240*
  soybeans, 257–262, 280
  tepary, 68
Bear, 61, 70, 264
Béchamel sauce, 104
Beef, 59, 215, 281, 349, 350, 359
  Hindu prohibitions, 45, 339
Beer, 100, 147, 155, 215
Beets, 141, 160
Beignets, 109
Beitzah, 27
Belongingness, food habits and, 4
Bel paese cheese, 124
Bénédictine, 101
Betel nuts, 308, 351, 354
  leaves, 351, 354
Bhelpuri, 345
Bibingka, 303
Bigos, 151
Birth rate,
  Mexicans, 223–224
  Puerto Ricans, 243
Biryani, 343–344, *345*
Biscuits, 100, 189, 190
Bison, 66–67, *67*
Bisteeva (pastilla), 322
Bitter melon, *250*, 348
Bitters, 100
Black Americans, 171–199. *See also* West Africa.
  adaptations of food habits, 194
  breastfeeding, 196
  counseling, 197
  Creoles, 176
  cultural food groups table, *180–181*
  current demographics, 178
  diabetes, 196
  family, 179
  food habits,
    contemporary, 193–197
    traditional, 182–193
  foods, 172
    historical influences, 182–187
  glucose-6-phosphate dehydrogenase deficiency, 197
  hemolytic anemia, 197

"high" and "low" blood, 192, 197
history of, 174–178
hypertension, 196
immigration to U.S. of, 174–178
iron deficiency anemia, 196–197
lactose intolerance, 195
low-birthweight infants, 195–196
meal composition and cycle, 189–190, 194–195
nutritional intake, 195–197
obesity, 196
organizations of, 178–179
pica, 193, 197
religion, 179
role of food in society, 192
sickle-cell anemia, 197
socioeconomic status, 178
special occasions, 190
staples, 187–189
therapeutic use of food, 189, 192–193
Black beans, 233, 236, *240*, 257
Black-eyed peas, 183, 184, 190
Blini, 153
Blue cornmeal, 68, 75
Boar, wild, 146
"Boat people," 288–289. *See also* Vietnamese.
Bock beer, 147
Boeuf bourguignon, 102
Bok choy (chinese cabbage), *250*
Bolitos, 212
Bombay duck, 345
Bo nuong xa, 299
Boova shenkel, 154
Borsch, 148
Borscht, 151
Boston baked beans, 60
Bottle-mouth, 224
Bouillabaise, 103, 109, 119
Boxing Day, 107
Boxty, 99
Braceros, 205. *See also* Mexicans.
Brahmins, 340. *See also* Asian Indians.
Bratwurst, 146
Braunschweiger, 155
Bread. *See also* individual breads.
  pudding (capirotada), 219
  symbolic use of, 5, 24, 31, 141
Breadfruit, 233, 239
Bread pudding (pie), 189
Breakfast foods, 14. *See also* individual foods; meal composition and cycle of each group.

Breastfeeding,
  Black Americans, 196
  Caribbean Islanders, 244
  Mexicans, 224
Brie Cheese, 101
Briki, 326, *327*
British. *See also* Northern
    Europeans; Great Britain.
  adaptations of food habits in
    U.S., 108, 110–111
  cooking styles, 103–104
  counseling, 112
  current demographics in U.S.,
    92
  food habits, contemporary in
    U.S., 108, 110–111, 111–
    112
    traditional, 95–100, 103–
    104, 105, 107
  immigration to U.S. of, 88–89
  meal composition and cycle,
    105, 107
  nutritional intake in U.S., 111
  socioeconomic status in U.S.,
    92
  special occasions, 107
  staples and regional
    variations, 95–100
Brown bread, 60
Bruhwurst, 146
Brunswick stew, 66
Brussels sprouts, 14
Bubble and squeak, 99
Bûche de Noël, 30, 110
Buckwheat, 147
Buddhism, 47–50, 340–341
  dietary practices, 49–50
  Mahayana, 256, 291
  principles of, 48–49
  Pure Land, 256, 274
  sects, 49
  Theraveda, 291
  Zen, 49, 256
Buffalo. *See* Bison.
Buffalo berries, 67
Bulgar (burghul), 322
Buñelos, 219
Burrida, 124
Burritos, 213
Butter, 160, 239
  clarified (ghee), 343
  clarified (samana), 324

Cabbage, 100, 141, 160, 233,
    264
  salad, 298
  stuffed, 146, 153, 161
Cacoila, 124
Cactus, 68, 215
  therapeutic use of, 73
  Caesar salad, 215
Café con leche, 217

Caffe latte, 126
Cajuns, 91, 92, 94, 108
  foods, 109–110
Calas, 109
Calcium, alternative sources,
    284
Caldos, 212
Caldo verde, 124
Callaloo, 184, 236
Calvados, 100
Calzone, 125
Camass root, 70
Cambodia, history of, 287
Cambodians. *See also* Southeast
    Asians; Cambodia.
  immigration to U.S. of, 289
  socioeconomic status in U.S.,
    290
Camembert cheese, 101
Camomile, therapeutic use of,
    220
Cancer, Japanese, 284
Cannoli, 126
Capirotada, 219
Cappelleti, 125
Cappuccino, 126
Caraboa milk, 293
Cardamon, 164, 326, *334,* 351
Cardiovascular disease,
  Filipinos, 307
  Greeks/Middle Easterners, 331
  Japanese, 284
  Native Americans, 77
Caribbean Islanders. *See also*
    Cubans; Puerto Ricans;
    Caribbean Islands.
  adaptations of food habits in
    U.S., 241–243
  breastfeeding, 244
  counseling, 245
  cultural food groups table,
    234–237
  dental caries, 245
  food habits, contemporary in
    U.S., 241–245
    traditional, 232–241
  intestinal parasites, 244
  lactose intolerance, 244
  meal composition and cycle,
    239–241, 243
  nutritional intake in U.S., 243–
    245
  staples, 233–238
    regional variations, 238
  therapeutic use of food, 241
Caribbean Islands
  foods, 232–238, *234–237,*
    240–241
    Cuban, 238
    Puerto Rican, 238
  history of, 227–228
Caribou, 110

Carne asada, 212
Carnival, 241
Carp, 151
  sweet and sour, 263
Carrots, 59
  pudding, 345
Cashew apples, 232
Cassarep, 236
Cassata, 126, 127
Cassava, 182, *201,* 216, 232
  bread, 233
  gari, 183
  juice (cassarep), 236
Cassis, 102
Castagnaccio alla Fiorentina, 125
Caste system, 43–44, 339–340
Catfish, fried, 187, 188
Catsup, 14
Causerras, 129
Caviar, 4, 146–147, 148
  red, 70
Cecinas, 215
Celiac sprue, Irish, 112
Cena, 218
Central Americans, 201. *See also*
    Latinos.
  foods, 213, 216, 217, 219, 233
  immigration to U.S. of, 201,
    206, 207
  socioeconomic status in U.S.,
    230
Central Europe, foods of, *131,*
    141–154, *142–145*
Central Europeans. *See also*
    individual national groups;
    Central Europe.
  adaptations of food habits in
    U.S., 154–156
  cultural food groups table,
    142–145
  food habits, contemporary in
    U.S., 154–157
    traditional, 141–154
  meal composition and cycle,
    147–153, 155–156
    Russians, 148
  nutritional intake in U.S. and
    counseling, 156
  special occasions, Germans,
    149–150
    Hungarians and
    Czechoslovakians, 151–
    153
    Poles, 151
    Russians, 153–154
  staples and regional
    variations, 141–147
Cepes, 103
Ceviche, 236
Cha gio, 298
Challah, 24
Chalupas, 218

Chalupines, 216
Champagne (sparkling wine), 101
Chapatis, 344
Charcuterie, 101
Chayote squash, 109, *172*, 216, 233
Chazuke, 281
Cheese. *See* individual cheeses.
Chelo kebab, 324
Cherokee Indians, 66. *See also* Native Americans.
Cherries, therapeutic use of, 283
Chesire cheese, 98
Chestnut bread, 75
Cheyenne Indians, 66. *See also* Native Americans.
Chianti, 125
Chicanos, 205. *See also* Mexicans; Mexico.
Chicharrones, 212, 238
    de pollo, 238
Chicken, 146, 183, 185, 238, 292, 296, 343
    therapeutic use of, 266
Chicken biryani, 343, *345*
Chicken Kiev, 146
Chicken relleno, 296
Chick-peas (garbanzo beans), 119, *313*, 324, 348
    hummus, 324
Chicory, 109
Chilaquiles, 212
Chili con carne, 213
Chilis, 68, 109, 182, 189, 213, 216, 264, 299
    en nogada, 213
    paprika, 146
    rellenos, 213
    therapeutic use of, 73
China,
    foods, *250*, 256–267, *258–263*
        northern, 263
        southern, 264
    history of, 251–252
Chinese, 250–269. *See also* China.
    adaptations of food habits in U.S., 267–268
    age calculation, 265
    counseling, 268
    cultural food groups table, *258–263*
    cultural organizations, 254
    current demographics in U.S., 253–254
    etiquette, 265
    family, 256
    food habits, contemporary in U.S., 267–269
        traditional, 256–267
    hypertension, 268

immigration to U.S. of, 252–253
lactose intolerance, 268
meal composition and cycle, 264–267, 268
nutritional intake in U.S., 268
religion, 254–256
socioeconomic status in U.S., 253–254
special occasions, 265–266
staples, 257–263
    regional variations, 263–264
therapeutic use of food, 266–267
Ch'ing Ming, 266
Chippewa Indians, 74. *See also* Native Americans.
Chitterlings (chitlins), 185
Chocho. *See* Chayote squash.
Chocolate, 208, 209, 216
    hot, 105, 126, 127, 128, 215, 217
Chokecherries, 70
Chopsticks, 265, 292
Chorizo, 122, 212
Chouriço, 124
Christianity,
    Eastern Orthodox, 31–33
        fast days, 31–32, *31*
        feast days, 32–33, *32*
        principles of, 31
    Goan, 341
        principles of, 29
    Protestants, 33–36
        dietary practices, 34, 36
        Mormons, 34–35
        principles of, 33–34
        Seventh-Day Adventists, 35–36
    Roman Catholics, 29–31
        dietary practices, 30
        religious holidays, 30–31
    Syrian, 341
Christmas, 15, 30, 107, 127, 129, 148, 150, 151, 164–165, 219, 223, 240–241, 302, 329
    tree, *149*, 150
Christophene. *See* Chayote squash.
Christopsomo, 329
Chukuviki, 68
Chula, 356
Churros, 123
Chutney, 103, 343, *352*
Cilantro. *See* Coriander (fresh).
Cinnamon, 325
Cipate (cipaille, si-paille, six pates, sea-pie), 110
Clambake, 60
Clam chowder, 60
Cocido, 123

Cocoa, 208
Coconut, 293, 297–298, 348
    milk, 184, 297
Cocoyam, 184
Cod, 107
    dried salt, 85, 122, 124, 125, 160, 184, 238
    fritters, 236
    therapeutic use of, 74
Coffee, 148, 236–237, 242, 299, 326
    café con leche, 217, 239
    caffe latte, 126
    cappuccino, 126
    in Central Europe, 147
    with chicory, 109
    espresso, 126
    Middle Eastern, 326, *327*
    prohibitions against, 35, 36, 40
Colcannon, 100
Coleslaw, 155
Colombo (curry), 236
Comida, 127, 217
Commensality, rules of, 355
Confetti, 128
Confucianism, 255
    influence in Japan, 274–275
Congee, 257
Coocoo, 236
Coq au vin, 102
Core foods, 13–14
Coriander (fresh), *201*, 213, 216, 238, 298
Corn, 13, 51, 59, *60*, 61, 185, 187, 189, 209
    grits, 66, 185
    hominy, 66, 68, 185, 189
    masa harina, 209, 213
    nixtamal, 209
    pozole, 213
    symbolism of, 68
    therapeutic use of, 73
Cornbread, 189
Corn flakes, 36
Cornish pasty, 104
Cornmeal, 185
    blue, 68, 75
Cortados rellenos de cidra, 129
Cottage (shepherd's) pie, 99
Coui, 233
Couscous, 126, *313*, 322
Cow peas, 184. *See also* Black-eyed peas.
Cows, sacred in India, 339
Crab, therapeutic use of, 268, 283
Cranberries, 51, 58, 61
Cream,
    crème fraîche, 101
    double, 99
    fleurette, 101

sour, 141, 160
whipped, 141
Creek Indians, 66. *See also*
  Native Americans.
Crema Dania cheese, 160
Creole cooking, 109
Creoles, 176, 204
Crêpes Suzette, 102
Creton, 110
Croissant, 105
  tuna sandwich, 18
Croûtes, 107
Crow Indians, 66. *See also* Native
  Americans.
Cuba libre, 237
Cubans,
  current demographics in U.S.,
    230
  family, 232
  immigration to U.S. of, 229–
    230
  iron deficiency anemia, 244
  malnutrition, 244
  religion, 232
  socioeconomic status in U.S.,
    230–231
Cultural food groups tables,
  Asian Indian, *346–349*
  Black American, *180–181*
  Caribbean Islander, *234–
    237*
  Central European, *142–145*
  Chinese, *258–263*
  Filipino, *294–297*
  Japanese, *276–279*
  Mexican, *210–213*
  Native American, *62–65*
  Northern European, *96–99*
  People of Greece and the
    Middle East, *320–323*
  Scandinavian, *162–165*
  Southern European, *120–
    123*
Cultural perspective, 9–11
Cultural relativity, 11
Culture, 5
Curaçao, 238
Curanderos, 225
Curry, 236, 343, 348
  aviyal, 348
Cuscus (couscous), 126
Czechs. *See also* Central
    Europeans;
    Czechoslovakians;
    Slovaks.
  cultural organizations, 139–
    140
  current demographics in U.S.,
    138–139
  family, 141
  immigration to U.S. of, 136–
    137

religion, 140
socioeconomic status in U.S.,
  138–139

Daikon, *269*
Dakota Indians, 66. *See also*
  Native Americans.
Dals, 348, 357
  therapeutic use of, 356
Danbo cheese, 160
Danes, 167. *See also* Denmark;
  Scandinavians.
  current demographics in U.S.,
    159
  immigration to U.S. of, 158–
    159
  socioeconomic status in U.S.,
    159
Danish blue cheese, 160
Danish pastry, 164
Daquiris, 237
Dasheen, 233
Dashi, 281
Deer. *See* Venison.
Demi-glace, 104
Denmark. *See* Scandinavia.
Dental caries,
  Caribbean Islanders, 245
  Mexicans, 225
  Native Americans, 78
  Vietnamese, 308
Desayuno, 217
Dessert, 14. *See also* individual
    desserts; meal
    composition and cycle of
    each group.
Deviled kidneys, 105
Dhansak, 350
Diabetes,
  Black Americans, 196
  Filipinos, 308
  Mexicans, 225
  Native Americans, 77
Digger Indians, 70. *See also*
  Native Americans.
Dijon mustard, 102
Dilis (daing), 296
Dill, 325
  therapeutic use of, 356
Dim sum, 264
Dinu-guan, 296, 303
Dirty rice, 109
Divali, 47, 354
Doboschtorte, 145
Dog meat, 11, 13
Dolmas, 324
Dosas, 248
Doughnuts, 145, 151, 154–155,
    161
Duck, 349
  Bombay, 345
  Peking, 263

smoked, 264
  wild, 61
Dumplings, 125, 144, 151, 257,
    264, 266, 281
Durian, 298
Dussehra, 47, 354

East Asians. *See* Asian Indians.
Easter, 30, 33, 107, 127, 129,
    148, 150, 151, 153, 223,
    302, 328–329
Eastern Orthodox, 31–33. *See
    also* Christianity.
  fast days, 31–32, *31*
  feast days, 32–33, *32*
Eau de vie de framboise, 101
Edo, 233
Eel, 126, 146
  therapeutic use of, 283
"Eggetarians," 358
Eggplant, 122, 324
  Chinese, 250
  Japanese, *269*
  therapeutic use of, 306
Egg rolls, 257, 298
Eggs, Easter, 151, 152, 153, 154,
    328
  symbolic use of, 33
Eggs, prohibitions against, 183
Egusi, 184
Egyptians. *See* Greeks/Middle
    Easterners.
Eid al-Azha, 40, 41
Eid al-Fitr, 40, 41
Eintopf, 146
Emic viewpoint, 11
Empanadas, 213
Enchiladas, 212, *222*
Enculturation, 5
Entrees, 14. *See also* individual
    entrees; meal composition
    and cycle of each group.
Escabeche, 236
Escargot, 102
Eskimos. *See* Inuits.
Espagnole sauce, 104
Espresso, 126
Ethnic identity, food habits and,
    4, 5, 7–8
Ethnocentrism, 11, 16
Etic viewpoint, 11
Europe, *82–83*
  early history of, 81–85
Europeans, 85–167. *See
    also* individual national
    groups.
  Central, 132–156
    cultural food groups table,
      142–145
  Northern, 85–112
    cultural food groups table,
      96–99

Europeans (cont.)
  Scandinavians, 156–167
    cultural food groups table,
      162–165
  Southern, 112–131
    cultural food groups table,
      120–123

Falafal, 324
Fan (grains), 265
Fast food, 4, 7, 8, 195, 359
Fasting, 15
  in Hinduism, 46, 354
  in Islam, 38, 40
  in Judaism, 25, 28–29
Fastnachts, 154–155
Fava beans, 324
Feasting, 15
  in Hinduism, 46, 353–354
Feast of Lanterns, 266
Feast of the Most Blessed
    Sacrament, 130
Fen, 262
Fennel seed, 351
Feta cheese, 313, 325
Fettucine Alfredo, 125
Fiambre, 219
Fiesta de los Santos Reyes, 219
Filé powder, 66, 185
Filet de boeuf béarnaise, 102
Filipinos. See also Philippines;
    Southeast Asians.
  alpha thalassemia, 308
  cardiovascular disease, 307
  cultural food groups table,
      294–297
  diabetes, 308
  glucose-6-phosphate
      dehydrogenase deficiency,
      308
  hyperuricemia, 308
  hypochromic microcytic
      anemia, 308
  lactose intolerance, 308
  renal disease, 307
Filo, 313, 319
Finland. See Scandinavia.
Finns. See also Scandinavians.
  foods, 160
  immigration to U.S. of, 158
Fish,
  paste, 297
  sauce, 297, 298
Fish and chips, 95
Fish and seafood. See individual
    fishes, seafoods.
Flan, 123, 214, 222, 240, 292
  leche, 293
Fontina cheese, 166
Food. See also Food habits.
  availability, 5, 7
  definition of, 3

symbolic use of, 5, 19
taboos, 13
Food habits,
  acculturation, 5
  age and, 8–9
  Aryan classification of foods,
      356
  cultural perspective, 9–11
  definition of, 3
  education and, 7
  ethnic identity and, 4, 5, 7–8
  etiquette, 4, 265, 328, 352–
      353
  factors that influence, 5–9, 6
  Four Food Groups, 12
  hot-cold classification of
      foods, 219–220, 241, 306,
      330
  household structure and, 9
  income and, 7
  Maslow's theory of human
      maturation, 3–4
  nutrition and, 15–17
  occupation and, 7
  religious beliefs and, 8, 19
  sex and, 9
  state of health and, 9
  survival and, 310
  ways to categorize, 12–15
    core foods, 13–14
    edible or inedible, 13
    meals and meal cycles, 14–
        15
  yin-yang classification of
      foods, 266–267, 283, 306
Foofoo, 236
Fork, development of, 125
Four Food Groups, use of in food
    habits study, 12
France. See also French.
  foods, 100–103, 104
    Alsace-Lorraine, 101
    Bordeaux, 102–103
    Brittany and Normandy,
        100–101
    Burgundy, 102
    Champagne, 101
    Ile-de-France, 101–102
    Provence, 103
    Touraine, 101
    in U.S, 109–110, 111
  history of, 87–88
Franco-Americans, 91, 92–93,
    95
  foods, 110
Frankfurters, 146, 155
French. See also France;
    Northern Europeans.
  adaptations of food habits in
      U.S., 109–110, 111
  cooking styles, 104
  counseling, 112

cultural organizations, 93
current demographics in U.S.,
    92–93
family, 94
food habits, contemporary in
    U.S., 109–110, 111
  traditional, 100–103, 104,
      105–106, 107
haute (grande) cuisine, 100
immigration to U.S. of, 91
meal composition and cycle,
    105–106, 107
nutritional intake in U.S., 111
provincial cooking, 100
religion, 94
socioeconomic status in U.S.,
    92–93
special occasions, 107
staples and regional
    variations, 100–103
French bread, 292
French fries, 1, 17
French toast, 110
Fricadeller, 161
Frijoles refritos, 209, 222
Frogs, 238
Fruit. See individual fruits.
Fry bread, 71
Fufu, 182
Fugu, 13
Ful medames, 324
Funnel cake, 154, 155

Gajar halva, 345
Game meat, 58, 61, 67, 70, 71,
    146, 185, 187. See also
    individual meats.
Garbanzo beans. See Chick-
    peas.
Gari, 183
Garlic, 103, 122, 123, 264, 281,
    292, 299, 325
  therapeutic use of, 220, 356
Gazpacho, 123
Gelatin, 22
Gelato, 126
Germans. See also Central
    Europeans; Germany.
  current demographics in U.S.,
      138
  immigration to U.S. of, 135–
      136
  religion, 140
  socioeconomic status in U.S.,
      138
Germany. See also Germans.
  foods in U.S., 154–155
  history of, 132–133
Ghee, 334, 343, 357
Ginger, 250, 299, 334
  therapeutic use of, 356
Glogg, 165

Glucose-6-phosphate
    dehydrogenase deficiency,
    Black Americans, 197
    Filipinos, 308
Gnocchi, 125
Gohan, 280
Goi go, 298
Gokul Ashtami, 354
Goldwasser, 147
Good Friday, 241
Goose, 58, 150, 152, 165
Gordos, 212
Gorgonzola cheese, 124
Goulash, 146
Granita, 126
Grapes, 58, 129, 303
    leaves, 324
Gravlax, 160
Grazing, 9, 10
Great Britain. See also British.
    foods, 95–100, 103–104
    in U.S., 108, 110–111
    history of, 86–88
Greece. See Greeks/Middle
    Easterners; Middle East.
Greeks. See Greeks/Middle
    Easterners; Middle East.
Greeks/Middle Easterners,
    adaptations of food habits in
        U.S., 330–331
    cardiovascular disease, 331
    counseling, 331–332
    cultural food groups table,
        320–323
    cultural organizations, 317–
        318
    current demographics in U.S.,
        317
    etiquette, 328
    family, 318
    food habits, contemporary in
        U.S., 330–332
    immigration to U.S. of, 316–
        317
    lactose intolerance, 325
    meal composition and cycle,
        326–330, 331
    nutritional intake in U.S., 331
    religion, 318
    socioeconomic status in U.S.,
        317
    special occasions, 328–329
    staples, 319–325
        regional variations, 325–
            326
    therapeutic uses of food, 330
Greens, 184, 185, 187–189, 213
    pot likker, 189
Grissini, 124
Grits, 66, 185, 189
Gulyás (goulash), 146
Gum arabic, 325

Gumbo, 109, 187
    z'herbes, 185

Haggis, 107
Haitians. See Caribbean
    Islanders.
Halibut, therapeutic use of, 74
Halloween, 110–111
Halo-halo, 293
Halusky, 151
Halvah, 325
Ham, 105, 107, 110, 146, 150,
    152, 189, 190
    prosciutto, 125
    Westphalian, 146
Hamantashen, 25
Hamburgers, 1, 155
Hanukkah, 25
Haroset, 28
Haute cuisine, 100
Havarti cheese, 160, 166
Health food, 4
Hemolytic anemia in Black
    Americans, 197
Herbs, therapeutic use of, 267
Herring, 131, 146
Hickory nut cream, 66
"High" and "low" blood in Black
    Americans, 192, 197
Hijiki, 281
Hinduism, 41–47, 340
    caste system, 43–44
    dietary practices, 45–47
    fasting, 46, 354
    feasting, 46, 353–354
    principles of, 41–45
    religious holidays, 46–47
    sects, 44–45
Hinkel welschkarn suup, 154
Hoecakes, 185
Hoisin sauce, 257
Holi, 46, 354
Holidays,
    Asian Indian, 353–354
    Black American, 190
    British, 107
    Caribbean Islander, 240–241
    Chinese, 265–266
    Czechoslovakian, 151–153
    Eastern Orthodox, 31–33
    Filipino, 299–303
    French, 107
    German, 149–150
    Greeks/Middle Easterners,
        328–329
    Hungarian, 151–153
    Hindu, 46–47
    Irish, 107
    Italian (festas), 127–128
    Japanese, 283
    Jewish, 24–29
    Mexican, 219

Muslim, 40–41
    Native American, 72
    Polish, 151
    Portuguese, 129–130, 129
    Roman Catholic, 30–31
    Russian, 153–154
    Scandinavian, 164–165
    Spanish, 128–129
    Vietnamese, 304–306
Holubjy, 151
Holy Ghost Festival, 129
    soup of, 130
Holy Week, 128
Hominy, 66, 68, 185, 189
Honey, 66, 151, 154
    therapeutic use of, 220, 224
Hopi Indians, 68. See also Native
    Americans.
Hornos, 71, 72
Horse meat, 13
Horseradish, symbolic use of, 27,
    151
Hot-cold classification of foods,
    Arab, 330
    Caribbean Islander, 241
    Filipino, 306
    Mexican, 219–220
Hot and sour soup, 264
Houska (vanocka), 151
Hrudka, 152
Hua diao, 262
Huckleberries, therapeutic use
    of, 74
Huevos reales, 214
Hummus, 324
Hungarians. See also Central
    Europeans.
    current demographics in U.S.,
        138
    immigration to U.S. of, 136–
        137
    socioeconomic status in U.S.,
        138
Hypertension,
    Black Americans, 196
    Chinese, 268
Hyperuricemia, Filipinos, 308
Hypochromic microcytic anemia,
    Filipinos, 308

Ice cream, 126
Idli, 348
Iftar, 329
India, 335
    foods, 334, 343–356, 346–349
        coastal, 345
        northern, 343–345
        religious variations, 349–
            350
        southern, 345–348
    history of, 334–337
Indian pudding, 61, 108

Indians. *See* Asian Indians;
    Native Americans.
Infectious diseases,
    Native Americans, 78
    Vietnamese, 308
International Society for Krishna
    Consciousness (ISKON),
    45, 342, 356
Intestinal parasites,
    Caribbean Islanders, 244
    Vietnamese, 308
Inuits, 69. *See also* Native
    Americans.
Iranians (Persians). *See* Greeks/
    Middle Easterners.
Iraqis. *See* Greeks/Middle
    Easterners.
Ireland. *See also* Irish.
    foods, 95–100, 103–104
    in U.S., 108, 110–111
    history of, 87
Irish. *See also* Northern
    Europeans; Ireland.
    adaptations of food habits in
        U.S., 108, 110–111
    alcoholism and, 112
    celiac sprue, 112
    cooking styles, 103–104
    counseling, 112
    cultural organizations, 93
    current demographics in U.S.,
        92
    family, 94
    food habits, contemporary in
        U.S., 108, 110–111, 111–
        112
        traditional, 95–100, 103–
        104, 105, 107
    immigration to U.S. of, 89–
        91
    meal composition and cycle,
        105, 107
    nutritional intake in U.S., 111–
        112
    religion, 94
    socioeconomic status in U.S.,
        92
    special occasions, 107
    staples and regional
        variations, 95–100
Irish Catholics, 89–91, 92, 93
Iron deficiency anemia,
    Black Americans, 196–197
    Cubans, 244
Iroquois Indians, 66. *See also*
    Native Americans.
Isca de fígado, 124
Islam, 36–41, 340
    dietary laws, 39–40
    fasting, 38, 40
    feast days, 41
    principles of, 37–38

religious holidays, 40–41
    sects, 38–39
Israelis. *See* Greeks/Middle
    Easterners, Jews.
Issei, 272. *See also* Japanese.
Italians. *See also* Southern
    Europeans; Italy.
    adaptations of food habits in
        U.S., 130
    counseling, 131
    cultural organizations, 117
    current demographics in U.S.,
        116
    family, 117–118
    food habits, contemporary in
        U.S., 130–131
        traditional, 119, 120, 124–
        126, 127–128
    immigration to U.S. of, 115
    meal composition and cycle,
        126, 127–128
    nutritional intake in U.S., 130
    religion, 118
    socioeconomic status in U.S.,
        116
    special occasions, 127–128
    staples, 119, 122
        regional variations, 124–126
Italy. *See also* Italians.
    foods, 119, 122, 124–126,
        127–128
        northern, 122, 124–125
        southern, 122, 125–126
    in U.S., 118–119
    history of, 114–115

Jackfruit, 348
Jainism, 341
Jalebis, 348
Jambalaya, 109
Janmashtami, 354
Japan. *See also* Japanese.
    foods, *269, 275–283, 276–279*
    history of, 270–271
Japanese, 269–284. *See also*
    Japan.
    adaptations of food habits in
        U.S., 283–284
    cancer, 284
    cardiovascular disease, 284
    counseling, 284–285
    cultural food groups table,
        276–279
    cultural organizations, 273–
        274
    current demographics in U.S.,
        272–273
    family, 274–275
    food habits, contemporary in
        U.S., 283–285
        traditional, 275–283
    immigration to U.S. of, 272

lactose intolerance, 284
meal composition and cycle,
    281–283
nutritional intake in U.S., 284
religion, 274
socioeconomic status in U.S.,
    272–273
special occasions, 283
staples and regional
    variations, 279–281
therapeutic use of food, 283
Jaternice, 146
Jati, 339–340, 355
Jelita, 146
Jerky, *52,* 67
Jerusalem artichokes, 66
Jews. *See also* Greeks/Middle
    Easterners; Judaism.
    immigration to U.S. of, 21
Jhuta foods, 355
Jícama, *201,* 216
Jollof rice, 182
Jordanians. *See* Greeks/Middle
    Easterners.
Judaism, 20–29. *See also* Jews.
    congregations, 21
    dietary laws (Kashrut), 21–24
    fasting, 25, 28–29
    principles of, 20–21
    religious holidays, 24–29
    sects, 20
Juneteenth, 190

Kaaba, 38
Kababs, 344
Kaccha foods, 355
Kalamata olives, 324
Kari-kari, 297
Karpas, 28
Karp po zydowsku, 151
Kaseri cheese, 325
Kasha, *131,* 138, 148
Kashrut, Jewish dietary laws,
    21–24
Kataif, 329
Kerry (curry), 236
Kheer, 345
Khir, 351
Kibbeh, 322
Kielbasa, 146
Kim chee, 281
Kippers, 95
Kirsch, 101, 145
Kitchen God, 265–266
Klejner (klener, klenatter), 165
Kletski, 144
Klobasa, 152
Knedliky, 144
Knockwurst, 146
Knödel, 144
Kolaches, 151, *153*
Kola nuts, 184

Koliva, 31
Kombu, 281
Koreans, 248, 281. *See also*
  Asians.
  foods, 281
Korma, 344
Kosher, definition of, 22
Koulourakia, 329
Krendel, 154
Kshatriyas, 340. *See also* Asian
  Indians.
Kulfi, 351
Kulich, 153
Kutia, 154
Kvas, 148
Kwakiutl Indians, 69. *See also*
  Native Americans.

Laban, 325
  zabadi, 325
Lactose intolerance, 11
  Black Americans, 195
  Caribbean Islanders, 244
  Chinese, 268
  Filipinos, 308
  Greeks/Middle Easterners, 325
  Japanese, 284
  Native Americans, 76
  Southern Europeans, 130
  Vietnamese, 308
Lager, 147
Lamb (mutton), 14, 263–264,
  325, 329, 343–344, 350
Lambropsomo, 329
Laos, history of, 287. *See also*
  Laotians.
Laotians. *See also* Southeast
  Asians; Laos.
  immigration to U.S. of, 289
  socioeconomic status in U.S.,
  290
Lard, 185
Lasagna verdi al forno, 124–125
Lassi, 352
Latin America, *202*
Latinos, 200–247. *See also*
  Caribbean Islanders;
  Mexicans.
Latkes, 25
Lebanese. *See* Greeks/Middle
  Easterners.
Lebkuchen, *149,* 150
Lechon, 297
Lederkranz cheese, 141
Lefser, 161
Lemon grass, *285,* 299
Lent, 30, 32, 107, 128, 152, 153,
  241
Lentils, *334,* 348
Licuado, 222
Limburger cheese, 141
Linguiça, 124

Liver, 14
Liverwurst, 155
Lobster, 58
  à l'américaine, 101
Long beans, *250*
Lotus root, *250,* 264
Low-birthweight infants,
  Black Americans, 195–196
  Puerto Ricans, 243
  Vietnamese, 308–309
Lox, 160
Lumpia, *293, 299*
Lupine seeds (tremecos), 124
Lutefisk, 160

Main courses. *See* Entrees.
Makowiec, 151
Malanga, 232
Malassadas, 124
Malnutrition,
  Asian Indians, 359
  Cubans, 244
  Mexicans, 224
  Vietnamese, 308
Malzbier, 146
Mamey, 216
Mandarin pancakes, 263
Mangos, 348, 354
Manioc. *See* Cassava.
Manju, 281
Maple syrup, 51, 58, 60, 110
Mardi Gras, 107, 111
Marielitos, 230. *See also* Cubans.
Maronite church, 318. *See also*
  Eastern Orthodox;
  Christianity.
Marror, 27
Marsala, 126
Marzenbier, 147
Marzipan, 119, 150, 164
  figurines, *150*
Masa harina, 213
Masala chicken, 344
Masalas, 343
Maslenitas (Butter Festival), 153
Massa sovada, 130
Mast, 325
Mastic, 325
Matzo bread, 27
Mayeritsa, 328
Mazanec, 151
Meals and meal cycles, 14–15
Melkite church, 318. *See also*
  Eastern Orthodox;
  Christianity.
Menudo, 212
Merienda, 127, 217–218, 299
Mescal, 209, 215
Metate, 209
Metaxia, 325
Mexicans, 201–226. *See also*
  Latinos; Mexico.

adaptations of food habits in
  U.S., 221–223
birth rate, 223–224
Braceros, 205
breastfeeding, 224
Chicanos, 205
counseling, 225–226
Creoles, 204
cultural food groups table,
  210–213
cultural organizations, 207
current demographics in U.S.,
  205–206
dental caries, 225
diabetes, 225
family (Chicano), 208
food habits, contemporary in
  U.S., 221–226
  traditional, 208–220
immigration to U.S. of, 205–
  207
malnutrition, 224
meal composition and cycle,
  217–219, 223
mestizos, 203
mortality rate, 225
nutritional intake in U.S., 223–
  225
obesity, 225
religion, 207
role of food in society, 219
  in U.S., 226
socioeconomic status in U.S.,
  206–207
special occasions, 219
staples, 209–215
  regional variations, 215–216
therapeutic uses of food, 212,
  219
undocumented aliens, 205
Mexico. *See also* Latinos;
  Mexicans.
  foods, 208–216, *210–213,* 219
  Aztec, 208–209
  plains, 215–216
  southern, 216
  tropical, 216
  in U.S., 213, 221, 222
  Yucatan, 216
  history of, 203–204
Mezze, 326
Microcytic anemia, Vietnamese,
  308
Middle East, *314. See also*
  Greeks/Middle Easterners.
  foods, *313,* 318–330, *320–333*
Mien ga, 299
Milk, 11
  curds, 264, 348
  therapeutic use of, 283
  water buffalo (caraboa), 293
Milkfish (bangus), 296

Mincemeat pie, 104, 107, 110
Minestra, 126
Minority groups, food habits of, 2–3, 17–18
Mint, 299, 325, 326
  jelly, 103
  therapeutic use of, 73, 356
Mirepoix, 103
Mirin, 280
Miso, 280
Misoshiru, 281
Miwok Indians, 71. See also Native Americans.
Mixtas, 233
Mochi, 283
  -gashi, 281
Molasses, 237–238
Moles, 216
Moon cakes, 266
Moon Festival, 266
Morcillas, 236
Mormons, 34–35
Mortadella, 125
Mother's Day, 107
Mountain chicken, 238
Mou tai, 262
Mozzarella cheese, 125
Mushimono, 282
Mu shi pork, 263
Mushrooms, shitake, 269
Muskmelons, 68
Muslim. See Islam.

Naan, 345
Nabemono, 282
Nachos, 221
Namasu, 282
Nam pa, 298
Naoc mam, 298
Native American,
  foods, 52, 58–59, 62–65, 74–75
    northeastern, 59–61
    Northwest Coast/Alaskan Native, 69–70
    plains, 66–67
    southern, 61, 66
    southwestern, 68–69
Native Americans,
  adaptation of food habits, 74–76
  alcoholism, 78
  cardiovascular disease, 77
  commodity foods and, 75
  counseling, 78–79
  cultural food groups table, 62–65
  cultural organizations, 55–56
  current demographics, 55
  dental caries, 78
  diabetes, 77
  family, 57

food habits, contemporary, 74–76
  traditional, 57–74
  history of, 52–54
  infectious diseases and, 78
  lactose intolerance, 76
  meal composition and cycle, 71–72, 75–76
  nations, 51, 53, 54
  nutritional intake, 76–78
  obesity, 77
  religion, 56–57
  role of food in society, 72–73
  socioeconomic status, 55
  special occasions, 72
  staples, 59
    regional variations, 59–71
  therapeutic use of food, 73–74
  worldview, 56–57
Nau-Roz, 41
Nau Roz, 329–330
Navajo Indians, 53, 68. See also Native Americans.
New Year's, 129, 151, 303, 304, 306, 329, 354
  Chinese, 265–267
  Japanese, 283
  Vietnamese, 304–306
Niaga, 302
Nimono, 282
Nisei, 272. See also Japanese.
Nixtamal, 209
Noodles, 251, 293
  pancit, 293
  pasta, 122
  rice, 257, 298
Nootka Indians, 74. See also Native Americans.
Nopales (nopalitos), 68, 215
Nori, 269, 281
North Africans. See Greeks/Middle Easterners.
Northern Europeans, foods of, 85, 95–107, 96–99
Norway. See Norwegians; Scandinavia.
Norwegians. See also Scandinavians.
  current demographics in U.S., 159
  immigration to U.S. of, 157, 158
  socioeconomic status in U.S., 159
Nuoc cham, 298
Nuoc mam, 285, 298
Nutrition, food habits and, 15–17

Oatmeal, 99, 105, 161
Obesity,
  Black Americans, 196

Mexicans, 225
  Native Americans, 77
  Puerto Ricans, 244
Obon Festival, 282, 283
Okra, 172, 183, 184, 185, 233
Oktoberfest, 147, 149–150
Olive oil, 103, 123, 292, 324
Olives, 32, 119, 324
Omega-3-fatty acids, 70
Ong Tao (Spirit of the Hearth), 306
Oplatky, 151
Oregano, 325
  therapeutic use of, 220
Ostiones, 238
Otoso, 283
Ouzo, 325
Oyster sauce, 250, 262
Ozoni, 283

Paan, 351
Pachadi, 343, 352
Paczki, 151
Padek, 298
Paella, 122
Pain perdu, 110
Pakka foods, 355
Palestinians. See Greeks/Middle Easterners.
Palm,
  hearts of, 298
  oil, 183
Palm Sunday, 30, 33, 128
Pan bagna, 103
Pancakes, 152
  blini, 153
  crêpes, 102
  Mandarin, 263
Pancit, 293, 303
Pan de muerto, 219
Pan de sol, 293
Pan doce, 113, 124
Pan dulce, 217, 222
Panettone, 30, 124, 127, 128
Papaya, 184, 232
  therapeutic use of, 220
Pappadams, 348
Paprika, sweet Hungarian, 146
Paratha, 344
Parmesan cheese, 125
Pascha, 153
Paska, 152
Passover, 15, 25–28
  Seder plate, 26, 27–28
Pasta, 122
  e fagiole, 125
Pastel de Navidad, 129
Pasteles, 240, 242
Pastilla (bisteeva), 322
Pâté, 101, 292
  creton, 110
  de foie gras, 101

Patis, 297
Pawnee Indians, 66. *See also*
    Native Americans.
Pawpaw, 184
Peaches, 59
Peanuts, 182, 184, 185
    therapeutic uses of, 220
Pebernødder, 165
Peking duck, 263
Pellegra, 185, 221
Pemmican, 67
Pennsylvania Dutch, 138, 140
    foods, 154–155
Pepparkakor, 165
Pepper, Szechwan (fagara), 264
Pepper cookies, 165
Pepper pot, 236
Peppers,
    pimento, 119
    sweet, 122, 189, 233
Persians (Iranians). *See* Greeks/
    Middle Easterners.
Persimmons, 58, 66, 67
    oriental, 264
        therapeutic use of, 268
Pesto, 124
Pfeffernüsse, *149*, 150
Philippines, history of, 287–
    288
Philippino. *See* Filipino.
Pho, 299
Phosphoron, 31
Pibil, 216
Pica,
    Black Americans, 193, 197
    in West Africa, 193
Picadillo, 238, *240*
Pickapeppa sauce, 238
Piki, 68
Pilaf, 323
Pilsner beer, 147
Pima Indians, 68. *See also* Native
    Americans.
Piñatas, 219
Pineapples, 298
Pine nuts, 68, 215
Piñon seeds. *See* Pine nuts.
Pirog, 144
Pirozhki, 144
Pita bread, *313*, 319
Pizza, 119, 125
Plantains (bananas), 183, *201*,
    216, 232, 238, 298, 348,
    354
Planter's punch, 237
Ploughman's lunch, 98
Plum pudding, 104, 107
Plums, 209, 215
    pickled, 281
        therapeutic use of, 283
Poland, history of, 134
Polenta, 124

Poles. *See also* Central
    Europeans; Poland.
    cultural organizations, 139
    current demographics in U.S.,
        138
    family, 141
    immigration to U.S. of, 136
    religion, 140
    socioeconomic status in U.S.,
        138
Polo, 323
Pomo Indians, 71. *See also*
    Native Americans.
Pone, 185
Ponhaus (scrapple), 154
Pont-l'Eveque cheese, 101
Poppy seeds, 151, 152
Pork, 59, *108*, 141, 146, 187,
    209, 264, 296, 298, 349
    barbecued, 187, 191
    chitterlings, 185
    hocks, 185
    Islamic prohibitions, 39
    Jewish prohibitions, 22
    lard, 185, 239, 262, 292
    maw, 185
    mu shi, 263
    salt, 184
    therapeutic use of, 266
Port, 100
Portugal. *See also* Portuguese.
    foods, 124, 129–130
    history of, 114
Portuguese. *See also* Southern
    Europeans; Portugal.
    adaptations of food habits in
        U.S., 130
    counseling, 31
    cultural organizations, 117
    current demographics in U.S.,
        116
    family, 118
    food habits, contemporary in
        U.S., 130–131
        traditional, 124, 127, 129–
            130
    immigration to U.S. of, 115
    meal composition and cycle,
        127, 129–130
    nutritional intake in U.S., 130–
        131
    religion, 118
    socioeconomic status in U.S.,
        116
    special occasions, 129–130
    staples, 124
Posadas, 219
Potage St. Germain, 102
Potato bread (lefser), 161
Potato chips, 76
Potatoes, 58, 99, 160, 208, 213,
    256, 299

Potlach, 58
Pot likker, 189
Potted meats, 105
Poulet rôti a là créole, 238
Powhatan Indians, 66. *See also*
    Native Americans.
Pozole, 68, 213
Prahoc, 298
Pralines, 109
Pretzels, 155
    symbolic use of, 141
Prosciutto, *113*, 125
Protestants, 33–36. *See also*
    Christianity.
Provolone cheese, 125
Prunes, 14
Pubs, in Great Britain, 98
Puchero, 297
Pudding, in Great Britain, 104
Pueblo Indians, 68. *See also*
    Native Americans.
Puerto Ricans. *See also*
    Caribbean Islanders.
    birth rate, 243
    current demographics in U.S.,
        230
    family, 232
    immigration to U.S. of, 228–
        229
    low-birthweight infants, 243
    obesity, 244
    religion, 232
    socioeconomic status in U.S.,
        230–231
Pulque, 215
Pumpkin, 58, 61, 182, 215
    pie, 60, 108
Pupusas, 213
Purim, 25
Puto, 293
    bumbong, 303

Quesadillas, 213, *222*
Queso blanco (cheese), 215
Queso fresca (cheese), 215
Quiche Lorraine, 101

Rabbit, 146
Ragú Sauce, 125
Raisins, 129
Raki, 325
Ramadan, 15, 40, 329
Ratatouille, 103
Raytas, 343, *352*
Red beans and rice, 109
Refried beans, 209, *222*
Religion. *See* Buddhism,
    Christianity, Hinduism,
    Islam, Judaism.
Renal disease,
    Filipinos, 307
    Vietnamese, 308

Retsina, 325
Rice, 119, 343, *344,* 345–348,
    354
  basmati, 324, *334*
  and beans, 109, 233, 240
  cakes, 281, 283, 293, 306
  long grain, 257, 293, 298, 323
  noodles (sticks), 257, *285,* 298
  paper, *285,* 298
  pudding, 219, 345
  saffron, 343
  short grain, 280, 293, 298
  therapeutic use of, 283
  vinegar, 280
  wild, 67
  wine, 280, 282, 283
Ricotta cheese, 125
Risotto, 119, 124
  à la Milanese, 119
Rowhurst, 146
Roman Catholics, 29–31. *See
    also* Christianity.
  dietary practices, 30
  immigration to U.S. of, 29–30
  religious holidays, 30–31
Romano (pecorino) cheese, 125
Romescu sauce, 123
Rosca de reyes, 219
Rosh Hashanah, 24
Roti, 344, 348, 357
Rouille, 103
Roux, 104
  Cajun, 109
Rum, 237
  therapeutic use of, 241
Russians. *See also* Central
    Europeans; Soviet Union.
  current demographics in U.S.,
    139
  immigration to U.S. of, 137–
    138
  religion, 140–141
  socioeconomic status in U.S.,
    139
Rye bread, 144, 155, 161

Sabbath (Jewish), 24
Sachertorte, 145
Saffron, 119, 323, 343
  rice, 343
  rolls, 164
Saint Canute's Day, 164
Saint Patrick's Day, *90,* 107
Sake, 282
Salade Niçoise, 103
Salal, 70
Sally Lunn Bread, 108
Salmon, 70
  gravlax, 160
  smoked, 146, 160
  therapeutic use of, 74
Salsa, 209, *222*

Salt, therapeutic use of, 306
Saltimboca, 125
Salt pork, 184
Samana, 324
Sambar, 348
Samosas, 344, *350*
Samovar, 147
Sanbusak, 319–322
Sancocho, 238
Sansei, 272. *See also* Japanese.
Santerias, 232
Sashimi, 282
Sassafras, 66, 185
Sauerbraten, 146
Sauerkraut, 141, 155, 165
Sausage, 124, 146, 187, 212,
    350. *See also* individual
    sausages.
  blood, 236, 239
Scampi, 124
Scandinavia. *See also*
    Scandinavians; individual
    nationalities.
  foods, 160–161, *162–165,*
    164–165
  history of, 157
Scandinavians. *See also* Danes;
    Finns; Norwegians;
    Scandinavians; Swedes.
  counseling, 166–167
  cultural food groups table,
    162–165
  cultural organizations, 159
  family, 159–160
  food habits, adaptations in
    U.S., 165
  contemporary in U.S., 165–
    167
  traditional, 160–165
  meal composition and cycle,
    161, 164–165
  nutritional intake in U.S., 166–
    167
  religion, 159
  special occasions, 164–165
  staples and regional
    variations, 160–161
Schmierkaes, 154
Schnecken, 154
Schnitzel, 146
Schnitz un knepp, 154
Schwarzwälder Kirschtorte,
    145
Scones, 98
Scotch-Irish, 89, 92
Scotland. *See* Great Britain.
Scrapple (ponhaus), 154
Seaweed (aonoriko, hijiki,
    kombu, nori, wakame),
    269, 281
Security, food habits and, 3
Seder plate, *26, 27*–28

Self-realization, food habits and,
    4
Seminole Indians, 66. *See also*
    Native Americans.
Sesame seeds, 183, 184, 325
Seventh-Day Adventists, 35–36
Shab-i-Barat, 41
Shark fin soup, 306
Shchi, 148
Shea oil, 183
Shepherd's (cottage) pie, 99
Sherry, 100, 123
Shintoism, 274
Shish kebab, 325
Shoofly pie, 154
Shoyu (soy sauce), 280
Shrewsbury simnel, 107
Shurbut, 352
Sickle-cell anemia, Black
    Americans, 197
Side dishes, 14. *See also*
    individual side dishes;
    meal composition and
    cycle of each group.
Sikhs, 337, 341. *See also* Asian
    Indians.
Sinigang, 296
Sioux Indians, 71. *See also*
    Native Americans.
Slovaks. *See also* Central
    Europeans; Czechs;
    Czechoslovakians.
  cultural organizations, 139
  current demographics in U.S.,
    139
  family, 141
  immigration to U.S. of, 136–
    137
  religion, 140
  socioeconomic status in U.S.,
    139
Smoked duck, 264
Smörgåsbord, 161
Smørrebrød, 161, *166*
Snails. *See* escargot.
Soda bread, 98–99
Sofrito, 238
Sopas-secas, 212
Soshone Indians, 71. *See also*
    Native Americans.
Soul food, 4, 192
Soupe dorée, 107
Soursop, 232
South Americans, 201. *See also*
    Latinos.
  foods, 213, 233, 236
  immigration to U.S. of, 201,
    206
  socioeconomic status in U.S.,
    230
Southeast Asia, foods, *285,* 292–
    307

Southeast Asians, 285–311. *See also* Cambodians; Filipinos; Laotians; Southeast Asia; Vietnamese.
adaptations of food habits in U.S., 307
counseling, Filipinos, 309
Vietnamese (mainland Southeast Asians), 309
cultural food groups tables, Filipino, *294–297*
Vietnamese (mainland Southeast Asians), *300–303*
cultural organizations, 290–291
current demographics in U.S., 289–290
family, 291
food habits, contemporary in U.S., 307–309
traditional, 292–307
immigration to U.S. of, 288–289
meal composition and cycle, Filipino, 299, 302–303
Vietnamese, 299, 304–306
nutritional intake in U.S., Filipino, 307–308
Vietnamese, 308–309
religion, 291–292
socioeconomic status in U.S., 290
special occasions, Filipino, 299, 302–303
Vietnamese, 304–306
staples, Filipino, 293–298
Vietnamese, 298–299
therapeutic use of food, Filipino, 306
Vietnamese, 306–307
Southern cooking (Black American), 187–189, 189–190, 192
Southern Europe, foods, 113, *120–123*
Southern Europeans. *See also* Italians; Portuguese; Southern Europe; Spaniards.
cultural food groups table, *120–123*
lactose intolerance, 130
Southern-fried foods, 187, *188*
Souvlaki, 325
Soviet Union. *See also* Russians; Central Europeans.
history of, 134–135
Soybeans, 257–262, 280
soup, 306
tofu, 14, 257, 266, 280, 298
Soy milk, 257

Soy sauce, 257, 280
Spaetzle, 144
Spaghetti, 119
Spain,
foods, 122–123, 126, 128
history of, 114
Spaniards. *See also* Southern Europeans; Spain.
adaptations of food habits in U.S., 130
counseling, 131
cultural organizations, 117
current demographics in U.S., 116
food habits, contemporary in U.S., 130–131
traditional, 119, 122–124, 126, 127, 128–129
immigration to U.S. of, 116
meal composition and cycle, 127, 128–129
nutritional intake in U.S., 130
socioeconomic status in U.S., 116
special occasions, 128–129
staples, 122–123
regional variations, 126
Spicebush, 66
Spirit of the Hearth (Ong Tao), 306
Spring rolls (egg rolls), 257
Spumone, 126
Squash, 51, 59, 68, 109, 216, 233
blossoms, 68
Stamp and go, 236
Status,
commensality, 355
food habits and, 4
Steak tartare, 146
Sticky buns, 154
Stilton cheese, 98
Stir-fried foods, 263, 264, 292
Stollen, 150
Stout, 100
Streuselkuchen, 154
Strudel, apple, 145
Sturgeon, 146–147
Succotash, 60, *61*
Sudras, 340. *See also* Asian Indians.
Sugar cane, 227–228
Suimono, 282
Sukiyaki, 282
Sukkot, 25
Sumac, 325
berries, 66, 75
Sunomono, 282
Sushi, 280, *280*
Sweden, *see* Scandinavia; Swedes.

Swedes. *See also* Scandinavians.
current demographics in U.S., 159
immigration to U.S. of, 158
socioeconomic status in U.S., 159
Sweet potatoes, 58, 184, 189, 233
Sweets and sours, 155
Syllabub, 108
Symbolic use of food, 5, 19
Syrek, 152
Syrians. *See* Greeks/Middle Easterners.
Szechwan pepper, 264

Ta'amia, 324
Tabasco Sauce, 109
Tabouli, 322
Tacos, 212, *222*
Tahini, 325
Tamale pie, 221
Tamales, 213, 223, 242
Tamarind, 233, *334*
Tandoor, 345
Tanier, 233
Taoism, 255–256
Tapas, 126
Tapioca, 232
Taro, 183, 184, 233, 236, 239, 264, *285*
Tea,
in Central Europe, 147
ceremony in Japan, 280
Chinese (green, black, oolong), 262
in Great Britain, 100, 105, *106*
High, 105
Japanese (green), 280–281
Native American, 66
prohibitions against, 35, 36, 40
therapeutic use of, 283
Tempura, 282
Tequila, 209, 215
Teriyaki sauce, 280
Terrine, 101
Tet, 15, 304–306
Tex-Mex foods, 221
Thalis, 352, *352*
Thanksgiving, 15, 110–111, 223, 241
Thuringer, 155
Tiffin, 351
Tiger bones, therapeutic use of, 307
Tlingit Indians, 69. *See also* Native Americans.
Tofu, 14, 257, 266, 280, 298
lasagne, *17*, 18
Tomatillos, *201*, 216

Tomatoes, 58, 103, 109, 119, 122, 123, 182, 213, 233, 256, 324
sauce, 104
Torrone, 127
Tortas de aceite, 128
Tortellini, 125
Tortillas, 16, 68, 75, 209, 212, *214*, 222
in Spain, 122
Tostados, 218
Tourtière, 111
Tremecos (lupine seeds), 124
Trifle, 104
Tripe, 5, *85*
menudo, 212
Ts'ai (e.g., meats, vegetables), 265
Tsoureki, 329
Tsukemono (pickled vegetables), 281, 282
Tuba, 297–298
Tuk-trey, 298
Tunas, 68
Turkey, 58, 61
Turks. *See* Greeks/Middle Easterners.
Turmeric, 323, *334*
Tybo cheese, 160

Ukha, 148
Ukoy, 296
Umeboshi, 281
Untouchability, in India, 340
Uppama, 345

Vaisyas, 340. *See also* Asian Indians.
Vanocka (houska), 151, *152*
Vasilopitta, 329
Veal Oscar, 157
Vegetables. *See* individual vegetables.
Vegetarianism, 4, 8, 36, 45, 49, 358–359
Velouté sauce, 104
Venison, 58, 146

Vietnam, history of, 286
Vietnamese. *See also* Southeast Asians; Vietnam.
age calculation, 308
dental caries, 308
infectious diseases, 308
intestinal parasites, 308
lactose intolerance, 308
low-birthweight infants, 308–309
malnutrition, 308
microcytic anemia, 308
renal disease, 308
Vietnamese (mainland Southeast Asians), cultural food groups table, *300–303*
Vodka, 147
Voodoo. *See* Santerias.

Wakame, 281
Walnuts, paste, 264
Water chestnuts, 264, *285*
Watermelon, 183, 184
seeds, 184, 306
therapeutic use of, 283
West Africa, *175*
days of week, 182
foods, 182–184
history of, 172–174
wunkirle spoon, 192
Wheat, 319
bulgar (burghul), 322
couscous, 126, 184, *313*, 322
symbolic use of, 31
Whiskey, 100, 110
Scotch, 100
Wienerbrød, 164
Wieners, 146
Wild rice, 67
Wine,
Central European, 147
Chinese, 262
French, 101, 102, 103, 104
fruit, 190
Greek, 325
Italian, 125, 126

kosher, 27
Mexican, 215
Portuguese, 127
rice, 280, 282, 283
Spanish, 123
Wok, 263, 292
Wontons, 257, 298
papers, 257
Worchestershire sauce, 103
Wunkirle spoon, 192, *192*
Wurst, 146

Yakhini (yiachni), 324
Yakimono, 282
Yams, 182
Yemas de San Leandro, 129
Yiachni (yakhini), 324
Yin-yang,
classification of disease, 267, 269, 306
classification of foods, 266, 283, 306
principles of, 255–256
Yogurt, 14, 141, 264, 325, 343, 357
Yokan, 281
Yom Kippur, 15, 24–25
Yonsei, 272. *See also* Japanese.
Yorkshire pudding, 85
Yuca. *See* Cassava.

Zabaglione, 126
Zakuski, 148
Zapote (sapodilla), 216
Zarzuela, 123
Zen, Buddhism, 49, 256
macrobiotics, 49
Zeppole, 126
Zinc deficiency, Asian Indians, 360
Zoroastrianism, 341
Z'roah, 27
Zuni Indians, 68. *See also* Native Americans.
Zuppa di pesce alla marinara, 119